TAKE TWO PLANTS

TAKE TWO PLANTS

The Gardener's Complete Guide to Companion Planting

NICOLA FERGUSON

CONTEMPORARY BOOKS

PHOTOGRAPHY CREDITS

The photographs in this book were taken by Nicola Ferguson (see Acknowledgements, page 260) with the following exceptions: Page 2 Steven Wooster/Garden Picture Library; page 6-7 Clive Nichols/The Old Vicarage, Norfolk; page 18 Gil Hanly/Garden Picture Library; page 28 Charles Quest-Ritson (bottom); page 40 Ron Evans/Garden Picture Library; page 42 Clive Nichols/designer: Jill Billington (top); page 58 Sunniva Harte/Garden Picture Library; page 77 Clive Nichols/Swinton Lane, Worcs; page 78 Sunniva Harte/Garden Picture Library; page 80 Charles Quest-Ritson (top); page 94 Howard Rice/Garden Picture Library; page 106 Brian Carter/Garden Picture Library; page 118 Jerry Harpur/Beth Chatto Gardens; page 128 Roger Hyan/Garden Picture Library; page 142 Steven Wooster/Garden Picture Library; page 151 JS Sira/Garden Picture Library (bottom); page 162 Lamontagne/Garden Picture Library; page 165 Clive Nichols (top); page 166 Clive Nichols/Manor House, Walton in Gordano (top); page 167 Ron Evans/Garden Picture Library (top); page 169 Photos Horticultural (top); page 171 Clive Nichols/Harcourt Arboretum, Oxford (top); page 174 Ron Sutherland/Garden Picture Library; page 176 Clive Nichols (top); page 178 Clive Nichols (bottom); page 186 Ron Evans/Garden Picture Library; page 188 Photos Horticultural (bottom); page 192 Photos Horticultural (top); page 198 Photos Horticultural; page 211 Clive Nichols/Wollerton Old Hall, Shropshire; page 212 JS Sira/Garden Picture Library; page 221 John Glover/Garden Picture Library; page 222 John Glover/Garden Picture Library; page 224 Clive Nichols/Barnsley House, Glos (top); page 224 Clive Nichols/Graham Strong (bottom); page 225 Photos Horticultural (bottom); page 226 Clive Nichols/Beth Chatto Gardens, Essex (top); page 228 Photos Horticultural (top); page 229 Clive Nichols (bottom); page 234 JS Sira/Garden Picture Library; page 237 Charles Quest-Ritson (bottom); page 246 Geoff Dann/Garden Picture Library.

NOTE: Throughout the book the time of year is given as a season to make the reference applicable to readers all over the world. In the northern hemisphere the seasons may be translated into months as follows:

Early winter	December	*Early spring*	March	*Early summer*	June	*Early autumn*	September
Midwinter	January	*Mid-spring*	April	*Midsummer*	July	*Mid-autumn*	October
Late winter	February	*Late spring*	May	*Late summer*	August	*Late autumn*	November

Published in the United States in 1999 by Contemporary Books
A division of NTC/Contemporary Publishing Group, Inc.
4255 West Touhy Avenue, Lincolnwood (Chicago), Illinois 60646-1975 U.S.A.

International Standard Book Number:
0-8092-2768-1 (cloth)
0-8092-2767-3 (paper)

A David & Charles Book
Published in the United Kingdom in 1998 by David & Charles,
Brunel House, Newton Abbot, Devon, England

Illustrations by Coral Mula
Design by Sally Adkins
Page make-up by Ian Muggeridge
Printed in Italy by Lego SpA

Library of Congress Cataloging-in-Publication Data

Ferguson, Nicola. 1949-
    Take two plants : the gardener's complete guide to companion planting / Nicola Ferguson.
        p.   cm.
    Includes index.
    ISBN 0-8092-2768-1 (cloth). -- ISBN 0-8092-2767-3 (pbk.)
    1. Color in gardening.   2. Landscape plants.   3. Landscape plants-
-Pictorial works.   I. Title.
SB454.3.C64F47   1999
635.9'63--dc21
                                                                98-29273
                                                                CIP

CONTENTS

INTRODUCTION

Creating a garden that delights the eye and satisfies the soul requires you to do more than buy some plants you like, dig some holes and pop the plants in the holes. Success cannot be relied upon even if you have got the 'bones' of your garden right: the paths and steps and the largest, most permanent plants may be perfectly positioned, but if you plant up the spaces in between, in a piecemeal fashion, with a bit of what you fancy here and there, the garden as a whole can still be disappointing. Whether you already have an existing garden or are starting out with a more or less bare plot, it is essential to plan before you plant.

If you have a garden that is visually unsatisfying, you will probably be able to see that there are at least two problems. First of all, some of the flowers – or berries or unusually coloured leaves – that look so attractive at close range, may merge dishearteningly with their surroundings when viewed at a distance. Other plants may behave in quite the opposite manner and assume an awkward, uncomfortable prominence among the existing plants. The trick to creating a successful garden is to stop considering individual plants in isolation from one another and to start visualizing them in harmonious and interesting combinations.

Needless to say, combining plants successfully requires careful observation and some practice. Real groups of plants growing in real gardens provide the most tangible evidence of which combinations work and which do not, and garden visiting is certainly the most pleasurable way of learning about the creative side of horticulture. In particular, gardens belonging to painters, photographers and flower arrangers will normally have been designed with a more than usually expert eye for form and colour. Magazines, books and television programmes too can illustrate, with glorious photography, whole borders in famous and not-so-famous gardens.

Photographs of plantings on a more modest scale – even just pairs of plants – can be almost as instructive and inspiring as those of large-scale plantings. Because the number of plants is limited, you may find it easier to see how some of the ideas behind successful plant combining really work. This can also make it easier for you to visualize actually carrying out some of these planting ideas. Few of us have the opportunity or the means to re-create the white garden at Sissinghurst Castle or the twin red borders at Hidcote Manor; smaller groups that may include familiar plants make the whole concept of companion planting seem more feasible.

For those gardeners who like to work from small beginnings, who find that it is duets, trios and quartets of plants that kindle the creative spirit, this book offers over four hundred ideas to stimulate the imagination. The plant combinations were photographed in almost a hundred gardens, created by inspired gardeners. These particular winning combinations are not garden designs, but they are sources of information and inspiration that will make the designing of gardens easier. Above all perhaps, these photographs provide convincing evidence of how the plants in our gardens, so beautiful in themselves, can appear still more beautiful when provided with flattering companions.

USING THE BOOK

Even if you are the sort of person who normally never reads the instructions before opening the packet, a short time spent looking at this section of the book will be useful. It contains, first of all, a few general points that are worth bearing in mind whenever you carry out any new planting. Following these points there are some suggestions as to how to use this book most effectively, including how to expand some of the planting ideas contained in the combinations. Finally, there is a description of the layout of the book and an explanation of the terms used to summarize details of plants.

PLANNING AND PLANTING

You may be using the combinations in this book as starting points for quite large planting schemes, or as a way of adding just one or two plants to an existing group. In either case, you should have made all the important decisions about the style of the garden, the siting of focal points and the handling of changes of level within the garden, before contemplating any details of planting. What is going on elsewhere in your garden, and especially what is flowering, must be kept in mind when you add new plants to any part of it.

When you do reach the stage of thinking about what to plant, try not to be so beguiled by the colour of plants that you overlook texture and, most importantly, shape. The colours of plants are wonderful, but planting schemes based on colour alone can sometimes be disappointing. Interesting shapes and, in particular, interesting combinations of shapes, can also act as successful garden enliveners.

Unless an overriding principle of 'keep it simple' is applied, flower and foliage colour, texture and form can all be taken into account and still the end result can be nothing much more than a bitty muddle. Successful groupings of plants are often strong and simple in design. This does not necessarily mean restricting the number of different plants in a garden, but it does mean limiting the range of colours and shapes and textures amongst these plants so that repetition arises. Repetition sets up a rhythm in a garden, making the garden simultaneously easy on the eye and interesting. The repetition of colours and shapes gives extra impact to plants by emphasizing their particular decorative features. It also has the effect of making individual plants seem as if they are 'meant' to be there. This in turn lends cohesion to a garden.

Repetition need never be boring. You can, of course, simply repeat one plant or a combination of two or three plants at various points in your garden, but you can also repeat a combination of colours, shapes or textures. For instance, you could repeat a combination of purple and yellow-green by having groups of purple leaves and yellow-green flowers as well as groups of purple flowers and yellow-green leaves.

The end product of this planning and organizing will not instantly be a fully-fledged planting scheme. Nor will any group of plants remain static once it has reached maturity – it will always be developing and changing. Well before senility sets in, renovations and replacements will be needed. Even quite immature plantings need more than routine maintenance since, if the visual balance of ingredients within a group of plants is allowed to alter too much, the group as a whole 'disintegrates'. Allowing one very vigorous plant to dominate its neighbours, for instance, soon results in a whole planting scheme slipping out of focus. The combining of plants should, therefore, be regarded as a continuing process.

USING THE COMBINATIONS

The book can be used in several different ways. It can, of course, simply be browsed through as if it were a garden with an especially large number of successful planting ideas, or it can be used as a source of more specific information. When, for example, a planting scheme of a particular colour is being planned, only certain chapters will be directly relevant. Many of the chapters are loosely related to each other and this is reflected in the running order. Because many gardeners like to use grey foliage with cool-coloured flowers, for example, the sections dealing with these two features appear next to each other for easy cross-reference. However, bear in mind that combinations with white-variegated foliage (in the Variegated Foliage section) or with foliage of tranquil, green colouring (in the Decorative Green Foliage section) will also be worth looking at in this context.

The book can also act as inspiration for ways to 'lift' existing schemes. It features numerous well-known plants which, with carefully chosen partners, can be made the most of and given extra impact. However, the huge range of garden plants available means that gardeners often encounter unfamiliar plants. Attractive new plants have a special appeal, and most gardeners will find that ideas for combinations involving these plants will be of particular interest.

Many of the planting ideas in these combinations can be treated quite flexibly and there will often be a number of suitable substitutes for one of the suggested plants in a combination. However, in gardening as in cookery, the adding, subtracting and substituting of ingredients should be carried out cautiously: sometimes an alteration will produce a more successful result than if the original recipe had been followed exactly, equally it can unbalance the whole concoction. When contemplating a substitution, it is important to compare all the details of the original plant and the proposed substitute, including habit of growth and any particular growing requirements.

Expanding the Combinations

Whether the combinations are copied exactly or interpreted more loosely, these small groups of plants will not, by themselves, make an entire garden. They can, however, take their place in wider schemes, and be expanded into larger, and more complex designs. Examples of such larger planting plans follow in Building Borders (see opposite).

When incorporating a combination into an existing group of plants it is, of course, very important that some forethought is given to how the shapes and colours of the new plants will blend in. A simple but effective method of avoiding clashes is to consider exactly what each plant in a proposed group will be doing season by season. In this way, a clash between, for instance, bright mauve-pink autumn flowers and scarlet berries can be avoided. The shapes of some plants vary little with the seasons, but adding a new shape to an existing group of plants also needs a certain amount of imaginative forethought.

Using the combinations as starting points for devising completely new plantings in fairly large areas will involve expanding and developing the combinations. Sometimes this will be quite straightforward. When a very simple scheme is required, the components of a particular combination can remain unaltered and it will be simply a case of, say, doubling or trebling the numbers of each plant so that the combination covers a larger area. A different type of expansion might use the repetition of a particular combination. A whole bed or border could consist of one combination repeated again and again though, in practice, it is more often the case that a combination is repeated or mirrored at only a few points in the planting area. However, when quite large areas need to be planted

from scratch, the repetition of a single combination is very unlikely to produce enough variety for most gardeners' tastes. In these circumstances, a single combination is still useful, but it needs to be treated as a starting point for further developments. Both the index of botanical names and the summaries of plant details in the main body of the book are useful sources of inspiration and information about combinations that make good bases for larger planting schemes.

Building Borders

The botanical names index reveals that some plants appear in several combinations in this book. These plants tend to be particularly good at blending with other plants. Remember that, when hunting amongst combinations for ideas to develop a particular combination, it is most important to take note of the sun and shade requirements and the soil preferences of individual plants.

The following planting plans offer suggestions for creating larger schemes, using more than one successful combination. The numbers given after each of the listed plants (for example, x 3) indicate the suggested number of plants required to fill the total planting area.

A Versatile Hosta

1 *Fuchsia magellanica gracilis* x 1
2 *Dicentra spectabilis* 'Alba' x 1
3 *Viola* 'Desdemona' x 3
4 *Hosta undulata albomarginata* x 1
5 *Lamium maculatum* 'White Nancy' x 3

Total planting area approximately 3.5-4m²/3.5-4yd²

Hostas are amongst the most versatile plants for creating combinations. White-variegated *H. undulata albomarginata*, for example, appears several times in this book. It looks especially attractive, perhaps, with the dangling flowers of *Dicentra spectabilis* 'Alba' (see 1.36). To expand this combination into a sizeable group, other pairings which feature the hosta can be used as inspiration. Combinations 9.30 and 9.31, for instance, show two further plants which make flattering additions to this partnership. Incorporated here, the pale leaves of a lamium (see 9.31) and the delicate flower colour of a viola (see 9.30) both emphasize the cool elegance of the hosta and dicentra partnership. In addition, the lamium's low carpet of growth balances the whole group very satisfactorily and the viola's long flowering season is a considerable asset. The lamium also appears, in 9.22, with a brilliant red and violet fuchsia which would bring warmth and late colour to the scheme – as well as a good, shrubby shape and added height. The enlarged group is illustrated here as it would appear in early summer. All the plants thrive in light shade and in moist but well-drained soil.

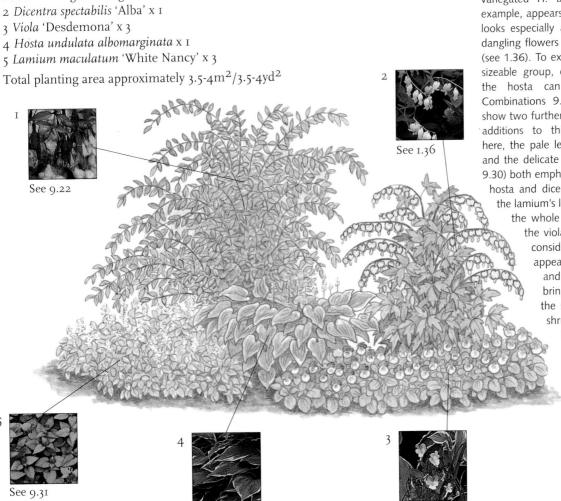

See 9.22

See 1.36

1

2

5
See 9.31

4
See 9.31

3
See 9.30

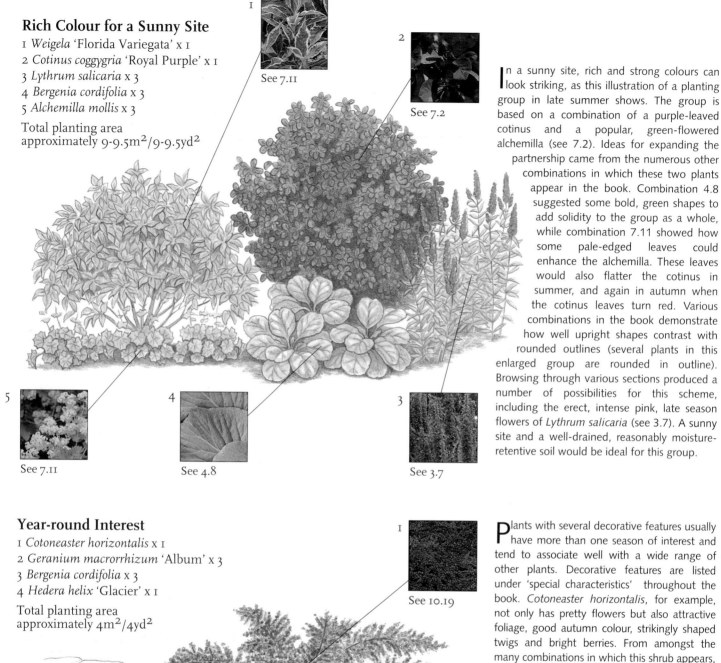

Rich Colour for a Sunny Site

1 *Weigela* 'Florida Variegata' x 1
2 *Cotinus coggygria* 'Royal Purple' x 1
3 *Lythrum salicaria* x 3
4 *Bergenia cordifolia* x 3
5 *Alchemilla mollis* x 3

Total planting area
approximately 9-9.5m²/9-9.5yd²

See 7.11

See 7.2

In a sunny site, rich and strong colours can look striking, as this illustration of a planting group in late summer shows. The group is based on a combination of a purple-leaved cotinus and a popular, green-flowered alchemilla (see 7.2). Ideas for expanding the partnership came from the numerous other combinations in which these two plants appear in the book. Combination 4.8 suggested some bold, green shapes to add solidity to the group as a whole, while combination 7.11 showed how some pale-edged leaves could enhance the alchemilla. These leaves would also flatter the cotinus in summer, and again in autumn when the cotinus leaves turn red. Various combinations in the book demonstrate how well upright shapes contrast with rounded outlines (several plants in this enlarged group are rounded in outline). Browsing through various sections produced a number of possibilities for this scheme, including the erect, intense pink, late season flowers of *Lythrum salicaria* (see 3.7). A sunny site and a well-drained, reasonably moisture-retentive soil would be ideal for this group.

5 See 7.11

4 See 4.8

3 See 3.7

Year-round Interest

1 *Cotoneaster horizontalis* x 1
2 *Geranium macrorrhizum* 'Album' x 3
3 *Bergenia cordifolia* x 3
4 *Hedera helix* 'Glacier' x 1

Total planting area
approximately 4m²/4yd²

1 See 10.19

Plants with several decorative features usually have more than one season of interest and tend to associate well with a wide range of other plants. Decorative features are listed under 'special characteristics' throughout the book. *Cotoneaster horizontalis*, for example, not only has pretty flowers but also attractive foliage, good autumn colour, strikingly shaped twigs and bright berries. From amongst the many combinations in which this shrub appears, additional plants, shown here in late autumn, have been chosen to flatter the shrub throughout the year. So, for instance, from combinations 15.18 and 10.19, there are pale ivy leaves to emphasize the cotoneaster's summer flowers and its dark winter twigs and, from a hardy geranium, more pale flowers as well as a contrastingly low carpet of leaves. To avoid overall fussiness, there is bold foliage from a spring-flowering bergenia (see 8.19). All four plants are easily grown in sun or partial shade, and in almost any soil with reasonable drainage.

4 See 15.18

3 See 8.19

2 See 10.19

Long-lasting Flowers for Late Colour

1 *Cornus alba* 'Elegantissima' x 1
2 *Nerine bowdenii* x 15
3 *Stachys byzantina* x 3
4 *Aster* × *frikartii* 'Mönch' x 3
5 *Lavatera* 'Rosea' x 1

Total planting area approximately 8.5m²/8.5yd²

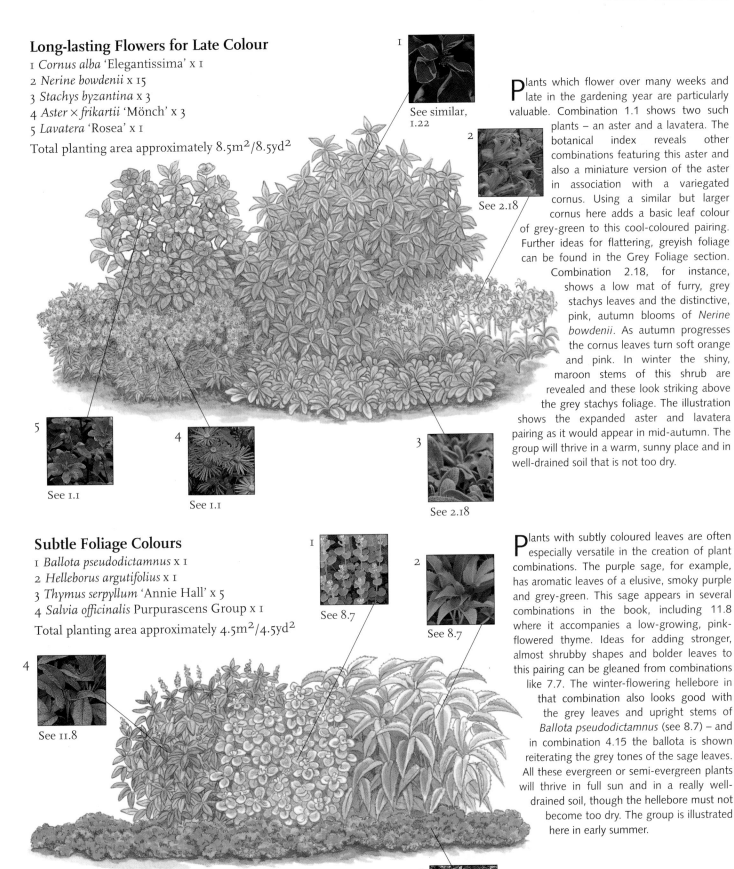

See similar,
1.22

See 2.18

See 1.1

See 1.1

See 2.18

Plants which flower over many weeks and late in the gardening year are particularly valuable. Combination 1.1 shows two such plants – an aster and a lavatera. The botanical index reveals other combinations featuring this aster and also a miniature version of the aster in association with a variegated cornus. Using a similar but larger cornus here adds a basic leaf colour of grey-green to this cool-coloured pairing. Further ideas for flattering, greyish foliage can be found in the Grey Foliage section. Combination 2.18, for instance, shows a low mat of furry, grey stachys leaves and the distinctive, pink, autumn blooms of *Nerine bowdenii*. As autumn progresses the cornus leaves turn soft orange and pink. In winter the shiny, maroon stems of this shrub are revealed and these look striking above the grey stachys foliage. The illustration shows the expanded aster and lavatera pairing as it would appear in mid-autumn. The group will thrive in a warm, sunny place and in well-drained soil that is not too dry.

Subtle Foliage Colours

1 *Ballota pseudodictamnus* x 1
2 *Helleborus argutifolius* x 1
3 *Thymus serpyllum* 'Annie Hall' x 5
4 *Salvia officinalis* Purpurascens Group x 1

Total planting area approximately 4.5m²/4.5yd²

See 8.7

See 8.7

See 11.8

See 11.8

Plants with subtly coloured leaves are often especially versatile in the creation of plant combinations. The purple sage, for example, has aromatic leaves of a elusive, smoky purple and grey-green. This sage appears in several combinations in the book, including 11.8 where it accompanies a low-growing, pink-flowered thyme. Ideas for adding stronger, almost shrubby shapes and bolder leaves to this pairing can be gleaned from combinations like 7.7. The winter-flowering hellebore in that combination also looks good with the grey leaves and upright stems of *Ballota pseudodictamnus* (see 8.7) – and in combination 4.15 the ballota is shown reiterating the grey tones of the sage leaves. All these evergreen or semi-evergreen plants will thrive in full sun and in a really well-drained soil, though the hellebore must not become too dry. The group is illustrated here in early summer.

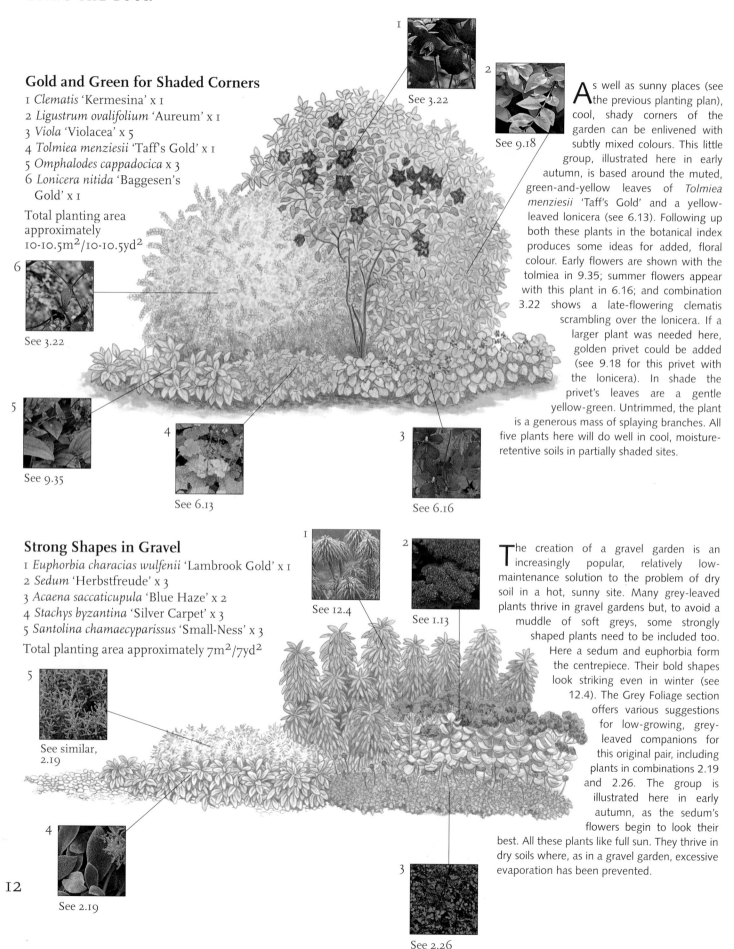

Gold and Green for Shaded Corners

1 *Clematis* 'Kermesina' x 1
2 *Ligustrum ovalifolium* 'Aureum' x 1
3 *Viola* 'Violacea' x 5
4 *Tolmiea menziesii* 'Taff's Gold' x 1
5 *Omphalodes cappadocica* x 3
6 *Lonicera nitida* 'Baggesen's Gold' x 1

Total planting area approximately 10-10.5m²/10-10.5yd²

As well as sunny places (see the previous planting plan), cool, shady corners of the garden can be enlivened with subtly mixed colours. This little group, illustrated here in early autumn, is based around the muted, green-and-yellow leaves of *Tolmiea menziesii* 'Taff's Gold' and a yellow-leaved lonicera (see 6.13). Following up both these plants in the botanical index produces some ideas for added, floral colour. Early flowers are shown with the tolmiea in 9.35; summer flowers appear with this plant in 6.16; and combination 3.22 shows a late-flowering clematis scrambling over the lonicera. If a larger plant was needed here, golden privet could be added (see 9.18 for this privet with the lonicera). In shade the privet's leaves are a gentle yellow-green. Untrimmed, the plant is a generous mass of splaying branches. All five plants here will do well in cool, moisture-retentive soils in partially shaded sites.

See 3.22

See 9.18

6
See 3.22

5
See 9.35

4
See 6.13

3
See 6.16

Strong Shapes in Gravel

1 *Euphorbia characias wulfenii* 'Lambrook Gold' x 1
2 *Sedum* 'Herbstfreude' x 3
3 *Acaena saccaticupula* 'Blue Haze' x 2
4 *Stachys byzantina* 'Silver Carpet' x 3
5 *Santolina chamaecyparissus* 'Small-Ness' x 3

Total planting area approximately 7m²/7yd²

The creation of a gravel garden is an increasingly popular, relatively low-maintenance solution to the problem of dry soil in a hot, sunny site. Many grey-leaved plants thrive in gravel gardens but, to avoid a muddle of soft greys, some strongly shaped plants need to be included too. Here a sedum and euphorbia form the centrepiece. Their bold shapes look striking even in winter (see 12.4). The Grey Foliage section offers various suggestions for low-growing, grey-leaved companions for this original pair, including plants in combinations 2.19 and 2.26. The group is illustrated here in early autumn, as the sedum's flowers begin to look their best. All these plants like full sun. They thrive in dry soils where, as in a gravel garden, excessive evaporation has been prevented.

1
See 12.4

2
See 1.13

5
See similar, 2.19

4
See 2.19

3
See 2.26

12

Designing with a Single Colour

1 *Acer palmatum* x 1
2 *Hosta plantaginea* x 5
3 *Tellima grandiflora* Rubra Group x 7
4 *Epimedium* × *versicolor*
  'Sulphureum' x 7
5 *Dryopteris filix-mas* x 3

Total planting area approximately
13-14m²/13-14yd²

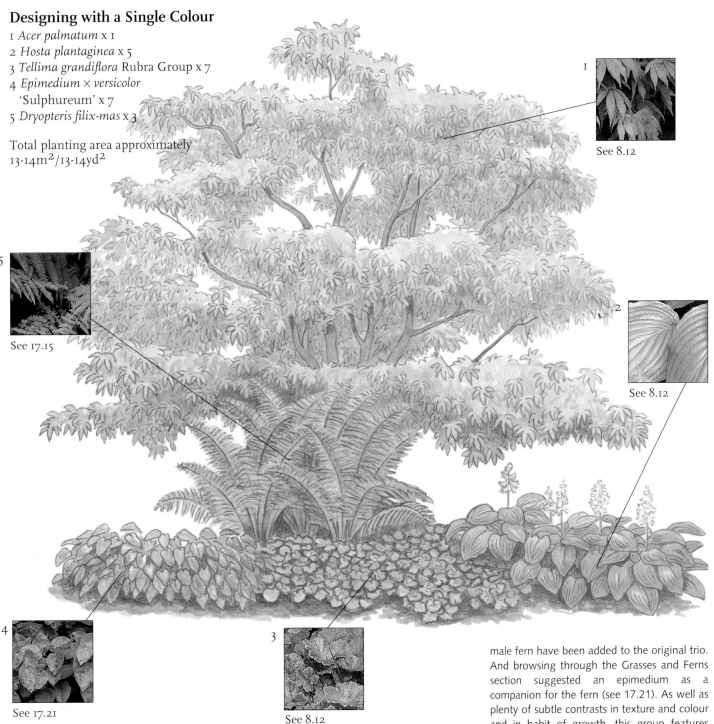

I
See 8.12

5
See 17.15

2
See 8.12

4
See 17.21

3
See 8.12

Areas of visual 'calm' are important in any garden, and all-green combinations in particular can do much to impart an air of cool composure. One of the most serene and elegant combinations in the book is a trio of plants, in the Decorative Green Foliage section, which is centred around *Acer palmatum* (see 8.12). Taking an idea from another combination featuring a form of this maple (see 17.15), the upright fronds of the male fern have been added to the original trio. And browsing through the Grasses and Ferns section suggested an epimedium as a companion for the fern (see 17.21). As well as plenty of subtle contrasts in texture and colour and in habit of growth, this group features early flowers, autumn leaf colour and late, fragrant blooms. The plants are illustrated here in late summer. Ideally, they should be given a lightly shaded, sheltered site and an acid to neutral, moisture-retentive soil.

13

A Cool, Shady Wall

1 *Hydrangea anomala petiolaris* x 1
2 *Polygonatum hybridum* x 7
3 *Dryopteris filix-mas* x 3

Total planting area
approximately
5.5-6m²/5.5-6yd²

1

See 15.20

3

See similar,
17.19

2

See 15.20

Cool, shady walls are often regarded as problematic planting positions, and *Hydrangea anomala petiolaris* is often seen as the solution to the problem. This magnificent climber can clothe a wall beautifully, but the area at ground level can then seem contrastingly bare and uninteresting. Two combinations in the book – 15.20 and 17.19 – feature this hydrangea. If both the crested form of the male fern in 17.19 and the Solomon's seal in 15.20 were planted at the base of the hydrangea there would be several interesting contrast in foliage and habit of growth. There would not, however, be any brash or bright colours to distract attention from the hydrangea. Particularly as the hydrangea matures, the ground beneath it can become rooty and rather dry. The crested form of fern in combination 17.19 is at its best in fairly moist conditions and it may, therefore, be a better long-term decision to use the ordinary male fern (see 17.15) in this planting. This too is a strikingly shaped plant, and it is tough and tolerant as well. Solomon's seal is a very accommodating plant. The illustration shows the three plants in early summer, when the hydrangea is in full flower.

14

See 13.6

See 15.11

See 11.6

See 11.6

Fragrant Features

1 *Rosa* 'Constance Spry' x 1
2 *Clematis viticella x 1*
3 *Lavandula angustifolia* 'Hidcote' x 1
4 *Lychnis coronaria* Atrosanguinea Group x 3

Total planting area
approximately
3-3.5m²/3-3.5yd²

Carefully orchestrated plant combinations can do much to extend the period of interest of individual plants in the garden. The rose 'Constance Spry', for example, produces quantities of pink, fragrant flowers, but only for about two weeks in the year. Aromatic, grey leaves certainly enhance these blooms

see 13.6), but aromatic, grey-leaved plants with late flowers would be even more decorative. Searching in the Aromatic Foliage section reveals a lavender and lychnis pairing (see 11.6) which would flower until late summer. Using the rose to support a later-flowering climber opens up other possibilities.

The Climbing Plants section contains various suggestions for climbers to grow through other plants – including a clematis, in 15.11, which would echo the lavender's flower colour. This group of plants, illustrated here in late summer, needs a sunny site and a reasonably fertile, well-drained soil.

15

LAYOUT OF THE BOOK

All seventeen sections of the book are organized in the same way. First, each section is divided into three sun or shade categories. Every combination in the section is allocated to one or other of these categories. Then, within each of the sun or shade categories, combinations are organized according to the minimum height of the tallest plant in each combination. Combinations featuring tall plants appear before combinations featuring small plants. This means that when you are looking for combinations of small plants for sunny places, you are not diverted by irrelevant combinations featuring tall plants for cool, shady places.

Each combination has a number. The first combination in the first section has the number 1.1. It is immediately followed by combination 1.2 and so on. These numbers are used in any cross-reference. They are also used at the end of each section to refer to further, relevant combinations in other sections. For example, at the end of the Climbing Plants section, all other combinations featuring climbers are listed by their numbers.

All the plants featured in these combinations are garden plants, rather than plants which are only suitable for growing under cover. They are all perennial plants of some sort or another.

Nearly all the plants are readily available, if not from every garden centre, then at least from most suppliers with a good range of general stock as well as from specialist nurseries. For a short list of nurseries and suppliers, see page 260.

SUMMARIES OF PLANT DETAILS

Basic details about every plant are summarized in several lines of information. Additional information – about habit of growth, growing conditions and, for instance, the colour of autumn foliage – are given in the description of the combination. The summaries of plant details always take the same form. They usually consist of at least seven separate items of information.

Name

First, the botanical name of the plant is given. The usual conventions have been followed: in the name *Berberis thunbergii*, for instance, the first word refers to the genus of the plant and the second word refers to the species. Sometimes species vary so much that distinct variants and cultivated varieties are recognized and these are given names. *Berberis thunbergii* f. *atropurpurea* denotes a purple-leaved forma (or botanical form) that arose naturally. The abbreviations 'ssp' and 'var' indicate subspecies and varietas (botanical or naturally occurring variety) respectively. If a variety was selected in cultivation, then its name appears in single, inverted commas, as in *Berberis thunbergii* 'Aurea' and *Berberis* 'Rubrostilla'. A multiplication sign (eg *Aster* × *frikartii* 'Mönch') indicates that a plant is a recognized hybrid.

Many plants have alternative botanical names. Where necessary, any synonymous names appear, in italics, after the main botanical name of a plant. The synonyms are preceded by the abbreviation 'syn'. Synonymous names which have been superceded by newer names, are particularly useful when consulting older gardening books and some plant catalogues.

Where appropriate, a common name follows the botanical name or names of a plant in brackets. For instance, the common name 'holly' appears below *Ilex aquifolium* 'Silver Queen'. This plant is a cultivated variety of the common or English holly with pale cream margins to its leaves. Where no common name is given either the plant has no widely recognized common name or its botanical name is better known than its common name.

Sun and Shade Requirements

It is worth bearing in mind that a soil's ability to retain moisture will sometimes affect the sun and shade requirements of plants. For example, in a moisture-retentive soil many plants will be able to withstand greater exposure to sun than they could if they were grown in a very light, free-draining soil.

There are other complicating factors too. For example, if you live in a cold district, or at the colder end of a plant's climate range, you may find certain plants need a sunnier site than is usually recommended. Unless some plants have sufficient sun and warmth, their wood will not ripen and there will be few flowers. Similarly many plants need shelter from cold winter winds or desiccating summer ones, but shade does not always equal shelter. A shaded site that is also draughty will be much colder and less congenial to good plant growth than a shaded place that is really sheltered and protected. Wherever necessary, the particular likes and dislikes of plants are noted in the accompanying text.

The sun and shade requirements of individual plants and of combinations are noted by means of symbols. The symbols for combinations appear at the top of each page. Where there is a single symbol, both combinations on the page have the same sun or shade requirements. If a page is headed with two symbols, for example ○ | ○ ◐, this means that the first combination needs a sunny site and the second one can be planted in either sun or partial shade. The following symbols are used for sun and shade requirements:

○ = sun. This means that the plant or the combination must receive sun during all, or almost all, the day in the summer months; in some cases the sunniest possible position is needed, and this sort of detail is mentioned in the text accompanying each combination.

○ ◐ = sun or partial shade. This means that the plant or the combination will do equally well in sun and in partial shade. Partially shaded sites receive dappled shade or they receive shade for only part of the day.

◐ = partial shade (as defined above). A few plants or combinations marked with this symbol will not object to being fully shaded all day and this is noted in the text accompanying the combination.

Combinations requiring a sunny site appear at the beginning of each section, followed by combinations that can be grown in either sun or partial shade, and finally by those needing partial shade. As mentioned under Layout of the Book, within each sun and shade category the combinations are arranged in order of height, based on the minimum height of the tallest plant in a combination.

Type of Plant

Immediately below the sun and shade requirements of each plant, there is a very brief description of the type and hardiness of the plant. So, for example, a plant may be described as a 'hardy bulb' or a 'slightly tender shrub'. Where a plant's habit of growth or hardiness varies according to, for instance, climate or maturity, this variability is indicated by the use of an oblique (for example, 'hardy shrub/tree' and 'hardy/slightly tender perennial'). Some plants are variably classified, sometimes being described as perennials, sometimes being called shrubs and so on. An oblique is used in these cases too.

Hardiness

The hardiness (that is, resistance to cold) of a plant depends on many factors. In addition to general climate, the amount of shelter available has a marked effect on the survival of plants in very cold weather. Even within a particular garden, there will some sites which are more sheltered than others. Soil also affects hardiness. Heavy soils tend to be both wet and cold in winter. Some plants find this combination of conditions very uncongenial. Then there are factors such as altitude and snow cover which need to be taken into consideration too. However, as a general rule: 'slightly tender' means that, in very cold weather, superficial damage (such as the browning of leaves) will occur but the plant is unlikely to die; in colder districts of the British Isles the plant may need some protection, though it is likely to be hardy in most parts of Australia, New Zealand, South Africa and the southern states of the USA. 'Hardy' means that, unless there are prolonged periods of very cold weather, the plants needs no special protection anywhere in the British Isles or in the coldest parts of Australia, New Zealand or South Africa.

Zonal Range

Each plant carries a hardiness zone rating, '(zone 8)', or rating range, '(zones 4-9)'. The United States Department of Agriculture's plant hardiness zone map, which is based around minimum winter temperatures, appears on page 259. Where a single figure, rather than a range, is given, this indicates the coldest area in which a plant will survive. In much of Western Europe the climate is a maritime one, and these USDA zones for a large, continental mass are of limited value.

In the Southern hemisphere, where heat and drought are as likely to limit the growth of plants as cold, the system of hardiness zones is not used. It is more useful to give a general description of the type of climate to which the plant is best suited. This is indicated by the following abbreviations: T (tropical), ST (sub-tropical), WT (warm-temperate), CT (cool-temperate), and C (cold). Most plants can be grown in a range of climates. If a plant is designated C-WT, for example, this indicates it will do well in any climate from cold to warm-temperate. Boundaries between climate zones are not hard and fast; a plant rated 'zone 8', for instance, may well be successful also in the warmest parts of zone 7, or one rated 'warm-temperate', in the cooler parts of the sub-tropical zone.

Flowering Time

Most of the summaries of details give the flowering times of plants. Where there is no information about flowering time and flower colour, then either the plant does not flower at all, or its flowers are generally considered inconspicuous. In some years the onset and length of flowering seasons vary.

Flower Colour

If two or more colours are present in a single flower, these appear with a plus sign (for example, white + green). Certain plants are variable in their flower colour and this is noted where relevant.

Height

An estimate of the eventual height of each plant is given. Where applicable, these figures include the height of the plant's flowers (particularly in the case of many perennials, the flowers may be held well above the leaves of the plant).

The eventual height of a plant is subject to many, variable factors such as the climate of a particular district, the richness and moisture-retentiveness of the soil, the aspect of the site and the care with which initial planting was carried out. Other factors such as pruning and the proximity of other, larger plants also have to be taken into consideration. The figures given here represent the eventual height of plants grown in at least reasonably good conditions.

Special Characteristics

Where relevant, each plant summary gives information about the plant's special characteristics. These are mainly decorative features, such as foliage that colours well in autumn. Where no special characteristics are given, the plant's sole, decorative feature will be its flowers. Two other pieces of important information are also given here: if a plant requires an acid soil, or if it is evergreen or semi-evergreen this is noted. Semi-evergreen plants are normally evergreen, but in a cold district or during an unusually cold winter they may lose some or all of their leaves.

Photographs of Combinations

Some photographs of combinations show the plants intermingling. However, in many photographs, one plant is clearly either to the left of the other plant or, alternatively, above it. In almost all cases, this plant's name and details are given first. (See, for instance, the chrysanthemum in combination 1.7 and the eryngium in 1.8.)

1 Cool-coloured Flowers

Planting schemes in which blues harmonize with other blue-toned colours are beguiling in their dreamy, far-away coolness. While the hotter colours of red, orange and yellow seem to advance towards the viewer, colours such as blue, mauve, lilac and pale, blue-tinged pink appear more distant than they really are. White flowers are perhaps best regarded as occupying a midpoint. They can certainly give an impression of coolness, both when they are associated with cool-coloured flowers and when they are planted alongside blooms of hotter hues, but rather than receding from the viewer they stand out conspicuously from their surroundings.

Grey leaves are one of the classic accompaniments of cool-coloured flowers, and combinations of pale pink flowers and grey leaves are especially popular (see Grey, Blue or Silver Foliage, pages 41-57). Grey foliage is frequently furry or hairy and therefore adds a soft texture to planting schemes, as well as a rather understated, almost inert coolness. However, there are plants – many sedums and some hebes and irises, for instance – with grey foliage that is smooth.

White-variegated foliage and glaucous leaves can also help to create a cool effect. When white-variegated leaves are combined with the chilly brilliance of white flowers a rather crisp, clean look emerges, while blue flowers combined with distinctly blue-toned leaves create cool harmonies.

Hot and Cold Combinations

A quite different approach to cool-coloured flowers is to combine them with contrastingly hot colours, such as bright oranges and reds. Both in this section and particularly in Hot-coloured Flowers (see pages 59-76) there are examples of such combinations. When hot and cold colours are set side by side the hot colours tend to appear hotter and the cool colours cooler, though of course the overall effect of a particular hot and cold combination depends upon the balance of colours in the combination. Touches of white among a mass of intense orange amounts to a hot combination, while the occasional dash of orange in a sea of white gives quite a cool impression overall.

As a complicating factor, light can have a marked effect upon the appearance of some cool colours, and the balance of hot and cold combinations can therefore alter considerably according to the time of day and the nature of the weather. In shade, and at dusk, white flowers gleam enticingly, whereas red flowers are quickly lost in the gloom as the light fades. Blue flowers look especially cool in shade; in full midday sun their coolness is diminished. As for white flowers, their light-reflecting qualities mean that they can appear disappointingly harsh and flat in the glare of full sun.

Adding Warmth

In combinations where only cool flower colours are present, touches of subdued warmth can be added in the form of purple or reddish leaves. Such foliage can also contribute drama and weight to plantings of cool pastels, especially if it is dark. Purple – which in many instances can be regarded as a warmer blue – harmonizes beautifully with blue and blue-tinged flowers, while the red tones in it ensure that it also blends very attractively with pale, cool pinks and with mauves and lilacs (see 4.7). When white blooms and purple foliage are combined the result is often particularly sparkling (see 4.18).

Another source of gentle warmth to add to cool-coloured flowers is yellow or yellow-variegated foliage. With this foliage, white flowers look clean and simple and blue flowers exude an exhilarating cheerfulness (see 17.13). Yellow flowers have a similar effect.

Using Green

At its yellowest, green foliage behaves with cool-coloured flowers in much the same way as yellow foliage does. In its darkest, richest manifestations, green foliage acts rather as dark purple foliage does, adding substance and weight to groups of pretty, cool-coloured blooms. The mid-greens generally have a straightforward, calming effect. Green flowers of pale or delicate shades give freshness to partnerships featuring cool-coloured blooms (see 7.14 and 7.15), whereas blooms of a sharper, yellower green have the effect of brightening and enlivening them (see 1.32).

Green foliage is available in a very wide range of shapes and sizes as well as tones (see Decorative Green Foliage, pages 129-141). Some of the bolder shapes and larger sizes of green leaves can be used to prevent the soft harmonies of the coolest flower colours from becoming simply misty muddles of too closely related shades.

Definition and Focus

Other means of adding definition to potentially ill-defined plantings include the introduction of some conspicuous flower shapes. In this section alone there are, for instance, the dramatic, prickly-looking flowers of eryngiums (sea hollies), the very erect flower spikes of ajugas (bugles) and the strikingly dense globes of *Echinops ritro*. Flowers of a really bright and dazzling white and those that are very vividly blue can also give focus to undifferentiated swathes of closely harmonized, cool flower colours.

Whether soft, quiet flower colours are used in romantic interminglings of blues and nearly-blues or pale pinks and whites, or employed more dramatically as counterpoints to blooms of hotter hues, the choice of cool-coloured material is huge. There are plants of every size, from trees to low-growing perennials with a wide range of shrubs, climbers, bulbs and taller perennials in between. Gardeners who find fragrant flowers particularly attractive will soon discover that many scented blooms are pale or cool-coloured (see Fragrant Flowers, pages 199-210).

The range remains substantial even in the coldest months. In winter, reds and oranges are to be found outdoors only among berries and barks, but there are winter flowers in all the cool colours, including the pale pinks of viburnums and the delicate lavender-blues of *Crocus tommasinianus* (see 14.9) and *Iris unguicularis* (syn *I. stylosa*), as well as the whites of classic winter flowers such as snowdrops and *Helleborus niger* (Christmas rose). So, from snowdrops onwards, there are many interesting and appealing ingredients with which to concoct schemes of ethereal coolness, of crisp, clean freshness or, indeed, of exciting hot-and-cold contrasts.

1.1 Lavatera & Aster

Lavatera 'Rosea'
(syn *L. arborea* 'Rosea')
(tree mallow, bush mallow)
sun/shade ○
type of plant slightly tender shrub
zonal range 8-11 (C-ST)
flowering time early summer to mid-autumn
flower colour pink
height 1.8-2.4m (6-8ft)

Aster × frikartii 'Mönch'
sun/shade ○
type of plant hardy perennial
zonal range 5-8 (C-WT)
flowering time late summer to mid-autumn
flower colour lavender-blue
height 90cm (3ft)

Seen here in mid-autumn, the lovely, slim-petalled, cool-coloured flowers of this aster are only just beginning to show signs of fading. The lavatera that accompanies them in this instance is another plant with an exceptionally long flowering season. As well as an appealing contrast in flower shape, this partnership features a highly successful blending of colours, mainly because the hints of blue in the lavatera's pink blooms provide a link with the fine blue rays of the aster.

In addition to a long succession of flowers, this vigorous, if fairly short-lived lavatera contributes a certain firmness of structure to the planting; with its lobed, slightly grey leaves, its dark, upright stems and its subshrubby constitution, it prevents the whole picture from being simply a mass of pretty flowers. The aster is of finer habit altogether, although its well-branched stems are strong and self-supporting.

This combination needs to be given a warm, sunny site, especially in colder districts. During prolonged periods of frosty weather the lavatera's top growth will die. However, there will usually be plenty of new growth the following spring, although the plant will stay quite small if regularly cut back by frost. Both plants like a fertile, well-drained soil that is reasonably moisture-retentive.

1.2 Crocosmia & Chrysanthemum

Crocosmia paniculata
(syn *Curtonus paniculatus*)
sun/shade ○
type of plant hardy corm
zonal range 6-9 (CT-ST)
flowering time late summer to early autumn
flower colour orange-red + orange
height 1.2m (4ft)
special characteristics decorative green foliage

Chrysanthemum maximum 'Mayfield Giant'
(syn *Leucanthemum × superbum* 'Mayfield Giant')
(Shasta daisy)
sun/shade ○
type of plant hardy perennial
zonal range 4-8 (C-ST)
flowering time early to late summer
flower colour white + yellow
height 1.2-1.5m (4-5ft)

The familiar Shasta daisies have petals of such a glacial white that they sparkle with other cool colours and – as here – with glowing oranges and reds. Despite the fact that the white is so pure, the overall effect is not flat. This is partly because the centre of each flower is usually yellow, but also because of the attractively uneven disposition of the petals, held on top of long, clear stems. All forms of Shasta daisy make excellent cut flowers. 'Mayfield Giant' is unusually tall; most varieties are about 60-90cm (2-3ft) high and would need to be placed in front of this crocosmia.

In complete contrast to these bright white daisies, the crocosmia's flowers consist of very richly coloured, curving trumpets poised on dark, branching stems. The whole appearance of this combination is considerably enhanced by the crocosmia's great sheaf of pleated greenery. The lance-shaped foliage of the Shasta daisy is a relatively unremarkable dark green.

As long as the Shasta daisy has good drainage, it will grow in most soils. However, when it is given the fairly fertile, moisture-retentive conditions which the crocosmia likes best, it will form good clumps of growth and flower well. For plenty of blooms, Shasta daisies – especially the double-flowered varieties – should be divided every few years.

1.3 Echinops & Aconitum

Echinops ritro
(globe thistle)
sun/shade ○
type of plant hardy perennial
zonal range 3-9 (C-WT)
flowering time mid- to late summer
flower colour blue
height 90-120cm (3-4ft)
special characteristics decorative green foliage

Aconitum × cammarum 'Bicolor'
(monkshood)
sun/shade ○ ◑
type of plant hardy perennial
zonal range 4-8 (C-WT)
flowering time mid- to late summer
flower colour white + violet
height 1.2m (4ft)

In this combination, the deep blue flowerheads of *Echinops ritro* look especially dense, spiky and symmetrical with a softly shaped crowd of frosty hoods behind them. The violet staining on the lips of these hoods brings out the touches of violet just present in the much darker flowers of the echinops. This echo of colouring links the two plants in a very successful blue and white partnership.

The jagged leaves of the echinops are aggressive-looking and of a good dark green (see 3.9), with white undersides. The monkshood's glossy, deeply divided foliage is also dark, but it is of a much softer texture. In contrast to the stiff stems and solid flowerheads of the echinops, the monkshood bears its loose masses of flowers on branching stems. All parts of the monkshood are very poisonous if eaten; hands should be washed after handling the plant.

Neither of these perennials is difficult to grow. The echinops thrives in all well-drained soils. Ideally, the monkshood should have a fertile, moisture-retentive soil; in dryish conditions, some shade is advisable.

The echinops' long-lasting flowerheads soften slightly in appearance as the plant begins to set seed and, as seedheads, they become attractive to birds. Earlier, the flowers are visited by butterflies and bees.

1.4 Lilium & Galtonia

Lilium lancifolium
(syn *L. tigrinum*)
(tiger lily)
sun/shade ○
type of plant hardy bulb
zonal range 3-8 (C-WT)
flowering time late summer to early autumn
flower colour orange
height 1.2m (4ft)
special characteristics needs acid soil

Galtonia candicans
(summer hyacinth, spire lily, cape lily)
sun/shade ○
type of plant hardy bulb
zonal range 7-10 (WT-ST)
flowering time late summer
flower colour white
height 1.05-1.2m (3½-4ft)

The impact of this combination comes in part from the similarities between these two late-season plants; though the arrangement of their leaves differs, both have hanging flowers on upright stems of approximately the same height. However, the difference in colour is spectacular. *Galtonia candicans* is all coolness: bare, rather pale green stems, slightly fragrant ice-white flowers with tinges of green, and glaucous blades of lax foliage. The lily, on the other hand, is hot and exotic. Its long, pendent buds transform themselves into glowing, spotted turk's caps, each about 10cm (4in) wide and complete with flamboyant stamens. The densely arranged, pointed leaves also add to the boldness of this plant.

Both of these plants perform well in fertile, well-drained but moisture-retentive soil. When well-suited, the galtonia self-seeds. *Lilium lancifolium* is easily increased from the bulbils found among its leaves. This lily and its forms need acid soil. Although these plants are prone to viral infection, they are usually robust enough to withstand its effects.

1.5 Anaphalis, Aster & Persicaria

Anaphalis margaritacea var. yedoensis

(syn *A. yedoensis*) (pearly everlasting)
sun/shade ○ **type of plant** hardy perennial
zonal range 4-8 (C-WT)
flowering time late summer to early autumn
flower colour white **height** 60cm (2ft)
special characteristics grey foliage

Aster novi-belgii 'Professor Anton Kippenberg'

(Michaelmas daisy)
sun/shade ○ **type of plant** hardy perennial
zonal range 4-8 (C-WT)
flowering time early to mid-autumn
flower colour mid-blue **height** 30-40cm (12-15in)

Persicaria amplexicaulis 'Atrosanguinea'

(syn *Polygonum amplexicaule* 'Atrosanguineum')
(bistort)
sun/shade ○ ◑ **type of plant** hardy perennial
zonal range 5-9 (CT-WT)
flowering time early summer to early autumn
flower colour deep red **height** 90-120cm (3-4ft)
special characteristics suitable for damp soils

If this combination were to consist of the cool-coloured anaphalis and Michaelmas daisy alone it would be a success. However, the addition of the bistort introduces interesting contrasts in shape as well as very effective touches of a warmer colour. First of all, there are the relatively large, bright green leaves of this plant, which differ markedly both from the Michaelmas daisy's clusters of dark green, close-textured foliage and from the slim, grey leaves of the anaphalis. Then there is the slenderness of the bistort's flower spikes, which contrasts with – but does not detract from – the more concentrated arrangement of the flowers of the other two plants. Finally, there is the bistort's much warmer flower colour, though the blueness in this deep red ensures that there is a link between it and the cooler colour of the Michaelmas daisy.

Although the three elements of this composition are quite distinct, the overall effect is one of well-matched partners – and the partnership has a long and late season of interest. Not only does the clump-forming bistort flower for many weeks, the crisp and papery flowers of the anaphalis continue to look decorative well after the end of their official flowering season. They are also conspicuous in bud, and the accompanying grey foliage and erect, pale stems look light and pretty for many months.

Ideally, this combination should be grown in a soil that is moist, fertile and well-drained. It is important that these late-flowering plants do not become dry in summer.

1.6 Sedum & Aster

Sedum 'Herbstfreude'

(syn *S.* 'Autumn Joy')
(stonecrop)
sun/shade ○
type of plant hardy perennial
zonal range 3-10 (C-ST)
flowering time late summer to mid-autumn
flower colour rose changing to salmon-pink, then bronze
height 45-60cm (1½-2ft)
special characteristics blue-green foliage, fruit

Aster × frikartii 'Mönch'

sun/shade ○
type of plant hardy perennial
zonal range 5-8 (C-WT)
flowering time late summer to mid-autumn
flower colour lavender-blue
height 90cm (3ft)

Well before its large, wide flowerheads colour up in autumn (see 1.13), this popular sedum may be said to be in bloom. This photograph shows the plant towards the end of summer, when the flowers are almost entirely green. Nevertheless, they already look very handsome and they create a lovely block of close-textured solidity in contrast to the airy mass of slim-petalled aster flowers. The sedum's dense clump of blue-green, fleshy foliage and erect stems (see 4.13) is a further source of firm shapes and contrasting texture. The aster's smaller-scale foliage and branching stems create an altogether slenderer structure. The sedum's leaves look bold and effective from early summer onwards.

The exceptionally long flowering season of the aster means that this is a combination that looks well over many weeks in early autumn. As a very late season bonus, the sedum produces seedheads of rich, reddish brown which make striking additions to the garden in winter (see 12.4).

Both these plants are easy to grow but they are at their best in fairly fertile, well-drained soils that retain moisture. The sedum in particular benefits from being divided from time to time to ensure a neat habit of growth and plenty of large flower-heads.

I.7 Chrysanthemum & Eryngium

Chrysanthemum maximum 'Shaggy'

(syn *Leucanthemum × superbum* 'Shaggy')
(Shasta daisy)
sun/shade ○
type of plant hardy perennial
zonal range 4-8 (C-ST)
flowering time early to late summer
flower colour white + yellow
height 90cm (3ft)

Eryngium × zabelii

(sea holly)
sun/shade ○
type of plant hardy perennial
zonal range 5-8 (C-CT)
flowering time mid- to late summer
flower colour violet-blue
height 60-75cm (2-2½ft)

The dense, teasel-like flowerheads and stiff, blue stems of *Eryngium × zabelii* emphasize the wonderfully wispy petals of these Shasta daisies. There is a certain wispiness about the thin, spiny bracts of the eryngium, too, but the stiffer and more solid parts of the plant prevent the whole combination from being too fussy. The striking association of a chilly, metallic blue and a brilliant white also tends to simplify and strengthen the whole composition.

Neither of the perennials here could be described as a foliage plant, although the jagged leaves of the eryngium certainly contribute to the plant's attractive, prickly appearance. The lack of any outstanding foliage is compensated for by two sets of flowers that look good over many weeks. The eryngium especially is effective over a long period, both before its flowers become fully coloured and after the blueness of the strikingly shaped flowerheads has faded.

Shasta daisies are easily grown in most well-drained soils but they flower most profusely when conditions are fertile and moisture-retentive. These growing conditions suit the eryngium as well, although it can tolerate some dryness.

'Phyllis Smith' is a variety of *Chrysanthemum maximum* that is similar to 'Shaggy'. Shasta daisies are normally self-supporting. Fairly frequent division helps to stimulate flower production.

I.8 Eryngium & Astrantia

Eryngium alpinum

(sea holly)
sun/shade ○
type of plant hardy perennial
zonal range 5-8 (C-CT)
flowering time midsummer to early autumn
flower colour mauve-blue
height 75cm (2½ft)

Astrantia maxima

(syn *A. helleborifolia*)
(masterwort)
sun/shade ○ ◖
type of plant hardy perennial
zonal range 4-8 (C-CT)
flowering time early to late summer
flower colour pink
height 60cm (2ft)

The rather prim flowers of *Astrantia maxima* contrast delightfully here with the extravagant ruffs of *Eryngium alpinum*, while the teaming of the latter's strong, cold, metallic colour with the lovely strawberry-mousse pink of the astrantia creates a pink and blue combination that is unusually deep-toned. The astrantia's fruity colouring is given further impact by the way in which the flowers appear in a fairly closely packed mass. The elaborate, mock-prickly thistles of the eryngium are, in contrast, quite widely spaced on their blue, branching stems.

The comparatively dense growth of the astrantia is also apparent in its foliage which, in moisture-retentive soils particularly, will form thick clumps. Each leaf is neatly divided into three lobes. The eryngium's basal foliage is large and heart-shaped, with slimmer, sharper-looking leaves at various points up the flowering stems.

The flowers of both these plants are decorative over a long period, and the astrantia's papery-textured blooms make good material for drying. The eryngium's flowers look handsome even before they become fully coloured (see 3.11).

Although the eryngium will tolerate some dryness, it grows best in a moist, fertile soil that is also well-drained – conditions that the astrantia enjoys, too.

23

1.9 Eryngium & Erigeron

Eryngium alpinum

(sea holly)
sun/shade ○
type of plant hardy perennial
zonal range 5-8 (C-CT)
flowering time midsummer to early autumn
flower colour mauve-blue
height 75cm (2½ft)

Erigeron cultivar

(fleabane)
sun/shade ○
type of plant hardy perennial
zonal range 5-8 (C-WT)
flowering time early to late summer
flower colour lilac-pink
height 45-60cm (1½-2ft)

Here the eye-catching ruffs of *Eryngium alpinum* are accompanied by blooms of a cooler, more lilac pink and a much softer texture than those of the astrantia shown in 1.8. The slight hints of blue in these erigeron flowers blend beautifully with the mauve tones of the eryngium. At the same time, there is a striking contrast between the eryngium's dramatic thistles, on their stout, blue, branching stems, and the erigeron's lower clump of demure, finely petalled, circular flowers. Neither plant has really decorative foliage. The jagged stem leaves and the large, heart-shaped basal leaves of the eryngium are, however, certainly more assertive than the very modest and rather sparse foliage of the erigeron.

The eryngium's thistles are so strikingly shaped that they make an impact even in early summer, when they are still green, while erigerons of the type shown here are all notably long-lasting in flower. The flowering and the general growth of both these perennials is best in fertile, well-drained soils that do not dry out in summer. Of the two plants, the eryngium is more tolerant of dryness.

The erigeron illustrated here seems close to an old variety called 'Festivity'. This is no longer readily available, but 'Quakeress' would make a very attractive, rather paler substitute of similar tone.

1.10 Polemonium & Nepeta

Polemonium caeruleum ssp. *caeruleum* f. *album*

(syn *P. c. album*)
(Jacob's ladder)
sun/shade ○ ◑
type of plant hardy perennial
zonal range 4-8 (C-WT)
flowering time late spring to midsummer
flower colour white
height 60cm (2ft)

Nepeta 'Six Hills Giant'

(catmint)
sun/shade ○
type of plant hardy perennial
zonal range 4-8 (C-WT)
flowering time early summer to early autumn
flower colour lavender-blue
height 60-75cm (2-2½ft)
special characteristics semi-evergreen, aromatic, grey-green foliage

When two plants have flowers that are arranged in a similar way, the eye is concentrated principally upon colour differences. Here there are two sets of spire-like flowers, each on erect stems of roughly the same height. With this repetition of shape, attention is focused upon the composition's blue and white colouring.

Though much of the charm of this combination is due to the clean, fresh coolness of its flower colours, the way in which the two plants mingle with one another is also important. This kind of interweaving nearly always creates an informal, rather soft appearance.

Both the leaves and the flowers of these plants are attractive, though the polemonium's ferny foliage is not produced in large quantities. The catmint will form a dense clump of curving stems and little, grey-green, minty-scented leaves, especially if it is cut back in midsummer, after its first flush of flowers. This treatment will also extend the plant's long flowering season still further.

Polemonium caeruleum and its forms are particularly at home in moist, fertile soils and they flower especially well in sunny positions. They are, however, easy-going plants that will often self-seed prolifically. *Nepeta* 'Six Hills Giant' needs a well-drained soil.

I.II Astrantia & Malva

Astrantia maxima
(syn *A. helleborifolia*)
(masterwort)
sun/shade ○ ◑
type of plant hardy perennial
zonal range 4-8 (C-CT)
flowering time early to late summer
flower colour pink
height 60cm (2ft)

Malva moschata f. alba
(musk mallow)
sun/shade ○
type of plant hardy perennial
zonal range 4-8 (C-WT)
flowering time early summer to early autumn
flower colour white
height 60cm (2ft)
special characteristics aromatic, decorative green foliage

It is the pretty colouring of this combination – the luscious, fruity pink paired with clean white – that catches the eye first. The beautifully scrolled buds of the mallow, the centre of each delicate flower and also the faded flowers are all tinged with palest pink, forming subtle but significant links with the astrantia.

However, this is not simply a partnership of pretty colours. There are several interesting differences in the shape and texture of the flowers of these two plants. The astrantia has crisp-textured, dome-centred flowers. In contrast, the mallow's comparatively simple blooms are open-faced and of a moister texture.

The astrantia produces a clump of clearly defined, tripartite leaves, above which the flower stems rise erectly, while the mallow grows much more loosely, forming a mass of lax stems and very finely divided, musk-scented foliage.

Both these plants flower best in rich, moisture-retentive soils that have good drainage. Moist conditions also ensure that the astrantia grows densely. Although it can look well in light shade, a position in full sun helps to keep the mallow from sprawling too openly. This mallow and its forms are short-lived perennials, but they self-seed prolifically.

I.I2 Geranium & Nepeta

Geranium pratense 'Mrs Kendall Clark'
(meadow cranesbill)
sun/shade ○ ◑
type of plant hardy perennial
zonal range 5-8 (C-WT)
flowering time early to mid-summer
flower colour pale grey-blue
height 60cm (2ft)
special characteristics decorative green foliage, autumn foliage

Nepeta × faassenii
(catmint)
sun/shade ○
type of plant hardy perennial
zonal range 4-8 (C-WT)
flowering time early summer to early autumn
flower colour lavender-blue
height 30-45cm (1-1½ft)
special characteristics semi-evergreen, aromatic, grey-green foliage

Gentle, harmonizing colours, soft flower shapes and pretty foliage all contribute to the charm of this combination. The pale blue of the geranium is almost a misty, far-away version of the catmint's flower colour. This link in colouring is heightened by the way in which the slim, rather floppy stems and open-faced flowers of the geranium entangle themselves beguilingly in the catmint's more upright flower spikes.

The leaves of both these plants are also attractive. The overall effect of the geranium's deeply cut foliage is one of finely textured, massed greenery. In autumn, this foliage turns shades of yellow, orange and red. The catmint's little leaves are softly hairy and mint-scented, and both the leaves and the curving stems of the plant are grey-green.

If the stems of the catmint are cut back in spring and the plant is in well-drained soil, all this greyish growth will be neat and dense. Cutting the plant back a second time, after the first flush of flowers, will encourage it to bloom for several months.

Hot, dry conditions suit the catmint but, for the sake of the geranium, this combination needs to be given a soil that does not become too parched in summer. Like all the single-flowered meadow cranesbills, *Geranium pratense* 'Mrs Kendall Clark' self-seeds prolifically.

25

1.13 Sedum & Anaphalis

Sedum 'Herbstfreude'

(syn *S.* 'Autumn Joy')
(stonecrop)
sun/shade ○
type of plant hardy perennial
zonal range 3-10 (C-ST)
flowering time late summer to mid-autumn
flower colour rose changing to salmon-pink, then bronze
height 45-60cm (1½-2ft)
special characteristics blue-green foliage, fruit

Anaphalis triplinervis

(pearly everlasting)
sun/shade ○
type of plant hardy perennial
zonal range 4-9 (C-ST)
flowering time late summer to early autumn
flower colour white
height 30-45cm (1-1½ft)
special characteristics grey foliage

The pearly everlastings, including the popular form shown here, are useful sources of long-lasting grey and white coolness. *Anaphalis triplinervis* forms a clump of slightly curving, pale stems clothed with white-backed, grey leaves. The flowers too have a long season of interest (the photograph here shows them in mid-autumn).

Here this anaphalis has been paired with another perennial that looks good over many months. As the erect stems of *Sedum* 'Herbstfreude' lengthen in late spring and early summer, the glaucous, fleshy foliage starts to form a strikingly firm clump of growth. The flowerheads above these leaves are large and solid and handsome, even in their green state (see 1.6). In autumn, they are richly coloured and the soft rustiness in their pink, coupled with the frosty anaphalis flowers, gives a definite autumnal feel to the combination. In winter the sedum flowers are transformed into rich red-brown seedheads (see 12.4).

The anaphalis bears its numerous flowers in dense clusters, but the overall appearance of this plant is a good deal looser than that of the sedum.

This combination needs a soil that is well-drained but moisture-retentive and reasonably fertile. The anaphalis does not prosper in dry conditions, and the sedum will not flower well in poor soils.

1.14 Alchemilla & Centaurea

Alchemilla mollis

(lady's mantle)
sun/shade ○ ◑
type of plant hardy perennial
zonal range 4-8 (C-WT)
flowering time early to mid-summer
flower colour yellow-green
height 45cm (1½ft)
special characteristics decorative green foliage, suitable for damp soils

Centaurea montana carnea

(syn *C. m. rosea*)
(mountain knapweed)
sun/shade ○
type of plant hardy perennial
zonal range 3-8 (C-WT)
flowering time late spring to midsummer with some later flowers
flower colour lilac-pink
height 45cm (18in)

The familiar, deep blue flowers of *Centaurea montana* itself would also look well combined with alchemilla, but the cool pink blooms of this form produce an especially gentle association of colours. Indeed, this is altogether a soft, relaxed partnership that would blend prettily with many other plants. The knapweed in particular has rather floppy stems, and as the alchemilla's foam of tiny green stars expands and loosens, that plant too tends to become slightly more lax and untidy. However, cutting the alchemilla right back after its first flush of flowers will produce a new and neater clump of foliage and, sometimes, a small, second crop of flowers, too.

The knapweed's spreading mat of narrow leaves has a greyish cast to it, but compared with the lovely, lime-green suede of the alchemilla's scalloped foliage (see 8.21) it is not particularly decorative. However, the knapweed's density of growth makes a pleasing background for the plant's large, elegantly wispy flowers. The alchemilla also grows densely and older specimens create especially impenetrable mounds of roots and stems.

Alchemilla mollis will grow – and self-seed with abandon – in almost any soil. The knapweed is at its best in well-drained, preferably alkaline soils that retain moisture.

1.15 Penstemon & Osteospermum

Penstemon 'Catherine de la Mare'

sun/shade ○
type of plant slightly tender perennial
zonal range 7-8 (CT-WT)
flowering time midsummer to mid-autumn
flower colour violet-blue
height 30-40cm (12-15in)
special characteristics semi-evergreen

Osteospermum jucundum 'Langtrees'

(syn *O.* 'Langtrees')
sun/shade ○
type of plant slightly tender perennial
zonal range 9-11 (WT-ST)
flowering time early summer to mid-autumn
flower colour mauve-tinged pink
height 23-30cm (9-12in)
special characteristics semi-evergreen

Except in very mild districts, this combination of two exceptionally long-flowering plants needs a really warm and sheltered position. Neither plant has foliage that is very remarkable, but this hardly matters in view of the fact that there are numerous flowers over a period of several months.

Compared with the slender trumpets of the penstemon, the osteospermum's broad-petalled flowers are large – about 5cm (2in) wide. However, the wonderful blue of the penstemon, with its vivid violet undertones, means that these smaller flowers are not eclipsed by the larger daisies of the osteospermum. Interestingly, some of the penstemon's violet undertones are reiterated both in the inner mauveish-pink surfaces and, more definitely, in the dark outer surfaces of the osteospermum's petals.

To prosper, these plants need a fertile soil that is both well-drained and moisture-retentive, although the osteospermum can survive periods of drought. The osteospermum is not long-lived, but vigorous young specimens form quite thick tangles of narrow leaves. The penstemon is a bushier plant than the osteospermum and its leafy growths are more conspicuously upright. The colouring of this penstemon (and of other similar hybrids such as *P.* 'Margery Fish') varies somewhat according to soil and climate and to the maturity of the plant.

1.16 Hebe & Erigeron

Hebe 'Youngii'

(syn *H.* 'Carl Teschner')
sun/shade ○
type of plant slightly tender shrub
zonal range 8-11 (WT-ST)
flowering time midsummer
flower colour violet-blue
height 23cm (9in)
special characteristics evergreen

Erigeron karvinskianus

(syn *E. mucronatus*)
(fleabane)
sun/shade ○
type of plant hardy perennial
zonal range 5-10 (CT-ST)
flowering time early summer to mid-autumn
flower colour white changing to soft pink
height 23-30cm (9-12in)
special characteristics evergreen

The dense, very widespreading hummock of neat little leaves produced by this hebe is characteristically covered in flowers and buds. In charming, informal contrast, a dwarf fleabane threads its slender way through this mass of close-set, tidy growth. This fleabane is another profuse flowerer, its many-petalled daisies, carried on top of very thin, curving stems, appearing over an exceptionally long period. The plant self-seeds happily and is particularly at home in cracks and crevices.

When the hebe's numerous flowers have faded, the little fleabane continues to light up the shrub's greyish foliage. However, the hebe is not unattractive out of flower and it is a useful plant in some foliage combinations (see, for example, 8.6).

This particular combination is growing on top of a drystone wall, and both plants are enjoying the sunshine and good drainage provided there. As they spill down the sides of the wall they meet a delightful mixture of other plants, including some ferns and the reddish-leaved *Heuchera micrantha diversifolia* 'Palace Purple'.

1.17 Hebe & Lithodora

Hebe pinguifolia 'Pagei'

sun/shade ○ ◗
type of plant hardy/slightly tender shrub
zonal range 8-10 (WT-ST)
flowering time late spring to early summer
flower colour white
height 15-30cm (6-12in)
special characteristics evergreen, blue-grey foliage

Lithodora diffusa 'Heavenly Blue'

(syn *Lithospermum diffusum* 'Heavenly Blue')
sun/shade ○
type of plant hardy shrub
zonal range 6-8 (CT-WT)
flowering time late spring to early summer
flower colour intense blue
height 10-15cm (4-6in)
special characteristics evergreen, needs acid soil

The clear blue of these lithodora flowers looks wonderful against the plant's own dense carpet of deep green. Adding another close mat of leaves which, in this case, has a distinctly blue cast to it, does nothing to detract from this penetrating flower colour and much to enhance it. Not only is there a pleasing reiteration of blueness, but the hebe's exceptionally neat, rounded, almost fleshy leaves contrast nicely with the lithodora's quite differently shaped and coloured foliage. The hebe's trim little flower spikes also contribute to the success of this partnership, adding a 'blue and white china' freshness to the whole combination. After all the flowers have faded, the tapestry created by these two sets of leaves will continue to look well for many months. However, the lithodora will not look its best in winter and in cold areas particularly may be only semi-evergreen.

In well-drained soils and sunny sites, both these plants will grow neatly and densely. The lithodora must have an acid and, ideally, a humus-rich soil in order to thrive and flower really profusely. When well-suited it may spread over 60cm (2ft) or more. In time, the almost prostrate, rooting stems of the hebe may extend at least as far.

1.18 Embothrium & Magnolia

Embothrium coccineum Lanceolatum Group 'Norquinco'

(syn *E. c. lanceolatum* 'Norquinco Valley')
(Chilean fire bush)
sun/shade ○ ◗
type of plant slightly tender tree/shrub
zonal range 8-10 (CT-WT)
flowering time late spring to early summer
flower colour scarlet
height 4.5-9m (15-30ft)
special characteristics semi-evergreen, needs acid soil

Magnolia × soulangeana 'Brozzoni'

sun/shade ○ ◗
type of plant hardy tree/shrub
zonal range 5-9 (CT-WT)
flowering time mid- to late spring
flower colour white + purple-pink
height 6-7.5m (20-25ft)

The large, upright flowers of this late-flowering variety of magnolia are only faintly tinged with purplish-pink at their bases. They therefore appear dazzlingly white and especially so since the plant has virtually no leaves at this stage. This spectacular show of blossom has been made still more dramatic by being combined with flowers of a sizzling scarlet. Here, early in the last month of spring, the flowers on this Chilean fire bush have not yet fully expanded. However, the contrasts between hot and cold colours, and between dense clusters of thin, tubular flowers and large, smoothly shaped petals, are already striking.

Brilliant though this combination is at flowering time, its period of glory is fairly short-lived. Nevertheless, both plants have the sort of rich green foliage that makes a good background for other, smaller plants. The magnolia usually forms a small tree of sweeping, generously spreading branches, while the Chilean fire bush is very much narrower and more erect in outline.

The relatively late flowering period of this magnolia makes its flowers less vulnerable to frost damage, but both plants benefit from a sheltered site. The Chilean fire bush must have an acid or neutral, moist, well-drained and at least moderately fertile soil. These conditions also suit the magnolia.

1.19 Eucryphia & Monarda

Eucryphia glutinosa

sun/shade ○ ◐
type of plant slightly tender shrub/tree
zonal range 8-9 (WT)
flowering time mid- to late summer
flower colour white + yellow
height 3.6-5.4m (12-18ft)
special characteristics semi-evergreen/
deciduous, autumn foliage, needs acid soil

Monarda 'Prärienacht'

(syn *M*. 'Prairie Night')
(sweet bergamot, bee balm, Oswego tea)
sun/shade ○ ◐
type of plant hardy perennial
zonal range 4-9 (C-WT)
flowering time midsummer to early autumn
flower colour violet-pink
height 1.2m (4ft)
special characteristics aromatic foliage

On well-established specimens *Eucryphia gluti-nosa* becomes smothered with beautifully simple, cool white flowers. Here its glossy-leaved growths, weighed down with blossom, are accompanied by patches of strong, blue-tinged pink. These frizzes of stronger colour, emerging from solid, reddish calyces and carried on conspicuously erect stems, emphasize the cool simplicity of the eucryphia's slightly fragrant flowers. In addition to this wonderfully generous display of blossom, the eucryphia produces a spectacular burst of colour in late autumn, when its numerous dark green leaflets turn rich shades of orange and red.

Eucryphia glutinosa is not a plant for impatient gardeners; it grows slowly, especially when young. It also requires some care in its cultivation and must have a reasonably sheltered position and an acid or neutral soil with good drainage. Its roots should always stay cool and moist, and this is especially important if it is grown in sun. The monarda is less demanding in its requirements and indeed is less dependent on moisture than some species and forms of its genus. However, it will thrive, and produce good clumps of its clean-scented foliage, in the same conditions as the eucryphia.

1.20 Viburnum & Ajuga

Viburnum plicatum 'Lanarth'

(syn *V. tomentosum* 'Lanarth')
sun/shade ○ ◐
type of plant hardy shrub
zonal range 6-8 (CT-WT)
flowering time late spring to early summer
flower colour white
height 2.4-3m (8-10ft)
special characteristics autumn foliage

Ajuga reptans 'Catlin's Giant'

(bugle)
sun/shade ○ ◐
type of plant hardy perennial
zonal range 3-9 (C-ST)
flowering time late spring to early summer
flower colour deep blue
height 23cm (9in)
special characteristics evergreen/semi-
evergreen, purple foliage

The distinctive, horizontally branched growth of this viburnum creates eye-catching layers of leaves and lace-cap flowers. Shown here in late spring, the flowers are not yet fully open but at their peak they will cover this very wide-spreading shrub with undulating waves of foamy white blossom. It is then that the contrast between the conspicuously upright and richly coloured flower spikes of the accompanying bugle and the pale, tiered blossom of the viburnum will be at its most striking.

This particular form of *Ajuga reptans* is altogether larger than other varieties. When the 15-20cm (6-8in) flower spikes have faded, the new leaves lengthen, often up to 15cm (6in) or so. 'Catlin's Giant' is, therefore, a suitably scaled underplanting for the large and emphatically shaped viburnum. The summer and early autumn foliage of this bugle is a rich chocolate-purple, the best leaf colour occurring on plants in positions where there is a reasonable amount of sunshine.

In the moisture-retentive soils that both these plants like, the bugle will form dense mats of overlapping leaves. In autumn, the viburnum's foliage turns wine in colour (see also 3.4 *Viburnum plicatum* 'Mariesii').

29

1.21 Brunnera & Camellia

Brunnera macrophylla
sun/shade ◑
type of plant hardy perennial
zonal range 4-8 (C-WT)
flowering time early to late spring
flower colour bright blue
height 45cm (18in)

Camellia × williamsii 'Donation'
sun/shade ○ ◑
type of plant hardy shrub
zonal range 7-9 (CT-WT)
flowering time early to mid-spring
flower colour pink
height 1.8-3m (6-10ft)
special characteristics evergreen, decorative green foliage, needs acid soil

Even if they are quite small, flowers of a really bright, icy blue can make a very effective contrast to pretty, rather sweet pinks. The mass of large (12cm/5in) blooms produced by *Camellia* 'Donation' is accompanied here by sprays of tiny brunnera flowers. These do not detract from the showiness of the camellia's blooms, but they are so intensely blue that they introduce an interesting note of biting coolness beside the camellia's pink confectionery. When both sets of flowers have faded, the brunnera's clump of larger, rougher, lighter green leaves looks well beside the elegant, glossy smoothness and the dark green colouring of the camellia's foliage.

Each of these plants appreciates a moisture-retentive, well-drained soil which, for the sake of the camellia, must be acid. Though its blooms are less liable to frost-thaw damage than those of some other camellias, this camellia's flowers do need shelter from early morning sun as well as from severe frosts and cold winds. In certain years and in ideal conditions the long succession of flowers may begin in late winter. If this vigorous, rather upright camellia is given a sunny site, the brunnera will need to be planted on the shrub's most shaded side. The brunnera's foliage becomes coarser during the summer, but fresh young leaves will appear if the plant is cut right back.

1.22 Cornus & Aster

Cornus alba 'Sibirica Variegata'
(red-barked dogwood)
sun/shade ○ ◑
type of plant hardy shrub
zonal range 3-8 (C-CT)
height 1.2-1.5m (4-5ft)
special characteristics variegated foliage, autumn foliage, fruit, ornamental twigs, suitable for damp or wet soils

Aster thomsonii 'Nanus'
sun/shade ○ ◑
type of plant hardy perennial
zonal range 4-9 (C-WT)
flowering time late summer to mid-autumn
flower colour lilac-blue
height 40-45cm (15-18in)

Mingled with creamy-edged leaves, the flowers of this aster look even more delicate and pretty than usual. These little pastel stars appear over a period of several months, and the combination of ornamented foliage and pale blooms is therefore a very long-lasting one.

Even when the last of the aster flowers finally do fade, the cornus continues to perform right through autumn and winter. In mid-autumn its leaves turn shades of rather winey pink, against which the plant's numerous clusters of palest blue berries stand out effectively. After leaf-fall, the upright growths, with their shiny red bark, gleam richly throughout the coldest months. Since young stems have the most colourful bark, a proportion of the stems should be cut back each year to encourage new growth, but not all if fruit is required.

This particular variety of *Cornus alba* is smaller than the more widely grown *C. a.* 'Elegantissima'. Like all the red-barked dogwoods, however, it is a very easily grown shrub that prospers in a wide variety of soils. If the aster is to produce plenty of flowers over its clump of greyish foliage, it needs a fertile, well-drained soil that does not dry out in summer.

For an illustration of a taller, blue aster with a yellow-variegated variety of *Cornus alba*, see 9.4.

1.23 Artemisia & Potentilla

Artemisia lactiflora
(white mugwort)
sun/shade ○ ◐
type of plant hardy perennial
zonal range 4-9 (C-WT)
flowering time late summer to mid-autumn
flower colour creamy white
height 1.2-1.5m (4-5ft)
Special characteristics aromatic foliage

Potentilla fruticosa 'Princess'
(syn *P. f.* 'Blink', *P.* 'Pink Panther')
(shrubby cinquefoil)
sun/shade ○ ◐
type of plant hardy shrub
zonal range 3-8 (C-WT)
flowering time late spring to early autumn
flower colour pale pink
height 75cm (2½ft)

The shrubby potentillas are noted for their exceptionally long flowering season, and here a prettily coloured variety has been paired with the long-lasting, late-season plumes of *Artemisia lactiflora*. As well as an attractive colour combination, there is a pleasing contrast between the stiffly upright flower stalks of the artemisia and the softer, rounded shape of the potentilla. As the artemisia's slightly fragrant flowers age, they become creamier in colour. The rich green, deeply cut leaves of this plant emit a resinous scent when bruised.

Both the potentilla and the artemisia like a site with some sun. However, the artemisia is liable to droop unless the soil is reasonably moist and the potentilla's flowers fade almost to white in strong light. A position with some shade is therefore more practical. Although the potentilla does well in light and chalky soils, it is not a fussy plant and it will be quite happy in the fairly moist, fertile conditions required by the artemisia. In time, the more vigorous artemisia will need to be restrained if it is not to overwhelm the potentilla.

1.24 Euonymus & Geranium

Euonymus fortunei 'Silver Queen'
sun/shade ○ ◐
type of plant hardy shrub/climber
zonal range 5-9 (CT-ST)
height 90cm (3ft) as a shrub
special characteristics evergreen variegated foliage

Geranium himalayense
(syn *G. grandiflorum*)
(cranesbill)
sun/shade ○ ◐
type of plant hardy perennial
zonal range 4-8 (C-WT)
flowering time early to mid-summer
flower colour violet-blue
height 30-40cm (12-15in)
special characteristics decorative green foliage, autumn foliage

When the flowers of this geranium begin to open, the variegated euonymus foliage beside them is at its yellowest, and the resulting combination of strong blue and rich cream is very striking. Later, when the leaf margins of the euonymus become whiter, the partnership of plants is still attractive and it remains so even when no flowers are present. The geranium's deeply veined leaves have slightly overlapping lobes and these give the plain, dark green foliage an almost frilly look.

Having looked so attractive all summer, the geranium also manages to put on an autumn performance. At this stage in the year the leaf colour changes to a bright mixture of yellows, oranges and reds. Cold weather also affects the appearance of the euonymus and the dark-centred leaves of this plant often become tinged with purplish pink.

The euonymus is initially a very slow-growing plant with a bushy and hummocky habit, while the geranium enlarges its spreading mat of growth rather quickly. Well-established specimens of the euonymus often produce self-clinging, climbing shoots that may reach as much as 3m (10ft) high.

Neither the geranium nor the euonymus is difficult to grow; almost any soil that is not waterlogged will give good results.

31

1.25 Paeonia & Astrantia

Paeonia lactiflora 'Festiva Maxima'

(peony)

sun/shade ○ ◑

type of plant hardy perennial

zonal range 3-9 (C-CT)

flowering time early summer

flower colour white + crimson

height 90cm (3ft)

special characteristics decorative green foliage, fragrant flowers

Astrantia major

(masterwort)

sun/shade ○ ◑

type of plant hardy perennial

zonal range 4-8 (C-WT)

flowering time early to late summer

flower colour white + pale green, sometimes tinged pink

height 60cm (2ft)

The wonderful, flamboyant ruffles of this peony are in marked contrast to the crisp, prim flowers of the accompanying astrantia. Though the form, texture and size of their flowers are so different, there is a subtle link in colour between these two plants. *Astrantia major* varies in flower colour, and some specimens, including the one shown here, have pink tinges on their very long-lasting, papery blooms. In this case, these little touches of soft rose-pink form a charming, low-key complement both to the gentle brown-reds of the peony's buds and stems and to the flecks of crimson on the inner petals of its great blooms. (For a pinker or redder effect altogether, one of the stronger-coloured forms of *Astrantia major*, such as *A. m. rosea* or *A. m. rubra*, could be used here.)

Its strong-stemmed, 15cm (6in) flowers, with their light, fresh fragrance, are obviously this peony's outstanding feature. Unfortunately they do not last for very long, though the plant's smooth and shapely foliage looks handsome over many weeks. The astrantia's leaves are divided into jagged lobes.

In the fertile, moist and well-drained conditions required by the peony, both plants here will thrive and create substantial clumps of greenery. The peony is a notably long-lived plant which takes several years to settle down and start flowering well.

1.26 Persicaria & Aster

Persicaria campanulata

(syn *Polygonum campanulatum*)

(knotweed)

sun/shade ○ ◑

type of plant hardy perennial

zonal range 5-9 (CT-ST)

flowering time midsummer to mid-autumn

flower colour pale pink

height 90cm (3ft)

special characteristics decorative green foliage, suitable for damp soils

Aster thomsonii 'Nanus'

sun/shade ○ ◑

type of plant hardy perennial

zonal range 4-9 (C-WT)

flowering time late summer to mid-autumn

flower colour lilac-blue

height 40-45cm (15-18in)

Each of the plants in this combination flowers for many weeks late in the gardening year, the knotweed's haze of tiny bobbles hovering well above the aster's neat and simple blue stars. Both plants produce good quantities of bushy, leafy growth on their erect stems. The knotweed's foliage is especially attractive, with its fine but conspicuous veining and its unusual, soft green colouring. On emerging in spring, the leaves create a low mat of crimson-stained greenery (some of this crimson colouring can still be seen, mainly on the midribs of the leaves, in this late summer photograph). The aster's foliage is less remarkable, but it has a greyish cast to it which associates well with the knotweed's soft leaf colour.

If these two plants are to grow and flower well, they need a moist, fertile soil that does not dry out in summer.

For this aster in another long-lasting combination, see 1.22.

I.27 Chaerophyllum & Polemonium

Chaerophyllum hirsutum 'Roseum'

(syn *C. h.* 'Rubrifolium')
sun/shade ○ ◖
type of plant hardy perennial
zonal range 5-8 (CT-WT)
flowering time late spring to early summer
flower colour lilac-pink
height 60-75cm (2-2½ft)
special characteristics decorative green foliage, suitable for damp soils

Polemonium 'Lambrook Mauve'

(syn *P. reptans* 'Lambrook Manor')
sun/shade ○ ◖
type of plant hardy perennial
zonal range 4-8 (C-WT)
flowering time late spring to early summer
flower colour lilac-blue
height 30-40cm (12-15in)

The softness of both these flower colours, with their just perceptible hints of mauve, and the careful matching of the depth of colour in each plant make for a particularly harmonious partnership. There is also a very appealing lightness about the whole combination. The polemonium's little flowers are carried in open sprays and its mounds of foliage are composed of numerous small leaflets. The chaerophyllum, though more emphatically shaped, also gives an impression of lightness and airiness since its wide heads of tiny flowers are supported by erect, branching stems and its handsome foliage is toothed and ferny.

A moist, fertile soil with good drainage will give good results with both these plants. Though it is a close relation of the familiar, prolifically self-seeding Jacob's ladder (*Polemonium caeruleum*), the polemonium shown here does not self-seed.

I.28 Geranium & Astrantia

Geranium 'Johnson's Blue'

(cranesbill)
sun/shade ○ ◖
type of plant hardy perennial
zonal range 4-8 (C-WT)
flowering time early to mid-summer
flower colour clear blue
height 45cm (18in)
special characteristics decorative green foliage

Astrantia major

(masterwort)
sun/shade ○ ◖
type of plant hardy perennial
zonal range 4-8 (C-WT)
flowering time early to late summer
flower colour white + pale green, sometimes tinged pink
height 60cm (2ft)

Hardy geraniums in general are outstandingly useful perennials for creating attractive combinations with other plants. The particular variety shown here has flowers that are remarkably clear in colour and delicate in shape. Beneath these flowers, the deeply divided leaves and slightly lax stems form a mass of greenery that mingles with the flowers and foliage of other plants in a gentle, flattering manner.

Here these leaves and flowers are paired with the simpler, lobed foliage and the much crisper-looking blooms of *Astrantia major*. The long-lasting, papery flowers of this astrantia vary in colour, and some specimens – including the one shown here – have pink-tinged bracts that look particularly pretty with blue flowers. (In the form *A. m. rosea*, all parts of the flower are distinctly pink.)

Moist but well-drained soils suit these plants best. In these conditions, they usually form good, weed-suppressing clumps of growth.

For other combinations that include blue-flowered hardy geraniums see 1.24, 5.17 and 12.11.

33

1.29 Cotoneaster & Geranium

Cotoneaster horizontalis

(fishbone cotoneaster)
sun/shade ○ ◑
type of plant hardy shrub
zonal range 5-8 (C-WT)
flowering time early summer
flower colour pinkish white
height 60cm (2ft), up to 2.4m (8ft) against a wall
special characteristics decorative green foliage, autumn foliage, fruit, ornamental twigs

Geranium macrorrhizum 'Album'

(cranesbill)
sun/shade ○ ◑
type of plant hardy perennial
zonal range 4-8 (C-WT)
flowering time late spring to midsummer
flower colour pinkish white
height 30-40cm (12-15in)
special characteristics semi-evergreen, aromatic, decorative green foliage, autumn foliage

All forms of *Geranium macrorrhizum* are highly efficient and very decorative smotherers of weeds. The variety shown here has the special attraction of unusually pale flowers. It is, however, the soft pink stems and calyces of these flowers that make this combination of plants so successful. The fishbone cotoneaster has such attractive red berries, foliage which reddens so richly and reliably in autumn and – as its common name suggests – such a distinctive arrangement of twigs that its flowers tend to get overlooked, but here the pink of the geranium accentuates the numerous pink-tinged buds and flowers of the cotoneaster.

Once these two sets of complementary flowers have faded, the plants' dissimilarities in leaf and in habit of growth become particularly conspicuous. Whereas the geranium's dense carpet of light green, pungently aromatic foliage is composed of quite large, deeply lobed leaves, the cotoneaster's heap of 'fishbones' is covered in tiny, gleaming leaves of a deep, rich green. This light-and-dark contrast is also present in the autumn foliage of these two plants (see 10.19).

Most soils and sites are suitable for these easily grown plants, though neither of them tolerates waterlogged conditions. Given vertical support, the cotoneaster will fan its twigs and branches upwards.

1.30 Polemonium & Geranium

Polemonium caeruleum ssp. *caeruleum* f. *album*

(syn *P. c. album*)
(Jacob's ladder)
sun/shade ○ ◑
type of plant hardy perennial
zonal range 4-8 (C-WT)
flowering time late spring to midsummer
flower colour white
height 60cm (2ft)

Geranium × *magnificum*

(cranesbill)
sun/shade ○ ◑
type of plant hardy perennial
zonal range 4-8 (C-WT)
flowering time early to mid-summer
flower colour violet-blue
height 45cm (18in)
special characteristics decorative green foliage, autumn foliage

These two very free-flowering plants produce such good blocks of colour that the clean white of one and the vivid, dark-veined blue of the other are both enhanced. When a softer blue intermingles with this white-flowered polemonium, the effect is much gentler and less dramatic (see 1.10).

Geranium × *magnificum* is a vigorous cranesbill that is more robustly constructed than many of its relations. In addition to its numerous, intensely coloured flowers, it produces a spreading, ground-covering clump of handsome, dark green leaves. Though deeply cut into a series of lobes, these leaves are basically rounded in outline. They therefore contrast well with the polemonium's airier, ferny foliage which is carried on clustered, upright stems. In most years, the geranium also looks very colourful in autumn, when its foliage turns shades of red and orange.

Both these plants will flower profusely if they are given a sunny position, though they will also perform well in a little shade. Neither plant is fussy about soil. The polemonium is a short-lived perennial but it renews itself by self-seeding. It is at its very best in moist, fertile soils. The geranium is satisfied in most soils with reasonable drainage.

1.31 Veronica & Trollius

Veronica gentianoides
(speedwell)
sun/shade ○ ●
type of plant hardy perennial
zonal range 5-8 (C-WT)
flowering time late spring to early summer
flower colour pale grey-blue
height 45cm (18in)

Trollius × *cultorum* 'Lemon Queen'
(globe flower)
sun/shade ○ ●
type of plant hardy perennial
zonal range 4-8 (C-WT)
flowering time late spring to early summer
flower colour pale yellow
height 60cm (2ft)
special characteristics decorative green foliage, suitable for damp and wet soils

Poised on top of upright, unbranching stems, both these sets of lovely pale flowers stand out beautifully against a mass of gleaming, rich green foliage. The globe flower produces a generous clump of toothed and strikingly lobed leaves. The veronica's little rosettes of thick-textured foliage are less remarkable, but they knit into a low, close mat of dark greenery.

It is, however, the flowers of these plants that form the chief attraction of this combination; not only the colours but also the shapes combine very pleasingly. Both plants carry their flowers on erect, more or less clear stems of approximately the same height and this similarity emphasizes the difference in flower shape. Placed next to the crowded flower spikes of the veronica, the generous, spherical blooms of the globe flower seem especially composed and serene.

Neither of these plants does well in dry situations and ideally the combination should be grown in a fertile, well-drained and moisture-retentive soil. The globe flower is also suitable for planting in damp and boggy ground.

1.32 Alchemilla & Geranium

Alchemilla mollis
(lady's mantle)
sun/shade ○ ●
type of plant hardy perennial
zonal range 4-8 (C-WT)
flowering time early to mid-summer
flower colour yellow-green
height 45cm (18in)
special characteristics decorative green foliage, suitable for damp soils

Geranium × *magnificum*
(cranesbill)
sun/shade ○ ●
type of plant hardy perennial
zonal range 4-8 (C-WT)
flowering time early to mid-summer
flower colour violet-blue
height 45cm (18in)
special characteristics decorative green foliage, autumn foliage

Yellowish-green and blue is an interesting variation on the usual yellow-and-blue theme. In this particular combination, as so often, the citrus tones of *Alchemilla mollis* enliven and enhance – but do not upstage – another plant. The brilliantly coloured, dark-veined flowers of *Geranium* × *magnificum* seem especially incisive beside the acid greens of the alchemilla.

As the summer progresses, the alchemilla's flowerheads will expand into frothy, airy masses of tiny flowers. The foliage of both plants makes good, dense ground cover and both sets of leaves are more or less rounded in outline. However, the foliage of this vigorous, spreading geranium is deeply toothed, whereas the soft, lime-green leaves of the alchemilla are almost circular. (This photograph shows the alchemilla's foliage after a shower of rain and, characteristically, the leaf surfaces appear to be decorated with moonstones.) In most years, the geranium's foliage turns orange and red in autumn.

Neither of these plants is difficult to grow. The alchemilla is a remarkably adaptable plant and one that self-seeds almost anywhere. *Geranium* × *magnificum* thrives in all well-drained soils, but it will prosper elsewhere, too.

For a blue and white combination using this geranium, see 1.30.

35

1.33 Acer & Rhododendron

Acer palmatum var. *dissectum* Dissectum Viride Group
(Japanese maple)
sun/shade ○ ◖
type of plant hardy shrub
zonal range 5-8 (CT-WT)
height 1.5-2.4m (5-8ft)
special characteristics decorative green foliage, autumn foliage

Rhododendron 'Dreamland'
sun/shade ◖
type of plant hardy shrub
zonal range 5-8 (C-CT)
flowering time late spring to early summer
flower colour pink fading to white
height 60cm (2ft)
special characteristics evergreen, needs acid soil

*R*hododendron yakushimanum is the parent of many popular dwarf hybrids, including the variety shown here. Though these plants are neatly dome-shaped, free-flowering and small enough for most gardens, their flowerheads can in some cases seem rather too sweetly coloured and too firmly shaped. Here the wonderful, pale green laciness of a cut-leaved maple counteracts any possible heaviness of form or sugariness of colour. It also enlivens the rhododendron's foliage, which can look rather dull. At the same time, of course, the rhododendron's comparative stiffness and density and its smooth-edged, leathery foliage enhance the apparent insubstantiality of the maple. This combination has a splendid second burst of colour, in autumn, when the maple's rounded mound of pendent foliage glows gold and orange (see 10.16).

The moist but well-drained, lime-free soil needed by this rhododendron also suits the maple, though the maple can also be grown in neutral soil. Both plants require some shelter from the effects of biting winds and spring frosts. With some care, this combination can be grown in sun. The maple in particular is a very slow-growing plant. 'Pink Cherub' is another *Rhododendron yakushimanum* hybrid with flowers similar in colouring to those of 'Dreamland'.

1.34 Rhododendron & Pulmonaria

Rhododendron williamsianum
sun/shade ○ ◖
type of plant slightly tender/hardy shrub
zonal range 7-8 (CT)
flowering time mid- to late spring
flower colour pink
height 90-150cm (3-5ft)
special characteristics evergreen, bronze young foliage, needs acid soil

Pulmonaria officinalis
(spotted dog, soldiers and sailors, lungwort)
sun/shade ◖
type of plant hardy perennial
zonal range 4-8 (C-CT)
flowering time early spring to late spring
flower colour pink changing to blue
height 25cm (10in)
special characteristics evergreen, variegated foliage

*D*espite the fact that the rhododendron flowers shown here are gently disintegrating, this is still a very pretty combination of pinks, blues and pale, silvery green variegation. In full flower, the rhododendron is covered in a mass of flared pink bells (see 2.8). These blooms are quite large and rather formal in shape, and there is a good contrast here between these flowers and the much smaller and simpler flower sprays of the lungwort.

The lungwort leaves also add a lighter, more diffuse element to the composition. Not only are these leaves dappled with palest, silvery green, but they are, overall, less dark than the foliage of the rhododendron. After flowering, the rhododendron produces a new set of neat, rounded leaves. These emerge a rich bronze (see 4.12) which also contrasts interestingly with the lungwort's foliage. At all stages, the combination of a dense, spreading mound of plain, smooth foliage and lower clumps of speckled greenery is a pleasing one.

In the moist, fertile soils it enjoys most, the lungwort will cover substantial areas with its long, raspy-textured leaves. The rhododendron also appreciates moisture. As well as needing a lime-free soil, it should be given some shelter in order to protect its early flowers and young foliage from spring frosts.

1.35 Polemonium & Hosta

Polemonium caeruleum
(Jacob's ladder)
sun/shade ○ ◖
type of plant hardy perennial
zonal range 4-8 (C-WT)
flowering time late spring to midsummer
flower colour blue
height 60cm (2ft)

Hosta sieboldiana var. *elegans*
(plantain lily)
sun/shade ◖
type of plant hardy perennial
zonal range 3-9 (C-WT)
flowering time early to mid-summer
flower colour palest lilac
height 75-90cm (2½-3ft)
special characteristics blue-grey foliage,
suitable for damp soils

Ferny leaves and loose bunches of cool-coloured flowers give *Polemonium caeruleum* a very attractive air of freshness and lightness. Here this insubstantiality has been contrasted with the solidity of big, bold hosta leaves. However, the two plants, so different in many ways, blend successfully because of the conspicuous blueness in the hosta's foliage. When the hosta's flowers appear they do not interfere with the composition, since they are carried in dense heads, are very pale and emerge just above the level of the foliage.

Moist soils, including heavy ones, suit both these plants. The polemonium is a short-lived perennial, but one which self-seeds prolifically. The longest-lived specimens occur on fertile soils. When soils are constantly moist as well as fertile, the hosta's leaves are often over 30cm (12in) wide. Some shade helps to conserve moisture, and it also ensures that this plant's foliage remains a good blue-grey over a long period. In autumn it briefly turns a beautiful shade of yellow before withering. The seedheads of this plant are also attractive. Though prettily shaped, the polemonium's foliage is not produced in large quantities. The similar but slightly taller-growing *P. foliosissimum* has feathery leaves.

For a smaller-scale version of a blue flowers and blue leaves combination, see 1.38.

1.36 Dicentra & Hosta

Dicentra spectabilis 'Alba'
(bleeding heart, Dutchman's breeches)
sun/shade ○ ◖
type of plant hardy perennial
zonal range 3-8 (C-CT)
flowering time late spring to midsummer
flower colour white
height 75cm (2½ft)
special characteristics decorative green foliage

Hosta undulata var. *albomarginata*
(syn *H.* 'Thomas Hogg')
(plantain lily)
sun/shade ◖
type of plant hardy perennial
zonal range 3-9 (C-WT)
flowering time early to mid-summer
flower colour pale lilac
height 60-90cm (2-3ft)
special characteristics variegated foliage,
suitable for damp soils

For freshness and elegance, this early-summer combination of whites and cool greens could hardly be improved upon. The outstanding feature of the partnership is the highly successful repetition of the white of the dicentra flowers in the white margins of the hosta's foliage. Equally important, however, is the contrast between the airiness of the dicentra and the dense solidity of the hosta, which produces a thick clump of big, bold leaves.

These plants create a lovely association of new leaves early in the gardening year. *H. undulata albomarginata* is one of the earliest hostas to come into leaf; the dicentra is notable for the abundance of its fresh green foliage even by mid-spring (though the foliage starts to die back early, too – usually in mid-summer). The hosta flowers slightly later than the dicentra and its tall spires of trumpet-shaped flowers boost the midsummer appearance of this combination.

Ideally, these two plants should be given a cool position and the sort of spongy-textured soil that is moist but not heavy. The combination can be planted in sun, but only if there is a constant supply of moisture and the plants are not exposed to drying winds. Both plants do especially well in fertile soils.

For another combination of a white-flowered plant with a white-variegated hosta, see 16.18.

1.37 Gentiana & Astilbe

Gentiana asclepiadea var. *alba*
(willow gentian)
sun/shade ◖
type of plant hardy perennial
zonal range 6-9 (C-CT)
flowering time late summer to early autumn
flower colour white
height 60-75cm (2-2½ft)
special characteristics decorative green foliage,
autumn foliage

Astilbe 'Sprite'
(false goat's beard)
sun/shade ◖
type of plant hardy perennial
zonal range 4-8 (C-WT)
flowering time midsummer to early autumn
flower colour pale pink
height 25-30cm (10-12in)
special characteristics decorative green foliage,
suitable for damp soils

A very pretty combination of flower colours is not the only attraction of this partnership, for the willow gentian and its various forms are exceptionally elegant and stylish plants. Their stems emerge upright, but as they lengthen they arch conspicuously. This habit of growth sets off to perfection the paired and pointed leaves and lovely, slender flower-trumpets. It also allows the plants to mingle most attractively with other, lower-growing flowers and leaves.

In the combination shown here, a white-flowered form of *Gentiana asclepiadea* bends down to meet the pink sprays and glossy, dark green foliage of a small astilbe. The young leaves of this trim little plant are slightly bronze. When fully expanded, they form a close-knit mat of greenery (see 16.3), in complete contrast to the much more open, arching growths of the gentian. In autumn, the astilbe's flowers turn into long-lasting, bright tan seedheads. These look particularly well beside the gentian in mid-autumn, since the leaves of this plant turn yellow at this stage.

A cool position and a moist, humus-rich, woodland soil are preferable for both these plants.

1.38 Viola & Hosta

Viola 'Belmont Blue'
(syn *V.* 'Boughton Blue')
(violet)
sun/shade ○ ◖
type of plant hardy perennial
zonal range 5-7 (C-CT)
flowering time mainly late spring to
midsummer
flower colour blue
height 15-23cm (6-9in)
special characteristics evergreen

Hosta sieboldiana Elegans Group
(plantain lily)
sun/shade ◖
type of plant hardy perennial
zonal range 3-9 (C-WT)
flowering time early to mid-summer
flower colour white
height 60-75cm (2-2½ft)
special characteristics blue-grey foliage,
suitable for damp soils

In all their different guises, violas and hostas are very versatile perennials for creating plant combinations. They also look well together. In all cases, there will be a very attractive contrast between the beguiling simplicity of little viola flowers and the boldness of hosta foliage.

In this combination there is the bonus of a striking link in the colouring of the two plants, so that the whole combination is bathed in blue. Hostas in the Elegans Group, including the form shown here, have a lovely glaucous bloom over their puckered and ribbed leaf surface which gives the foliage its beautiful, silvery, sea-green appearance. However, unless the hosta is positioned in some shade, this surface covering and therefore the leaf colouring are relatively short-lived. The bell-shaped flowers of hostas in the Elegans Group are typically pale in colour and usually appear just above the leaves.

Both plants in this combination are most at home in cool, moist conditions; they also appreciate a fertile soil with good drainage. In these conditions they will form dense clumps of foliage and make good ground cover. Fertile soils will additionally encourage the viola to flower well over a long period. The flowering season can be extended still further by regular dead-heading and by cutting back most of the growths in late summer.

1.39 Ajuga, Vinca & Tolmiea

Ajuga reptans 'Atropurpurea'

(bugle)

sun/shade ○ ◐
type of plant hardy perennial
zonal range 3-9 (C-ST)
flowering time late spring to early summer
flower colour deep blue
height 15-20cm (6-8in)
special characteristics evergreen/semi-evergreen, purple foliage

Vinca minor 'Aureovariegata'

(syn *V. m.* 'Variegata Aurea')
(lesser periwinkle)

sun/shade ○ ◐
type of plant hardy shrub/perennial
zonal range 4-9 (C-ST)
flowering time mid-spring to early summer
flower colour blue
height 10-15cm (4-6in)
special characteristics evergreen, variegated foliage

Tolmiea menziesii 'Taff's Gold'

(piggyback plant)

sun/shade ◐
type of plant hardy perennial
zonal range 6-9 (CT-ST)
flowering time late spring to early summer
flower colour coppery brown
height 20cm (8in) (leaves)
special characteristics semi-evergreen, yellow/yellow-variegated foliage

Surrounded by yellow, the intense, deep blue of this bugle's flowers looks splendidly bright and cheerful. These flowers add conspicuous, upright shapes to the predominantly horizontal lines created by three dense, carpeting plants. The flowers of the other two plants are less eye-catching than those of the bugle; in the dappled shade most suitable for this combination, the periwinkle will not produce large quantities of its starry blooms, and the tolmiea's wispy wands of brown are not, in any case, especially decorative.

Even when the bugle's flowers have faded completely, this is still a very lively association of leaves of different shapes, sizes and colours. As long as there is a reasonable amount of light the tolmiea's relatively bold foliage will be generously marked with yellow. Though smaller, neater and less flamboyant, the yellow and green leaves of the periwinkle echo the tolmiea's colouring. Most of the youngest leaves of this vinca are entirely yellow, the variegation developing as the foliage matures.

As a dramatic counterpoint to this pair of yellows, there is the dark, glossy foliage of the bugle. Plain and deeply coloured, this close carpet of blunt-nosed leaves also has an important calming, steadying influence upon the whole combination.

All three plants are vigorous and likely to spread widely – rooting as they go – in the sort of cool, moist and well-drained conditions that encourage them to produce plenty of good-looking foliage (though this variegated form of *Vinca minor* is not nearly as energetic as the green-leaved species). All the plants in this combination are tolerant of at least some sunshine but they are not suitable for hot, dry places. With more sun the tolmiea's leaves will be yellower and only faintly mottled, and all the plants will flower more freely.

2 Grey, Blue or Silver Foliage

Perhaps there have been too many sub-Sissinghurst attempts to create white gardens but, whatever the reason, there is now a definite feeling among some gardeners that grey-leaved plants – which are often a major ingredient of white gardens – are monotonous, difficult to please and altogether less desirable than they used to be. It is true, of course, that large-scale plantings in white and grey alone demand considerable skill in design, but small-scale groupings of grey leaves or the use of grey-leaved plants in small quantities with other colours is something we can all have success with.

In all their wonderful diversity of scale, texture, shape – and indeed colour – and in their undisputed ability to enhance and emphasize many other flower and foliage colours, grey-leaved plants are invaluable. Some of the most popular and readily available garden plants have grey leaves, including the fashionable hostas and euphorbias; the cottage-garden favourites lamb's lug or lamb's ears (*Stachys byzantina*) and blue rue (*Ruta graveolens* 'Jackman's Blue'); and that standby of all but the coldest gardens, *Brachyglottis* (Dunedin Group) 'Sunshine' – previously known as *Senecio* 'Sunshine' and *S. laxifolius*. All of these plants are featured in combinations in this section.

The Wide Range of Greys

Grey-leaved plants offer the gardener a diverse and interesting palette of shapes, sizes, textures and colours to choose from. In horticultural terms 'grey' ranges from the strong grey-green of plants like the pearly everlastings (*Anaphalis*), through the steely blue-grey of some conifers and several hostas, to the so-called silver or palest grey of, for instance, certain artemisias. Even among the small number of plants just mentioned, leaf size and shape vary greatly, from the tiny needles of junipers to the great, heart-shaped paddles of a hosta like *H. sieboldiana elegans* (see 2.31) and the featheriness of many artemisias (see 2.4).

As far as texture is concerned, grey-leaved plants are particularly varied. This is partly because the greyness of many plants arises from the presence of hairs on the leaf surface. These hairs may create a deep, soft woolliness but they can also produce a close-textured, flannelled feel; they may even give a silken sheen to foliage. However, other grey-leaved plants, notably the sedums, are of a squeaky, succulent smoothness, while some grasses feel quite hard and dry.

This wide variation in texture, shape and size means that all-grey planting schemes need not be monotonous. Even in quite large groups of grey – with nothing more colourful than some white-flowered plants perhaps – the addition of a few plants with a striking habit of growth can quickly enliven a too-quiet scheme. For example, among small plants, there is the conspicuous spikiness of the blue-leaved grass *Festuca glauca* (for a variety of this grass, see 2.1); medium-sized plants with blue- or grey-green foliage and a striking habit of growth include some very narrow, upright junipers and also some spurges (see 6.1), the leaves of which are arranged in large, eye-catching whorls; on a much larger scale, there are several taller upright forms of grey- and blue-leaved conifers, including cultivars of Lawson cypress (*Chamaecyparis lawsoniana*) and juniper, and the larger willows with their huge hanging curtains of grey foliage.

Plants with very large leaves can also enliven monochrome planting schemes and, apart from the hosta mentioned above, there are several other grey-leaved plants with bold foliage. The enormous, thistle-like cardoon (*Cynara cardunculus*, see 2.3) must be one of the most imposing of all perennials and other notable plants with large grey leaves include some verbascums (mulleins) and yuccas.

Grey in Multi-coloured Schemes

Of course, you may prefer to use grey foliage simply as one ingredient in a planting scheme of several colours. When it comes to combining them with other flower and foliage colours, grey leaves demonstrate their versatility by making dark, rich colours richer and more glowing and pale colours still more delicate and pretty. The feathery paleness of *Artemisia* 'Powis Castle' makes the maroon-y-red purple foliage of *Heuchera micrantha diversifolia* 'Palace Purple' look splendidly solid and dark (see 2.13), but combined with the pink rose 'Constance Spry' (see 13.6) it has the effect of enhancing a general impression of paleness and prettiness.

Grey or glaucous foliage can make cool blues and nearly-blues look especially peaceful (see 2.20 and 1.38). It contrasts with – and thereby emphasizes – the strong reds and oranges of hot-coloured flowers (see 3.8 and 3.12) and glowing autumn leaves (see 10.3). With variegated leaves the subdued, rather inert quality of some grey foliage can be enlivened. When the variegation is yellow, a soft warmth is added to grey leaves; with glaucous foliage (see 2.26), yellow appears bright as well as warm. Grey and glaucous leaves have similar effects upon yellow flowers and wholly yellow foliage.

The use of grey leaves is one way of 'lifting' a sea of mainly green foliage which, without this contrast, might seem nothing but a blur of green for much of the year. However, grey leaves always need to be used carefully. Grey – in particular pale or silvery grey – is eye-catching and can throw a planting off balance. Unless some mid-tones have been provided, one or two pale greys will stand out uncomfortably among large quantities of deeper-toned foliage. The main reason that white flowers and white-variegated leaves work well with pale grey leaves is that white is eye-catching, too, and is therefore able to hold its own.

Growing Conditions

Most of the plants in this section need plenty of sun to do well. However, there are grey-leaved plants – for example, some hostas, columbines and a few rhododendrons (*R. cinnabarinum* and some of its subspecies and hybrids – see 10.20) which must have moister, shadier conditions if they are to thrive.

So, not only do grey-leaved plants vary widely in appearance, but they also vary considerably in their growing requirements. As a group, therefore, they are an excellent source of material for all sorts of plantings. There are grey leaves for both large and small planting schemes, for multi-coloured and monochrome schemes, for schemes with hot or cool colours, and for places that are moist and shady as well as for places that sizzle in the sun.

2.1 Picea & Festuca

Picea pungens 'Koster'
(blue spruce)
sun/shade ○
type of plant hardy conifer
zonal range 3-8 (C-CT)
height 7.5-9m (25-30ft)
special characteristics evergreen, blue-grey foliage

Festuca glauca 'Elijah Blue'
(blue fescue)
sun/shade ○
type of plant hardy perennial (grass)
zonal range 4-8 (C-WT)
flowering time late spring to early summer
flower colour blue-grey
height 25-30cm (10-12in)
special characteristics evergreen, blue-grey foliage

Monochromatic plantings make the most of differences in texture and form. In this combination there are stout 'sausages' of stiff, coniferous foliage and very fine, curving blades of grass. The contrast is especially arresting because the two sets of leaves are of a remarkably similar blue-grey colour. Even the blue-tinged flower panicles of the grass, just beginning to ripen here into soft gold seedheads, conform to this colour scheme.

Apart from the marked difference in their textures (and, of course, in their heights), the two plants here are also completely different in overall shape. The spruce's habit of growth is as firm and solid as its foliage and it eventually forms a fairly narrow, stiffly branched cone with a rather irregular outline. In contrast, the grass's dense, 15cm (6in) clump of leaves arches gently and symmetrically and the plant is altogether quite soft in appearance.

Picea pungens and its varieties are at their best in lime-free soils. They like good drainage, but conditions must also be moist. In this particular combination, competition from the roots of the conifer will make the surrounding soil rather dry, providing optimum conditions for the grass.

2.2 Olearia & Hebe

Olearia × macrodonta
(New Zealand holly, daisy bush)
sun/shade ○
type of plant slightly tender shrub
zonal range 9-10 (WT-ST)
flowering time early to mid-summer
flower colour white
height 2.4-3.6m (8-12ft)
special characteristics evergreen, sage-green foliage

Hebe pinguifolia 'Pagei'
sun/shade ○ ◑
type of plant hardy/slightly tender shrub
zonal range 8-10 (WT-ST)
flowering time late spring to early summer
flower colour white
height 15-30cm (6-12in)
special characteristics evergreen, blue-grey foliage

Being paired with a distinctly blue-grey hebe has emphasized the greyish tones in this olearia's sage-green foliage. Because the leaf colours of these two shrubs appear rather similar, attention is focused on differences in leaf shape and habit of growth. The olearia's shining, leathery leaves have prickly, holly-like edges and white-felted undersides, whereas the hebe's foliage is on a much smaller scale and is smoother, rounder and almost fleshy in texture. The olearia's branches are rather upright; in contrast, the hebe forms an almost prostrate carpet of stems.

The combination is shown here in early summer. At this stage the hebe is producing the last of its pretty flower spikes, while some of the first of the olearia's numerous heads of daisy-like flowers are beginning to open. Unfortunately, some people find that the musky scent emitted by the olearia's leaves overpowers the honey fragrance of the plant's flowers.

Both of the plants in this combination are well-equipped to withstand the effects of salt-laden winds in exposed seaside gardens. While both shrubs appreciate good drainage, the olearia in particular needs some moisture, too. In inland regions this quick-growing shrub will require a warm and sheltered site.

2.3 Cynara & Paeonia

Cynara cardunculus
(cardoon)
sun/shade ○
type of plant hardy/slightly tender perennial
zonal range 7-9 (CT-WT)
flowering time early to mid-summer
flower colour purple
height 1.8-2.4m (6-8ft)
special characteristics silver foliage

Paeonia lactiflora 'Bowl of Beauty'
(peony)
sun/shade ○ ◑
type of plant hardy perennial
zonal range 3-9 (C-CT)
flowering time early summer
flower colour pink + cream
height 90cm (3ft)
special characteristics decorative green foliage

The huge, silvery-grey leaves of *Cynara cardunculus*, and particularly those produced at the base of the plant, reach well over 90cm (3ft) long. Foliage of this stature needs partners which themselves make some impact, and here the large, strikingly shaped flowers of one of the Imperial peonies are suitably effective. Once established, this peony will produce quantities of its 12cm (5in) blooms.

Although some gardeners like to treat the cardoon as a foliage plant and remove its stout flower stalks, it produces large and impressive, thistle-like flowers which make good material for dried arrangements. However, the foliage of this plant is undoubtedly its most striking feature; when the plant is prevented from flowering the elegantly arching leaves, deeply divided into a series of sharply pointed, jagged lobes, make a mound about 1.2-1.5m (4-5ft) high. The peony's clumps of foliage are also handsome, the leaves being divided into smooth, shining lobes of rich green.

Both of these plants are at their best in a fertile, well-drained and moisture-retentive soil. They may both need staking, and it is as well to remember that the cardoon will require at least a square metre/yard of space in which to grow. Young specimens of the cardoon may need some protection in their first winter.

2.4 Lavatera & Artemisia

Lavatera 'Barnsley'
(tree mallow, bush mallow)
sun/shade ○
type of plant slightly tender shrub
zonal range 8-11 (CT-WT/ST)
flowering time early summer to mid-autumn
flower colour pink + red
height 1.8-2.4m (6-8ft)

Artemisia 'Powis Castle'
sun/shade ○
type of plant slightly tender perennial/shrub
zonal range 5-8 (C-ST)
height 60-90cm (2-3ft)
special characteristics evergreen/semi-evergreen, aromatic, silver foliage

Grey leaves and pink flowers make flattering partners and there are several examples of this popular combination in this section – see, for example, 2.8 and 2.18. None of these combinations, however, is as long-lasting as the one shown here. *Lavatera* 'Barnsley' flowers prolifically over many weeks and the gentle colouring both of its blooms and of its soft, sage-green, lobed leaves is made still prettier by the presence of this silvery artemisia.

Since the artemisia flowers only rarely, its stems and feathery foliage remain tidy. It is an evergreen or semi-evergreen plant, depending on climate. In any case, its pungently scented foliage looks attractive for a considerable part of the year and the plant is unlikely to be seriously damaged in winter, except after heavy falls of snow.

The lavatera is much more sensitive to the effects of frosts; during periods of prolonged frost, its top growth will die. However, this openly branched, upright shrub is very vigorous and fast-growing and will easily make over 90cm (3ft) of new growth in a season.

Both the artemisia and the lavatera like well-drained soils and the artemisia will thrive in hot, dry conditions. The lavatera performs best in fertile soils, and a warm site in full sun is advisable. It is a fairly short-lived plant.

2.5 Brachyglottis & Olearia

Brachyglottis rotundifolia

(syn *Senecio reinoldii*)
sun/shade ○
type of plant slightly tender shrub
zonal range 9-10 (WT-ST)
height 1.2-1.8m (4-6ft)
special characteristics evergreen, decorative green foliage

Olearia moschata

(daisy bush)
sun/shade ○
type of plant slightly tender shrub
zonal range 9-10 (WT-ST)
flowering time mid- to late summer
flower colour white
height 90cm (3ft)
special characteristics evergreen, aromatic, silver foliage

The light, silvery foliage of *Olearia moschata* strikes just the right note of delicacy and brightness in this combination of contrasting textures. Both the leaves and the stems of this musk-scented plant are covered in a close, distinctly grey felt and the general air of lightness is emphasized by upright stems and upward-pointing foliage.

In contrast, the much larger, rounded leaves of the brachyglottis are unusually thick and leathery and of a gleaming, rich green. The foliage is carried on stout, slightly curving branches. The lower surfaces of the leaves are covered in pale, yellow-beige felt and, along with the white-felted flower shoots and their buds, they provide an interesting link with the matt silver of the olearia. As well as its pretty foliage, the olearia produces a mass of white daisies. The brachyglottis' petal-less, yellow-tinged flowers are not decorative, but the felted flower buds have a certain charm.

Both these plants are well-equipped to withstand the effects of salt-laden winds and they will thrive in mild coastal areas. In colder regions they need a warm, sheltered spot. Both plants will grow in any well-drained soil.

2.6 Phlomis & Sedum

Phlomis fruticosa

(Jerusalem sage)
sun/shade ○
type of plant slightly tender shrub
zonal range 8-9 (CT-WT)
flowering time early to mid-summer
flower colour bright yellow
height 1.2m (4ft)
special characteristics evergreen, grey foliage

Sedum spectabile 'Brilliant'

(stonecrop)
sun/shade ○
type of plant hardy perennial
zonal range 4-9 (C-ST)
flowering time early to mid-autumn
flower colour bright pink
height 45cm (18in)
special characteristics blue-grey foliage

This association of plants is altogether bolder and brighter than the *Phlomis fruticosa/Geranium wallichianum* combination in 2.7. The phlomis has, in both cases, been closely clipped and is, therefore, looking very satisfactorily dense and grey. However, the sharper colouring and more solid construction of the sedum produce a partnership that is quite different from the soft, pretty pairing of phlomis and geranium.

Even before they acquire their brilliant colouring, the wide, firm flowerheads of the sedum look striking. The clumps of glaucous, succulent foliage and rather upright stems are also bold and decorative, and in summer both the leaves and the unripened flowers make a pleasing grey-and-green grouping with the phlomis. (The photograph accompanying 4.13 shows *Sedum* 'Herbstfreude' in late summer, at which stage *S. spectabile* 'Brilliant' looks similar.) The flowers of *S. s.* 'Brilliant' are very attractive to butterflies.

A well-drained and reasonably fertile soil suits this sedum best and the phlomis will be happy in these conditions, too. For further details about the phlomis, see 2.7.

2.7 Phlomis & Geranium

Phlomis fruticosa
(Jerusalem sage)
sun/shade ○
type of plant slightly tender shrub
zonal range 8-9 (CT-WT)
flowering time early to mid-summer
flower colour bright yellow
height 1.2m (4ft)
special characteristics evergreen, grey foliage

Geranium wallichianum 'Buxton's Variety'
(syn G. 'Buxton's Blue')
(cranesbill)
sun/shade ○ ◑
type of plant hardy perennial
zonal range 4-8 (C-WT)
flowering time midsummer to mid-autumn
flower colour lavender-blue + white
height 30cm (12in)
special characteristics decorative green foliage

Left to its own devices, *Phlomis fruticosa* forms a sprawling mass of curving, rather upright stems and woolly, grey-green leaves. When clipped closely, as it has been here, it becomes altogether denser, the foliage tends to be particularly pale and there are few, if any, of the whorls of mustard-yellow flowers. This smaller, rounded and very densely leaved mound makes an excellent background for cool and for warm colours (see 2.6).

The exceptionally long flowering season of this particular geranium means that this is a combination that looks good almost all summer long and well into autumn. Throughout these months, the pretty blue of this trailing plant combines charmingly with the soft grey of the phlomis. The small touches of red from the calyces and stalks of the geranium add liveliness, and the neatly lobed leaves are of an excellent bright, rich green.

Although the phlomis will tolerate hot, dry conditions, this combination is best planted in a well-drained soil that does not dry out too readily. If the phlomis is not clipped and is left to grow taller and more openly it is important not to choose a very windy site, since the stems of this shrub are rather brittle. Despite its common name, the foliage of *Phlomis fruticosa* is only slightly aromatic.

2.8 Rhododendron & Salix

Rhododendron williamsianum
sun/shade ○ ◑
type of plant hardy/slightly tender shrub
zonal range 7-8 (CT)
flowering time mid- to late spring
flower colour pink
height 90-150cm (3-5ft)
special characteristics evergreen, bronze young foliage, needs acid soil

Salix helvetica
(willow)
sun/shade ○
type of plant hardy shrub
zonal range 6-7 (C-CT)
flowering time mid-spring
flower colour silver-grey
height 90-120cm (3-4ft)
special characteristics grey foliage

The bright, silvery grey of this willow's new leaves make the pink bells of *Rhododendron williamsianum* look even prettier than usual. When the willow's foliage lengthens and expands, there is a striking contrast between its soft greyness and the smooth, deep bronze of the rhododendron's newest leaves (see 4.12)

These two slow-growing shrubs continue to look well together throughout summer and most of the autumn. The willow forms a bowl shape of rather upright branches and oval leaves, whereas the rhododendron makes a wide, dense dome of distinctly rounded, mid-green foliage. In autumn, the willow's leaves usually turn buff and soft yellow before falling.

Both of these plants like a moisture-retentive soil, which for the sake of the rhododendron must be well-drained and lime-free. Although this rhododendron will do well in sun, as long as it is not very hot and there is a constant supply of moisture, its earliest flowers and new leaves can be damaged if they thaw quickly after spring frosts. The plants shown here are growing in a large rock garden, with the willow placed just above the rhododendron in a position where it can receive plenty of sun. The rhododendron's lower – and slightly shadier – position offers more protection.

45

2.9 Brachyglottis & Persicaria

Brachyglottis (Dunedin Group) 'Sunshine'

(syn *Senecio greyi*, *S. laxifolius*)
sun/shade ○
type of plant slightly tender shrub
zonal range 9-10 (WT-ST)
flowering time early to mid-summer
flower colour yellow
height 90-120cm (3-4ft)
special characteristics evergreen, grey foliage

Persicaria amplexicaulis 'Rosea'

(syn *Polygonum amplexicaule* 'Roseum')
(bistort)
sun/shade ○ ◐
type of plant hardy perennial
zonal range 5-9 (CT-ST)
flowering time early summer to early autumn
flower colour pink
height 90-120cm (3-4ft)
special characteristics suitable for damp soils

One of the most reliable and handsome of all grey-leaved shrubs, *Brachyglottis* (Dunedin Group) 'Sunshine' is also a very versatile plant for creating attractive plant combinations. At its best, it forms a dense, ground-covering mound of grey-green, white-backed leaves and pale stems.

Here this rounded shrub has been teamed with a thicket of contrastingly slender and upright pink flower spikes. It would look equally good with the more readily available deep red form of this bistort which is shown in 3.24. In all its forms, *Persicaria amplexicaulis* has an exceptionally long flowering season.

Many gardeners find the ragwort-like daisies of the brachyglottis rather garish. If this shrub is pruned fairly hard in mid-spring each year (or at least every other year) it will produce very few flowers. More importantly, this treatment ensures that the plant will remain neat and dense and that there will be plenty of pale new leaves.

Though well-drained conditions are ideal, this easily grown shrub will do well in a wide range of soils. The bistort is only slightly more demanding in its requirements in so far as it needs a soil that does not dry out too readily. In moist, fertile conditions this plant's clumps of rich green leaves tend to spread quite rapidly.

2.10 Euphorbia & Cotoneaster

Euphorbia characias ssp. *wulfenii* × *E. characias* seedling

(spurge)
sun/shade ○
type of plant slightly tender/hardy shrub/perennial
zonal range 7-10 (CT-WT/ST)
flowering time mid-spring to early summer
flower colour yellow-green
height 90-120cm (3-4ft)
special characteristics evergreen, blue-green foliage

Cotoneaster horizontalis

(fishbone cotoneaster)
sun/shade ○ ◐
type of plant hardy shrub
zonal range 5-8 (CT-WT)
flowering time early summer
flower colour pinkish white
height 60cm (2ft), up to 2.4m (8ft) against a wall
special characteristics decorative green foliage, autumn foliage, fruit, ornamental twigs

Euphorbia characias and most of its subspecies and forms produce bold, blue-green bottlebrushes of foliage. These need to mature for a year or so before they become topped with great cylindrical heads of flowers (see 7.5), but even in their flowerless state they are strikingly handsome.

Underplanting these imposing, upright shapes with the flatter, fishbone fans of *Cotoneaster horizontalis* has created a very well-balanced composition and one that looks interesting throughout the year. Although the cotoneaster's rows of little flowers are pretty in early summer, its bright red autumn fruits are even more decorative and they look especially well with the cool blue of the euphorbia's foliage (see 12.3). When, later in autumn, the cotoneaster's little, shiny, green leaves turn rich shades of crimson and burnt orange, there is another pleasing contrast between warm and cool colours. Later still, the dark spikiness of the cotoneaster's fishbone arrangement of leafless twigs shows up well against the smooth blue-green of the euphorbia.

The cotoneaster is a very tolerant plant suitable for almost all soils and sites; the euphorbia should have a warm, sheltered position and a well-drained soil. The cut stems of the euphorbia exude juices that may irritate the skin and eyes.

2.11 Salix & Ajuga

Salix helvetica
(willow)
sun/shade ○
type of plant hardy shrub
zonal range 6-7 (CT)
flowering time mid-spring
flower colour silver-grey
height 90-120cm (3-4ft)
special characteristics grey foliage

Ajuga reptans 'Atropurpurea'
(bugle)
sun/shade ○ ◖
type of plant hardy perennial
zonal range 3-9 (C-ST)
flowering time late spring to early summer
flower colour deep blue
height 15-20cm (6-8in)
special characteristics evergreen/semi-evergreen, purple foliage

Salix helvetica is a much underrated, easily grown shrub with attractive, soft, grey foliage covering a shapely bowl of fairly upright branches. It lends itself to combinations of many sorts and looks pretty with, for example, pinks (see 2.8), rich bronzes (see 4.12) and other greys, as well as blues of many shades – including the deep, intense colour shown here.

In addition to its striking, upright flower spikes, the bugle in this combination also has rich purple foliage which forms a dense carpet of fairly large, shining leaves. Even after both sets of flowers have faded, therefore, this is an appealing partnership of erect greyness and horizontal purple. The willow's flowers are silky catkins which appear with the young, pale foliage of the plant. In autumn, the leaves of this shrub often turn soft yellow and beige before falling and, though this colour change is not spectacular, it is an added attraction.

Both these plants like a moisture-retentive soil and an open position. The bugle makes good, dense ground cover provided its roots are cool and moist. When well-suited, it is a vigorous plant. The most richly coloured leaves are produced in full sun. For an association of this bugle with a smaller, grey-leaved plant, see 2.25.

2.12 Artemisia & Erigeron

Artemisia absinthium 'Lambrook Silver'
(wormwood)
sun/shade ○
type of plant hardy perennial/shrub
zonal range 4-9 (C-ST)
flowering time mid- to late summer
flower colour yellow
height 75cm (2½ft)
special characteristics evergreen/semi-evergreen, aromatic, silver foliage

Erigeron karvinskianus
(syn *E. mucronatus*)
(fleabane)
sun/shade ○
type of plant hardy perennial
zonal range 5-10 (CT-ST)
flowering time early summer to mid-autumn
flower colour white, changing to soft pink
height 15-23cm (6-9in)
special characteristics evergreen

Deeply cut and of a most attractive, very silvery, pale grey, the foliage of this artemisia is an obvious candidate for inclusion in combinations featuring plants with smoothly shaped leaves that are either deep purple or really dark green. However, it also looks well when, as here, it is paired with a plant of a similarly soft and fine-textured appearance.

Erigeron karvinskianus is a delightful, wispy, wiry self-seeder with an exceptionally long flowering season. Here, in early autumn, its thin, curving flower stems and loose clusters of leaves are still covered in a mass of daisies.

The flowers of the artemisia are small and carried in long, branched spikes; they are interspersed with tiny, grey leaves. Some gardeners like to remove the spent flower spikes – the plant shown here has been treated in this way – so that the remaining upright stems and their leaves continue to look neat and tidy. With the flower spikes removed, the plant is about 30-40cm (12-15in) high.

Artemisia absinthium is a good deal hardier than some other popular plants of this genus and it can tolerate soils that are not especially well-drained. However, the silveriest and most pungently scented foliage is produced in dryish soils and warm places. Good drainage and warmth also suit the erigeron.

47

2.13 Artemisia & Heuchera

Artemisia 'Powis Castle'

sun/shade ○
type of plant slightly tender perennial/shrub
zonal range 5-8 (C-WT)
height 60-90cm (2-3ft)
special characteristics evergreen/semi-evergreen, aromatic, silver foliage

Heuchera micrantha var. *diversifolia* 'Palace Purple'

sun/shade ○
type of plant hardy perennial
zonal range 6-8 (CT-WT)
flowering time mid- to late summer
flower colour pale pink
height 45-60cm (1½-2ft)
special characteristics evergreen, purple foliage

Placed against a background of bold, red-purple leaves, the feathery fingers of this artemisia appear even paler and more delicately divided than usual. The plant seldom flowers and for this reason remains tidier than some others in the genus. The heuchera produces a haze of pale flowers (see 3.14) which turns into an attractive mass of soft pink seedheads. Its flower stems rise well clear of the solid mound of lustrous, crinkled leaves, the backs of which are a surprising light magenta. As well as providing good contrasts with greys, these leaves are popular ingredients in hot colour schemes. The lacy paleness of the artemisia is also good with pale pinks (see 13.6). The leaves of this plant are sharply aromatic.

Artemisia 'Powis Castle' is at its very best and its hardiest in hot, dry soils. In cold winters some top growth may be damaged and stems may break under snow. Although it too likes good drainage, the heuchera needs slightly more moisture than the artemisia and a very dry site would not, therefore, be suitable for this combination.

2.14 Nepeta & Stachys

Nepeta 'Six Hills Giant'

(catmint)
sun/shade ○
type of plant hardy perennial
zonal range 4-8 (C-WT)
flowering time early summer to early autumn
flower colour lavender-blue
height 60-75cm (2-2½ft)
special characteristics semi-evergreen, aromatic, grey-green foliage

Stachys byzantina

(syn *S. lanata*, *S. olympica*)
(lamb's tongue, lamb's ear, lamb's lug)
sun/shade ○
type of plant hardy perennial
zonal range 4-9 (C-WT)
flowering time midsummer
flower colour mauve-pink
height 30-45cm (12-18in)
special characteristics evergreen, silver foliage

The non-flowering form of lamb's tongue (see, for example, 2.24) is a popular edging plant, but there are situations in which the woolly, leafy flower stems of the species look good. Here, rising palely against a catmint's haze of blue, these stems have the effect of intensifying an already deep and cool flower colour. In addition, their relatively solid shape contrasts nicely with the softer, mistier impression created by the catmint.

Even when the faded flower stems of the lamb's tongue have to be removed, this combination will continue to look attractive. The catmint has an exceptionally long flowering season and throughout this time the carpet of furry, silver-grey foliage produced by the lamb's tongue enhances the catmint's blooms. This mat of pale grey also looks well against the catmint's clump of curving stems with their little grey-green leaves, which emit a slightly fusty, minty scent when bruised.

Both the plants in this combination need a well-drained soil and both are tolerant of hot, dry conditions. The catmint will readily produce later flowers if it is cut back after the first crop of flowers has faded. This treatment will also encourage good, dense, ground-covering growth.

2.15 Euonymus & Santolina

Euonymus fortunei 'Emerald 'n' Gold'

sun/shade ○ ◐
type of plant hardy shrub/climber
zonal range 5-9 (C-ST)
height 60cm (2ft) as a shrub
special characteristics evergreen, variegated foliage

Santolina pinnata ssp. neapolitana

sun/shade ○
type of plant slightly tender shrub
zonal range 7-9 (WT-ST)
flowering time midsummer
flower colour bright lemon-yellow
height 60-75cm (2-2½ft)
special characteristics evergreen, aromatic, grey-green foliage

Soft, wispy and graceful, the lovely grey-green foliage of this santolina has been combined here with much bolder and more colourful leaves. The euonymus's foliage is quite differently constructed and, especially in full sun, its yellow edges are a strong, bright yellow. The warm colouring of these leaf margins can make the cool grey of the santolina's foliage look almost blue.

The euonymus is an erect and bushy plant which, in maturity, may produce self-clinging, climbing shoots about 1.8-2.4m (6-8ft) high. It is at first slow-growing. In contrast, the santolina's close-textured, spreading hummock of pungently scented growth matures quickly, and it needs pruning each year to prevent it from becoming open and lanky. The brightly coloured, button-like flowers of this plant appear in large numbers and more or less cover the plant. Once faded, these flowers should all be removed to encourage the production of plenty of good-looking foliage for autumn and winter.

During the colder months, the euonymus's leaves will often become tinged with purplish-pink. This colour change is most likely to take place on specimens grown in full sun, and in any case an open, sunny position is what the santolina requires. The euonymus will grow in almost any soil, but the santolina must have good drainage.

2.16 Hebe & Ruta

Hebe rakaiensis

sun/shade ○
type of plant hardy/slightly tender shrub
zonal range 8-10 (WT-ST)
flowering time early to mid-summer
flower colour white
height 60cm (2ft)
special characteristics evergreen, decorative green foliage

Ruta graveolens 'Jackman's Blue'

(rue)
sun/shade ○
type of plant hardy shrub
zonal range 6-8 (CT-WT)
flowering time mid- to late summer
flower colour yellow
height 45-60cm (1½-2ft)
special characteristics evergreen, aromatic blue-grey foliage

Both sets of leaves in this combination are rather similar in size and shape. In addition, the outline of both shrubs is alike: the hebe naturally forms a neat dome, and the rue makes much the same sort of shape if hard pruned in spring and if any later flower spikes are pinched out. Preventing the rue from flowering produces better quality foliage as well as a much more shapely plant.

When mature, the hebe will cover about twice the area of the rue but, apart from size, the only significant differences between these two plants are those of leaf texture and colour: the hebe's densely packed, light green leaves are shiny, whereas the rue's sprays of sharply pungent foliage are an intense, matt blue-grey. Only when the hebe becomes rather irregularly sprinkled with little white flower spikes is another colour introduced.

These minimal differences make for the kind of restrained yet interesting combination of plants that looks well in quite formal surroundings.

Both plants like a sunny position, and full sun produces the best and bluest foliage on the rue. Both plants also need well-drained soil but, for the sake of the hebe, conditions must not be too dry.

It is advisable to protect your hands when cutting the rue as it can irritate the skin.

49

2.17 Heuchera, Sisyrinchium & Juniperus

Heuchera micrantha var. diversifolia 'Palace Purple'

sun/shade ○ **type of plant** hardy perennial
zonal range 6-8 (CT-WT)
flowering time mid- to late summer
flower colour pale pink
height 45-60cm (1½-2ft)
special characteristics evergreen, purple foliage

Sisyrinchium striatum

(syn *Phaiophleps nigricans*)
sun/shade ○ **type of plant** hardy perennial
zonal range 7-8 (CT-ST)
flowering time early to mid-summer
flower colour pale yellow
height 60cm (2ft)
special characteristics evergreen, grey-green foliage

Juniperus squamata 'Blue Star'

(juniper)
sun/shade ○ **type of plant** hardy conifer
zonal range 5-8 (CT-ST)
height 30-45cm (12-18in)
special characteristics evergreen, blue-grey foliage

The pale grey-green leaves and charming flowers of *Sisyrinchium striatum* are very effectively outlined here against a mound of rich red-purple. In front, the almost prostrate growth of a slow-growing blue juniper steadies the whole group with its hard, close-textured foliage and the more or less horizontal arrangement of its branches. All of these plants are evergreen and, although only the juniper's foliage looks really good in winter, this is a combination that is attractive for many months.

There are numerous pleasing contrasts in texture and form: the sisyrinchium's leaves are smooth, slim and upright; the heuchera's gleaming, crinkled foliage is rounded and the individual leaves are quite large; and the juniper's tiny needles are dry and densely packed. Despite all these differences, however, the combination does not appear cluttered and busy. This is due partly to the presence of the very dark foliage of this well-coloured form of *Heuchera micrantha diversifolia* 'Palace Purple' and partly to the fact that there is a conspicuous link between the greyish leaves of the sisyrinchium and the grey-blue needles of the juniper. Though some gardeners might find that the heuchera's long-stemmed flower-sprays interfered with other ingredients in this group, they are certainly attractive and especially so perhaps as pinkish seedheads.

In winter, the juniper's leaves become a darker, steely grey.

None of the plants here is difficult to grow. They all appreciate good drainage, though for the heuchera to perform well the soil must not be too dry. The sisyrinchium self-seeds in most soils.

2.18 Nerine & Stachys

Nerine bowdenii

sun/shade ○
type of plant slightly tender bulb
zonal range 8-10 (WT-ST)
flowering time early to late autumn
flower colour pink
height 45-60cm (1½-2ft)

Stachys byzantina

(syn *S. lanata, S. olympica*)
(lamb's tongue, lamb's ear, lamb's lug)
sun/shade ○
type of plant hardy perennial
zonal range 4-9 (C-ST)
flowering time midsummer
flower colour mauve-pink
height 30-45cm (12-18in)
special characteristics evergreen, silver foliage

The woolly, silver-green foliage of lamb's tongue makes an excellent companion for many pink-flowered plants. This is particularly true if the flowers, like those of *Nerine bowdenii*, have a distinct silveriness about them. As well as enhancing the colour of the nerine's lovely, curly flowers, the lamb's tongue also helps to furnish its bare stems (most of the nerine's strap-shaped leaves are produced well after the plant has flowered and they die down in summer). The nerine's flowers are especially welcome since they appear so late in the season and are so different in form and colour from many autumn blooms. It is a bonus indeed that they are also very long-lasting as cut flowers. For a photograph of these flowers with pink autumn foliage, see 10.10.

In order to produce a really long display of numerous flowers, the nerine must have a position where it receives plenty of sun and is really warm during its summer dormancy. It also requires well-drained soil. The lamb's tongue thrives in these conditions too and, especially in areas with relatively mild winters, it will look spruce and silvery almost all year long. The foliage benefits from having the woolly flower stems removed as soon as the flowers have faded.

2.19 Santolina & Stachys

Santolina chamaecyparissus
(syn *S. incana*)
(cotton lavender)
sun/shade ○
type of plant hardy shrub
zonal range 6-9 (CT-ST)
flowering time midsummer
flower colour bright yellow
height 45-60cm (1½-2ft)
special characteristics evergreen, aromatic, silver foliage

Stachys byzantina 'Silver Carpet'
(syn *S. lanata* 'Silver Carpet', *S. olympica* 'Silver Carpet')
(lamb's tongue, lamb's ear, lamb's lug)
sun/shade ○
type of plant hardy perennial
zonal range 4-9 (CT-ST)
height 10-15cm (4-6in)
special characteristics evergreen, silver foliage

Combinations involving only grey-leaved plants can sometimes look rather drab, but if strong textural contrasts are provided the whole effect can be surprisingly lively. In this particular combination, the very neat, almost crisp-looking foliage of *Santolina chamaecyparissus* is completely different in size and shape from the broad, softly furred and smoothly edged leaves of the lamb's tongue. In addition, there is an attractive contrast in habit of growth: the santolina's bushy, rounded outline is formed by fairly upright stems, whereas the lamb's tongue consists of a low, dense carpet of foliage.

Since both these plants keep their leaves through the winter months, this is a long-lasting combination of interesting contrasts. However, by the end of winter in colder regions, the lamb's tongue may look rather scruffy and need tidying up. In all areas the santolina benefits from a springtime clipping. This means that few flowers are produced, but in any case many gardeners do not like these brightly coloured buttons. Like many grey-leaved plants, this shrub has foliage which is pungently scented.

Both the santolina and the lamb's tongue enjoy well-drained conditions and plenty of sun; they do well in hot, dry places. *Stachys byzantina* 'Silver Carpet' is a virtually non-flowering form of lamb's tongue that combines well with many other plants.

2.20 Viola & Anaphalis

Viola 'Blue Carpet'
(violet)
sun/shade ○ ◖
type of plant hardy perennial
zonal range 5-8 (C-WT)
flowering time late spring to mid-autumn
flower colour bright violet-blue
height 20-30cm (8-12in)

Anaphalis triplinervis
(pearly everlasting)
sun/shade ○
type of plant hardy perennial
zonal range 4-9 (C-WT)
flowering time late summer to early autumn
flower colour white
height 30-45cm (12-18in)
special characteristics grey foliage

The number of grey-leaved plants that do well in moisture-retentive soils is limited. *Anaphalis triplinervis* is, therefore, particularly welcome for creating combinations such as the one shown here, where the companion plant must have moisture to grow and flower well.

In addition to its attractive, white-backed leaves, and pale, somewhat curving stems, the anaphalis has numerous, crisp-textured everlasting flowers. Because of their texture, these blooms often look good even when the main flowering period is over (here the plant is shown in mid-autumn). They are useful in dried flower arrangements.

The viola can be encouraged to produce plenty of flowers over a long season by being provided with a well-drained but moist soil, and by having all its initial crop of flowers and any long growths removed. A sunny position and regular dead-heading also encourage the viola to flower prolifically. At all times the splendid richness of the viola's flower colour is intensified by the good, solid grey of the anaphalis foliage. When growing well, both of these clump-forming plants make good ground cover.

Other, more readily available violas of a similar rich, strong colouring include *Viola* 'Huntercombe Purple' and *V.* 'Martin'.

2.21 Stachys & Juniperus

Stachys byzantina 'Silver Carpet'

(syn *S. lanata* 'Silver Carpet', *S. olympica* 'Silver Carpet')

(lamb's tongue, lamb's ear, lamb's lug)

sun/shade ○
type of plant hardy perennial
zonal range 4-9 (C-ST)
height 10-15cm (4-6in)
special characteristics evergreen, silver foliage

Juniperus squamata 'Blue Carpet'

(juniper)

sun/shade ○
type of plant hardy conifer
zonal range 5-8 (C-CT)
height 30-45cm (12-18in)
special characteristics evergreen, blue-grey foliage

With such a restricted colour range, all attention is focused on the strong contrasts in leaf shape, size and texture in this combination. The form of lamb's tongue used here seldom produces the familiar, woolly-stemmed flowers of the species, and this concentrates the eye still further. At almost all times of the year this combination looks good, though in colder districts the lamb's tongue can look rather battered by the end of winter.

Both the hard blue needles of the juniper and the soft grey hairiness of the much larger leaves of the lamb's tongue withstand hot, dry conditions well. Full sun produces these plants' best foliage colour and their densest, ground-covering growth.

Juniperus squamata 'Blue Star' is another ground-covering conifer of very similar colouring to *J. s.* 'Blue Carpet' (see 2.17). *J. s.* 'Blue Carpet' may need pruning to keep its branches prostrate; it can eventually spread up to 1.5m (5ft) wide. In winter the foliage of this conifer may become tinged with purple. *Stachys byzantina* and *S. b.* 'Silver Carpet' are very useful front-of-the-border perennials which will blend well with plants of many different colours and shapes.

2.22 Thymus & Celmisia

Thymus × citriodorus 'Variegatus'

(lemon-scented thyme)

sun/shade ○
type of plant hardy shrub (herb)
zonal range 6-8 (CT-ST)
flowering time early to mid-summer
flower colour mauve
height 20cm (8in)
special characteristics evergreen, aromatic, variegated foliage

Celmisia spectabilis

sun/shade ○
type of plant slightly tender perennial
zone 9 (WT)
flowering time early summer
flower colour white + yellow
height 30cm (12in)
special characteristics evergreen, silver foliage

Many celmisias, including the species shown in 2.23, produce bold bursts of grey foliage. The leaves of *Celmisia spectabilis* are silvery green above, but below they are white and this makes the plant appear quite grey overall. Here this plant is accompanied by rounded masses of tiny, citrus-scented thyme leaves. Each of these leaves is edged with creamy white and the general impression is one of lightness and delicacy.

In contrast, the celmisia's broad, greyish blades have a much clearer-cut outline. The boldness of this plant is emphasized both by the eye-catching white undersides of the leaves and by the way in which the foliage is arranged in rosettes. Among these leaves may be seen the developing flower buds, which will open out into large daisies with stiff, pale stems and conspicuous yellow centres. When the thyme flowers, it produces a cloud of small, lipped blooms which often covers the plant completely.

While the thyme is easily grown in any sunny place with good drainage, the celmisia is rather more fussy; it too must have a well-drained soil but its roots must not become hot and parched. Ideally it should have an open-textured yet moisture-retentive soil. It also needs a protected but light and sunny position.

2.23 Geranium & Celmisia

Geranium × traversii var. elegans

(cranesbill)
sun/shade ○
type of plant slightly tender perennial
zonal range 8-9 (CT-WT)
flowering time early summer to mid-autumn
flower colour pink
height 15cm (6in)
special characteristics semi-evergreen, decorative green foliage

Celmisia coriacea

sun/shade ○
type of plant slightly tender perennial
zonal range 8-9 (WT)
flowering time early to mid-summer
flower colour white + yellow
height 40cm (15in)
special characteristics evergreen, silver foliage

Like several plants of its genus, this celmisia produces a stiff rosette of tough, silvery, white-backed leaves that could hardly be more different in character from the long geranium stems which traipse lazily over and around it. This pairing of plants is one that will give pleasure for many months, for the pretty flowers of the geranium, flattered here by the celmisia's silvery leaves, are produced over an exceptionally long season (the photograph shows the combination in mid-autumn). The lobed and slightly fleshy leaves of this plant are also attractive, and they have a distinctly grey cast to their basic green colouring. The foliage that grows from the central rootstock of this plant is rounder and larger than that produced on the trailing stems. The celmisia has daisy-like, yellow-centred flowers on stiff stems, which again contrast with the much more relaxed demeanour of the geranium.

Unfortunately, this striking partnership of disparate personalities is not easily accommodated in every garden. Both plants are rather tender and need full sun and perfect drainage. To make matters more difficult, the celmisia will not tolerate hot, dry conditions. The necessary combination of warmth, plenty of light and a cool, peaty or humus-rich soil seems to occur most often in regions with cool summers.

2.24 Stachys & Aethionema

Stachys byzantina 'Silver Carpet'

(syn *S. lanata* 'Silver Carpet', *S.olympica* 'Silver Carpet')
(lamb's tongue, lamb's ear, lamb's lug)
sun/shade ○
type of plant hardy perennial
zonal range 4-9 (C-ST)
height 10-15cm (4-6in)
special characteristics evergreen, silver foliage

Aethionema grandiflorum

(Persian stone cress)
sun/shade ○
type of plant hardy perennial
zonal range 5-8 (C-WT)
flowering time late spring to midsummer
flower colour pink
height 15-23cm (6-9in)
special characteristics evergreen/semi-evergreen, grey foliage

Grey foliage and pink flowers nearly always make a successful combination (for a grey-and-pink partnership using larger plants than those shown here, see 2.8). In this case, bold grey leaves are combined with tiny pink flowers and very narrow, trailing, grey foliage.

S. b. 'Silver Carpet' differs from the species in a number of ways: not only is it virtually non-flowering, but it produces a more densely leafy carpet of growth, its leaves are larger and longer-stemmed and – as shown here in late spring – its foliage is less woolly in spring and early summer. Here, the relative smoothness and largeness of the leaves are advantages, since they emphasize the appealing fussiness of the stone cress.

During the ensuing weeks, the rounded flowerheads of the stone cress will become looser and more elongated. Even when all the flowers have faded, the two sets of leaves in this combination continue to look attractive together.

Really good drainage and plenty of sun will produce the best specimens of both these plants. However, even in ideal conditions, the stone cress is a rather short-lived plant.

2.25 Stachys & Ajuga

Stachys byzantina 'Silver Carpet'
(syn *S. lanata* 'Silver Carpet', *S. olympica* 'Silver Carpet')
(lamb's tongue, lamb's ear, lamb's lug)
sun/shade ○
type of plant hardy perennial
zonal range 4-9 (C-ST)
height 10-15cm (4-6in)
special characteristics evergreen, silver foliage

Ajuga reptans 'Atropurpurea'
(bugle)
sun/shade ○ ◐
type of plant hardy perennial
zonal range 3-9 (C-ST)
flowering time late spring to early summer
flower colour deep blue
height 15-20cm (6-8in)
special characteristics evergreen/semi-evergreen, purple foliage

The previous photograph shows *Stachys byzantina* 'Silver Carpet' in its relatively smooth-leaved, late spring condition. During early summer, the foliage will have acquired the lovely, soft covering of silky, silvery hairs evident here in early autumn. This most attractive, downy paleness is enhanced by the presence of another low, ground-covering plant of quite different colouring and texture. The foliage of *Ajuga reptans* 'Atropurpurea' is glossy, veined and, particularly when it is grown in positions with plenty of light, very richly coloured. Indeed, the colouring can be so dark and rich that the leaves tend to disappear among ordinary greens. Here, however, they are conspicuous against the pale fur of the lamb's tongue.

The flowers, as well as the foliage, of this bugle are strongly coloured (see 5.8) and they too look very good against the lamb's tongue. 'Silver Carpet' is a virtually non-flowering variety of *Stachys byzantina*. The lack of flowers helps to make it an especially versatile edging plant.

Neither of these perennials is difficult to grow but, although the lamb's tongue thrives in hot, rather dry places, the soil should not be too dry for the sake of the bugle. Provided it is well-drained, any ordinary garden soil will be suitable for this combination.

2.26 Thymus & Acaena

Thymus × citriodorus 'Golden King'
(lemon-scented thyme)
sun/shade ○
type of plant hardy shrub (herb)
zonal range 6-8 (CT-WT)
flowering time early to late summer
flower colour mauve
height 15-20cm (6-8in)
special characteristics evergreen, aromatic, variegated foliage

Acaena saccaticupula 'Blue Haze'
(syn *A.* 'Pewter')
sun/shade ○
type of plant hardy perennial
zonal range 6-8 (CT-WT)
height 10-15cm (4-6in)
special characteristics semi-evergreen, blue-grey foliage, fruit

The tiny, ferny leaflets of this acaena are an excellent blue-grey, and the blueness in their smoky colouring is heightened when they intermingle with yellow leaves. By the same token, the gold and green of this thyme's citrus-scented foliage looks particularly sharp and yellow when seen with blue.

The flowers of these two plants are not as striking as their leaves. The thyme's tiny blooms are less freely produced than those of *Thymus × citriodorus* itself. The acaena's long-stalked flowerheads, seen here in early summer, are not considered decorative – though, in late summer, they ripen into burrs of a good red-brown.

The acaena is a vigorous plant and its rooting carpet of stems may well need some restraining if it is not to overwhelm the thyme's bushier, less spreading dome of growth. The foliage of this particular form of lemon-scented thyme is apt to revert occasionally; any plain, green-leaved shoots should be removed. Both plants need really well-drained soil and an open, sunny position to look as neat and colourful as they do here.

2.27 Chamaecyparis & Euonymus

Chamaecyparis lawsoniana 'Pembury Blue'

(Lawson cypress)
sun/shade ○ ◑
type of plant hardy conifer
zonal range 6-7 (C-WT)
height 10m (30ft)
special characteristics evergreen, blue-green foliage

Euonymus fortunei 'Emerald Gaiety'

sun/shade ○ ◑
type of plant hardy shrub/climber
zonal range 5-9 (C-ST)
height 60-90cm (2-3ft) as a shrub, 2.1-3m (7-10ft) as a climber
special characteristics evergreen, variegated foliage

When fully mature this form of Lawson cypress produces foliage which is a deep, glaucous green tipped with vivid silver-blue. Despite the bright frosting, the size and density of this plant can produce quite a ponderous impression. However, by planting a variegated euonymus nearby and allowing it to clamber among the larger plant's branches, the relatively sombre foliage of this conifer has been lightened and animated considerably.

In contrast to the cypress's dark and slender cone of growth, the euonymus's foliage, with its sprightly combination of greyish green and white, is frothy and frilly. Since both sets of leaves are evergreen, this is a partnership of differing colours, shapes and textures that looks good throughout the year. In winter the leaves of the euonymus often become tinged with pink during cold weather. This euonymus is usually seen as a low hummock of bushy growth, but older specimens of this slow-growing plant will often produce climbing stems.

Each of the plants in this combination is easy to grow. However, the Lawson cypress will become established most quickly and will grow best in soils which are both moisture-retentive and well-drained. After ten years it can be expected to reach about 3m (10ft) or more in height.

2.28 Rosa & Lilium

Rosa glauca

(syn *R. rubrifolia*)
(rose)
sun/shade ○ ◑
type of plant hardy shrub
zonal range 4-8 (C-WT)
flowering time early summer
flower colour pink + white
height 1.8-2.4m (6-8ft)
special characteristics grey/purple foliage, fruit

Lilium martagon

(turk's cap lily, martagon lily)
sun/shade ○ ◑
type of plant hardy bulb
zonal range 4-8 (C-CT)
flowering time early to mid-summer
flower colour variable shades of pink-purple
height 90-150cm (3-5ft)

The foliage of *Rosa glauca* is always a subtle mixture of grey and plummy red. This elusiveness of colouring accounts for its ability to blend very successfully with a wide range of other plants. In partial shade, as here, the grey tones predominate, but an undercurrent of mauve-red is present and it is enhanced by the maroon colouring both of the leaf stalks and of the long, arching, almost thornless stems.

These subordinate reddish tones are also heightened by the soft pink-purple of the lily's attractively shaped but rather unpleasantly scented, turk's cap flowers. The leaves of the lily are whorled and green.

As the lily reaches its main period of flower, the sharp pink blooms of *Rosa glauca* begin to fade. They are followed, from late summer onwards, by dusky orange-red hips, and in mid-autumn the leaves of this rose turn briefly yellow before falling.

Lilium martagon is an easily grown, self-seeding plant which is not nearly as fussy as most lilies. Although it prefers acid or neutral soils, it is lime-tolerant. It does not require perfect drainage to grow well. In order to produce plenty of new, well-coloured shoots and good quality foliage, *Rosa glauca* needs to be pruned fairly hard and to be given a fertile, moisture-retentive soil.

2.29 Vitis & Athyrium

Vitis coignetiae

(ornamental vine)
sun/shade ○ ◖
type of plant hardy climber
zonal range 5-9 (C-WT)
height 15-24m (50-80ft)
special characteristics decorative green foliage, autumn foliage

Athyrium niponicum var. *pictum*

(syn *A. n. metallicum*, *A. goeringianum* 'Pictum')
(Japanese painted fern)
sun/shade ◖
type of plant hardy fern
zonal range 3-8 (C-CT)
height 40cm (15in)
special characteristics grey foliage

As well as being one of the most beautiful of all ferns, *Athyrium niponicum pictum* is a useful source of grey foliage for shady places. Here its clumps of almost horizontally held, silvered fronds have been set at the foot of a magnificent and vigorous vine. Where the fern is all laciness and subtle gradations of colour, the vine is big and bold and straightforwardly green.

In autumn, and especially in light soils and sunny sites, the vine's foliage turns deep, tawny shades of yellow, orange and purple-crimson. Each leaf is rough-textured above and brown-felted below, and may be up to 30cm (12in) wide. The fern's foliage is delightfully delicate in comparison. As each new frond unfurls, it changes from maroon to silvery grey in colour, although an attractive maroon-purple is retained on the stems and on the mid-ribs of the fronds.

This fern is at its leafiest and most luxuriant in sheltered, partial shade and in spongy, moisture-retentive soils. The vine also needs good drainage and moisture, and, if it is to establish quickly, the soil needs to be fairly fertile. After just ten years this plant can be as much as 4.5-6m (15-20ft) tall. However, if necessary, its growth can be easily restricted by winter pruning. Young plants of this tendrilled climber need assistance to cling to supports.

2.30 Berberis & Hosta

Berberis temolaica

(barberry)
sun/shade ○ ◖
type of plant hardy shrub
zonal range 6-9 (CT-WT)
flowering time early summer
flower colour pale yellow
height 1.8-3m (6-10ft)
special characteristics blue-grey foliage, fruit

Hosta Tardiana Group

(plantain lily)
sun/shade ◖
type of plant hardy perennial
zonal range 3-9 (C-CT)
flowering time mid- to late summer
flower colour mauve
height 45cm (18in)
special characteristics blue-grey foliage, suitable for damp soils

These two sets of leaves match beautifully in colour and contrast interestingly in size and shape. There are also striking differences in habit of growth in this combination: *Berberis temolaica* has an open structure of curving branches and this slightly ungainly sparseness is quite different from the lush solidity of the hosta. In addition, the berberis has little, rounded leaves, whereas the hosta's foliage is elegantly pointed and relatively large.

Here, in late spring, the berberis is decorated with small grey flower buds. These open into yellow flowers. Later there are red berries frosted with a greyish bloom. The flowers of hostas in the Tardiana Group are not usually much taller than the leaves. An especially good, readily available form of hosta in this group is *H.* 'Halcyon' (see 17.11).

Though easy to grow in most soils, *Berberis temolaica* is difficult to propagate and therefore expensive. Some forms are a good deal less attractive than others. Some pruning prevents too much lankiness, and it also encourages the growth of plenty of pale new stems and leaves. The hosta should be given a soil that remains constantly moist. A little shade will help conserve moisture, and it will also ensure that the leaf colour of this plant lasts well throughout the growing season.

2.31 Hosta & Sorbus

Hosta sieboldiana var. *elegans*
(plantain lily)
sun/shade ◐
type of plant hardy perennial
zonal range 3-9 (C-ST)
flowering time early to mid-summer
flower colour palest lilac
height 75-90cm (2½-3ft)
special characteristics blue-grey foliage, suitable for damp soils

Sorbus reducta
(rowan, mountain ash)
sun/shade ○ ◐
type of plant hardy shrub
zonal range 5-7 (C-CT)
flowering time late spring to early summer
flower colour white or palest pink
height 45-75cm (1½-2½ft)
special characteristics decorative green foliage, autumn foliage, fruit

Big, bold and very blue, the smooth-edged leaves of *Hosta sieboldiana elegans* contrast strikingly here with the numerous, ferny little leaflets of a sorbus. And beside the much fleshier clump of growth produced by the hosta, the sorbus's thicket of upright, unusually suckering stems is a conspicuously shrubby presence.

The combination was photographed late in the first month of summer. At this stage, the flower clusters of the sorbus have faded and the berries have already formed. Later these fruits will ripen to a lovely, bright pink (see 12.16). From mid-autumn, the slightly blue-tinged leaves of this shrub take on rich tones of maroon, bronze and red. The hosta's puckered foliage colours a splendid, buttery yellow, but only briefly, in early autumn. The flowers of the hosta are thickset and short-stalked; as seedheads, they are most attractive.

A fertile, moisture-retentive soil is needed if the foliage of the hosta is to look good (in rich, damp soils the leaves can be well over 30cm/1ft wide). The foliage colour lasts longest in some shade. Though the sorbus is a vigorous, occasionally invasive shrub that will tolerate drier conditions than the hosta, it will also thrive in soils that are moist – as long as they are reasonably well-drained.

2.32 Hosta & Geranium

Hosta sieboldiana var. *elegans*
(plantain lily)
sun/shade ◐
type of plant hardy perennial
zonal range 3-9 (C-ST)
flowering time early to mid-summer
flower colour palest lilac
height 75-90cm (2½-3ft)
special characteristics blue-grey leaves, suitable for damp soils

Geranium renardii
(cranesbill)
sun/shade ○ ◐
type of plant hardy perennial
zonal range 6-8 (CT-WT)
flowering time early summer
flower colour pale grey + soft mauve
height 23-30cm (9-12in)
special characteristics decorative green foliage

The soft fringing of sage-green provided by *Geranium renardii* seems just the right sort of modest – but not too modest – accessory for the enormous, assertive foliage of this hosta. It does not detract from the hosta's striking blue-grey colour or from its great, ribbed and seersuckered surfaces, yet its felted leaves are interestingly shaped, and its flowers are conspicuous against both its own and the hosta's foliage.

In fertile soils that remain permanently damp, the hosta's leaves may be well over 30cm (1ft) in diameter. However, most moisture-retentive soils will give good results. The geranium will do well in much poorer, more sharply drained soils than the hosta, but it will also be happy and form substantial clumps of growth in the cooler, moister places which suit the hosta best. For further details about the hosta, see 2.31.

3 Hot-coloured Flowers

The recent renewal of enthusiasm for plants with hot-coloured flowers will be viewed with misgiving by some gardeners; there will be those who shudder at the thought of burning reds, bright oranges and eyeball-scorching carmines. However, the new planting schemes featuring hot colours are not the visual assault courses that used to be constructed by some municipal parks departments. The reds and oranges and magentas that interest gardeners now are predominantly hot but not harsh. Equally importantly, there is now at least as much emphasis on foliage as on flowers, and in all the most finely judged, delicately balanced plantings with hot-coloured flowers there are significant amounts of, for instance, plain green and dark, rich purple foliage.

The hottest colours among flowers are the vermilions and scarlets and the strong, intense oranges. These colours grab our attention and appear to advance towards us. But there are other hot – or, at least, very warm – colours that are almost equally striking, and, in the garden, they too seem nearer than they really are. They include penetrating magenta-pinks, with their perceptible blue tones (seen in the flowers of *Geranium psilostemon* in 3.5, for instance), and the deep, richly glowing reds, crimsons and clarets of, for example, some weigelas and certain roses.

Designing with Hot Colours

Exciting planting schemes can be devised using flowers of hot colours only, or the heat of red and orange flowers can be augmented with the radiant, cheerful warmth of yellow blooms and yellow leaves. In late-season schemes of hot colours, red and orange berries and flame-coloured autumn leaves can raise the visual temperature still further.

Using several hot colours together can, however, create visual confusion, though there are various methods of ensuring that this is minimized. To avoid disturbing visual jumps between hot or warm colours, mid-tones can be used as links between the colours. Orange can create a smooth transition between neighbouring reds and yellows, for instance, without lowering the overall heat of a planting scheme. Alternatively, the reds in a hot scheme can be steadied with, for instance, dark purple foliage (see, for instance, the dramatic pairing in 3.3, as well as the combination in 3.17). And, finally, jarring confusions can be simplified and brought to order by using strong shapes. Plants with conspicuously shaped flowers in hot colours include most kniphofias (red hot pokers) and some tulips and astilbes (for examples of which, see 3.2, 3.18 and 16.15, respectively).

When hot-coloured flowers are combined with relatively cool colours, a number of different effects are produced. With the bright, light-reflecting brilliance of white flowers and, to a lesser extent, with the crispness of white-variegated foliage, hot-coloured blooms look smart and sharp. At least, this observation is true if the plants are viewed in the middle of the day. As light fades towards evening, however, reds in particular start to disappear, while whites gleam conspicuously in the half light. The balance of any red-and-white combination alters substantially, therefore, according to the time of day.

Cool blue flowers and glaucous leaves also contrast with hot-coloured flowers, but here the effect is softer and less bright and brash than it is with white. Blue and orange are complementary colours that magnify the differences between each other. For this reason, combinations of blue and orange or blue and orange-red have a special intensity about them (see, for instance, 12.19 and 3.9). This intensity is diluted somewhat when purples and violet-blues, with their red tones, are used with oranges and reds.

A much quieter, subtler look is achieved if hot colours are combined with grey or dark purple foliage. Grey, grey-blue or silver leaves often have a gentle, cooling effect on hot colours, whereas the resonating harmonies set up between dark, plum-coloured foliage and reds and rich oranges amount more nearly to an impression of deep, glowing radiance.

Green leaves usually have a calming effect on other colours. However, red is the complementary colour of green. Like orange and blue, red and green contrast intensely one with the other and highlight their differences. Greens need to be really deep in colour to introduce tranquillity to hot planting schemes. Light, yellowy, lime greens, on the other hand, can cool reds and oranges, though they tend also to keep these colours sharp and bright (see, for example, 8.4).

A Plant for Every Place

All-red borders or borders containing only hot-coloured flowers seem always to be packed with sun-loving plants like salvias, poppies and penstemons, and sometimes these borders also appear to have a high proportion of short-lived and tender plants. All the combinations in this book feature plants that are perennial and that do not need to be brought under cover during the winter months in the British Isles and other temperate climates. Furthermore, this section alone shows and describes several plant combinations that are suitable for growing in shaded sites.

In shade, hot colours seem to simmer rather than boil fiercely – the partnership of crocosmias and ferns shown in 3.30, demonstrates this in an appealingly informal, vibrant partnership. Other plants which appreciate shade and have hot-coloured flowers include some rhododendrons and some primulas (see 3.29 and 3.31).

Finally, there are hot-coloured flowers for almost every season. True, in the coldest months reds and oranges are found mainly among berries and coloured bark, but it is a popular misconception that hot-coloured flowers belong principally to late summer and early autumn. Well before crocosmias and heleniums and kniphofias glow in our borders, there will have been tulips, oriental poppies and primulas, as well as orange-flowered euphorbias, early red roses like *Rosa* 'Geranium' (see 3.23) and a mass of azaleas and rhododendrons in bright, hot colours.

The colouring of all these spring and early summer flowers can be sharpened with acidic greens, or they can be made to look more fiery still with, for instance, the red foliage of *Photinia* × *fraseri* 'Red Robin' or the orange leaves of *Spiraea japonica* 'Goldflame' (see 4.23 and 4.14, respectively.) In just the same sort of way, but at the other end of the gardening year, late-flowering plants with hot-coloured flowers can have their colours boosted by the presence of berries (see, for example, 3.2) or radiant autumn foliage.

3.1 Chamaecyparis & Lychnis

Chamaecyparis pisifera 'Squarrosa'

(Sawara cypress)
sun/shade ○
type of plant hardy conifer
zonal range 5-8 (CT-WT)
height 9m (30ft)
special characteristics evergreen, blue-grey foliage

Lychnis coronaria

(rose campion)
sun/shade ○
type of plant hardy perennial
zonal range 4-8 (C-WT)
flowering time mid- to late summer
flower colour bright magenta-pink
height 60-75cm (2-2½ft)
special characteristics grey foliage

The searingly bright flower colour of *Lychnis coronaria* is this plant's most striking feature. Here the flowers have a softly textured and coolly coloured background against which to burn. The flowers are carried on airy, branching stems, which means that, from a short distance, they look like a series of hot pinpoints on a backdrop of frosted fluffiness.

As well as the cypress's soft, blue-grey foliage, there are also the pale grey leaves of the lychnis itself. These leaves are pointed and oval, and they grow in a clump below the plant's pale, felted flower stems. Together with the cypress's foliage, they create an interesting combination of two similarly coloured but differently textured greys.

In time, the cypress will grow into a small, broadly cone-shaped tree, but it will do so very slowly. The lychnis is a short-lived plant which seeds itself freely in the well-drained soils that suit it best. The cypress may be grown in any ordinary soil, though it does not enjoy the very dry, infertile conditions which the lychnis can tolerate.

3.2 Rosa, Kniphofia & Rudbeckia

Rosa 'Geranium'

(rose)
(syn *R. moyesii* 'Geranium')
sun/shade ○ ◐ **type of plant** hardy shrub
zonal range 6-8 (CT-WT)
flowering time early summer
flower colour scarlet
height 2.1-2.4m (7-8ft)
special characteristics fruit

Kniphofia linearifolia

(red hot poker, torch lily)
sun/shade ○
type of plant hardy perennial
zonal range 7-10 (WT-ST)
flowering time late summer to mid-autumn
flower colour orange + yellow
height 1.5m (5ft)
special characteristics evergreen

Rudbeckia fulgida var. deamii

(coneflower)
sun/shade ○ **type of plant** hardy perennial
zonal range 4-9 (C-ST)
flowering time midsummer to early autumn
flower colour yellow
height 60-75cm (2-2½ft)

The three plants in this most attractive, early autumn combination are different in shape, but they are all linked by their warmth of colouring. The long, shapely hips of *R.* 'Geranium', orange-red and shiny, dangle above the upright orange and yellow poker-heads of the kniphofia, while the yellower parts of these flowers are echoed in the coneflower's dazzling, dark-eyed daisies.

Flowers and fruits are the stars of this performance, but the arching branches and small-scale foliage of the rose, the stout stems of the kniphofia and the anchoring mound of greenery produced by the coneflower are all part of an important supporting cast. The rose is by far the largest and most wide-spreading of the plants here. It pays for its consumption of space by also producing a large crop of beautifully simple, single flowers of an exceptionally attractive scarlet (see 3.23).

All three plants are vigorous and easy to please. For this combination to be at its best, there must be plenty of sun and a well-drained, reasonably moisture-retentive soil. *Rudbeckia fulgida sullivantii* 'Goldsturm' is a more widely available form of rudbeckia that is similar to *R. fulgida deamii*. If *Kniphofia linearifolia* is difficult to obtain, the variety *K.* 'Royal Standard' would make a good substitute. Both these kniphofias have grassy foliage.

3.3 Alstroemeria & Cotinus

Alstroemeria aurea
(syn *A. aurantiaca*)
(Peruvian lily)
sun/shade ○
type of plant slightly tender perennial
zonal range 7-10 (CT-ST)
flowering time early to mid-summer
flower colour variable – yellow to orange-bronze
height 90cm (3ft)

Cotinus coggygria Rubrifolius Group
(syn *C. c.* 'Foliis Purpureis')
(smoke tree, Venetian sumach)
sun/shade ○
type of plant hardy shrub/tree
zonal range 5-9 (C-WT)
fruiting time mid- to late summer
fruit colour purplish
height 1.8-3m (6-10ft)
special characteristics purple foliage, autumn foliage, fruit

The wonderful, rich colour and the elegant flower shape of *Alstroemeria aurea* persuade many gardeners to excuse this plant its vigorous, spreading nature and its tendency to seed itself everywhere. Here it has been given a dramatic, dark background which outlines every curve and point of its petals and against which its flowers glow. After flowering, its attractively leafy, upright stems begin to die back.

The accompanying cotinus is a flattering companion to a remarkably wide range of other plant colours. It and other purple-leaved forms of *Cotinus coggygria* look well with pinks, yellow-greens (see 7.2), and greys (see 4.9), for example.

As the alstroemeria finishes flowering, the cotinus's cloud of tiny flowers ripen and the fruits within this haze become rosier and more purple. However, flowers only appear in sizeable quantities on mature wood and some gardeners like to remove most of this each year in order to get plenty of good quality foliage on young shoots.

This cotinus is late into leaf and will not look well-clothed until early summer. In light and rather poor soils particularly, the leaves of this rounded shrub or small tree turn red in mid-autumn. Not too dry a soil would, however, be most suitable for this combination since the alstroemeria does not thrive if parched. It also likes some warmth and shelter.

3.4 Kniphofia & Viburnum

Kniphofia linearifolia
(red hot poker, torch lily)
sun/shade ○
type of plant hardy perennial
zonal range 7-10 (WT-ST)
flowering time late summer to mid-autumn
flower colour orange + yellow
height 1.5m (5ft)
special characteristics evergreen

Viburnum plicatum 'Mariesii'
(syn *V. tomentosum* 'Mariesii')
sun/shade ○ ◑
type of plant hardy shrub
zonal range 6-8 (C-WT)
flowering time late spring
flower colour white
height 1.8-2.4m (6-8ft)
special characteristics autumn foliage

With their thick stems and assertive shape, the flame-coloured flowers of many kniphofias are striking embellishments of the garden in autumn. Here the orange and yellow of *K. linearifolia* have been paired, not with similarly coloured autumn leaves, among which they might get lost, but with contrasting, wine-tinted foliage.

Since this purplish autumn colour belongs to a variety of *Viburnum plicatum*, there is also an interesting difference between the very upright, long-stemmed kniphofia flowers and the conspicuous horizontal line of the viburnum's branches. This is a contrast that is evident well before the kniphofia comes fully into flower. The habit of growth and the pretty, lace-cap flowers of a very similar viburnum – *V. p.* 'Lanarth' – are shown in 1.20.

Another slightly smaller kniphofia, which would have the same effect in this combination, is *K.* 'Royal Standard'. Both these kniphofias have grassy and rather untidy leaves. Apart from needing plenty of sun and good drainage, *K. linearifolia* is easy to please. However, it does not perform well if its roots are very dry, and the viburnum too likes some moisture. Both the plants in this combination thrive in alkaline soils.

For purplish viburnum leaves combined with cool, very blue foliage, see 10.20.

61

3.5 Crambe, Inula & Geranium

Crambe cordifolia
sun/shade ○
type of plant hardy perennial
zonal range 6-9 (C-WT)
flowering time early to mid-summer
flower colour white
height 1.8m (6ft)

Inula magnifica
sun/shade ○
type of plant hardy perennial
zonal range 4-8 (C-WT)
flowering time midsummer to early autumn
flower colour yellow
height 1.8m (6ft)
special characteristics decorative green foliage, suitable for damp and wet soils

Geranium psilostemon
(syn *G. armenum*) (cranesbill)
sun/shade ○ ◐ **type of plant** hardy perennial
zonal range 4-8 (C-WT)
flowering time early to late summer
flower colour magenta-pink + black
height 90-120cm (3-4ft)
special characteristics decorative green foliage, autumn foliage

Even with the enormous white cloud of flowers of the crambe and huge rough leaves of the inula to compete with in this combination, the searing, black-eyed flowers of *Geranium psilostemon* more than hold their own. In this photograph, the very large, bright yellow daisies of *Inula magnifica* have yet to appear (though the purple-brown buds will soon be looking interesting). However, the immense leaves and sturdy stems of this plant play an important role in this planting. The leaves stabilize what might be too fussy a pairing of two relatively small-flowered plants.

The crambe too has very large leaves but these form a fairly low mound beneath the branching flower stems. The geranium's foliage is on a different scale and attractively divided and lobed. It grows in rather lax clumps and turns red in autumn.

All three of these robust and fairly vigorous plants may need staking. Though the inula can be grown in damp and boggy soils and the geranium does especially well in fertile conditions, an ordinary, well-drained soil is most suitable for this combination. The flowers of *Crambe cordifolia* have a rather oily scent which is usually noticeable only at close range.

3.6 Rosa & Nepeta

Rosa 'Conditorum'
(syn *R. gallica* 'Conditorum')
(rose)
sun/shade ○
type of plant hardy shrub
zonal range 4-9 (C-WT)
flowering time early to mid-summer
flower colour bright crimson
height 1.2-1.8m (4-6ft)
special characteristics fragrant flowers

Nepeta × faassenii
(catmint)
sun/shade ○
type of plant hardy perennial
zonal range 4-8 (C-WT)
flowering time early summer to early autumn
flower colour lavender-blue
height 30-45cm (12-18in)
special characteristics semi-evergreen, aromatic, grey-green foliage

Roses of many types bear flowers that are brilliant red or crimson and catmint makes a low, tidy, greyish-leaved companion for them all. It is especially suitable for planting beneath shrub roses, since these plants are often bushy and flower-covered more or less to ground level, and the contrast between their bright blooms and the cool, soft colours of the catmint is therefore accentuated.

The rose shown here is not very readily available. More popular gallica varieties such as 'Tuscany Superb' and 'Cardinal de Richelieu' have a good deal more purple in their colouring – though purplish roses look good with catmint, too (see 13.7). Gallica-type roses with bright crimson-scarlet flowers include *R.* 'Scharlachglut' (syn 'Scarlet Fire') and *R.* 'James Mason'. Their flowers are richly and sweetly scented. All these roses will tolerate soils that are not particularly fertile.

Catmint can be grown in any well-drained soil. With good drainage, sunshine and pruning in spring it forms a dense clump of grey-green stems and leaves. To make sure that the plant flowers well over several months, the stems that have carried the first flush of flowers should be trimmed off. The leaves have a slightly musty, minty smell.

3.7 Aconitum & Lythrum

Aconitum 'Spark's Variety'

(monkshood)
sun/shade ○ ◑
type of plant hardy perennial
zonal range 4-8 (C-WT)
flowering time mid- to late summer
flower colour dark violet-blue
height 1.2-1.5m (4-5ft)

Lythrum salicaria

(purple loosestrife)
sun/shade ○
type of plant hardy perennial
zonal range 4-9 (C-ST)
flowering time midsummer to early autumn
flower colour bright mauve-pink
height 1.2m (4ft)
special characteristics suitable for damp and wet soils

Conventional companions for the loosestrife's erect spikes of intense pink might include either some cooling grey foliage or more, hot-coloured flowers and leaves. The use of exceptionally dark blue flowers here creates an unusually smart and sophisticated combination.

The most striking feature of this partnership is the contrast between a very dark and a very bright colour, but there is an interesting colour link here, too. The sharp and piercing pink of the loosestrife's flowers is tinged with blue and quite similar to magenta, an intermediary colour which is very close to violet, the colour which suffuses the dark blue of the monkshood's flowers.

The stiff, erect nature of the loosestrife flowers is emphasized still further by the contrastingly soft shapes of the monkshood. Its more flexible, branching stems, deeply divided foliage and little hooded flowers all create a quieter, more retiring impression than the bold spikes of the loosestrife. The loosestrife's slender leaves form a clump of growth.

Both plants in this combination appreciate a moisture-retentive soil and the monkshood likes fertile conditions. The lythrum can also be grown in damp and wet ground. All parts of the monkshood are very poisonous.

3.8 Crocosmia & Artemisia

Crocosmia paniculata

(syn *Curtonus paniculatus*)
sun/shade ○
type of plant hardy corm
zonal range 6-9 (WT-ST)
flowering time late summer to early autumn
flower colour orange-red + orange
height 1.2m (4ft)
special characteristics decorative green foliage

Artemisia ludoviciana

(syn *A. palmeri*)
(white sage)
sun/shade ○
type of plant hardy perennial
zonal range 4-9 (C-WT)
height 90-120cm (3-4ft)
special characteristics aromatic, silver foliage

The rich, luminous flowers of *Crocosmia paniculata* and their dark stems are in marked contrast to the slender, silvery growths of this artemisia. The main effect of the pale foliage, shown here in late summer, is to make the crocosmia's curving trumpets glow still more brightly. However, for a much longer period it also accentuates the similarly upright but quite differently coloured leaves of the crocosmia. These great sheaves of pleated greenery are a striking shape in any setting, and their bold outline is emphasized by the artemisia's lightness and delicacy.

Whereas the crocosmia grows quite thickly, the artemisia spreads, with moderate vigour, into patches of very variable density. The crocosmia likes a moisture-retentive but well-drained and fertile soil. However, for the sake of the artemisia, conditions should not be too moist since the leaves of this cleanly aromatic plant are palest and most strongly scented when the roots of the plant are fairly dry.

Forms of *Artemisia ludoviciana* with particularly pale or broad leaves are less tall and slender than the species.

3.9 Crocosmia & Echinops

Crocosmia paniculata

(syn *Curtonus paniculatus*)
sun/shade ○
type of plant hardy corm
zonal range 6-9 (WT-ST)
flowering time late summer to early autumn
flower colour orange-red + orange
height 1.2m (4ft)
special characteristics decorative green foliage

Echinops ritro

(globe thistle)
sun/shade ○
type of plant hardy perennial
zonal range 3-9 (C-ST)
flowering time mid- to late summer
flower colour blue
height 90-120cm (3-4ft)
special characteristics decorative green foliage

Though, as in the preceding combination, the glowing orange-red of *Crocosmia paniculata* appears very striking, here the curvaceous, dark-stemmed trumpets have a much more solidly built partner competing for attention. *Echinops ritro* produces dense, rich blue globes, nearly 5cm (2in) in diameter, on strong and conspicuously pale stems. Even before they become distinctly blue, these spherical flowerheads are effective. They are attractive to bees and butterflies and the seedheads are often visited by birds.

The stems of the echinops are covered with dark, very jagged, prickly leaves and the rather bright green of the crocosmia's pleated foliage stands out well against this darker growth. There is also a pleasing contrast in overall shape between the very definite, upright leaves of the crocosmia and the echinops' more randomly disposed prickliness. Both sets of foliage are attractive well before either of these plants comes into flower. The crocosmia's leaves in particular make a very bold shape.

Well-drained soils of all sorts suit the echinops. In this instance, the soil should be reasonably moisture-retentive for the crocosmia to perform well.

For an illustration of the flowers of this crocosmia with autumn leaves, see 10.6.

3.10 Juniperus & Euphorbia

Juniperus × pfitzeriana 'Pfitzeriana Aurea'

(syn *J. × media* 'Pfitzeriana Aurea')
(juniper)
sun/shade ○
type of plant hardy conifer
zonal range 4-9 (C-WT)
height 90-150cm (3-5ft)
special characteristics evergreen, yellow foliage

Euphorbia griffithii 'Fireglow'

(spurge)
sun/shade ○ ◖
type of plant hardy perennial
zonal range 4-9 (C-WT)
flowering time late spring to early summer
flower colour bright orange-red
height 60-90cm (2-3ft)
special characteristics autumn foliage

The intense colour of this euphorbia is at its brightest in late spring and early summer but, like many spurges, *Euphorbia griffithii* 'Fireglow' has flowers that are conspicuous both before and after the main flowering season. Here they have been teamed with a form of juniper that has bright yellow young foliage, and the two hot colours emphasize each other.

Shown here in late spring, the young, scaly leaves of the juniper have yet to lengthen. As they mature, they also become greener, but the two plants continue to look well together since there are interesting contrasts in texture and habit of growth. The euphorbia is a bushy, leafy, red-stemmed plant with foliage which is much fleshier than that of the juniper. In time, the juniper builds up into a very wide-spreading, irregular mound of layered, somewhat pendulous main branches with attractively arching tips.

In autumn the leaves of the euphorbia may turn orange and yellow before falling (see 10.17). Both these plants are vigorous. The juniper does particularly well where there is good drainage. The euphorbia is easily pleased in most soils.

The cut stems of *E. g.* 'Fireglow' exude a milky juice which can irritate the skin and eyes.

3.11 Geranium & Eryngium

Geranium psilostemon
(syn *G. armenum*)
(cranesbill)
sun/shade ○ ◖
type of plant hardy perennial
zonal range 4-8 (C-WT)
flowering time early to late summer
flower colour magenta-pink + black
height 90-120cm (3-4ft)
special characteristics decorative green foliage, autumn foliage

Eryngium alpinum
(sea holly)
sun/shade ○
type of plant hardy perennial
zonal range 5-8 (CT-WT)
flowering time midsummer to early autumn
flower colour mauve-blue
height 75cm (2½ft)

Geranium psilostemon has one of the most dazzling flower colours of all medium-sized perennials. Here the cool, mock-prickliness of a sea holly emphasizes the heat of this colouring and makes a stylishly elaborate contrast to the neat, rounded flowers. In a couple of weeks' time, right in the middle of summer, these flowers, with their large and intricate ruffs, will be fully suffused with a steely mauve-blue (see 1.8) and the colour contrast will be even greater.

Though this combination is at its very best in midsummer, the texture of the eryngium flowers means that they are attractive both before and after their official flowering period. There are also the pleasures, over many weeks, of the eryngium's erect blue stems and the jagged leaves that decorate these stems. The geranium's foliage is even more attractive; the leaves are lobed and divided and they turn red in autumn. They form rather loose clumps of growth which may need staking.

A deep, fertile soil with good drainage will produce excellent specimens of both the eryngium and the geranium. However, the eryngium in particular will do well in drier conditions.

3.12 Alstroemeria & Anaphalis

Alstroemeria aurea
(syn *A. aurantiaca*)
(Peruvian lily)
sun/shade ○
type of plant slightly tender perennial
zonal range 7-10 (CT-ST)
flowering time early to mid-summer
flower colour variable – yellow to orange-bronze
height 90cm (3ft)

Anaphalis margaritacea 'Neuschnee'
(syn *A. m.* 'New Snow')
(pearly everlasting)
sun/shade ○
type of plant hardy perennial
zonal range 3-8 (C-CT)
flowering time midsummer to mid-autumn
flower colour white
height 40cm (15in)
special characteristics grey foliage

Alstroemeria aurea varies somewhat in colour, and there are some named varieties, but all the forms are of a warm or – as here – a rich and dominant colour. In this combination, the radiance of the alstroemeria's shapely funnels has been cooled with white flowers and slim grey foliage. (For a rather different treatment see 3.3, where the alstroemeria has been teamed with the deep purple foliage of a cotinus.)

There is a pleasing similarity both in the upright stems and in the leaf arrangement of both these plants, though the leaf colour differs. The alstroemeria's foliage tends to die back in late summer and, since the plant is a very prolific self-seeder, its seedpods should be removed. The anaphalis then takes centre stage and its crisply textured, everlasting flowers widen and reveal their yellow eyes.

A. m. 'Neuschnee' is approximately half the size of the typical species. Like the species, it needs a well-drained soil that stays moist in summer. These conditions, along with some shelter and warmth, suit the alstroemeria, too. The latter is a very vigorous plant and it may be advisable to sink some sort of large, bottomless container into the soil where it is to be planted so that its roots are prevented from invading those of nearby plants.

65

3.13 Hemerocallis & Eryngium

Hemerocallis 'Stafford'

(daylily)

sun/shade ○
type of plant hardy perennial
zonal range 4-9 (C-ST)
flowering time midsummer to early autumn
flower colour mahogany red + yellow
height 90cm (3ft)
special characteristics semi-evergreen, green foliage, suitable for damp soils

Eryngium × *oliverianum*

(sea holly)

sun/shade ○
type of plant hardy perennial
zonal range 5-8 (C-WT)
flowering time mid- to late summer
flower colour blue
height 75-90cm (2½-3ft)

The most conspicuous ingredient of this combination, at least at first glance, is the vivid spiciness of the daylily's flowers. However, the elegant, sculpted shape of these blooms and the excellent contrast between them and the cool, blue spikiness of the eryngium are every bit as important in terms of the success of the partnership.

The flowers of the daylily are individually short-lived, but the numerous buds open over a long period. Both plants have fairly upright, branching flower stems: those of the eryngium are a striking violet-blue, while the daylily's stems rise above a dense, ground-covering clump of arching, strap-shaped leaves. The eryngium will probably need staking, especially as flowering time approaches, and because of this it may be best to try to hide its lower stems among some of the daylily leaves. The basal foliage of the eryngium is jagged and rather dark, and is not as decorative as that of the daylily.

The eryngium is best in a fertile soil and it must have good drainage. The daylily is a more adaptable plant, but as long as conditions are not too dry it will do well. It too thrives in fertile soils. For another combination involving hot-coloured flowers and an eryngium, see 3.11.

3.14 Heuchera & Hemerocallis

Heuchera micrantha var. *diversifolia* 'Palace Purple'

sun/shade ○
type of plant hardy perennial
zonal range 6-8 (C-WT)
flowering time mid- to late summer
flower colour pale pink
height 45-60cm (1½-2ft)
special characteristics evergreen, purple foliage

Hemerocallis 'Golden Chimes'

(daylily)

sun/shade ○ ◗
type of plant hardy perennial
zonal range 4-9 (C-ST)
flowering time early to late summer
flower colour yellow + red-brown
height 75cm (2½ft)
special characteristics semi-evergreen, green foliage, suitable for damp soils

The foliage of *H. m. d.* 'Palace Purple' varies from red-purple to the browner colour seen here. In this instance, a browner-leaved specimen has been carefully chosen in order to complement the mahogany-backed, rich yellow petals of a daylily. The combination exudes a lovely deep warmth.

As well as an interesting colour match, this pair of plants features excellent foliage contrasts. In this particular colour form, the heuchera's bold clump of dark, rounded leaves could look rather glum, but the slender, arching foliage of the daylily lends an especially light elegance to the whole composition. In milder districts the leaves of the daylily, as well as those of the heuchera, will be evergreen.

An impression of airiness also emanates from the flowers of these both plants. The heuchera's pale, insubstantial sprays float above its gleaming foliage and the daylily's small but numerous flowers are held gracefully on branching stalks. Individually, the daylily's blooms are short-lived, but they open in succession over many weeks. Some gardeners find the pink seedheads of the heuchera even more attractive than the earlier flowers.

A fertile, moisture-retentive soil would be ideal for this combination. The daylily is especially easy to grow, but the heuchera needs reasonably well-drained conditions.

3.15 **Rhododendron & Iris**

Rhododendron 'Vuyk's Rosyred'
(azalea)
sun/shade ○ ◑
type of plant hardy shrub
zonal range 6-8 (CT)
flowering time late spring to early summer
flower colour bright rose-pink
height 60-75cm (2-2½ft)
special characteristics evergreen, needs acid soil

Iris laevigata 'Variegata'
sun/shade ○
type of plant hardy perennial
zonal range 5-9 (C-WT)
flowering time early to mid-summer
flower colour violet-blue
height 60-75cm (2-2½ft)
special characteristics variegated foliage, suitable for water gardens, requires damp or wet soil

Strong pink and white is an eye-catching combination in most circumstances, and here it is particularly striking because of the very upright and conspicuously striped nature of the iris leaves. These leaves do not, however, overwhelm the azalea's ruffle-edged blooms, partly because the latter are such a penetrating pink, but also because the green part of the iris leaves is a soft, greyish colour. The flowers of the iris are a pretty blue which is especially attractive with this grey-green and white foliage. Even when both sets of flowers in the combination have faded, the long-lasting variegation of the iris continues to look well with the azalea's spreading mass of smaller, oval foliage.

Iris laevigata and its forms like moist and wet soils and they will grow in shallow water. Though the azalea likes moisture-retentive conditions it cannot be grown in waterlogged soil, so here it has been placed above the iris in a drier position on a pond bank. Most streams and ponds would allow a similar arrangement. If the azalea is in a sunny position, the need for coolness at its roots is especially important. This slow-growing plant also needs acid soil and some shelter.

For a similarly coloured combination, featuring a pink-magenta primula and a white-variegated euonymus, see 3.31.

3.16 **Tulipa & Muscari**

Tulipa Darwin hybrid
(tulip)
sun/shade ○
type of plant hardy bulb
zonal range 5-7 (C-CT)
flowering time mid-spring
flower colour bright red
height 60-75cm (2-2½ft)

Muscari armeniacum
(grape hyacinth)
sun/shade ○
type of plant hardy bulb
zonal range 4-9 (C-WT)
flowering time mid- to late spring
flower colour mid-blue
height 20-25cm (8-10in)
special characteristics fragrant flowers

The sheer exuberance and brightness of this springtime combination compensate for its relatively short period of interest. Placing spikes of strong blue beneath these flamboyant, large-flowered tulips makes their wonderful colour seem especially vibrant, and the difference in flower shape – the tightly packed little heads of muscari flowers and the smooth and shapely tulip petals – emphasizes still further the bold contrast between these two smart, paintbox colours.

If the tulip is to produce plenty of large flowers from year to year, it must have a really well-drained soil and a site that receives plenty of sun in summer. Almost any soil with reasonable drainage will suit the muscari. This vigorous plant often increases rapidly, to the extent that it may become something of a nuisance. Its leaves first emerge in autumn, and by the time the flowers open, the foliage is usually rather straggly. In warm weather the muscari flowers release a soft, sweet scent.

'Apeldoorn' and 'Oxford' are two readily available Darwin hybrid tulips which have flowers of a similar colouring to the tulip shown here. The size of all these flowers makes them vulnerable to wind damage and they must therefore be given a fairly sheltered site.

67

3.17 Heuchera & Viola

Heuchera micrantha var. *diversifolia* 'Palace Purple'

sun/shade ○
type of plant hardy perennial
zonal range 6-8 (CT-WT)
flowering time mid- to late summer
flower colour pale pink
height 45-60cm (1½-2ft)
special characteristics evergreen, purple foliage

Viola 'Jackanapes'

(violet)
sun/shade ○ ◖
type of plant hardy perennial
zonal range 5-7 (C-CT)
flowering time late spring to early autumn
flower colour yellow + maroon
height 10-15cm (4-6in)
special characteristics evergreen/semi-evergreen

Both the upper and the lower petals of *Viola* 'Jackanapes' are warmly coloured, and in this combination the deep maroon of the upper petals is echoed in the foliage colour of *H. m. d.* 'Palace Purple'. Giving the viola a yellow-leaved partner has a quite different effect – see 5.14.

The heuchera is a variable plant. However, all forms – including those with quite red leaves (see 2.13) – are useful for lending weight and depth to planting schemes involving hot colours. Here the bold, crinkled foliage, coupled with the rich yellow of the viola's cheery flowers, radiates a deep, opulent glow.

This is a combination that looks attractive over a long period. The viola is in bloom for many weeks and is especially free-flowering if grown in fertile, moisture-retentive soil and regularly deadheaded. After the main flush of summer flowers, the spreading, dark-leaved stems of this plant can be cut right back. This encourages the production of blooms well into autumn. The heuchera's tiny flowers are carried in airy sprays well above the plant's clump of foliage. They ripen into pretty, pinkish seedheads.

The heuchera needs a moisture-retentive, reasonably well-drained soil to produce plenty of good-quality foliage. Moisture is important for the viola too, particularly if it is grown in sun.

3.18 Tulipa & Euphorbia

Tulipa 'Queen of Sheba'

(tulip)
sun/shade ○
type of plant hardy bulb
zonal range 5-8 (C-CT)
flowering time late spring
flower colour deep orange-red + yellow
height 45cm (18in)

Euphorbia polychroma

(syn *E. epithymoides*)
(spurge)
sun/shade ○ ◖
type of plant hardy perennial
zonal range 4-9 (C-WT)
flowering time mid- to late spring
flower colour bright yellow
height 45cm (18in)
special characteristics autumn foliage

Against a neat dome of acid yellow the tapering and curving of these tulip petals and their splendidly rich, warm colour are clearly delineated, and the difference in colouring between the two plants – the sharpness of one and the full, deep glow of the other – is mutually enhanced.

Euphorbia polychroma is a bright accompaniment to tulips of many colours, including the very dark purple varieties such as 'Black Parrot' and 'Queen of Night'. 'Queen of Sheba' is classified as a lily-flowered tulip. Another variety in this group which also has glowing red and yellow colouring is 'Dyanito', and more readily available reds such as 'Apeldoorn', 'Madame Lefeber' (syn 'Red Emperor') and *T. praestans* 'Fusilier' would also look very well with this euphorbia.

All these tulips demand really good drainage and sunshine especially if their bulbs are not to dwindle away in a year or two. The euphorbia will also do well in these conditions, although it is quite happy in most soils with reasonable drainage.

The euphorbia's foliage frequently turns an interesting mixture of apricot, yellow and pink in autumn. Gardeners with sensitive skin must be especially careful when handling the cut stems of this plant, as the milky juice which the stems exude can be a severe irritant.

3.19 Geranium & Origanum

Geranium 'Ann Folkard'

(cranesbill)
sun/shade ○
type of plant hardy perennial
zonal range 5-8 (C-WT)
flowering time early summer to early autumn
flower colour bright magenta
height 40-45cm (15-18in)
special characteristics yellow young foliage

Origanum vulgare 'Aureum'

(golden marjoram)
sun/shade ○
type of plant hardy perennial (herb)
zonal range 4-8 (C-WT)
height 23cm (9in)
special characteristics evergreen/semi-evergreen, aromatic, yellow foliage

In spring the new leaves of this weaving, trailing geranium are a bright, greenish yellow, and throughout the growing season there is a fair proportion of younger, lime-green foliage. With a background as sharp and acidic as this, the intensely coloured, black-eyed flowers of the plant seem especially hot and penetrating. These dazzling flowers appear in profusion over a very long period.

Adding a second yellow-leaved plant that retains its foliage colour for longer than the geranium makes sure this combination sizzles for several months. It also provides some interesting contrasts in texture: the geranium's thickly tangled long, lax stems are clothed in deeply divided leaves, whereas the marjoram produces a close-knit clump of erect growths set with neatly arranged ovals of aromatic foliage. As summer progresses, the marjoram's leaves become more khaki in colour. When bruised, the foliage emits the usual peppery, marjoram scent. In this yellow-leaved form, *Origanum vulgare* seldom produces many of its tiny flowers.

Sun and good drainage are important for this marjoram, but in very dry conditions the yellow foliage is apt to become scorched. The geranium will spread up to 1.2m (4ft) wide. It is happy in a wide range of soils, as long as there is reasonable drainage.

3.20 Calluna & Juniperus

Calluna vulgaris 'Firefly'

(heather or ling)
sun/shade ○
type of plant hardy shrub
zonal range 5-7 (C-CT)
flowering time late summer to early autumn
flower colour cerise-crimson
height 30-45cm (12-18in)
special characteristics evergreen, red foliage, autumn/winter foliage, needs acid soil

Juniperus squamata 'Blue Star'

(juniper)
sun/shade ○
type of plant hardy conifer
zonal range 5-8 (C-WT)
height 30-45cm (12-18in)
special characteristics evergreen, blue-grey foliage

The dazzling combination of flower and foliage in *Calluna vulgaris* 'Firefly' could hardly be more different from the chilly silver-blue of this prickly-leaved juniper. As the heather's flower spikes lengthen they will make even more impact, but throughout summer and early autumn the very bright, russet-orange foliage of this dense and hummocky plant will compete for attention. In winter, the heather's leaves become a darker, deeper red and at this time the juniper is also more deeply and soberly coloured. Even without any flowers, and despite the fact that they both have small leaves and a rather dry texture, these two plants create a conspicuously contrasting pair.

The juniper is a slow-growing plant. It is neat, dense and almost prostrate and usually not very much wider than it is tall. The heather, however, needs to be clipped over early in spring each year if it is to stay dense and tidy. It must have a lime-free soil and one that is well-drained but not bone-dry. The juniper can tolerate drier conditions than the heather, but it will be quite happy in the rather moister soils that suit the heather best.

Another, popular variety of *Calluna vulgaris* with leaves that are gold, orange or red – depending on the time of year – is *C. v.* 'Robert Chapman'. Its flowers are purple.

69

3.21 **Prunus & Chaenomeles**

Prunus domestica 'Victoria'

(plum)
sun/shade ○ ◑
type of plant hardy shrub/tree
zonal range 5-9 (C-WT)
flowering time mid-spring
flower colour white
height 3-4.5m (10-15ft)
special characteristics fruit

Chaenomeles speciosa

(syn *C. lagenaria, Cydonia japonica*)
(Japanese quince, japonica)
sun/shade ○ ◑
type of plant hardy shrub
zonal range 5-9 (C-WT)
flowering time early to late spring
flower colour scarlet
height 1.8-2.4m (6-8ft)
special characteristics fruit

Many of the newer forms of Japanese quince have pale flowers, but the long-cultivated species shown here has large blooms of a rich, warm red. If this vigorous plant's tangle of spiny branches is trained against a wall, flowering may well begin during winter and the plant may reach about 3.6m (12ft) high. Intermingled with the bright, white stars of a Victoria plum, these richly coloured flowers seem especially spicy. At the same time, the plum's snow-white blossom is provided with a contrasting glow.

As well as flowers that coincide, these two plants have fruit that ripens at about the same time. In late summer and early autumn, fragrant yellow quinces appear and the plum bears heavy crops of pinkish-red fruits. The quinces are sharp and sour and are best made into jelly, but the plums are good both for cooking and for eating fresh.

The chaenomeles' profusion of branches and the rather loose structure of the plum both benefit from being trained against a wall. Any aspect is suitable, but the plum in particular will fruit more success-fully in fairly sunny positions. To encourage good fruiting, the plum should be given a fertile, well-drained but moisture-retentive soil. The chaenome-les is a tough and tolerant shrub that can be grown in almost any soil.

3.22 **Lonicera & Clematis**

Lonicera nitida 'Baggesen's Gold'

(shrubby honeysuckle)
sun/shade ○ ◑
type of plant hardy shrub
zonal range 7-9 (WT-ST)
height 1.2-1.8m (4-6ft)
special characteristics evergreen, yellow foliage

Clematis 'Kermesina'

sun/shade ○ ◑
type of plant hardy climber
zonal range 5-9 (C-CT)
flowering time midsummer to early autumn
flower colour claret + white
height 3-3.6m (10-12ft)

Though the richly coloured clematis shown here will, with suitable support, grow quite tall, in this combination it is in effect as tall as the lonicera that it is scrambling over. It and related *viticella* vari-eties are excellent climbers for growing through shrubs, having a light structure of stems and small leaves that is unlikely to smother medium-sized hosts. In addition, their late flowering season means that early each spring they need to be cut right back. This pruning ensures that whatever sup-ports one of these climbers has a period during which it receives all the available light with no competition from the clematis.

The lonicera is more or less rounded in shape but it has some long, spiky shoots and these make an excellent framework for the clematis. Teaming these smallish (5cm/2in), claret-coloured flowers with a yellow-leaved shrub has resulted in a combi-nation with a bright glow.

Neither the lonicera nor the clematis likes hot, dry conditions and the roots of the clematis should be cool. This can be most easily achieved by plant-ing the clematis on the shaded side of the lonicera. A well-drained, fertile and moisture-retentive soil would suit this combination best.

The lonicera is especially good at blending with other plants (see, for example, 5.5, 6.4, and 9.18).

3.23 Rosa & Hosta

Rosa 'Geranium'

(syn *R. moyesii* 'Geranium')
(rose)
sun/shade ○ ◑
type of plant hardy shrub
zonal range 6-8 (CT-WT)
flowering time early summer
flower colour scarlet
height 2.1-2.4m (7-8ft)
special characteristics fruit

Hosta sieboldiana var. elegans

(plantain lily)
sun/shade ◑
type of plant hardy perennial
zonal range 3-9 (C-WT)
flowering time early to mid-summer
flower colour palest lilac
height 75-90cm (2½-3ft)
special characteristics blue-grey foliage,
suitable for damp soils

The smart, sharp red of this rose seems perfectly complemented by the plant's pretty, slightly blue-green leaflets and its graceful, arching growth. Adding large-scale, very glaucous foliage has the effect of emphasizing not only the hot clarity of this wonderful red but also the rose's overall air of grace and delicacy.

Sadly, the flowers of this rose make only a single, brief appearance, but in late summer and autumn there is a profusion of curvaceous, orange-red hips (see 3.2), each about 5cm (2in) long. In autumn, too, the foliage of the hosta will briefly turn an excellent, buttery yellow before dying. Shown here in early summer, these large, puckered leaves have yet to expand fully – in really rich, damp soils they can be over 30cm (12in) across. However, they are already forming a substantial clump. Soon the thickset, almost white flowers of this plant will be appearing just above the blue foliage. Later, these flowers form attractive seedheads.

'Geranium' is a vigorous, wide-spreading rose that can thrive in most ordinary soils as well as in well-cultivated, fertile conditions. If this combination is planted in a sunny position, it is important to place the hosta on the shaded, moister side of the rose.

3.24 Hydrangea & Persicaria

Hydrangea aspera Villosa Group

(syn *H. villosa*)
sun/shade ○ ◑
type of plant hardy shrub
zonal range 7-9 (CT-WT)
flowering time late summer to early autumn
flower colour rich violet + pale rose-lilac
height 1.8-3m (6-10ft)

Persicaria amplexicaulis 'Atrosanguinea'

(syn *Polygonum amplexicaule* 'Atrosanguineum')
(bistort)
sun/shade ○ ◑
type of plant hardy perennial
zonal range 5-9 (CT-ST)
flowering time early summer to early autumn
flower colour deep red
height 90-120cm (3-4ft)
special characteristics suitable for damp soils

By placing a small forest of richly coloured flower spikes in front of this imposing hydrangea, the warm, pinkish tones in the hydrangea's flower colour are emphasized; planting it with, for instance, the blue globes of *Echinops ritro* or with white Japanese anemones would draw attention to the cooler, bluer tones which are also present. Illustrated here in summer, the hydrangea flowers are neither as richly and brightly coloured nor as large as they will be later. When fully mature, the blooms may be 20cm (8in) or more in diameter. However, they are already conspicuous and looking well with the exceptionally long-flowering bistort.

The hydrangea is a rounded, wide-spreading shrub with rather upright branches that in older specimens have peeling bark. The large, softly hairy leaves do not unfurl until late spring. The bistort's leaves are of a much brighter green and they form a dense clump of growth that is likely to spread fairly quickly. The erect flower spikes are in marked contrast to the flat, horizontal shape of the hydrangea's mature flowers.

The bistort will enjoy the cool, moist, fertile conditions required by the hydrangea. Although this particular hydrangea is lime-tolerant, it will not thrive in shallow soils over chalk. It also needs some shelter in order to grow really well.

3.25 Mahonia & Primula

Mahonia japonica
sun/shade ○ ◑
type of plant hardy shrub
zonal range 7-9 (CT-WT)
flowering time late autumn to early spring
flower colour pale yellow
height 1.8-2.4m (6-8ft)
special characteristics evergreen, decorative green foliage, fragrant flowers

Primula bulleyana
sun/shade ○ ◑
type of plant hardy perennial
zonal range 6-8 (C-CT)
flowering time early to mid-summer
flower colour orange
height 60cm (2ft)
special characteristics suitable for damp soils

Tiers of glowing flowers and red buds are provided here with a suitably emphatic background of large whorls of rich green, gently gleaming foliage. Many gardeners will associate this mahonia with sprays of winter flowers and a rich, lily-of-the-valley fragrance, but the leaves of this erect-stemmed plant, arranged like great, decorated spokes of wheels, are every bit as remarkable. Another, more minor attraction is its fruit, which ripens in early summer. The strings of dark purple berries are at first a beautiful sea-green.

The primula's upright candelabras of flowers are, of course, its main attraction. However, its substantially sized, crinkled foliage makes an attractive vertical contrast to the more horizontal lines of the mahonia's whorls of leaves.

For the very best quality foliage, the mahonia should be grown in a little shade and a moisture-retentive soil, conditions which also suit the primula. The primula will not do well in dry soils.

There should also be some shelter from cold winds, both for the leaves and for the winter flowers of the mahonia. In exposed places, the mahonia's general growth may be less good but, during the colder months, there will be the bonus of burnished foliage.

3.26 Ligularia & Monarda

Ligularia 'The Rocket'
sun/shade ○ ◑
type of plant hardy perennial
zonal range 4-8 (C-WT)
flowering time mid- to late summer
flower colour yellow
height 1.2-1.8m (4-6ft)
special characteristics decorative green foliage, suitable for damp soils

Monarda 'Cambridge Scarlet'
(sweet bergamot, bee balm, Oswego tea)
sun/shade ○ ◑
type of plant hardy perennial
zonal range 4-9 (C-WT)
flowering time mid- to late summer
flower colour crimson-red
height 60-90cm (2-3ft)
special characteristics aromatic foliage, suitable for damp soils

These splashes of red and shooting spires of yellow create an exciting and stylish combination of vibrant colours and contrasting flower shapes. The very dark, almost black stems of the ligularia are an important element in the composition, too, emphasizing the erectness of both plants and ensuring that the combination is more than just a dramatic firework display of colour. As well as its striking flowers, the ligularia has rounded, jagged, dark-veined leaves which are large and bold. The monarda's foliage emits a strong, clean scent when bruised.

To look so handsome and vigorous, both plants here must have a moist, fertile soil. In poor, dry conditions they will sulk, and the monarda will be particularly prone to mildew. Given the right soil, both plants can be expected to mature into clumps of growth of considerable size.

3.27 Rhododendron & Viola

Rhododendron Knap Hill-Exbury hybrid

(azalea)
sun/shade ○ ◐
type of plant hardy shrub
zonal range 6-8 (C-CT)
flowering time late spring to early summer
flower colour yellow-orange + red
height 1.2-1.8m (4-6ft)
special characteristics autumn foliage, needs acid soil

Viola riviniana Purpurea Group

(syn *V. labradorica*, *V. l. purpurea*)
(Labrador violet)
sun/shade ○ ◐
type of plant hardy perennial
zonal range 3-8 (C-WT)
flowering time mid- to late spring
flower colour purple-violet
height 10-15cm (4-6in)
special characteristics evergreen, purple foliage

The very thought of a combination of orange and purple is enough to make some gardeners wince. However, when the purple is as dark and dusky as it is in the case of the little heart-shaped leaves of this violet, the effect is rich and striking rather than discordant.

The numerous Knap Hill-Exbury hybrid azaleas include varieties with flowers that are more deeply coloured than the specimen shown here. 'Gibraltar' is a particularly popular form with vivid orange blooms, while others have glowing red or orange-red flowers. Many of these rather open, upright shrubs have coppery young leaves and the flowers of some varieties are fragrant. Almost all varieties have brightly coloured autumn foliage. The low carpet of purple foliage produced by the violet shown here would provide a good, dense, dark contrast to those varieties that produce a blaze of autumn leaf colour.

The roots of all these hybrid azaleas should be kept cool and moist in a humus-rich, open-textured, acid – or at least neutral – soil. Cool, moist soils also suit the violet, but it is a very tolerant plant which will thrive in most soils and sites. In sun its leaves tend to be especially well-coloured. Its little flowers frequently set seed, but any of the numerous, self-sown seedlings which are not wanted are easily uprooted.

3.28 Weigela & Viburnum

Weigela 'Eva Rathke'

sun/shade ○ ◐
type of plant hardy shrub
zonal range 5-8 (C-WT)
flowering time early to mid-summer
flower colour bright crimson
height 1.2-1.5m (4-5ft)

Viburnum tinus 'Variegatum'

(laurustinus)
sun/shade ○ ◐
type of plant slightly tender shrub
zonal range 9-10 (C-WT)
flowering time late autumn to early spring
flower colour white
height 1.2-1.8m (4-6ft)
special characteristics evergreen, variegated foliage

This low-key combination of warm colours involves no great contrast in overall habit of growth, and there is much cooling greenery as well as the weigela's rich crimson flowers and the creamy yellow markings on the viburnum's foliage. Nevertheless, the variegated leaves enliven the scene considerably, and when they are combined with the bright trumpets of the weigela there is a definite, luminous glow.

'Eva Rathke' flowers rather later and longer than other weigela hybrids and its dark foliage is in keeping with its deep, vivid flower colour. It is a fairly upright and slow-growing plant. The viburnum has a denser, bushier habit, but it too grows fairly slowly. Its flowers, like those of the plain, green-leaved laurustinus, open from pink buds during mild spells in the colder months. However, its coloured leaves are of a thinner texture than those of the species and they can become browned at the edges in icy winds and scorching sunshine.

A sheltered site is, therefore, advisable for this combination, and though both plants are tolerant of a wide range of soil types they are not at their best in very dry soils. If a sunny site is chosen, the flowering of the weigela is likely to be particularly prolific.

73

3.29 Rhododendron & Astilbe

Rhododendron Elizabeth Group

sun/shade ○ ◖
type of plant hardy shrub
zonal range 7-8 (CT)
flowering time mid- to late spring
flower colour bright scarlet-red
height 90-150cm (3-5ft)
special characteristics evergreen, needs acid soil

Astilbe chinensis var. *pumila*

(false goat's beard)
sun/shade ○ ◖
type of plant hardy perennial
zonal range 4-8 (C-CT)
flowering time midsummer to early autumn
flower colour mauve-pink
height 23-30cm (9-12in)
special characteristics decorative green foliage, suitable for damp soils

The glistening, frilled trumpets of *R.* 'Elizabeth' and its slight variants are of a particularly opulent colouring. However, like many rhododendrons, there is a stolidity about the foliage alone that makes a lighter, more airily constructed partner welcome. Here the newish leaflets of a vigorous, carpeting astilbe, with their lime-green tones and feathery edges, enliven the whole scene considerably. Later, when the rhododendron flowers have faded, the astilbe's foliage will lift the darker, rounded mass of the rhododendron's smooth-edged, leathery leaves. During summer, however, this darker, simpler foliage plays its part by providing an excellent background for the erect, dense and incisively pink flower spikes of the astilbe. Even in late autumn and winter the astilbe can provide some brightness, since its persistent seedheads are conspicuously russet.

It is important that the roots of both these plants remain moist and cool. This is often most easily achieved by choosing a site that is partially shaded. Partial shade – or shelter of some sort – will also ensure that the flowers of the rhododendron are protected from spring frosts. The astilbe can be grown in damp ground near water.

3.30 Dryopteris & Crocosmia

Dryopteris filix-mas

(male fern)
sun/shade ○ ◖
type of plant hardy fern
zonal range 4-8 (C-CT)
height 60-120cm (2-4ft)
special characteristics decorative green foliage

Crocosmia × *crocosmiiflora*

(common montbretia)
sun/shade ○ ◖
type of plant hardy corm
zonal range 5-9 (CT-ST)
flowering time mid- to late summer
flower colour orange + yellow
height 60cm (2ft)
special characteristics decorative green foliage

Hot-coloured flowers are usually dramatic and they tend to be used, often in association with coloured foliage, in the more formal areas of gardens. Here is a combination where glowing orange flowers look quite at home in a relaxed setting, planted in rough grass.

The rich green laciness of the fern's rather erect fronds and the arching sheaves of light, bright greenery produced by the montbretia both complement the two-toned heat of the montbretia's flowers. The fern's foliage remains remarkably fresh and green over a long period; it is often still very respectable in early winter. Even as a pairing of two sets of foliage this is a pleasing combination – one that is low-key, but with sufficient contrasts to make it interesting. When well-suited, both plants here will grow densely and the combination will be usefully weed-smothering as well as good-looking.

These two plants are very easily grown: the male fern is native to the British Isles and will tolerate a wide range of growing conditions, from dry shade to heavy clay; the common montbretia has become naturalized in the milder, wetter parts of Britain and Ireland and it may be mildly invasive in the moist, spongy soils it likes best.

3.31 Primula & Euonymus

Primula denticulata cultivar
(drumstick primrose)
sun/shade ○ ◀
type of plant hardy perennial
zonal range 6-8 (CT)
flowering time early to late spring
flower colour pink-magenta
height 30cm (12in)

Euonymus fortunei 'Emerald Gaiety'
sun/shade ○ ◀
type of plant hardy shrub/climber
zonal range 5-9 (C-ST)
height 60-90cm (2-3ft) as a shrub
special characteristics evergreen, variegated foliage

Among the gentle lavenders, blues and pinks available as forms of *Primula denticulata* there are also some vivid crimsons and purples. The crisp, cool colouring of this variegated euonymus provides a lively background of leafiness for the primula's solid flowerheads and stout stalks. After the primula has finished flowering, this white and grey-green foliage will also look good with many other plants, including those of more subdued colouring (see, for example, 9.25). In winter, the leaves often become tinged with pink.

Primula denticulata cultivars are all long-lived plants that prosper in a wide range of soils, provided there is a constant supply of moisture. They are particularly at home in acid or neutral soils. Their wrinkled leaves elongate considerably after flowering and they can form quite dense clumps of growth. Most soils also suit the rather slow-growing, hummocky euonymus. Mature specimens may produce longer, climbing shoots that will attach themselves to walls and other surfaces and grow up to 3m (10ft) high. Older plants may also flower, but the creamy bobbles are not very conspicuous among the variegated foliage.

3.32 Primula & Astrantia

Primula Polyanthus cultivar
(polyanthus)
sun/shade ○ ◀
type of plant hardy perennial
zonal range 6-8 (C-WT)
flowering time mid- to late spring
flower colour bright burgundy + yellow
height 23-30cm (9-12in)

Astrantia major 'Sunningdale Variegated'
(syn *A. m.* 'Variegata')
(masterwort)
sun/shade ○ ◀
type of plant hardy perennial
zonal range 4-8 (C-WT)
flowering time early to late summer
flower colour white or pinkish
height 60-75cm (2-2½ft)
special characteristics variegated foliage

The numerous strains of polyanthus include plants that produce flowers of really glowing and rich colours. These colours are often emphasized by contrasting yellow or orange centres. The cultivar shown here has had the intensity and brightness of its flower colour heightened still further by being partnered with a plant with crisply variegated, jagged-edged leaves.

This variegation of white and soft green is at its freshest and clearest in spring. By the time the flowers appear, the leaf markings will be yellower and, as summer progresses, the variegation will become considerably less pronounced. However, throughout the summer and into autumn, the leaves will continue to make a good clump of weed-suppressing foliage about 23cm (9in) high. Although this variegated form of *Astrantia major* is not as free-flowering as the species, it does produce charming, long-lasting, papery-textured flowers. The polyanthus's crinkled, oval leaves will lengthen somewhat after flowering and when the plant is growing well they will form a thick carpet of greenery.

Neither of these plants really thrives unless its roots are in moisture-retentive soil. The astrantia also appreciates reasonably good drainage. Some gardeners feel that a sunny position enhances the variegation of the astrantia.

3.33 Paeonia & Saxifraga

Paeonia officinalis 'Rubra Plena'
(peony)
sun/shade ○ ◐
type of plant hardy perennial
zonal range 3-9 (C-CT)
flowering time late spring to early summer
flower colour deep crimson
height 60-75cm (2-2½ft)
special characteristics decorative green foliage

Saxifraga × urbium
(London pride)
sun/shade ◑
type of plant hardy perennial
zonal range 6-7 (C-CT)
flowering time late spring to early summer
flower colour pale pink
height 23-30cm (9-12in)
special characteristics evergreen, decorative green foliage

The sumptuous flowers of this old-fashioned peony do have some blue in their colouring but, especially with the sun shining through their petals, there are cerise tones as well and altogether the effect is rich and warm. London pride's cloud of tiny flowers is dainty and cool in comparison, though there is a perceptible soft redness in the flower stems.

Both these plants have good-looking foliage so that the combination is interesting for several weeks before and after flowering. The low carpet of leathery, scallop-edged leaves of the smaller plant are arranged in neat rosettes. These show the peony's foliage to advantage both when it first emerges as erect, deep red shoots and later when it opens out into a loose structure of broad-fingered sprays. These sprays of mature foliage remain fresh-looking well into autumn.

The peony is a very long-lived plant that likes to be left undisturbed in fertile soil. London pride will grow in many sites and soils, but is at its very best in cool, moist shade. If this combination is planted in full sun, the peony will to some extent shade the London pride.

3.34 Acer & Trillium

Acer palmatum 'Garnet'
(Japanese maple)
sun/shade ○ ◐
type of plant hardy shrub
zonal range 5-8 (C-WT)
height 1.2-1.8m (4-6ft)
special characteristics purple foliage, autumn foliage

Trillium chloropetalum rubrum
(trinity flower, wood lily)
sun/shade ◑
type of plant hardy perennial
zonal range 5-9 (C-CT)
flowering time mid- to late spring
flower colour bright claret
height 30-40cm (12-15in)
special characteristics variegated foliage

With reddish-purple leaves to complement them, the flame-like flowers of this trillium seem particularly bright and glowing. Beneath each three-petalled flower there is a trio of marbled leaves, the markings of which may vary from pale grey to maroon. These comparatively large leaves and the very upright flowers provide interesting contrasts in shape and texture to the very finely cut, pendent leaves of the accompanying maple.

The trillium's clump of foliage lasts longest in cool, shaded places with moist, leaf-mouldy soil, but even given these conditions the plant will usually have begun to die back in early summer. The maple has a much longer season of interest. It retains its leaf colour throughout summer and into autumn, when the foliage turns shades of red and pink before dying. The dome of richly coloured, feathery leaves makes a good companion for many other plants (see, for example, a similar maple in 9.27).

The maple enjoys the same sort of growing conditions as the trillium and both plants are best in acid or at least neutral soils. The maple also requires a site that is sheltered from wind and late frosts. It is a very slow-growing plant, and the trillium takes several years to become established and flower freely.

Trillium sessile resembles *T. chloropetalum rubrum* very closely and it is a more readily available plant.

For other combinations featuring hot-coloured flowers, see:
COOL-COLOURED FLOWERS 1.2, 1.4, 1.5, 1.18 GREY FOLIAGE 2.6 DECORATIVE GREEN FOLIAGE 8.4 VARIEGATED FOLIAGE 9.22 AUTUMN FOLIAGE 10.6 AROMATIC FOLIAGE 11.6, 11.16 FRAGRANT FLOWERS 15.5, 15.12, 15.16, 15.17 DAMP AND WET SOILS 16.15

4 PURPLE, RED OR BRONZE FOLIAGE

There are leaves in this section that are indeed purple, red or bronze (see the sage in 4.15, the photinia in 4.10 and the astilbe in 4.27, respectively). However, there are also pink pieris leaves, chocolate-bronze rhododendron leaves and coppery spiraea leaves, as well as a few plants with foliage of such a deep purple that it is almost black. The largest group of commonly grown 'purple'-leaved plants contains plants that are, in fact, quite crimson or plum in colour. This group includes popular plants such as *Heuchera micrantha diversifolia* 'Palace Purple', *Berberis thunbergii atropurpurea*, various forms of *Cotinus coggygria* and many forms of *Acer palmatum*.

What the majority of these diversely coloured plants do have in common is a distinctive depth and richness of tone. This can produce dramatic effects when it is included in planting schemes of hot-coloured flowers, and it can also be used to achieve effective contrasts with paler foliage and flowers of cool colouring.

LIGHTENING THE EFFECT

Purple or red foliage that is very dark should be used with discretion. When planting schemes contain a high proportion of deep-coloured leaves, the overall effect can be heavy and drab. Often a more successful result is obtained if further rich reds and claret-purples are added in the form of flowers rather than foliage (see, for example, the combinations in 3.34 and 8.8). Alternatively, any dullness and heaviness can be lightened with grey leaves (see 4.12 and 4.15) or with white- or yellow-variegated foliage (see 9.3 and 11.7).

It should be borne in mind that, especially when viewed from a distance, small plants with very dark, purple leaves tend to disappear into the surrounding soil. Providing these plants with partners of much paler or lighter and brighter colouring usually overcomes this problem. It is also important to remember that not only do almost all purple- or red-leaved plants need full sun in order to produce good, rich leaf colour, but also that their foliage looks very much livelier and more colourful in a sunny place than in a shady corner.

VIBRANT SCHEMES

Although purple and red foliage has been popular for a long time, the re-awakening of interest in hot-coloured flowers has resulted in increased enthusiasm for these hues. In planting schemes of pulsating reds, oranges and bright yellows, purple leaves exude a deep, rich warmth which stabilizes hot colours without dulling their vibrancy. Red- or purple-leaved plants that are evergreen, and therefore suitable for accompanying bright autumn leaves, include the heuchera mentioned above and also, for instance, some forms of New Zealand flax such as *Phormium tenax* Purpureum Group.

The pairing of yellow and purple can be really eye-catching, especially when the yellow is bright and the purple is dark or rich (see 4.2). When the purple has a blue, almost violet-toned cast to it, the relationship between purple and yellow takes on a sharper intensity (see 6.2).

Some gardeners will find these yellow-and-purple combinations too strident. For them, purple leaves combined with slightly gentler and cooler yellow-greens or with pale apple-greens are usually more appealing (see 7.2 and 7.7). Rather livelier – but still not harsh –

partnerships are created when these greens are combined with red or copper, rather than purple leaves (see 16.12 and 4.14). Dark greens and dark purple foliage tend to merge uninterestingly, but striking partnerships can be devised using vibrant or richly coloured greens with purple leaves (see 4.8 and 8.1).

COOL CONTRASTS

When purple leaves and cool blues and violets are used together, combinations of a lovely luminosity can be created (see 4.19 and 15.7). Particularly if the foliage is plum-coloured, rather than a very red purple, and the flowers are pale, a distinct impression of coolness will prevail. The coolness of either blue-grey or grey foliage can also work well with purple leaves (see 2.17 and 2.25).

Contrasts between light and dark contribute to the success of many combinations of white or pale pink flowers with purple foliage. White flowers seem especially brilliant against dark, richly coloured leaves (see 4.18 and 8.17), and pale pinks look more than merely pretty when combined with deep purple foliage.

Not all purple, red and bronze leaves are dark, however, and among the plants in this section there are illustrations of very subtly shaded leaves. The elusive, wine-coloured staining of *Pseudowintera colorata* (see 4.26), and the plummy tones of *Rosa glauca* (when this plant is grown in sun) are examples of low-key red or purple leaf colouring.

USING VARIEGATION AND TEXTURE

There are also a few variegated plants either with a basic leaf colouring of red-purple (such as *Berberis thunbergii* 'Rose Glow', see 9.8) or with leaves suffused with red-purple (see *Fuchsia magellanica* 'Versicolor', 4.6). These plants give a lighter, less static impression than foliage that is entirely red or purple. The leaves of some plants in this section are richly or brightly coloured but only fleetingly so, and this too introduces variety into plantings. (For examples of plants with colourful young leaves, see 4.12, 4.14, 4.27 and 4.28.)

Finally, there are purple- or red-leaved plants with a size or texture of leaf that has an animating effect. Purple-leaved plants with lively, small-scale foliage include *Euphorbia dulcis* 'Chameleon' (see 4.18), while purple or red foliage plants with leaves that gleam or shine include *Ajuga reptans* 'Atropurpurea' (see 2.25) and *Photinia × fraseri* 'Red Robin' (see 4.10).

AUTUMN FOLIAGE

Relatively few plants with purple, red or bronze leaves have outstandingly attractive flowers. However, many of these plants, including the various forms of berberis, cotinus and acer shown in this section, have foliage which becomes very colourful in autumn. In addition, there is *Vitis vinifera* 'Purpurea', the beautiful, shapely leaves of which turn a rich, crimson red in autumn (see 5.1).

Purple foliage may conjure up scenes of large and ponderous copper beeches, but the plants in this section are generally of an altogether more manageable size, usually of a more interesting colour and always a good deal more versatile in their ability to flatter other plants.

4.1 Prunus & Philadelphus

Prunus cerasifera 'Pissardii'
(syn *P. pissardii*)
(purple-leaved plum)
sun/shade ○
type of plant hardy tree
zonal range 5-8 (C-WT)
flowering time early spring
flower colour pale pink fading to white
height 4.5-6m (15-20ft)
special characteristics purple foliage

Philadelphus coronarius 'Aureus'
(mock orange)
sun/shade ◐
type of plant hardy shrub
zonal range 5-8 (C-WT)
flowering time early to mid-summer
flower colour creamy white
height 1.5-2.1m (5-7ft)
special characteristics yellow-green foliage, fragrant flowers

Left unpruned, the purple-leaved plum grows into a bushy, round-headed tree. It is, however, a popular hedging or screening plant. Here it has been given an acidic partner, and because the size and shape of the two plants' leaves are roughly similar the result is a tapestry-like interweaving in which the stitches are either sharp yellow-green or rich red-purple.

The plum needs a sunny site for good leaf colour. In full sun the foliage of this bushy, rather upright philadelphus tends to be a strong yellow, until about midsummer when it becomes greener, and there may be some scorching of the leaf edges. However, in this combination, many of the philadelphus's leaves will be partially shaded by the growth of the plum and their colouring will be a less harsh and longer-lasting yellow-green.

Both these plants have beautifully simple flowers. The plum's pale, gauzy haze of blossom is soon joined by the coppery young leaves of the plant. The flowers of the philadelphus emit a rich, spicy-sweet scent.

Well-drained soils of most sorts suit these plants, but if there is to be plenty of good-quality foliage the conditions must be reasonably fertile and moisture-retentive, too. This particular variety of plum does not fruit reliably.

4.2 Acer & Rhododendron

Acer palmatum f. *atropurpureum*
(Japanese maple)
sun/shade ○
type of plant hardy shrub/tree
zonal range 6-8 (C-WT)
height 3.6-4.5m (12-15ft)
special characteristics purple foliage, autumn foliage

Rhododendron luteum
(syn *Azalea pontica*)
(azalea)
sun/shade ○ ◐
type of plant hardy shrub
zonal range 5-8 (C-CT)
flowering time late spring to early summer
flower colour yellow
height 1.8-3m (6-10ft)
special characteristics autumn foliage, fragrant flowers, needs acid soil

Such a bold pairing of the sunny and the sombre certainly makes a change from the sort of combination where purple foliage is used to enhance the delicacy of, for instance, pretty pinks or pale blues. Plants sold under the name *Acer palmatum* f. *atropurpureum* vary somewhat in leaf colour. The specimen shown here is a beautiful, dark, rich, maroon-purple. The overall impression is not, however, unattractively solid because, as with all Japanese maples, the foliage is both pendent and elegantly lobed and it is arranged on a canopy of spreading branches. The azalea is upright and open-habited with rather erectly held, slim leaves of a good, rich green.

Here, in early summer, the azalea is in full bloom, its mass of funnel-shaped flowers exuding a penetratingly sweet scent. In autumn the plant's leaves turn glowing oranges and reds. To add to the drama, the maple too changes colour, usually in mid-autumn, when its dying leaves become scarlet.

Rhododendron luteum is easily pleased; it often suckers and it is a prolific self-seeder. However, it does require a lime-free soil. It and the maple like moisture-retentive, well-drained, acid soils. The maple needs shelter from cold and drying winds, and it needs sun too for a rich, deep leaf colour. It is slow growing.

4.3 Acer & Epimedium

Acer palmatum f. atropurpureum

(Japanese maple)
sun/shade ○
type of plant hardy shrub/tree
zonal range 6-8 (C-WT)
height 3.6-4.5m (12-15ft)
special characteristics purple foliage, autumn foliage

Epimedium × rubrum

(barrenwort, bishop's hat)
sun/shade ◖
type of plant hardy perennial
zonal range 4-9 (C-WT)
flowering time mid- to late spring
flower colour crimson + cream
height 30cm (12in)
special characteristics red young foliage, decorative green foliage, autumn/winter foliage

The dense, slowly spreading mass of heart-shaped leaves produced by *Epimedium × rubrum* goes through a number of colour changes during the year – all of them complementary to the rich maroon of this maple. In early spring, the new leaves are a beautiful coppery red. Here, in late spring, the predominant pale green contrasts most effectively with the deep-toned foliage of the maple. In autumn, the leaves of both these plants change colour: the epimedium's foliage becomes a pink-tinged, deep red (and later, all through winter, a copper-brown); the maple turns scarlet.

At all stages, the leaf shapes and the habits of growth of these two plants look well together. The much smoother outline of the epimedium foliage emphasizes the elegant, pointed fingers of the maple leaves, and the maple's graceful, rounded canopy of airy foliage is interestingly different from the epimedium's mounds of low growth.

Although the epimedium is a tolerant plant which will even do quite well in dry shade, it is at its best in cool, moist soils. Here it is lightly shaded by the maple. Its delicate, wiry-stemmed flower sprays are hidden by the old foliage unless this is removed early in spring. For details of the maple see 4.2.

4.4 Cotoneaster & Berberis

Cotoneaster × watereri

sun/shade ○ ◖
type of plant hardy shrub/tree
zonal range 6-8 (C-WT)
flowering time early summer
flower colour white
height 3.6-4.5m (12-15ft)
special characteristics semi-evergreen/evergreen, fruit

Berberis × ottawensis 'Superba'

(syn *B. thunbergii* 'Atropurpurea Superba')
(barberry)
sun/shade ○
type of plant hardy shrub
zonal range 5-9 (C-WT)
flowering time late spring
flower colour yellow + red
height 1.8-2.4m (6-8ft)
special characteristics purple foliage, autumn foliage

Bigger, bolder and darker than the more commonly planted *B. thunbergii atropurpurea* (see 4.11), *B. × ottawensis* 'Superba' makes a splendid, weighty partner for this large cotoneaster. The two plants here are at their most spectacular in autumn, when the cotoneaster bears great, hanging bunches of red berries and the rounded leaves of the berberis turn orange-red and red. The berberis too may bear red berries, but many specimens of this variety do not fruit reliably.

Both plants look imposing earlier in the year as well. The cotoneaster has spreading, conspicuously arching branches and long leaves. These are considerably enhanced by the berberis's generous head of curving growths and glistening, almost metallic purple leaves. Here, as midsummer approaches, the cotoneaster's flowerheads are fading. The soft yellow flowers of the berberis are borne earlier, in small clusters.

Most well-drained soils suit these plants. Although they will both tolerate a certain amount of dryness, the berberis's foliage is not at its best in really parched conditions.

For illustrations of this vigorous, prickly berberis in combination with variegated foliage, yellow leaves and glowing crimson flowers, see 9.3, 6.2 and 15.5, respectively.

81

4.5 Ligustrum & Hebe

Ligustrum ovalifolium 'Aureum'
(golden privet)
sun/shade ○ ◑
type of plant hardy shrub
zonal range 6-11 (C-ST)
flowering time midsummer
flower colour white
height 2.7-3.6m (9-12ft)
special characteristics evergreen/semi-evergreen, yellow foliage/variegated foliage

Hebe 'Amy'
(syn H. 'Purple Queen')
sun/shade ○
type of plant slightly tender shrub
zonal range 9-10 (WT-ST)
flowering time midsummer to mid-autumn
flower colour violet-purple
height 75-90cm (2½-3ft)
special characteristics evergreen, purple foliage

There are a number of hebes with coppery or purple foliage, though in some cases the colouring is in fact a dark green tinged with purple. However, as with H. 'Amy', there are various ways in which the purplish tones can be enhanced.

First of all, a really sunny site and a well-drained, though not dry soil will produce the richest foliage colour. Secondly, the presence of some lighter foliage will help to make the leaves seem especially dark. If this additional foliage is yellow, it will, as a more or less 'opposite' or complementary colour, emphasize the purple tones in the leaves. Finally, if the hebe's own flowers are purplish, they will increase the overall impression of dusky purple. The dark, upright stems of H. 'Amy' are decorated with spikes of purple over a notably long period.

That the enriching, enlivening enhancer of this hebe should be the ordinary golden privet is an interesting illustration of how it is important not to overlook really familiar plants when devising combinations. In the sort of sunny place that suits the hebe best, the privet's leaves will be conspicuously variegated and brightly coloured. Grown informally, and not clipped, the privet has an open habit of growth that contrasts pleasingly with the denser appearance of the hebe. Golden privet will grow in almost any soil; self seeds prolifically in hot climates.

4.6 Fuchsia & Cotinus

Fuchsia magellanica 'Versicolor'
(syn F. 'Versicolor')
sun/shade ○
type of plant hardy/slightly tender shrub
zonal range 8-10 (WT-ST)
flowering time midsummer to mid-autumn
flower colour red + purple
height 90-150cm (3-5ft)
special characteristics variegated foliage

Cotinus coggygria 'Notcutt's Variety'
(smoke tree, Venetian sumach)
sun/shade ○
type of plant hardy shrub/tree
zonal range 5-9 (C-WT)
fruiting time mid- to late summer
fruit colour pink-purple
height 2.4-3m (8-10ft)
special characteristics purple foliage, autumn foliage, fruit

Most fuchsias have unremarkable leaves but some forms, including the bushy, rather erect variety shown here, do produce interesting foliage. The mature leaves of Fuchsia magellanica 'Versicolor' are grey-green, usually with thin margins of palest cream. The young foliage is a most attractive, smoky, crimson-purple colour which in this combination is boosted by the deep maroon-purple of a large-leaved form of Cotinus coggygria.

Though both these plants are late into leaf, between them they are decorative over a very long period. As well as two sets of good-looking foliage, there is a long succession of elegantly slim, fuchsia flowers and the cotinus's tiny, early summer flowers ripen into smoky clouds of seedheads. (If, however, the plant has been pruned hard to encourage plenty of good-quality foliage, these clouds will not develop and the whole, rounded shrub is likely to be relatively small and erect.) Late in mid-autumn, there is a dramatic glow of red and orange from the dying leaves of the cotinus (see 10.5).

The autumn colour of the cotinus is outstanding on light and rather poor soils; the fuchsia, however, needs a certain amount of moisture, as well as good drainage, to perform satisfactorily. In cold areas the fuchsia's top growth is likely to be cut back each year, but it will make new growth from the base.

4.7 Hydrangea & Cotinus

Hydrangea aspera Villosa Group
(syn *H. villosa*)
sun/shade ○ ◑
type of plant hardy shrub
zonal range 7-9 (CT-WT)
flowering time late summer to early autumn
flower colour rich violet + pale rose-lilac
height 1.8-3m (6-10ft)

Cotinus coggygria 'Royal Purple'
(smoke tree, Venetian sumach)
sun/shade ○
type of plant hardy shrub/tree
zonal range 5-9 (C-WT)
fruiting time mid- to late summer
fruit colour pink-purple
height 2.4-3m (8-10ft)
special characteristics purple foliage, autumn foliage, fruit

The purple-leaved forms of *Cotinus coggygria* are outstandingly versatile shrubs for combining with other plants (see, for example, 4.8, 4.9 and 7.2). Here, in summer, the flowerheads of the accompanying hydrangea have yet to open fully, but both at this stage and when the heads expand to 20cm (8in) and become a good deal bluer, the cotinus makes a wonderful, opulently coloured partner. As a bonus, the really dark red-purple of this foliage has the effect of making the hydrangea's leaves seem a particularly clear mid-green.

In addition to the lovely associations of colours, there are interesting contrasts in leaf shape in this combination. The cotinus's foliage is rounded and silky-smooth, whereas the hydrangea's leaves are long and soft, with a close covering of hairs. Both these shrubs are, however, late into leaf and do not appear well-clothed until early summer.

For the sake of the hydrangea this combination must be grown on a moist, fertile soil that remains cool during summer. In time, and in the sheltered positions it prefers, the hydrangea's rounded, spreading shape can become very substantial. On mature specimens the bark of the rather upright branches peels attractively. For further details relevant to the cotinus, see 4.6.

4.8 Cotinus & Bergenia

Cotinus coggygria 'Royal Purple'
(smoke tree, Venetian sumach)
sun/shade ○
type of plant hardy shrub/tree
zonal range 5-9 (C-WT)
fruiting time mid- to late summer
fruit colour pink-purple
height 2.4-3m (8-10ft)
special characteristics purple foliage, autumn foliage, fruit

Bergenia cordifolia
sun/shade ○ ◑
type of plant hardy perennial
zonal range 3-8 (C-ST)
flowering time early to mid-spring
flower colour mauve-pink
height 30-40cm (12-15in)
special characteristics evergreen, decorative green foliage, autumn/winter foliage

Grey, variegated and yellow leaves are all flattered by the purple foliage of varieties of *Cotinus coggygria* such as 'Royal Purple', and it is easy to overlook the fact that plain, green leaves can also look most attractive with these very dark-leaved shrubs. In this partnership, the green of the bergenia's foliage appears really fresh and vibrant and at the same time the deep red-purple of the cotinus is enhanced.

The leaf shape of these two plants is not dissimilar: the bergenia's leaves are almost circular and the cotinus has conspicuously rounded foliage. However, at about 23-30cm (9-12in) wide, the bergenia's leathery, often puckered leaves are four or five times the width of the cotinus's smoother and much thinner-textured leaves. When there are marked differences in the size, texture and colour of two sets of leaves, the reiteration of a calm, steady shape does much to contribute to the success of a combination.

In full sun, the bergenia's leaves will take on purplish tones in the colder months (see 8.19). The bergenia also looks well in spring, when its red-stalked flowerheads appear. For futher details relevant to the cotinus, see 4.6.

83

4.9 Cotinus & Artemisia

Cotinus coggygria Rubrifolius Group

(syn *C. c.* 'Foliis Purpureis')
(smoke tree, Venetian sumach)
sun/shade ○
type of plant hardy shrub/tree
zonal range 5-9 (C-WT)
fruiting time mid- to late summer
fruit colour purplish
height 1.8-3m (6-10ft)
special characteristics purple foliage, autumn foliage, fruit

Artemisia 'Powis Castle'

sun/shade ○
type of plant slightly tender perennial/shrub
zonal range 5-8 (C-WT)
height 60-90cm (2-3ft)
special characteristics evergreen/semi-evergreen, aromatic, silver foliage

Dark purple-leaved forms of *Cotinus coggygria* make especially dramatic backgrounds for the foliage and flowers of paler plants. The silky, rounded leaves of the specimen shown here are of an exceptionally deep shade, against which the foliage of the accompanying artemisia is etched in filigree paleness. In poor, light soils particularly, this dark purple turns to bright red in mid-autumn and then there is a different kind of contrast, this time between glowing heat and cool, frosty-looking grey.

Artemisia 'Powis Castle' seldom flowers and this ensures that its clump of sharply aromatic foliage is tidy and fairly dense. The well-drained soils and sunny positions that produce the most colourful autumn colour on the cotinus also suit this artemisia. Under these conditions its foliage will be really silvery and it will survive all but the coldest winters.

For further details relevant to this continus, see 4.6. Named varieties of *Cotinus coggygria* with very dark purple foliage include 'Velvet Cloak'.

For a smaller-scale combination involving this artemisia and a purple-leaved perennial, see 2.13.

4.10 Photinia & Euphorbia

Photinia × fraseri 'Red Robin'

sun/shade ○ ◗
type of plant slightly tender shrub
zonal range 8-9 (C-ST)
flowering time late spring to early summer
flower colour white
height 1.8-3m (6-10ft)
special characteristics evergreen, red young foliage

Euphorbia characias ssp. *wulfenii* and *E. characias* seedling

(spurge)
sun/shade ○
type of plant slightly tender/hardy shrub/perennial
zonal range 7-10 (C-WT)
flowering time mid-spring to early summer
flower colour yellow-green
height 90-120cm (3-4ft)
special characteristics evergreen, blue-green foliage

Euphorbia characias and its relations make excellent companions for red-leaved photinias, the clean green of their flowers being a splendid counterpoint to the rich colour of the photinias' new leaves (see also 4.23 for this colour association). In addition, the strong shapes of these large flower-heads, and of the big bottle-brushes of accompanying blue-green foliage (see 6.1), provide plenty of interest both earlier and later in the year when the photinias' leaves are less colourful.

This photograph shows the plants in late spring. By the end of summer the photinia's glossy leaves will be bronze; when fully mature they are deep green. Though it does become denser with age, this shrub is rather open in growth. In contrast, well-grown, young specimens of the euphorbia produce solid-looking clumps of upright stems which are thickly covered in foliage.

The euphorbia's flowers are long-lasting. Removing the faded flowerheads greatly improves the quality and quantity of the plant's foliage, though the milky juice exuded from the cut stems can be an irritant to skin and eyes. The photinia's clusters of little flowers are less striking than its young foliage.

Both plants appreciate some shelter and need a soil with good drainage. The photinia requires moisture to grow well.

4.11 Berberis & Olearia

Berberis thunbergii f. atropurpurea

(barberry)
sun/shade ○
type of plant hardy shrub
zonal range 5-8 (C-WT or ST)
flowering time mid- to late spring
flower colour pale yellow + red
height 1.2-1.8m (4-6ft)
special characteristics purple foliage, autumn foliage, fruit

Olearia × haastii

(daisy bush)
sun/shade ○
type of plant hardy/slightly tender shrub
zonal range 8-10 (CT-ST)
flowering time mid- to late summer
flower colour white
height 1.8m (6ft)
special characteristics evergreen

Both these shrubs are dense and rounded and have leaves of approximately the same size. These similarities focus attention on the foliage colour of each plant so that the overall effect, here in early summer, is of a swathe of green beside a swathe of rich purple-mahogany. In autumn the leaves of the berberis turn vivid red, and then the contrast becomes one of hot and cool rather than bright and dark.

Although the upper surfaces of the olearia's leaves are in fact quite a dark sage-green, the stems and the undersides of the leaves are white. These touches of paleness lighten the whole shrub. When the numerous, yellow-centred daisies appear, the plant becomes paler still and then the contrast between it and the berberis is magnified. Unfortunately, this mass of hawthorn-scented daisies turns unattractively brown as seed is set. The berberis's little flowers (see 9.6) have the advantage of ripening into pretty berries of a brilliant, shiny red.

This combination of plants can be grown in any well-drained soil as long as – for the sake of the berberis – it is not very alkaline. In all but the mildest districts, the olearia benefits from some shelter. For an illustration of this prickly berberis with a pale, variegated shrub, again see 9.6.

4.12 Salix & Rhododendron

Salix helvetica

(willow)
sun/shade ○
type of plant hardy shrub
zonal range 6-7 (C-CT)
flowering time mid-spring
flower colour silver-grey
height 90-120cm (3-4ft)
special characteristics grey foliage

Rhododendron williamsianum

sun/shade ○ ◖
type of plant slightly tender/hardy shrub
zonal range 7-8 (CT)
flowering time mid- to late spring
flower colour pink
height 90-150cm (3-5ft)
special characteristics evergreen, bronze young foliage, needs acid soil

Rhododendron williamsianum produces a mass of very pretty, bell-shaped flowers which more or less cover its neat dome of rounded, mid-green foliage. Once the flowers have faded, usually by late spring, the new growth emerges a rich, chocolatey red-brown. The colouring of these young leaves does not last very long, but a plant with soft grey foliage emphasizes its darkness and smoothness and makes the most of its decorative qualities.

For a photograph of this combination approximately two weeks earlier, see 2.8 where full details, including information about cultivation, are given. In 2.11, *Salix helvetica* is shown with a plant that retains its purple leaf colouring throughout the year.

4.13 Sedum & Rodgersia

Sedum 'Herbstfreude'
(syn S. 'Autumn Joy')
(stonecrop)
sun/shade ○
type of plant hardy perennial
zonal range 3-10 (C-ST)
flowering time late summer to mid-autumn
flower colour rose changing to salmon-pink, then bronze
height 45-60cm (1½-2ft)
special characteristics blue-green foliage, fruit

Rodgersia pinnata 'Superba'
sun/shade ○ ◖
type of plant hardy perennial
zonal range 5-8 (C-CT)
flowering time mid- to late summer
flower colour deep pink
height 90-120cm (3-4ft)
special characteristics purple foliage, suitable for damp and wet soils

Just as satisfying as the attractive contrast in leaf colour in this combination is the marked difference in texture between the two plants: the sedum's blunt-nosed, blue-green leaves are thick and fleshy, whereas the rodgersia's dark, purplish-green leaflets, with their crinkled, glossy, deeply veined surfaces, are so solid that they almost rattle when moved about against each other. Both these plants are stoutly constructed. However, the sedum produces a clump of conspicuously upright stems, whereas the rodgersia has clusters of curving, pointed leaflets, which look almost like upturned bells.

The rodgersia's large leaves are particularly well coloured when young, though in a sunny site they are a dusky purple-green throughout the growing season. (This photograph shows the plant in late summer.)

Both these perennials have splendid flowers and seedheads. The rodgersia bears roughly pyramid-shaped heads of flowers which ripen into good, coppery seedheads. The sedum's wide flowerheads are decorative over a very long period (see 1.13 and 12.4 for their autumn and their winter colouring).

Rodgersias grow well in rich, moisture-retentive soils and in damp or wet positions. The sedum likes fertile, well-drained soils that do not dry out.

4.14 Spiraea & Hebe

Spiraea japonica 'Goldflame'
sun/shade ○ ◖
type of plant hardy shrub
zonal range 4-9 (C-WT)
flowering time early to mid-summer
flower colour crimson-pink
height 75-90cm (2½-3ft)
special characteristics yellow foliage, orange when young

Hebe rakaiensis
sun/shade ○
type of plant hardy/slightly tender shrub
zonal range 8-10 (CT-ST)
flowering time early to mid-summer
flower colour white
height 60cm (2ft)
special characteristics evergreen, green foliage

The youngest leaves of this spiraea, seen here in mid-spring, are a wonderful, coppery red-orange. This colouring is brightest in sunny positions and before the shrub flowers. In light shade, the colouring is more subdued but still attractive – see 6.14. Combining the strong copper of these new leaves with light, apple-green foliage creates a lovely, fresh effect without any harshness.

As flowering time approaches, the spiraea's foliage becomes a more or less uniform yellow. After flowering, the leaves are quite green. Through all these alterations in leaf colour, the hebe's neat, dense bun of tidy little leaves makes an excellent partner for the more loosely shaped spiraea.

Not all gardeners like the strong pink of the spiraea's flowerheads with the yellow of the plant's leaves. Pinching out the flower buds not only averts this combination of colours but also promotes good, bushy growth. The hebe produces a rather uneven dusting of pale flower spikes.

This combination of plants can be grown in most well-drained soils, provided they are not too dry; in dry, sunny places the leaves of the spiraea may become scorched.

For photographs of this spiraea combined with yellow flowers and with grey leaves, see 5.16 and 6.6, respectively.

4.15 Ballota & Salvia

Ballota pseudodictamnus
sun/shade ○
type of plant slightly tender perennial/shrub
zonal range 7-9 (CT-WT)
flowering time early to mid-summer
flower colour mauve
height 45-60cm (1½-2ft)
special characteristics evergreen/semi-evergreen, grey foliage

Salvia officinalis Purpurascens Group
(purple sage)
sun/shade ○
type of plant slightly tender shrub/perennial (herb)
zonal range 7-9 (CT-ST)
flowering time early to mid-summer
flower colour violet-purple
height 60-75cm (2-2½ft)
special characteristics evergreen/semi-evergreen, aromatic, purple foliage

Lapping against a neat mass of white flower bobbles, pale stems and tidy, rounded leaves, this sage's tongues of dusky purple help to create a very effective, harmonious partnership.

The harmony is due mainly to the fact that both plants grow neatly and densely. The ballota is more obviously upright; though the sage too has erect stems, the leaf arrangement of this plant gives it a more rounded appearance. Secondly, there are unifying tones of grey in both sets of foliage. Indeed, the purple sage's subtle mixture of grey and purple blends exceptionally well with the colouring of many other plants (see, for example, 11.7 and 11.8). Finally, both sets of leaves here are soft to the touch, so that there is a similarity in foliage texture, too: the ballota's leaves are beautifully woolly, while the foliage of the sage feels more like thin velvet.

Flowers do not play a very important part in this combination. Compared with the rather more aromatic, plain-leaved species, the purple sage is not very free-flowering. In any case, this plant is neatest if clipped each spring and this treatment discourages flower formation. The ballota's tiny blooms, still in bud here in early summer, add suitably restrained touches of colour to the plant.

Apart from plenty of sun, good drainage is the most important consideration for this combination.

4.16 Heuchera & Polygonatum

Heuchera micrantha var. *diversifolia* 'Palace Purple'
sun/shade ○
type of plant hardy perennial
zonal range 6-8 (C-WT)
flowering time mid- to late summer
flower colour pale pink
height 45-60cm (1½-2ft)
special characteristics evergreen, purple foliage

Polygonatum × *hybridum* 'Striatum'
(syn *P.×h.* 'Variegatum')
(Solomon's seal, David's harp)
sun/shade ○ ◑
type of plant hardy perennial
zonal range 4-9 (C-ST)
flowering time late spring to early summer
flower colour white + green
height 60cm (2ft)
special characteristics variegated foliage

The large, bold, lustrous leaves of *H. m. d.* 'Palace Purple' provide just the right sort of richly coloured leafiness to show this variegated Solomon's seal to advantage, while the pale cream striping and edging of the latter plant in turn emphasize the deep colouring of the heuchera's foliage. This contrast in leaf colour is reinforced by the difference between the solidity of the heuchera's clump of foliage and the more openly arranged, arching growth of the Solomon's seal.

Both plants here have attractive flowers. The little green-tipped bells of the Solomon's seal dangle prettily beneath each curved stem with its topping of almost horizontally held foliage. In contrast, the heuchera's sprays of tiny flowers are held well above its leaves; they ripen into decorative, bronzed pink seedheads.

The heuchera needs a sunny position in order to develop a good, rich foliage colour. However, this is not a combination for hot, dry places; both plants need a soil that is well-drained but also moisture-retentive (although the Solomon's seal will tolerate dryness, provided there is also some shade).

The heuchera is a very useful source of fairly low-growing, bold, purple foliage. It looks good with cool-coloured flowers (see 4.19), grey foliage (see 2.17) and also hot-coloured blooms (see 3.17).

87

4.17 Euphorbia & Origanum

Euphorbia amygdaloides '**Purpurea**'
(syn *E. a.* 'Rubra')
(spurge)
sun/shade ○ ◑
type of plant hardy perennial
zonal range 7-9 (CT-WT)
flowering time mid-spring to early summer
flower colour yellow-green
height 45-60cm (1½-2ft)
special characteristics evergreen, purple foliage

Origanum vulgare '**Aureum**'
(golden marjoram)
sun/shade ○
type of plant hardy perennial (herb)
zonal range 4-8 (C-WT)
height 23cm (9in)
special characteristics evergreen/semi-evergreen, aromatic, yellow foliage

In spring the new growths of this euphorbia are a bright maroon and the combination of this colour and the acidic yellow-green of its flowerheads is very striking. Here this successful association of colours has been prolonged by giving the euphorbia a yellow-leaved marjoram as a partner.

The euphorbia's foliage colour deepens as the summer progresses until, as here, in early autumn, it is a mixture of dark green and beautiful, dusky red-purple. The marjoram's leaf colour also softens, at approximately the same time, from a radiant yellow to a greener shade. Though their colours may tone down, there are always pleasing contrasts between these two plants. The euphorbia's dark, sometimes upright, sometimes sprawling, stems are clothed in conspicuous whorls of slim leaves. In contrast, the marjoram's thick clumps of erect stems and peppery-scented leaves create a more uniform carpet of growth. There are usually only a few flowers on this yellow-leaved marjoram. The euphorbia's flowerheads are at least as attractive as its leaves. They are also very long-lasting.

Both plants like good drainage with reasonable moisture retention to protect the marjoram's leaves from scorching and the euphorbia from mildew. The cut stems of the euphorbia exude a milky juice that may irritate some people's skin and eyes.

4.18 Euphorbia & Anaphalis

Euphorbia dulcis '**Chameleon**'
(spurge)
sun/shade ○
type of plant hardy perennial
zonal range 4-9 (C-WT)
flowering time late spring to early summer
flower colour lime green
height 45-60cm (1½-2ft)
special characteristics purple foliage, autumn foliage

Anaphalis triplinervis
(pearly everlasting)
sun/shade ○
type of plant hardy perennial
zonal range 4-9 (C-WT)
flowering time late summer to early autumn
flower colour white
height 30-45cm (12-18in)
special characteristics grey foliage

Purple leaves make white flowers sparkle, and the long-lasting, papery little blooms of *Anaphalis triplinervis* look really clean and crisp among the very dark foliage of this euphorbia. The leaves of the anaphalis (see 4.20) are softly felted and held on white, curving stems; they are white below and grey above. They too combine very pleasingly with the euphorbia's bushy, slim-stemmed mass of deep purple.

A sharper colour is introduced by the flowers of the euphorbia (see 13.8). The contrast between the acidic green of these tiny blooms and the chocolatey purple of the surrounding leaves is strong, though it is usually only noticeable at close quarters. More conspicuous is the colour of the euphorbia's autumn foliage, which is most often a striking mixture of pinks and apricots. Although the anaphalis's clump of growth is inclined to open out rather untidily towards the end of the season, it will certainly be respectable enough to provide a good block of cool colour beside the euphorbia's bright autumn leaves.

Both the euphorbia and the anaphalis like well-drained soil. However, neither plant is at its best in very dry conditions. When cutting the euphorbia, it should be remembered that the milky juice that oozes from the stems can irritate skin and eyes.

4.19 Heuchera & Viola

Heuchera micrantha var. *diversifolia* 'Palace Purple'

sun/shade ○
type of plant hardy perennial
zonal range 6-8 (CT-WT)
flowering time mid- to late summer
flower colour pale pink
height 45-60cm (1½-2ft)
special characteristics evergreen, purple foliage

Viola 'Belmont Blue'

(syn *V.* 'Boughton Blue')
(violet)
sun/shade ○ ◖
type of plant hardy perennial
zonal range 5-7 (C-WT)
flowering time mainly late spring to midsummer
flower colour blue
height 15-23cm (6-9in)
special characteristics evergreen

The obvious companions for pretty blue violas such as these are plants with grey or blue-tinted leaves (see, for example, 1.38). Giving them instead big, crinkled, gleaming leaves of a really deep red-purple makes them look wonderfully misty and delicate. In their turn, the small, pale shapes of the viola flowers have the effect of throwing into relief what might, especially at a distance, be almost too dark and flat a foliage colour.

The heuchera's flowers are quite different from those of the viola. They are carried in hazy sprays, well above the level of the foliage, and are particularly attractive when they ripen into soft, bronze-pink seedheads.

Each of the plants here likes a fertile, moisture-retentive soil that is also well-drained. In these conditions, the heuchera will produce plenty of good-quality foliage and the viola will flower for many weeks. The flowering period of the viola can be extended if the plant is cut back hard in midsummer, after the first flush of flowers begins to fade. When growing well, both plants form thick clumps of foliage. The viola's little leaves are smooth and a fairly light green.

It is worth bearing in mind that *H. m. d.* 'Palace Purple' varies in leaf colour and that some forms are more brown and less red-purple than others.

4.20 Anaphalis & Sedum

Anaphalis triplinervis

(pearly everlasting)
sun/shade ○
type of plant hardy perennial
zonal range 4-9 (C-WT)
flowering time late summer to early autumn
flower colour white
height 30-45cm (12-18in)
special characteristics grey foliage

Sedum telephium ssp. *maximum* 'Atropurpureum'

(stonecrop)
sun/shade ○
type of plant hardy perennial
zonal range 5-9 (C-ST)
flowering time late summer to early autumn
flower colour buff-pink
height 45-60cm (1½-2ft)
special characteristics purple foliage

Purple-leaved plants with foliage of a fleshy texture are to be found mainly among sedums. The lovely maroon-purple of this particular variety seems especially rich because of the thickness and smoothness of the leaves, and here the colour is further enhanced by a clump of much paler, softer-textured and slimmer foliage. The flower colours of each of these perennials reinforce the differences in foliage: the anaphalis' papery, 'everlasting' blooms add to the ashen appearance of the plant, and the sedum's much more warmly coloured flowerheads harmonize particularly happily with its dusky leaves and very dark, erect stems.

Both the plants here look attractive over a long period. The sedum's foliage colour is at first more blue-green than purple, but the texture and shape of the plant are attractive from mid-spring onwards. Its flowers ripen into rich brown seedheads in mid-autumn, at which stage the anaphalis flowers will often still be decorative (see 9.11).

During the growing season, both plants in this combination tend to become more open. Both like a well-drained soil but neither will prosper in very dry conditions and, in particular, the anaphalis needs some moisture if it is not to wilt.

For a combination using a smaller purple-leaved sedum, see for instance 17.16.

4.21 Helleborus & Viola

Helleborus × sternii
(hellebore)
sun/shade ○
type of plant hardy perennial
zonal range 6-9 (CT-WT)
flowering time late winter to mid-spring
flower colour pink-purple + greenish cream
height 45cm (18in)
special characteristics evergreen, green foliage

Viola riviniana Purpurea Group
(syn *V. labradorica, V. l. purpurea*)
(Labrador violet)
sun/shade ○ ◑
type of plant hardy perennial
zonal range 3-8 (C-WT)
flowering time mid- to late spring
flower colour purple-violet
height 10-15cm (4-6in)
special characteristics evergreen, purple foliage

Delicately and subtly coloured, these hellebore flowers, with their hints of pink-purple, are certainly shown to advantage when surrounded by a pool of deep purple leaves. Because these leaves are so small and dark and closely packed, they also provide a good background for the hellebore's long, elegant, pointed leaflets, which are suffused with purplish maroon when new. The older leaves are a soft, rich green, often with pale veining (see 14.2, where a form of *H. × sternii* is shown).

Both these plants are evergreen, and while at the end of winter the viola may be looking slightly thin and worn, the hellebore's clump of foliage is tough and leathery and very frost-resistant. The flowers of the hellebore are another long-lasting feature of this combination. Here, in late spring, they are still very decorative.

Many hellebores thrive in shade, but this hybrid needs a sunny, sheltered site. The viola is a very tolerant and adaptable plant, though – as can be seen here – sunshine produces foliage of a particularly dark purple. Both these plants appreciate a moist but well-drained, humus-rich soil. The viola's numerous self-sown seedlings are easily removed.

This viola mixes well with many other plants (see, for example, 8.22 and also 3.27 where the viola's flowers are in evidence).

4.22 Acer & Geranium

Acer palmatum 'Bloodgood'
(Japanese maple)
sun/shade ○ ◑
type of plant hardy shrub/tree
zonal range 6-8 (CT-WT)
height 2.7-3.6m (9-12ft)
special characteristics purple foliage, autumn foliage, fruit

Geranium phaeum
(mourning widow, cranesbill)
sun/shade ○ ◑
type of plant hardy perennial
zonal range 4-8 (C-WT)
flowering time late spring to early summer
flower colour dark purple
height 60-75cm (2-2½ft)
special characteristics semi-evergreen, decorative green foliage, suitable for damp soils

The flowers of *Geranium phaeum* are very deeply and softly coloured and they are therefore not especially conspicuous. One way of making them more noticeable is to boost their colour by adding another plant of similar shade. Here a Japanese maple, with fingered foliage of a long-lasting, deep red-purple, picks the geranium's dark flowers out of obscurity. At the same time, the colour and shape of the maple's leaves are shown off beautifully by the geranium's mass of lobed and veined green foliage. This is true in autumn, too, when the maple's elegant, rounded canopy of foliage turns bright red. The small touches of bright red evident in this illustration are supplied by the maple's key-like fruits which follow tiny, reddish purple, spring flowers.

Like all forms of *Acer palmatum*, this maple is a slow-growing plant that needs a well-drained, moisture-retentive and preferably acid soil to do well. It also requires shelter from cold and drying winds. The geranium is less difficult to accommodate, but it too likes its roots to be cool and either moist or damp. If this combination is planted in a sunny position, it is important to place the geranium on the shady side of the maple.

Self-sown seedlings of the geranium will vary in colour. For a photograph of this very dark-flowered form with a white-variegated hosta, see 16.20.

4.23 Photinia & Helleborus

Photinia × fraseri 'Red Robin'
sun/shade ○ ◑
type of plant slightly tender shrub
zonal range 8-9 (WT-ST)
flowering time late spring to early summer
flower colour white
height 1.8-3m (6-10ft)
special characteristics evergreen, red young foliage

Helleborus argutifolius
(syn *H. lividus* ssp. *corsicus*)
(Corsican hellebore)
sun/shade ○ ◑
type of plant hardy perennial
zonal range 7-9 (CT-WT)
flowering time late winter to late spring
flower colour pale green
height 60cm (2ft)
special characteristics evergreen, decorative green foliage

The wonderful red of this photinia's newest growths could be combined with other bright colours – the reds and yellows of tulips, for instance. However, the delicately coloured hellebore shown here provides an interesting and more subtle contrast to the photinia's brilliant leaves. This particular hellebore has an exceptionally long and early flowering season, and its bold, pale-stalked, evergreen foliage (see 8.7) is very handsome, too.

Here, in late spring, the hellebore's large heads of sculpted, cup-shaped flowers are still looking very decorative. Overall, the rather lax stems and firmly shaped foliage of the hellebore give it a rounded shape and this shrubby solidity is effective at the base of the upright, fairly open branches of the photinia.

The bright colour of the photinia lasts into summer, the pointed, glossy leaves gradually becoming bronzer as they age, until in maturity they are a deep, rich green. In contrast, the hellebore's pale-stalked leaves are of an unusually soft, rich green. The photinia's dense heads of small flowers are not as dramatic as its leaves.

Both the plants in this combination grow best in soils that are well-drained but also moisture-retentive. In colder districts, both plants will appreciate shelter from cold winds.

4.24 Cimicifuga & Hosta

Cimicifuga simplex var. *simplex* Atropurpurea Group
(syn *C. racemosa* 'Purpurea')
(bugbane)
sun/shade ○ ◑
type of plant hardy perennial
zonal range 3-8 (C-CT)
flowering time early to mid-autumn
flower colour pink tinged white
height 1.2-1.8m (4-6ft)
special characteristics purple foliage, suitable for damp soils

Hosta fortunei var. *albopicta*
(plantain lily)
sun/shade ○ ◑
type of plant hardy perennial
zonal range 3-9 (C-WT)
flowering time midsummer
flower colour pale lilac
height 45-60cm (1½-2ft)
special characteristics variegated young foliage, suitable for damp soils

Foliage as dark and as deeply divided as this cimicifuga's looks especially good with smoothly shaped, pale leaves. Illustrated here a few weeks into summer, this popular hosta has already lost some of the light, bright yellow of its newest leaves. (For an illustration of the foliage earlier in summer, see 8.16.) Even when, after flowering, its colouring becomes still more subdued, the bold, ribbed foliage is always much paler than the blackish purple leaves of the cimicifuga.

By the time the hosta's spires of trumpet-shaped flowers appear, the cimicifuga's foliage is several feet high and provides a splendidly dark background for these pale blooms. It also looks well beneath the plant's own slender, bottle-brush flowers, some of which may be over 30cm (12in) long. The scent of these cimicifuga flowers is sometimes described as fragrant, but many people find the smell unpleasant. Of the two plants in this combination, the hosta produces the more solid clump of growth.

Both plants here thrive in rich, damp soil. They also do well in any soil that is reasonably fertile and moisture-retentive. The foliage colour of the cimicifuga will be particularly deep in sunny positions, but in sunshine the provision of moisture is especially important.

4.25 Euphorbia & Rodgersia

Euphorbia amygdaloides 'Purpurea'

(syn *E. a.* 'Rubra')
(spurge)
sun/shade ○ ◐
type of plant hardy perennial
zonal range 7-9 (CT-WT)
flowering time mid-spring to early summer
flower colour yellow-green
height 45-60cm (1½-2ft)
special characteristics evergreen, purple foliage

Rodgersia podophylla

sun/shade ○ ◐
type of plant hardy perennial
zonal range 5-8 (C-CT)
flowering time early to mid-summer
flower colour cream
height 90-120cm (3-4ft)
special characteristics bronze foliage (mainly young), decorative green foliage, autumn foliage, suitable for damp and wet soils

The rich red-purple leaves and green flowers of this euphorbia can be used to echo the colouring of other purple-and-green plants, such as *R. podophylla* with its reddish-bronze flushed, green foliage.

Seen here in midsummer, the euphorbia's colouring is quite soft; in spring its leaves are bright maroon and its flowers are an acid yellow-green. The rich maroon-bronze of the rodgersia's emerging foliage has faded, too but, in this sunny site, the great, long-stalked, jagged leaves have already assumed their midsummer bronzing. In autumn these leaves will become redder still.

There are interesting differences in the size, shape and texture of these plants' leaves. Whereas the rodgersia's foliage is bold and conspicuously veined, the euphorbia has small, slim, relatively smooth leaves. The euphorbia's bushy mass of usually upright stems also creates a quite different pattern to the rodgersia's large clumps of growth. The euphorbia's flowers are very long-lasting; the rodgersia's broad spires of tiny flowers are often rather sparsely produced.

In the absence of damp or marshy ground, the rodgersia will grow well in deep, moisture-retentive soil. It needs shelter. The euphorbia too appreciates moisture.

4.26 Pseudowintera & Alchemilla

Pseudowintera colorata

(syn *Drimys colorata*)
sun/shade ○ ◐
type of plant slightly tender shrub
zonal range 9-10 (WT)
height 60-90cm (2-3ft)
special characteristics evergreen, aromatic, red foliage, needs acid soil

Alchemilla mollis

(lady's mantle)
sun/shade ○ ◐
type of plant hardy perennial
zonal range 4-8 (C-WT)
flowering time early to mid-summer
flower colour yellow-green
height 45cm (18in)
special characteristics decorative green foliage, suitable for damp soils

The leaf colour of *Pseudowintera colorata* is so subtle and unusual that it needs a partner that will blend gently with it. *Alchemilla mollis* harmonizes beautifully with a wide range of plants and most gardeners forgive its energetic self-seeding nature on this account. Here, its foamy heads of yellow-green echo the creamy lime-green of the central parts of the pseudowintera's younger leaves. There is too a pleasing contrast between the soft mass of the alchemilla's flowers and the smooth, rather slim shapes of the pseudowintera's leathery, wine-edged leaves. These leaves, which are held on dark, spreading stems, emit an astringent, peppery smell when crushed. The alchemilla's dense mound of velvety, scalloped foliage (see 8.21) also adds to the charms of the pseudowintera.

Since the alchemilla will grow almost anywhere, only the needs of the pseudowintera require some attention. Conditions must be acid or neutral, and ideally a moist, spongy soil should be provided.

For other combinations featuring purple, red or bronze foliage, see:
COOL-COLOURED FLOWERS 1.20, 1.34*, 1.39 GREY FOLIAGE 2.8*, 2.11, 2.13, 2.17, 2.25. 2.28 HOT-COLOURED FLOWERS 3.3, 3.14, 3.17, 3.27, 3.34 YELLOW FLOWERS 5.1, 5.8, 5.16* YELLOW FOLIAGE 6.2, 6.5, 6.6*, 6.8, 6,12*, 6.14*, 6.19 GREEN FLOWERS 7.2, 7.4, 7.7 GREEN FOLIAGE 8.1, 8.8, 8.10, 8.16*, 8.17*, 8.21, 8.22 VARIEGATED FOLIAGE 9.3, 9.6, 9.10, 9.26, 9.27 AUTUMN FOLIAGE 10.2, 10.4, 10.5 AROMATIC FOLIAGE 11.1, 11.2, 11.7, 11.8, 11.17, 11.19* FRUIT 12.1, 12.7 FRAGRANT FLOWERS 13.8, 13.13, 13.14, 13.19 CLIMBING PLANTS 15.3, 15.5, 15.7, 15.8 DAMP AND WET SOILS 16.5*, 16.6*, 16.15*, 16.16* GRASSES AND FERNS 17.5, 17.9, 17.10, 17.15, 17.16, 17.21* * denotes colour in young leaves only.

4.27 Euonymus & Astilbe

Euonymus fortunei 'Variegatus'
(syn *E. f.* 'Silver Gem')
sun/shade ○ ◖
type of plant hardy shrub/climber
zonal range 5-9 (C-WT)
height 45-60cm (1½-2ft) as a shrub
special characteristics evergreen, variegated foliage

Astilbe × *arendsii* 'Fanal'
(false goat's beard)
sun/shade ○ ◖
type of plant hardy perennial
zonal range 4-8 (C-WT)
flowering time early to late summer
flower colour deep red
height 60cm (2ft)
special characteristics bronze young foliage, decorative green foliage, suitable for damp soils

Astilbes with deep-coloured flowers also tend to have dark, rich green foliage. In its immature, spring state, this foliage is coppery or bronze. Since these new leaves are only a few centimetres high they can, especially at a distance, merge all too readily with the soil around them. However, if they are provided with a paler partner such as the variegated euonymus shown here, they become much more visible. The grey-green and pale cream of the euonymus is also enhanced, since the gleaming mahogany of the astilbe leaves makes the variegated foliage look particularly light and lively.

The two plants continue to look good together throughout the summer months, when the astilbe's long-lasting, plume-like flowers stand erect above its ferny foliage. When these flowers fade, there are handsome, red-brown seedheads which remain decorative right through winter. In cold weather the euonymus's leaf margins may become flushed with pink.

The astilbe thrives and makes dense clumps of growth in moist or damp soils that are also fertile. Where conditions are dryish, a shaded position is advisable. The euonymus will do well in almost any soil. It is at first a slow-growing, bushy shrub, but mature specimens may produce self-clinging shoots, up to 3m (10ft) high.

4.28 Pieris & Arum

Pieris 'Forest Flame'
sun/shade ◖
type of plant hardy shrub
zonal range 6-8 (CT)
flowering time mid- to late spring
flower colour creamy white
height 1.8-3m (6-10ft)
special characteristics evergreen, red young foliage, needs acid soil

Arum italicum ssp. *italicum* 'Marmoratum'
(syn *A. i.* 'Pictum')
sun/shade ○ ◖
type of plant hardy tuber
zonal range 6-9 (CT-ST)
flowering time late spring
flower colour greenish cream
height 30-45cm (12-18in)
special characteristics variegated foliage, fruit

On first emerging, the slender leaves of *Pieris* 'Forest Flame' are bright pink-red and held rather erectly, so that the whole, dense, upright shrub does indeed look as if it is covered in little flames. As the new foliage expands, it turns pink and then cream – as here, in early summer. The mature leaves are a glossy, dark green. Through all these colour changes, the accompanying arum, with its clumps of boldly spear-shaped, grey-variegated foliage, makes a sophisticated and highly flattering companion for the pieris.

The leaves of the arum appear first in mid-autumn. Even if they become frozen in winter, they soon revive, unscathed, after thawing. They have usually died back completely by midsummer, but by autumn remarkable drumstick heads of poisonous, orange-red berries develop on thick, bare stems.

The cowl-shaped flowers of the arum are less decorative than the pieris' dense, drooping heads of slightly fragrant flowers.

Both of these plants thrive in moist, humus-rich soils and in sheltered sites. Cold, drying winds and late frosts can disfigure the new growths of the pieris. Altogether, the ideal growing conditions are easier to achieve in partially shaded places. The pieris must have a lime-free soil.

93

5 YELLOW FLOWERS

Yellow is the colour of daffodils and springtime and therefore, by association, of cheerfulness and optimism – but it is also the colour of autumn daisies, such as heleniums and rudbeckias, which conjure up thoughts of ripeness and mellowness and the passing seasons. In this section there are plants that produce flowers of a pure, clear, springtime yellow, including some tulips as well as daffodils, and also the rich, golden yellows of autumn from *Rudbeckia laciniata* and the charming autumn-flowering bulb *Sternbergia lutea*. Softer, more delicate yellows are present in the flowers of primroses, some daylilies (especially the species, rather than the garden hybrids) and certain forms of potentilla. These gentler yellows are more akin to creams, which also appear in some of the combinations below. *Sisyrinchium striatum* and *Rosa* 'Buff Beauty' both have blooms of palest, creamy yellow (although the roses are at first a beautiful shade of caramelized apricot). Of all the different kinds of yellow, it is with these creams and with the cooler, greener yellows that pink flowers look most comfortable.

COOL AND WARM YELLOWS

Despite the fact that yellow is nearly always regarded as a warm colour, the very brightest yellows and some paler ones are actually quite cool; very vivid golds and yellows can look harsh and brassy and almost cold. These shades of yellow can swamp more delicate shades of the colour. Lemony yellows appear cool and restrained because they are tinged with green. In contrast, the orange-tinted flowers of, for example, the geum in the final combination in this section are very definitely a warm yellow. Between these two extremes of coolness and warmth there are the pure, clear yellows that have a straightforward, sunny warmth about them.

The tonal variations in the colour yellow will, of course, affect how flowers of a particular yellow appear in combination with leaves and flowers of other colours. Even where partnerships of yellow leaves and yellow flowers are devised, quite a wide range of effects can be produced. For example, light, lemony flowers can be matched with lemony foliage (see 5.12) or they can be contrasted with rich orange-yellow leaves (see 5.16). Generally speaking, however, yellow or yellow-variegated leaves can be regarded as emphasizers of yellow flower colour.

CONTRASTING PARTNERS

For combinations of contrasts, rather than harmonies of similarities, the complementary or near-complementary colours of violet and blue are the first choices for use with yellow flowers. With blue flowers or very glaucous foliage, yellow flowers look clean and very bright. When blue warms into violet or purple, the overall effect is more dramatic, and with dark purple leaves there is often an air of weighty opulence.

Pure, mid-yellows combined with strong purples and violets can be too harsh for some gardeners, in which case the yellows can be replaced by the less emphatic yellow-greens of, for example, *Alchemilla mollis* and many euphorbias.

Still softer-looking but nevertheless sophisticated planting schemes can be created using grey leaves with yellow flowers. Some yellow-flowered plants have grey leaves of their own (see, for example, *Helichrysum* 'Schwefellicht' in 5.10). Other sources of rather cool foliage are plants with white-variegated leaves. They and plants with white flowers look pretty and fresh with yellow flowers.

When teamed with hot colours such as red and orange, yellow flowers manage to add further warmth and, at the same time, to introduce a certain lightness. As they are closer to each other in the colour spectrum, yellow and orange together create less startling effects than partnerships of yellow and red.

HARMONIZING COLOURS

Yellow's other next-door neighbour in the colour spectrum is green. Deep greens can produce rich effects with yellow, and attractive harmonies can be created using fairly sharp, yellowish greens with yellows. However, in this type of plant grouping there is the danger that from a distance the yellow and green will merge too readily with one another, especially in the case of the gentler, weaker yellows. To mitigate against this, green and yellow plantings can be pepped up with dashes of, for example, brilliant white or intensely contrasting violet and purple.

Another way of bringing definition to these plantings is to incorporate some strong shapes. Drifts of yellow daisies look pretty, but the smooth, goblet shapes of most tulips and the great, dark-stemmed spires of many ligularias, for example, have much greater visual impact. Boldly shaped foliage can give structure to amorphous plantings, too. As well as the wide range of green-leaved plants with bold foliage (see Decorative Green Foliage, pages 129-141), there are also a number of yellow or yellow-marked leaves that are strikingly shaped, for example those of the golden hop (*Humulus lupulus* 'Aureus', see 6.10) and of hostas such as *Hosta fortunei albopicta aurea* (see 6.19), which are large and conspicuous. Very large or otherwise eye-catching yellow-variegated leaves are another option to consider (see, for example, 6.13 and 14.4).

Yellow flowers may mean daffodils and forsythia to most people, but some of the best-loved winter flowers are also yellow, including winter jasmine, winter aconites and the deliciously fragrant blooms of mahonias and witch hazels. To follow on from the familiar flowers of spring, there are the beautifully scented yellow blooms of early summer, including azaleas, daylilies and roses, and yellow clematis blooming on into autumn.

5.1 Clematis & Vitis

Clematis tibetana vernayi
(syn *C. orientalis*)
sun/shade ○ ◑
type of plant hardy climber
zonal range 6-9 (CT)
flowering time late summer to mid-autumn
flower colour yellow
height 3.6-5.4m (12-18ft)
special characteristics fruit

Vitis vinifera 'Purpurea'
(claret vine, Teinturier grape, grape vine)
sun/shade ○
type of plant hardy climber
zonal range 6-9 (CT-WT)
height 3-4.5m (10-15ft)
special characteristics purple foliage, autumn
foliage, fruit

The thick-'petalled' flowers of this clematis peer down for many weeks from among ferny foliage and twining growths. By early autumn a substantial number of silky seedheads will have developed. Against the rich, crimson-claret of the accompanying vine every part of this clematis is shown to advantage. Not only do the flowers look well here, but there are pleasing contrasts in leaf shape and colour and the seedheads are also accentuated against the deep-toned leaves of the vine, which are about 10-15cm (4-6in) wide.

Earlier in the season, this vine's shapely foliage is a rather sombre purple, with the very newest growths grey (see 15.8). In autumn the leaves become redder and in good years and against really warm, sunny walls they will turn a bright, rich crimson. In mid-autumn, small bunches of black, bitter grapes will often form (see 12.1).

For these two twining climbers to perform well, they should be positioned against a warm wall in full sun. The roots of the clematis, however, should be cool and shaded – by being placed behind a lower-growing shrub, for example. The vine is slow-growing, particularly when young. The clematis is a rather variable species but, compared to the vine, all forms grow quickly. This combination is best in a well-drained, moisture-retentive and fertile soil.

5.2 Rudbeckia, Solidago & Tradescantia

Rudbeckia laciniata
(coneflower)
sun/shade ○
type of plant hardy perennial
zonal range 3-9 (C-WT)
flowering time midsummer to early autumn
flower colour yellow
height 1.8-2.1m (6-7ft)

Solidago 'Mimosa'
(goldenrod)
sun/shade ○ ◑
type of plant hardy perennial
zonal range 4-9 (C-WT)
flowering time late summer to early autumn
flower colour golden yellow
height 1.2m (4ft)

Tradescantia × *andersoniana* 'Isis'
(spiderwort)
sun/shade ○ ◑
type of plant hardy perennial
zonal range 5-9 (C-WT)
flowering time early summer to early autumn
flower colour bright royal blue
height 60cm (2ft)

This large-scale threesome of robust and easily grown plants has two contrasting layers of strong yellow anchored by a much lower, tangled mound of vibrant blue and green. All three plants bloom profusely late in the season (the goldenrod's plumes are just beginning to open here, in late summer).

The general air of autumnal sunshine in this group is created by the two larger plants. However, the intense, contrasting blue of the spiderwort has the effect of making the yellows look even more yellow. There are pleasing contrasts, too, in overall habit of growth. The coneflower is distinctively upright, whereas the upper parts of the goldenrod's stems have a softer, arching appearance and there are some horizontal lines in the spiderwort's strap-shaped foliage. Despite many differences, the principal connection between these plants – the yellowness of the goldenrod and the coneflower allied to the near-complementary primary colour blue – is sufficiently strong to unify the group most successfully.

All these plants will grow in ordinary soil as long as it is reasonably moisture-retentive. The group can be planted in a lightly shaded position but the coneflower and, to a lesser extent, the spiderwort need sun to flower really well.

'Goldenmosa' is a goldenrod of a similar size to 'Mimosa' and more readily available. The stems of 'Goldenmosa' do not, however, arch as attractively as those of 'Mimosa'. *Rudbeckia* 'Herbstsonne' (syn. *R.* 'Autumn Sun') would be a handsome substitute for the coneflower shown here.

5.3 Bupleurum & Berberis

Bupleurum fruticosum
sun/shade ○
type of plant slightly tender shrub
zonal range 7-10 (CT-ST)
flowering time midsummer to early autumn
flower colour greenish yellow
height 1.5-2.4m (5-8ft)
special characteristics evergreen, decorative green foliage

Berberis candidula
(barberry)
sun/shade ○ ◖
type of plant hardy shrub
zonal range 6-9 (C-WT)
flowering time mid- to late spring
flower colour yellow
height 90-120cm (3-4ft)
special characteristics evergreen, fruit

The flowers of *Bupleurum fruticosum* – shaped like those of cow-parsley but of a more definite colour – are its main attraction, but everything about this shrub is handsome. The loose structure of slightly curving, reddish-brown stems shows both the flowers and the leaves to advantage. Here the whole ensemble is enhanced by the much denser, darker growth of *Berberis candidula*.

There are a number of pleasing contrasts in this partnership. The berberis's habit of growth is wide-spreading and rounded but there is a distinct downward arch to its branches, whereas the bupleurum is basically upright. The latter's leaves are smoothly tongue-shaped, quite large and have a bluish cast; the berberis has contrastingly small, dark, prickly foliage. Some of the berberis's blue-black berries can be seen ripening here, in late summer, and there are even a very few of the flowers visible, too. The size and density of the berberis's small leaves provide an interesting link, in terms of scale, with the bupleurum's crowded flowerheads of little buttons.

The berberis is easily pleased in a wide range of growing conditions. The bupleurum needs sun, a light soil and a reasonably sheltered site in order to prosper. It will thrive near the sea.

5.4 Rosa & Ruta

Rosa 'Buff Beauty'
(rose)
sun/shade ○
type of plant hardy shrub
zonal range 6-10 (C-WT)
flowering time early summer to early autumn
flower colour apricot-yellow fading to palest yellow
height 1.5-1.8m (5-6ft)
special characteristics fragrant flowers

Ruta graveolens 'Jackman's Blue'
(rue)
sun/shade ○
type of plant hardy shrub
zonal range 6-8 (C-WT)
flowering time mid- to late summer
flower colour yellow
height 45-60cm (1½-2ft)
special characteristics evergreen, aromatic, blue-grey foliage

The warm, toffee tones of this rose's generous flowers are cooled here by the exceptionally blue leaf sprays of a popular variety of rue. The rose forms a loose mass of large-leaved growth as wide as it is high, and if the rue is kept neat and tidy it is contrastingly dense and close-textured.

Not all gardeners would feel that the acid yellow of the rue's little flowers complemented the rose's blooms, and pinching out the rue's flowering shoots helps to produce a more rounded, denser shape. Hard pruning in spring also assists matters. (In dealing with the rue's sharply pungent growths, it may be necessary to wear some protection, since sensitive skins may become irritated.)

In addition to their lovely colouring, the flowers of this hybrid musk rose have a sweet, full scent. They are at their very best in midsummer (they are shown here in early summer); the sprays of autumn flowers are a good deal less numerous.

In common with most roses, 'Buff Beauty' thrives in sun and in fertile, well-drained soils that retain moisture. The rue needs plenty of sun for its foliage to be a bright blue-grey, and good drainage is important if the whole plant is not to become thin and lanky.

5.5 Lonicera & Tulipa

Lonicera nitida 'Baggesen's Gold'

(shrubby honeysuckle)
sun/shade ○ ◑
type of plant hardy shrub
zonal range 7-9 (CT-ST)
height 1.2-1.8m (4-6ft)
special characteristics evergreen, yellow foliage

Tulipa 'Jewel of Spring'

(tulip)
sun/shade ○
type of plant hardy bulb
zonal range 5-7 (C-CT)
flowering time mid- to late spring
flower colour soft yellow
height 60cm (2ft)

The largeness and smoothness of this tulip's blooms are emphasized here by the close texture of the background planting. At the same time, the related colouring – the rich but soft yellow of the tulip and the subdued ochre-gold of the lonicera – unites the planting in a most agreeable way.

The exact colour of the lonicera's tiny, shining leaves varies a good deal, according to the time of year and how much light is available. The colour here is fairly typical for mid-spring and for a position that receives plenty of sun but is not in the very brightest, most exposed part of the garden (6.4 shows a specimen in summer, growing on a sunny slope). When allowed to grow freely, this form of *Lonicera nitida* makes a rounded shrub with a rather spiky outline. If it is lightly clipped, like the specimen shown here, the growth becomes denser.

Good drainage and sun are essential for the tulip. Even under such conditions, the bulbs of large-flowered forms like 'Jewel of Spring' may need to be lifted each year to prevent them from dwindling away completely. The lonicera should not have a very hot, dry position or its leaves may scorch.

T. 'Jewel of Spring' is a Darwin hybrid tulip. A more readily available, brighter yellow tulip of this sort is 'Golden Apeldoorn'.

5.6 Hebe & Mahonia

Hebe rakaiensis

sun/shade ○
type of plant hardy/slightly tender shrub
zonal range 8-10 (CT-ST)
flowering time early to mid-summer
flower colour white
height 60cm (2ft)
special characteristics evergreen, decorative green foliage

Mahonia aquifolium

(Oregon grape)
sun/shade ○ ◑
type of plant hardy shrub
zonal range 5-8 (C-WT)
flowering time early to late spring
flower colour yellow
height 90-120cm (3-4ft)
special characteristics evergreen, decorative green foliage, autumn/winter foliage, fruit

This mahonia's bunched heads of slightly fragrant yellow flowers are beginning to open here, in early spring. By combining them with the excellent, apple-green foliage of a hebe – which itself has plenty of yellow in its colouring – their cheerful tones are emphasized.

At the same time, the hebe's leaves enliven the rich, dark green of the mahonia's glossy foliage. This striking difference in leaf colour alters in autumn and winter when the mahonia's foliage often takes on bronze and red tints, especially if it is grown in a dryish soil and a sunny position.

The spiny foliage of *Mahonia aquifolium* varies somewhat in shape, but in any case, these leaves are much larger than those of the hebe and contrast well with them. There is also a contrast in habit of growth: the hebe forms an exceptionally tidy, dense dome of greenery, whereas the mahonia consists of a number of upright stems that sucker moderately. The hebe's fluffy little flower spikes coincide with the ripening blue-black berries of the mahonia.

Almost any soil and site will be adequate for the mahonia, but the hebe must have sun and a well-drained but reasonably moisture-retentive soil to do well.

5.7 Euphorbia & Doronicum

Euphorbia palustris

(spurge)

sun/shade ○
type of plant hardy perennial
zonal range 5-8 (C-WT)
flowering time late spring to early summer
flower colour strong green-yellow
height 90cm (3ft)
special characteristics autumn foliage, suitable for damp and wet soils

Doronicum plantagineum

(leopard's bane)

sun/shade ○ ◖
type of plant hardy perennial
zonal range 4-8 (C-WT)
flowering time mid-spring to early summer
flower colour yellow
height 60-75cm (2-2½ft)

The sharp, springtime yellow of this euphorbia has faded here, in early summer, but the long-lasting flowerheads are still attractive. Against this undulating foam of lime-green, the doronicum's summery-looking daisies seem especially precise and tidy. In common with most spurges, *Euphorbia palustris* has flowerheads that are decorative well before they open fully. Even in mid-spring they are a fresh, bright presence behind the doronicum and this is therefore a combination that looks good for several weeks. In autumn, the euphorbia's foliage turns yellow and sometimes orange, too.

Both plants have erect stems. However, the euphorbia's large flowerheads and leafy growths create an impression of bushiness, in contrast to the doronicum's much more open arrangement of branching stalks and large leaves.

To do well, the euphorbia and the doronicum need moist, fertile soil. Particularly if conditions are slightly too dry, a substantial proportion of the doronicum's leaves die back after flowering.

If this doronicum is not available, the popular, larger-flowered and slightly later-flowering *D.* × 'Harpur Crewe' would make a good substitute.

5.8 Ajuga & Potentilla

Ajuga reptans 'Atropurpurea'

(bugle)

sun/shade ○ ◖
type of plant hardy perennial
zonal range 3-9 (C-ST)
flowering time late spring to early summer
flower colour deep blue
height 15-20cm (6-8in)
special characteristics evergreen/semi-evergreen, purple foliage

Potentilla fruticosa 'Primrose Beauty'

(shrubby cinquefoil)

sun/shade ○
type of plant hardy shrub
zonal range 3-8 (C-WT)
flowering time early summer to mid-autumn
flower colour pale yellow + yellow
height 90cm (3ft)

Both the leaves and the flowers of this purple-leaved form of bugle are richly coloured, and although this is a combination of many contrasts, this strong colouring ensures that the overall effect is not fussy. The bugle forms a low mat of gleaming foliage that sits in a dark pool around the rather upright growths and spreading dome shape of the potentilla. These dark leaves are particularly well-coloured here since the plant is in a sunny position. The potentilla's foliage is quite different in shape, with its little sprays of tiny, slightly blue-grey leaves covering numerous twigs.

The flowers of the two plants are also unalike. The bugle's leafy spires of intense blue are composed of many, tiny, long-lipped blooms, whereas the potentilla's flowers are of a much simpler, more open design and, in colour, are contrastingly pale and luminous. The overall impression is one of lush darkness intensifying pretty lightness and softness, and vice versa.

Neither of these plants is difficult to grow. Well-drained soils of all sorts, as long as they are not very dry, are suitable. The bugle is a vigorous plant that spreads quite rapidly if its roots are constantly moist, but neither it nor the potentilla likes wet soils.

5.9 Tulipa & Milium

Tulipa 'Yellow Purissima'
(tulip)
sun/shade ○
type of plant hardy bulb
zonal range 5-7 (C-CT)
flowering time mid-spring
flower colour yellow
height 40cm (15in)

Milium effusum 'Aureum'
(Bowles' golden grass)
sun/shade ◖
type of plant hardy perennial (grass)
zonal range 5-8 (C-WT)
flowering time late spring to midsummer
flower colour yellow
height 60-75cm (2-2½ft)
special characteristics semi-evergreen, yellow-green foliage

Suffused with spring sunshine, these clear yellow Fosteriana tulips and the bright, greenish-yellow blades of grass all exude vitality and warmth. *Milium effusum* 'Aureum' is a versatile grass that flatters plants of many colours and shapes (see, for example, 17.12 and 17.13).

Here the rather sharp yellow of this grass, conspicuous beside the broad, greyish foliage of the tulip, animates the whole combination. In addition, its habit of growth gives it a lively texture and this makes the tulips seem particularly smooth and elegant. Bowles' golden grass is at its brightest and yellowest in spring and early summer, but its dense clump of leaves is an excellent, light lime-green at other times. The foliage is usually about 30cm (12in) high, with the haze of delicate, yellow-stemmed flowers about twice this height.

Though this grass thrives and will self-seed in moist soils and partially shaded sites, it can be grown in sunnier positions as long as conditions are not dry. Here both plants have been given the sunny position and well-drained soil that the tulip requires. However, nearby herbaceous and shrubby material, when fully grown, will shade the grass and keep it cool during the summer months.

5.10 Santolina & Helichrysum

Santolina chamaecyparissus
(syn *S. incana*)
(cotton lavender)
sun/shade ○
type of plant hardy shrub
zonal range 6-9 (C-WT)
flowering time midsummer
flower colour bright yellow
height 45-60cm (1½-2ft)
special characteristics evergreen, aromatic, silver foliage

Helichrysum 'Schwefellicht'
(syn *H.* 'Sulphur Light')
sun/shade ○
type of plant hardy perennial
zonal range 5-9 (C-WT)
flowering time mid- to late summer
flower colour pale yellow changing to mustard, then tawny yellow
height 30-45cm (12-18in)
special characteristics aromatic, grey foliage

Even when their official flowering season is over, the papery, 'everlasting' flowers of this helichrysum remain attractive for some weeks (the plant is shown here in early autumn). At all stages, their colouring looks well with the plant's own slim grey leaves and with the neat, dense, finely divided foliage of this santolina.

The santolina also has yellow flowers, but the whole appearance of this plant is much improved, and the plant's hardiness is increased, if it is clipped closely in spring. This treatment ensures a dense, rounded shape which shows off the texture of the silvery-grey foliage to perfection, but it prevents many of the flowers from developing.

The foliage of both these plants has a warm, pungent scent. The helichrysum's slender leaves are held in upright tufts and the general growth is much less dense than that of the santolina. Therefore, well before the first flowers of the helichrysum appear, this is a pleasing all-grey partnership with contrasts in leaf shape and size and in habit of growth. Indeed, just before flowering, the helichrysum makes an extra contribution by producing flower buds which, like the leaves and stems, are attractively covered in close, white felt.

Both the helichrysum and the santolina thrive in sunny, dry places.

5.11 Sisyrinchium & Buphthalmum

Sisyrinchium striatum
(syn *Phaiophleps nigricans*)
sun/shade ○
type of plant hardy perennial
zonal range 7-8 (CT-WT)
flowering time early to mid-summer
flower colour pale yellow
height 60cm (2ft)
special characteristics evergreen, grey-green foliage

Buphthalmum salicifolium
sun/shade ○
type of plant hardy perennial
zonal range 4-9 (C-WT)
flowering time early summer to early autumn
flower colour yellow
height 45-60cm (1½-2ft)

Between them, these two plants create a little forest of upright stems, the vertical lines of which are emphasized by the erect, sword-like leaves of the sisyrinchium. This grey-green foliage also gives substance to the combination throughout the buphthalmum's long flowering season.

The conspicuous similarity in habit of growth in this partnership has the effect of focusing attention on differences in the flowers of the two plants. In contrast to the buphthalmum's sunny yellow, the sisyrinchium's flower colour is soft and delicate, and whereas the buphthalmum's daisies are cheerful, slender-petalled circles, the little cupped flowers of the sisyrinchium are clustered neatly and rather elegantly into slim spires. However, overall this is not so much a combination of stark contrasts as a gentle and informal mingling of two harmonizing plants.

For the combination to work as it has here, a really well-drained, rather poor soil and a site in full sun are needed. In richer soils and in some shade, the buphthalmum in particular will be much more lax in growth with a mass of flopping, curving stems. Whatever the fertility of the soil, the sisyrinchium is likely to self-seed generously.

5.12 Stachys & Narcissus

Stachys byzantina 'Primrose Heron'
(syn *S. lanata* 'Primrose Heron', *S. olympica* 'Primrose Heron')
(lamb's tongue, lamb's ear, lamb's lug)
sun/shade ○
type of plant hardy perennial
zonal range 4-9 (C-WT)
flowering time mid- to late summer
flower colour mauve-pink
height 23-30cm (9-12in)
special characteristics evergreen, yellow-grey foliage

Narcissus 'Binkie'
(daffodil)
sun/shade ○ ◖
type of plant hardy bulb
zonal range 4-6 (C-CT)
flowering time early to mid-spring
flower colour palest yellow + lemon yellow
height 30cm (12in)

By adding another lemon-coloured plant, the fresh, clear yellow of these daffodils is made even more striking. *Stachys byzantina* 'Primrose Heron' is a recent form of lamb's tongue with leaves that are suffused with light, greenish-yellow in spring. The softly furred foliage is at its brightest early in the season but the colour is good almost all summer long. Like the popular, grey-leaved typical species, this plant makes a dense mat of foliage approximately 10-15cm (4-6in) high in well-drained soils and sunny sites.

Although the particular variety of daffodil used here looks very attractive, there are many other pale yellow forms that would look equally well in this combination. *N.* 'Binkie' is classified as a large-cupped variety. It might be worth considering some of the smaller-flowered forms of daffodil for this planting, particularly if they have less conspicuous foliage. *N.* 'Hawera' is an example of a lemon-yellow daffodil of the Triandrus group, with leaves that are relatively inconspicuous. Whichever variety of daffodil is chosen, a fertile soil and fairly frequent division will be needed if it is to flower really well.

5.13 Narcissus & Muscari

Narcissus 'February Gold'
(daffodil)
sun/shade ○ ◑
type of plant hardy bulb
zonal range 4-8 (C-CT)
flowering time early to mid-spring
flower colour yellow
height 30cm (12in)

Muscari armeniacum
(grape hyacinth)
sun/shade ○
type of plant hardy bulb
zonal range 4-9 (C-WT)
flowering time mid- to late spring
flower colour mid-blue
height 20-25cm (8-10in)
special characteristics fragrant flowers

Despite its name, this daffodil seldom flowers in late winter. It is, however, a most attractive cyclamineus variety which begins to bloom very early in spring and lasts for several weeks. Combining these sunny flowers with dense, blue spikes emphasizes their lovely colouring and the bright and breezy, comparatively open arrangement of their petals. The tightly packed flowers of the muscari also look good with the smooth shapes of most tulips – see 3.16.

Neither of the plants in this combination has a long season of interest. However, both of them are vigorous, easily grown plants that are suitable for naturalizing in what might otherwise be simply an area of rough grass. Planted where mowing is carried out only a few times each year, their foliage can die back naturally without looking unsightly. In addition, competition from the roots of grasses will ensure that the energy of the rather untidy-leaved muscari is curbed somewhat. In beds and borders, this plant can spread too widely for some gardeners' liking.

Any soil with reasonable drainage will be suitable for this combination, but the daffodil will not perform well in very dry conditions. On warm spring days the muscari's flowers exude a soft, sweet fragrance.

5.14 Origanum & Viola

Origanum vulgare 'Aureum'
(golden marjoram)
sun/shade ○
type of plant hardy perennial (herb)
zonal range 4-8 (C-WT)
height 23cm (9in)
special characteristics evergreen/semi-evergreen, aromatic, yellow foliage

Viola 'Jackanapes'
(violet)
sun/shade ○ ◑
type of plant hardy perennial
zonal range 5-7 (C-CT)
flowering time late spring to early autumn
flower colour yellow + maroon
height 10-15cm (4-6in)
special characteristics evergreen/semi-evergreen

The yellow-leaved form of marjoram is a popular and easily grown plant that forms a dense, weed-proof clump of more or less upright stems. It is especially useful as an edging. Both the acid yellow of its leaves in spring and early summer and the more khaki colour of its foliage later in the year look good with many different plants, including those with yellow or partly yellow flowers.

Here, in early summer, its bright young foliage is emphasizing the yellow petals of the bi-coloured flowers of *Viola* 'Jackanapes'. (Planting this viola with maroon-purple leaves draws attention to its dark, upper petals, see 3.17). The viola has an exceptionally long flowering season, and it can be persuaded to flower for longer still by being regularly dead-headed and then chopped right back at the end of summer.

The marjoram does not usually produce many of its tiny, mauve flowers. When bruised, the leaves of this plant emit the characteristic sweet and peppery scent of ordinary, green-leaved marjoram.

Though a well-drained soil and sun are needed for this herb to thrive, the plant must not become too hot and dry or else its leaves may scorch. In any case, the viola requires a moisture-retentive soil; if conditions are dry, its spreading clump of dark foliage will be thin.

5.15 Helianthemum & Sternbergia

Helianthemum 'Ben Nevis'

(sun rose, rock rose)

sun/shade ○
type of plant hardy shrub
zonal range 5-7 (CT-WT)
flowering time early to mid-summer
flower colour orange-gold + orange-bronze
height 20cm (8in)
special characteristics evergreen

Sternbergia lutea

sun/shade ○
type of plant hardy bulb
zone 7 (CT-WT)
flowering time early to mid-autumn
flower colour rich yellow
height 10-15cm (4-6in)

The wonderful, warm flower colour of *Sternbergia lutea* is quite different to the pinks, mauves and whites of other low-growing, autumn-flowering bulbs. The leaves of this bulb are a deep, shining green which is an ideal accompaniment to the yellow of the flowers. A larger, denser and differently textured block of this excellent dark colour is provided by a hummocky sun rose.

This little sub-shrub flowers much earlier than the sternbergia, producing large quantities of its fragile-looking, dark-centred blooms, though each of these is very short-lived. If it is clipped lightly after its midsummer flush of flowers, it often goes on to produce another, smaller crop of flowers.

Both these plants require a well-drained soil and plenty of sun. The sternbergia needs warm, dry conditions for its bulbs to ripen during the summer months. Since its leaves continue to elongate and develop after the flowers have faded, it should not be given a site that is too exposed to cold, winter winds.

Other sun roses with dark green leaves include 'Ben More', which has orange-red flowers over many weeks, and the double-flowered, yellow 'Jubilee'.

5.16 Spiraea & Primula

Spiraea japonica 'Goldflame'

sun/shade ○ ◐
type of plant hardy shrub
zonal range 4-9 (C-WT)
flowering time early to mid-summer
flower colour crimson-pink
height 75-90cm (2½-3ft)
special characteristics yellow foliage, orange when young

Primula vulgaris

(primrose)

sun/shade ◐
type of plant hardy perennial
zonal range 5-8 (C-CT)
flowering time early to late spring
flower colour pale yellow
height 10-15cm (4-6in)

By being tucked under the dense, rounded twigginess and the warm, orange-and-gold foliage of *Spiraea japonica* 'Goldflame', these primroses have been made to appear especially pale and beautiful. The dappled shade cast by the shrub also provides just the right sort of light conditions for primroses. These much-loved, occasionally fragrant little plants, with their close clumps of fresh green, crinkled foliage, thrive in cool places with moist, fertile soil. They can also be grown in sunny places, as long as the soil never dries out or they receive regular summer watering. In ideal conditions, they often self-seed liberally.

Most soils are suitable for the easy-going spiraea. The foliage of this shrub is brightest before flowering time; newer varieties, such as 'Golden Princess', keep their foliage colour rather longer. A sunny site encourages particularly strong colouring. After the flowers have faded, the leaves are a good deal greener. Some gardeners find the conjunction of pink flowers and yellow leaves so jarring that they prefer to pinch out the flower buds. This procedure has the beneficial effect of stimulating plenty of neat, leafy growth.

5.17 Hemerocallis & Geranium

Hemerocallis lilioasphodelus
(syn *H. flava*)
(daylily)
sun/shade ○ ◐
type of plant hardy perennial
zonal range 3-9 (C-ST)
flowering time early to mid-summer
flower colour yellow
height 75cm (2½ft)
special characteristics decorative green foliage, fragrant flowers, suitable for damp soils

Geranium 'Johnson's Blue'
(cranesbill)
sun/shade ○ ◐
type of plant hardy perennial
zonal range 4-8 (C-WT)
flowering time early to mid-summer
flower colour clear blue
height 45cm (18in)
special characteristics decorative green foliage

The pale, cool yellow of this daylily's slender and sweetly scented flowers is one of the best colours with which to associate the exceptionally pretty blue of this popular geranium. The whole combination is one of delicacy and elegant simplicity and, since the flowers of both plants are produced in succession over several weeks, this is a partnership that looks good during a substantial part of the summer.

As well as lovely flowers, these two plants have attractive leaves. The geranium's foliage is deeply divided and forms a light, leafy clump, while the daylily's bright green, strap-shaped leaves arch over this clump and contrast with it in a very flattering manner. Should the geranium's foliage start to look rather shabby towards the end of the flowering period, it can be cut right back at this time and fresh new growth will appear.

Both these plants make good ground cover as long as they are not grown in too dry a soil. Though the daylily will thrive in damp places and heavy soils, a moisture-retentive but well-drained soil would suit this combination best. For a further illustration of this daylily, growing in a damper, shadier position with a fern, see 13.17.

5.18 Corydalis & Asplenium

Corydalis lutea
sun/shade ○ ◐
type of plant hardy perennial
zonal range 5-8 (C-WT)
flowering time late spring to mid-autumn
flower colour yellow
height 23-30cm (9-12in)
special characteristics evergreen, decorative green foliage

Asplenium scolopendrium
(syn *Phyllitis scolopendrium*)
(hart's tongue fern)
sun/shade ◐
type of plant hardy fern
zonal range 4-8 (C-CT)
height 30-45cm (12-18in)
special characteristics evergreen, decorative green foliage

The common yellow corydalis has an exceptionally long flowering season. Its own clump of ferny, slightly blue-green leaves is a pretty accompaniment to its flowers, with the upright and relatively smooth foliage of the hart's tongue fern here making an interesting addition. The fern has been planted at a slightly lower level than the corydalis and its firmer shape makes a good anchor to the airier foliage and flowers of the corydalis. Although the two plants in this combination have dissimilar foliage, they are linked by the way in which the yellow of the corydalis's flowers is echoed in the yellowish-green of the fern's newest leaves.

Light shade and a moist, leafy, alkaline soil are ideal for both of these plants. In partial shade, the corydalis's flowering season is especially long and the fern grows lushly with mature fronds of a good, rich green. Each of these plants is, however, very easy to please in a wide variety of sites and soils. The corydalis is a prolific self-seeder.

5.19 Geum & Hosta

Geum 'Georgenburg'

(avens)

sun/shade ○ ◗

type of plant hardy perennial

zonal range 5-8 (C-CT)

flowering time late spring to early summer

flower colour orange-yellow

height 30cm (12in)

Hosta 'Hydon Sunset'

(plantain lily)

sun/shade ◗

type of plant hardy perennial

zonal range 3-9 (C-WT)

flowering time midsummer

flower colour purple

height 30cm (12in)

special characteristics yellow-green foliage, suitable for damp soils

The light yellow-green of these hosta leaves adds considerable zest to this combination. It also has the effect of intensifying the geum's colouring, enriching the egg-yolk yellow of its flowers and making the foliage seem an especially lively green.

Though the branching heads of dark-stalked flowers are the geum's main attraction, its crinkled and lobed foliage makes a very satisfactory clump and it remains remarkably fresh well into autumn. The hosta's foliage is indisputably its outstanding feature. 'Hydon Sunset' is a charming miniature variety with closely packed, heart-shaped leaves to a height of about 15-23cm (6-9in). The foliage gradually becomes greener during summer, but even when less yellow it continues to look attractive with the geum's quite differently shaped leaves.

Like some other hostas with plain yellow foliage, 'Hydon Sunset' needs shade – and some shelter from desiccating winds – in order to prevent its leaves from scorching. Even a fully shaded site is suitable, though there may be rather fewer of the bell-shaped flowers in such a position. The geum too needs a reasonable amount of light, and fairly frequent division and replanting, to flower well. Both plants like a soil that is well-drained but moisture-retentive. The hosta will also prosper in damp soils.

For other combinations featuring yellow flowers, see:

COOL-COLOURED FLOWERS 1.31 GREY FOLIAGE 2.17 HOT-COLOURED FLOWERS 3.2, 3.14, 3.17, 3.18, 3.26 PURPLE FOLIAGE 4.2 YELLOW FOLIAGE 6.14 VARIEGATED FOLIAGE 9.2, 9.6, 9.29 AROMATIC FOLIAGE 11.1 FRAGRANT FLOWERS 13.12, 13.17, 13.18, 13.21 WINTER FLOWERS 14.4, 14.9, 14.10 WATER GARDENS AND DAMP AND WET SOILS 16.2, 16.10, 16.13 GRASSES AND FERNS 17.12

6 Yellow or Yellow-green Foliage

Plants with yellow leaves form a select little group compared with the large range of variegated and grey-leaved plants available to gardeners, yet some of the most useful of all plants for creating attractive combinations fall into this category. They include golden marjoram (*Origanum vulgare* 'Aureum'), the yellow-leaved form of mock orange (*Philadelphus coronarius* 'Aureus') and of *Lonicera nitida* (*L. n.* 'Baggesen's Gold'), and the familiar golden privet (*Ligustrum ovalifolium* 'Aureum'), the leaves of which become almost entirely yellow-green in shaded places. All of these plants appear not only in this section but elsewhere in the book too. They are all easily grown and widely available.

Perhaps the most obvious use for yellow-leaved plants is as emphasizers of other yellows, whether these colours are present in flowers and or in the markings of yellow-variegated foliage. Combined with other yellows, the mood created is predominantly one of sunny cheerfulness. A different, softer warmth emanates from combinations of grey and yellow leaves, and there is a gentle cleanness and clarity about combinations of yellow leaves and white flowers. Yellow foliage with green gives an especially restful effect, but if the green is supplied by deeply coloured, glossy leaves the impression is quite a rich one, too. Richer still and more opulent and dramatic are combinations of purple and yellow, while the intense contrasts that arise when yellow leaves are placed beside blues and violets maximize the colours involved and make exhilarating viewing. With oranges and reds the heat is turned up and the whole picture sizzles.

Varying Colour, Size and Shape

Of course, these observations about the effect that yellow foliage has in combination with other colours are very broad generalizations. Yellow foliage varies considerably in colour – and therefore in the effect it has on other colours. In this section there are leaves that are particularly warm and orange-tinted, like those of *Spiraea japonica* 'Goldflame' and *Taxus baccata* 'Semperaurea'; there are leaves of a more straightforwardly sunny yellow, such as those of *Origanum vulgare* 'Aureum' and *Lysimachia nummularia* 'Aurea'; and vivid, acidic yellows are present in the leaves of, for example, *Berberis thunbergii* 'Aurea'. This variety of colouring in yellow-leaved plants is particularly evident in plantings that make a feature of yellow foliage and, in these cases, care is needed in arranging the individual plants so that the greener yellows do not appear over-acidic and bilious.

The exact colour of many yellow-leaved plants changes during the year. Some conifers and heathers become more richly or brightly coloured in winter but, generally speaking, deciduous yellow-leaved plants become greener as the growing season progresses. Leaf colour is also affected by how much light a particular plant receives. Deciduous yellow foliage tends to have a rather delicate texture, and in strong sunlight or very dry soils there may well be unsightly browning of the leaf edges. Some shade is, therefore, often advisable and though the leaf colour may not be so bright as it would be in full sun, it will be longer-lasting in cool, shaded places and the foliage will remain in better condition. The tougher, harder-textured leaves of conifers and heathers, on the other hand, can withstand full exposure and generally need plenty of sunshine to colour well.

Even though the range of yellow-leaved plants is not very extensive, there is a surprising variety of leaf size, shape and texture: from the bold, lobed, 15cm (6in) leaves of the golden hop (*Humulus lupulus* 'Aureus') and the smooth, elegant outlines of yellow-leaved hostas, through the slim, arching shapes of grasses like *Milium effusum* 'Aureum' (see 17.13) to the tiny, aromatic leaves of herbs such as golden marjoram and some of the thymes, there is a wide assortment of shapes and sizes to choose from. Texture varies considerably, too: in this section there are examples of prickly conifers (see 6.7), stringy conifers (see 6.1), and there are the veined leaves of *Tolmiea menziesii* 'Taff's Gold' and the smooth leaves of *Berberis thunbergii* 'Aurea'.

The choice of good flowering plants with yellow leaves is not very wide. However, given the brightness of most of these leaves, the lack of very decorative flowers is not, perhaps, a great drawback. Some yellow-leaved plants do have attractive blooms, including many of the heaths and heathers, some hostas and, notably, the beautifully fragrant, yellow-leaved form of mock orange (*Philadelphus coronarius* 'Aureus').

Nurseries specializing in foliage plants will stock yellow-leaved plants not illustrated here. Among the taller-growing plants there will be, for example, ivies such as *Hedera helix* 'Buttercup' and some trees (*Acer shirasawanum* 'Aureum', is particularly elegant, but the yellow-leaved forms of *Robinia pseudoacacia*, or false acacia, and *Gleditsia triacanthos*, or honey locust, are also very attractive). Smaller yellow-leaved plants include the popular shrub *Choisya ternata* 'Sundance' and the especially handsome, golden-yellow form of meadowsweet, *Filipendula ulmaria* 'Aurea'.

6.1 Chamaecyparis & Euphorbia

Chamaecyparis pisifera 'Filifera Aurea'
(Sawara cypress)
sun/shade ○
type of plant hardy conifer
zonal range 5-8 (C-CT)
height 4.5-6m (15-20ft)
special characteristics evergreen, yellow foliage

Euphorbia characias ssp. *wulfenii* × *E. characias* seedling
(spurge)
sun/shade ○
type of plant slightly tender/hardy shrub/perennial
zonal range 7-10 (CT-WT)
flowering time mid-spring to early summer
flower colour yellow-green
height 90-120cm (3-4ft)
special characteristics evergreen, blue-grey foliage

A cascade of green-gold filaments and a colony of icy blue-grey bottle-brushes make an imposing combination at any time, but in a midwinter fog they form a strikingly substantial and impressive partnership. However, this is an association of plants for the patient gardener. The euphorbia will grow quite quickly, seed itself and – as here – intermarry with other, closely related spurges. But the cypress is slow, especially when young – after ten years it may be about 90-120cm (3-4ft) high. Eventually it broadens into a wide-spreading cone of weeping growth.

As well as its splendid foliage, the euphorbia bears large, cylindrical heads of flowers on top of its upright stems. The flowers of the subspecies *wulfenii* are particularly broad and handsome, but in all forms the flowerheads make an impact for many weeks. The best-quality foliage is obtained by removing the faded flowers, but this operation can be hazardous for those gardeners whose skin is sensitive to the irritant, milky juices of these plants.

Sun and a well-drained but moisture-retentive soil are needed for this combination. Although the euphorbia does well in dry soils, the cypress dislikes dry conditions and requires sun for its foliage to be well-coloured. The euphorbia needs shelter from cold winds, but in hot climates it accepts light shade.

6.2 Cupressus & Berberis

Cupressus macrocarpa 'Lutea'
(Monterey cypress)
sun/shade ○
type of plant hardy/slightly tender conifer
zonal range 7-10 (CT-ST)
height 6-7.5m (20-25ft)
special characteristics evergreen, aromatic, yellow-green foliage

Berberis × *ottawensis* 'Superba'
(syn *B. thunbergii* 'Atropurpurea Superba')
(barberry)
sun/shade ○
type of plant hardy shrub
zonal range 5-9 (C-WT)
flowering time late spring
flower colour yellow + red
height 1.8-2.4m (6-8ft)
special characteristics purple foliage, autumn foliage

In maturity, *Cupressus macrocarpa* 'Lutea' makes a broad cone of feathery foliage coloured a lively, clean yellow-green. Here both the shape and the colour of this fast-growing conifer have been contrasted with a rounded mass of prickly, arching branches and rich purple foliage. The unusually dark leaves of *Berberis* × *ottawensis* 'Superba' – spangled here with raindrops after a recent shower – have an interesting blue-green cast to them. This accentuates their deep, dusky colouring and gives the whole plant considerable visual weight.

In autumn, these dark leaves turn orange-red and red. The colouring is often vivid and, combined with the cypress's fairly sharp yellow-green, it creates an especially bright, late-season association. Compared with forms of the familiar *Berberis thunbergii*, the autumn display of red berries produced by this bolder, more vigorous shrub is, however, often disappointing.

Almost any well-drained soil will suit both these plants, but conditions must not be dry. The cypress needs shelter from cold winds and is seen at its best in mild, moist areas near the sea. The most popular recent variety of this plant is 'Goldcrest'. When crushed, the leaves of *Cupressus macrocarpa* and its varieties emit a fruity, almost citrus scent.

6.3 Taxus & Hosta

Taxus baccata 'Semperaurea'
(yew)
sun/shade ○
type of plant hardy conifer
zonal range 6-7 (C-CT)
height 1.8-3m (6-10ft)
special characteristics evergreen, yellow foliage

Hosta sieboldiana var. elegans
(plantain lily)
sun/shade ◑
type of plant hardy perennial
zonal range 3-9 (C-WT)
flowering time early to mid-summer
flower colour palest lilac
height 75-90cm (2½-3ft)
special characteristics blue-grey foliage, suitable for damp soils

Taxus baccata 'Semperaurea' has spring growth of a remarkable orange-tinged yellow. Blue and orange are complementary colours which in proximity intensify each other. Here, in early summer, the remaining hints of orange – in what is now, basically, a leaf colour of long-lasting, bright, rich yellow – have been accentuated by the presence of some wonderful blue-grey hosta leaves.

This striking combination of two colours is enlivened by differences in leaf shape and habit of growth. The yew's tiny, strap-shaped leaves are held on rather upright, splaying branches which create an irregular, eventually wide-spreading outline. In contrast, the hosta's puckered and veined foliage forms a great, solid clump of very broad leaves. These leaves are, briefly, yellow in autumn. The short-stalked flowerheads of the hosta are followed by good seedheads.

Though this slow-growing yew needs plenty of sun to enhance its foliage colour, the leaves of the hosta are best in some shade. The hosta should, therefore, be planted on the most shaded side of the yew, and the combination should be given a fertile, moisture-retentive soil. Nearly every part of the yew is poisonous.

6.4 Hebe & Lonicera

Hebe hectorii
sun/shade ○
type of plant slightly tender shrub
zonal range 8-10 (CT-ST)
flowering time midsummer
flower colour white or pale pink
height 75cm (2½ft)
special characteristics evergreen, decorative green foliage

Lonicera nitida 'Baggesen's Gold'
(shrubby honeysuckle)
sun/shade ○ ◑
type of plant hardy shrub
zonal range 7-9 (CT-WT)
height 1.2-1.8m (4-6ft)
special characteristics evergreen, yellow foliage

Both the plants here are grown purely for their foliage. The hebe does flower, but only sparingly so and in this case a paucity of flowers is an advantage, since the little flowerheads tend to detract from the erect solidity and neatness of the shrub's overall shape.

Although this is effectively a leaves-only combination, it is a partnership that looks attractive throughout the year. As a considerable bonus, the foliage colour of the lonicera in particular combines especially well with other plants. Its tiny leaves, on their longish, branching shoots, can vary from a soft gold, as here, to a brighter old gold. The latter colouring is most evident in spring and is especially marked on plants grown in the sunniest positions. In winter the foliage can become bronzed. The hebe's contrasting cords of dark green are suffused with olive tones which are echoed in the yellow of the lonicera's foliage.

Both these plants appreciate well-drained soil. If conditions are too dry, however, the lonicera's leaves may become scorched. The hebe benefits from being sheltered from cold winds.

6.5 Berberis & Ophiopogon

Berberis thunbergii 'Aurea'
(barberry)
sun/shade ○
type of plant hardy shrub
zonal range 5-8 (C-WT)
flowering time mid- to late spring
flower colour yellow + pink
height 90-120cm (3-4ft)
special characteristics yellow foliage, autumn foliage, fruit

Ophiopogon planiscapus 'Nigrescens'
sun/shade ○ ◑
type of plant hardy perennial
zonal range 6-10 (CT-ST)
flowering time mid- to late summer
flower colour pale pink-mauve
height 15cm (6in)
special characteristics evergreen, purple foliage, fruit

This is not a combination for the timid gardener, who might prefer soft and subtle pastels to this emphatic contrast of bright, acid yellow and darkest purple-black. *Berberis thunbergii* 'Aurea' is a slow-growing shrub with thorny branches and red-tinged young shoots that create a rather irregular outline overall. The yellow leaf colour shown here in mid-spring becomes greener by the end of summer; in autumn, particularly in full sun, there is some rusty orange colour. There are some scarlet berries, too, in autumn.

The extraordinarily dark, grass-like leaves of *Ophiopogon planiscapus* 'Nigrescens' arch into heaps of foliage, which are particularly dense in moisture-retentive soils. The flowers are small and appear more or less amongst these leaves; they are followed by black berries which last all winter.

The berberis needs a position that is both sunny, to encourage good foliage colour, and sheltered, to prevent damage from wind and frost. It is less fussy about soil, although a very alkaline soil is not ideal. The ophiopogon likes moist, fertile, well-drained soil.

For a similar but smaller-scale combination using this ophiopogon, see 17.9.

6.6 Spiraea & Stachys

Spiraea japonica 'Goldflame'
sun/shade ○ ◑
type of plant hardy shrub
zonal range 4-9 (C-WT)
flowering time early to mid-summer
flower colour crimson-pink
height 75-90cm (2½-3ft)
special characteristics yellow foliage, orange when young

Stachys byzantina 'Silver Carpet'
(syn *S. lanata* 'Silver Carpet', *S. olympica* 'Silver Carpet')
(lamb's tongue, lamb's ear, lamb's lug)
sun/shade ○
type of plant hardy perennial
zonal range 4-9 (C-WT)
height 10-15cm (4-6in)
special characteristics evergreen, silver foliage

Oval is the most mundane of foliage shapes but if, as here, there are differences in colour, texture and habit of growth, a combination of two oval-leaved plants can be very pleasing. The photograph shows how, when grown in a sunny position and well-drained soil, the spiraea's leaves can take on some soft yellow and orange colouring in early autumn. This dense, rounded shrub is principally noted for the coppery orange and yellow of its younger leaves. The leaf colour is brightest before flowering time, after which the foliage becomes greener. Newer varieties such as 'Golden Princess', however, are colourful for a longer period.

Many gardeners feel that, when the spiraea's bright flowers first appear along with the summer foliage, the resulting combination of yellow and crimson-pink is not an attractive one. Pinching out the flower buds avoids this colour clash and promotes good, neat growth, too.

In well-drained soils and sunny sites the lamb's tongue forms a dense carpet of furry, overlapping leaves. This contrasts flatteringly with the larger, rounder shape and smoother foliage of the spiraea. *Stachys byzantina* 'Silver Carpet' rarely flowers.

The spiraea is happy in most soils, but in hot, dry conditions there may be some unsightly browning of the leaf edges.

6.7 Juniperus, Stachys & Salvia

Juniperus communis 'Depressa Aurea'

(juniper)
sun/shade ○ **type of plant** hardy conifer
zonal range 3-7 (C-CT)
height 30-45cm (12-18in)
special characteristics evergreen, aromatic, yellow foliage, autumn/winter foliage

Stachys byzantina 'Silver Carpet'

(syn *S. lanata* 'Silver Carpet', *S. olympica* 'Silver Carpet')
(lamb's tongue, lamb's ear, lamb's lug)
sun/shade ○ **type of plant** hardy perennial
zonal range 4-9 (C-WT)
height 10-15cm (4-6in)
special characteristics evergreen, silver foliage

Salvia officinalis 'Icterina'

(syn *S. o.* 'Variegata')
(golden sage)
sun/shade ○ **type of plant** slightly tender shrub/perennial (herb)
zonal range 7-9 (CT-WT)
height 60cm (2ft)
special characteristics semi-evergreen, aromatic, variegated foliage

The three components of this combination differ considerably in the size, outline and texture of their leaves, yet the linking of colours and the balancing of plant shapes has been so careful that the result is outstandingly successful.

Flowers play a virtually negligible role here, but most gardeners would feel that there is enough variety without them. In mild areas all three plants are evergreen and therefore this combination looks good throughout the year. In colder districts the sage and, to a lesser extent, the lamb's tongue may appear rather weary by the end of winter.

Precisely because it is the least colourful plant and the one with the largest, boldest foliage, the lamb's tongue acts as an important unifying and stabilizing element in this composition. The leaves of this non-flowering form of *Stachys byzantina* have the usual silvery fur but, compared to the typical species, they are broader and longer-stemmed and make a denser carpet of growth. Against this calm grey, the tiny, bright yellow leaves and downward curving branches of the juniper stand out strikingly. The plants are illustrated here in midsummer. As the season progresses, the juniper's foliage will become more golden until, with the onset of cold weather, it turns a rich orange-bronze. In time, this slow-growing conifer's prickly,

resinous needles and overlapping branches will spread densely up to 3m (10ft) wide.

Both the grey of the lamb's tongue and the yellow of the juniper are echoed in the subtly variegated leaves of the sage. The golden sage rarely flowers, but its leaves are as pungently scented as those of the typical species. The plant makes a mound of foliage and is neat and dense if it is given a light clipping each spring. This treatment, which is so beneficial to the appearance of the foliage, also removes any flowering shoots that may have formed.

Light, well-drained soils, including alkaline ones, suit all these plants, and all three do well in hot, dry conditions.

6.8 Origanum & Ajuga

Origanum vulgare 'Aureum'

(golden marjoram)
sun/shade ○
type of plant hardy perennial (herb)
zonal range 4-8 (C-WT)
height 23cm (9in)
special characteristics evergreen/semi-evergreen, aromatic, yellow foliage

Ajuga reptans 'Atropurpurea'

(bugle)
sun/shade ○ ◑
type of plant hardy perennial
zonal range 3-9 (C-WT)
flowering time late spring to early summer
flower colour deep blue
height 15-20cm (6-8in)
special characteristics evergreen/semi-evergreen, purple foliage

The cheerful colouring and the tight, whorled arrangement of the foliage on this yellow-leaved variety of marjoram make it a flattering companion for many plants. It is also very easy to grow in any well-drained soil that does not dry out completely. Planted with the glossy and relatively large leaves of a purple-leaved bugle, its bright colour and its neat, dense habit of growth are both shown to advantage.

The bugle is another easily grown plant. It can be fairly vigorous, especially in moist soils. Its foliage is most richly coloured in sunshine. Here, as midsummer approaches, its blue flowers are fading but they, like the plant's purple leaves, have the effect of intensifying the yellowness of the marjoram's foliage. At the same time, the dark carpet of leaves is set off nicely by the comparative lightness of the marjoram's foliage. Even when the marjoram's leaves become less yellow and more khaki-coloured later in summer, this is a successful combination of differing textures and colours.

The leaves of the marjoram have a warm, peppery scent when bruised and they are useful in cooking. In this yellow-leaved form, marjoram does not bloom very freely and the little flowers are not particularly attractive.

6.9 Colchicum & Thymus

Colchicum speciosum
(naked ladies)
sun/shade ○ ◑
type of plant hardy corm
zonal range 6-10 (C-WT)
flowering time early autumn
flower colour variable shades of purple, pink-purple, pink-lilac
height 15-20cm (6-8in); spring leaves 30-40cm (12-15in)

Thymus × citriodorus 'Bertram Anderson'
(syn *T.* 'Anderson's Gold', *T.* 'E. B. Anderson')
(lemon-scented thyme)
sun/shade ○
type of plant hardy shrub (herb)
zonal range 6-8 (C-WT)
height 8-10cm (3-4in)
special characteristics evergreen, aromatic, yellow foliage

*C*olchicum speciosum is a vigorous plant and well-suited to being naturalized in grass, though when it is grown in a border the shapeliness of its large, goblet-like flowers can more easily be appreciated. However, since the leaves of this plant appear in winter or spring and are over before its flowers are produced on long, bare tubes, the flowers all too often collapse during wet and windy autumn weather. A plant like the yellowish-leaved thyme shown here not only flatters the colour and the smooth shape of the colchicum's flowers but, importantly, gives them some support and thereby extends the period at which they look their best.

For the thyme to grow as a dense and effective prop, however, it must have full sun and a well-drained soil. It can be further encouraged to grow neatly by being cut back in spring. There are usually only a very few pale, mauvish flowers. The citrus-scented leaves are most brightly coloured in really sunny positions (here the foliage is shaded to some extent by taller plants nearby).

The colchicum will grow in partial shade but it tends to flower best in an open position. It too likes a well-drained soil. Some gardeners find its large, broad-bladed, shiny leaves difficult to cope with; other gardeners find them bold and handsome; slugs usually find them irresistible.

6.10 Humulus & Ligustrum

Humulus lupulus 'Aureus'
(golden hop)
sun/shade ○ ◑
type of plant hardy perennial climber
zonal range 5-9 (C-WT)
height 4.5m (15ft)
special characteristics yellow-green foliage

Ligustrum ovalifolium 'Aureum'
(golden privet)
sun/shade ○ ◑
type of plant hardy shrub
zonal range 6-11 (C-ST)
flowering time midsummer
flower colour white
height 2.7-3.6m (9-12ft)
special characteristics evergreen/semi-evergreen, yellow foliage/variegated foliage

*L*eft to its own devices, the familiar and often despised golden privet forms a shapely, rather upright and open shrub. With the large, lime-yellow leaves of the golden hop threading through it, it is transformed into a stylish and thoroughly desirable horticultural object. Since the hop is vigorous and has spreading roots, it is probably best to plant it so that it can twine over a small group or an informal hedge of the privet. Even though the hop dies down each year, it would probably obscure too much of a single privet's foliage for the shrub to grow well.

Golden privet is very tolerant of a wide range of soil types and it will thrive in sun, partial shade or even full shade. In hot climates it is a prolific self-seeder. The sunnier the position, the brighter its foliage will be; in full shade the leaves are often a uniform yellow-green. The hop will colour well in sun or partial shade but a little shade will produce a good colour and prevent possible scorching of the leaves. By late summer the foliage colour is green. Ideally this climber should be given a fertile soil. It is not at its best in cold or draughty positions.

The golden-leaved form of hop produces a few, greenish flowers in summer; the privet flowers have a heavy scent which many people dislike. A more floriferous companion for golden privet would be *Clematis alpina* (see 15.19) or one of its forms.

6.11 Philadelphus & Cassinia

Philadelphus coronarius 'Aureus'
(mock orange)
sun/shade ◐
type of plant hardy shrub
zonal range 5-8 (C-WT)
flowering time early to mid-summer
flower colour creamy white
height 1.5-2.1m (5-7ft)
special characteristics yellow-green foliage, fragrant flowers

Cassinia leptophylla ssp. *fulvida*
(golden heather)
sun/shade ○
type of plant slightly tender shrub
zonal range 9-10 (WT)
flowering time midsummer
flower colour off white
height 90-150cm (3-5ft)
special characteristics evergreen, yellow-green/green foliage

This is a most attractive combination of two differently textured sets of leaves which share a lovely, acid yellow-green colouring. Though the buds and stems of the cassinia are lime-yellow, the upper leaf surfaces of this shrub are a darker, olive-khaki green. This green introduces a contrasting depth of tone to the partnership. Habit of growth provides another contrast: the cassinia has a rather open structure of upright branches, while the philadelphus, though quite upright, too, is denser and twiggier.

Some compromise has to be made in order to meet the different light requirements of these two shrubs. The sort of warm but slightly shaded position needed is perhaps most easily found in gardens in mild areas. Both these plants like well-drained soils, but very dry conditions are not suitable; without a reasonable supply of moisture the philadelphus foliage would be rather sparse and, if the plant was positioned in full sun, the leaves would be likely to lose their colouring quite quickly and to brown at the edges. The flowers of this shrub have a charming simplicity. They emit a full, slightly spicy and very sweet scent. The cassinia produces tiny flowers in clusters.

6.12 Sambucus, Ligularia & Hosta

Sambucus racemosa 'Plumosa Aurea'
(elder)
sun/shade ○ ◐ **type of plant** hardy shrub
zonal range 4-7 (C-CT) **flowering time** mid-spring **flower colour** yellowish white
height 1.5-2.1m (5-7ft)
special characteristics yellow foliage, bronze when young, fruit, suitable for damp soils

Ligularia przewalskii
(syn *Senecio przewalskii*)
sun/shade ○ ◐ **type of plant** hardy perennial
zonal range 4-8 (C-WT) **flowering time** mid- to late summer
flower colour yellow **height** 1.2-1.8m (4-6ft)
special characteristics decorative green foliage, suitable for damp soils

Hosta fortunei var. *aureomarginata*
(syn *H.* 'Obscura Marginata', *H.* 'Yellow Edge')
(plantain lily)
sun/shade ○ ◐ **type of plant** hardy perennial
zonal range 3-9 (C-WT) **flowering time** mid-summer **flower colour** violet **height** 90cm (3ft)
special characteristics variegated foliage, suitable for damp soils

The various layers in this combination are all linked and at the same time contrasting. All three plants have yellow features in common. The elder's jagged leaves are an attractive greenish yellow particularly in cool, partially shaded sites, and the elegantly narrow, irregular edging of the hosta's leaves is a green-yellow colour which is notably long-lasting. In this photograph the ligularia's striking black stems are still covered in buds, but these will soon open into numerous yellow flowers.

In contrast, the toothed foliage of the ligularia is a distinctly different, dark ingredient which sharpens the elder's yellowness and helps to delineate the hosta's variegation. Another contrasting element is the smooth shape of the hosta's foliage, which emphasizes the pointed irregularity of the other two plants' leaves.

The hosta produces numerous spires of trumpet-shaped blooms that are held well clear of the plant's solid clumps of foliage. The elder flowers, too, but many gardeners prefer to cut back this shrub each year to ensure that plenty of foliage is produced, even though this means sacrificing the flowers and the subsequent red berries. Treated in this way, the elder slowly forms a rounded mound of growth.

All three plants enjoy moist or damp growing conditions, and the hosta and the elder in particular appreciate some shade. However, as long as there is constant moisture, all these plants will also grow well in sun. However, in dry, sunny positions the elder's leaves are a harsher colour and some scorching of the leaf edges may occur. Hot, dry positions are not suitable.

6.13 Tolmiea & Lonicera

Tolmiea menziesii 'Taff's Gold'
(piggyback plant)
sun/shade ◐
type of plant hardy perennial
zonal range 6-9 (CT-WT)
flowering time late spring to early summer
flower colour coppery brown
height 20cm (8in) (leaves)
special characteristics semi-evergreen, yellow/yellow-variegated foliage

Lonicera nitida 'Baggesen's Gold'
(shrubby honeysuckle)
sun/shade ○ ◐
type of plant hardy shrub
zonal range 7-9 (CT-WT)
height 1.2-1.8m (4-6ft)
special characteristics evergreen, yellow foliage

The two plants shown here are tolerant of quite a wide range of growing conditions. The tolmiea, in particular, is a fairly vigorous and generally unfussy plant. However, this cheerful, yellow-leaved combination will be at its best in not too sunny a position and in a well-drained soil that remains reasonably moist. The sunnier the site, the yellower the foliage of both the tolmiea and the lonicera will be. With some sun, the tolmiea produces a high proportion of pale yellow, faintly mottled leaves; in shadier positions, the whole effect is greener and more obviously variegated (see 9.35).

The lonicera's flowers are inconspicuous and the tolmiea's thin wands of brown flowers – visible here – have a rather subdued charm. But the excellent contrasts in leaf size and shape, and the way the tolmiea spreads and roots into a weed-proof carpet beneath the irregular, densely-leaved branches of the lonicera are all attractive. This pairing of two pretty yellows looks good from spring until the coldest months.

For floral colour to add to this combination, see 6.16.

6.14 Spiraea & Primula

Spiraea japonica 'Goldflame'
sun/shade ○ ◐
type of plant hardy shrub
zonal range 4-9 (C-WT)
flowering time early to mid-summer
flower colour crimson-pink
height 75-90cm (2½-3ft)
special characteristics yellow foliage, orange when young

Primula including Gold Laced Group
(polyanthus)
sun/shade ○ ◐
type of plant hardy perennial
zonal range 6-8 (C-WT)
flowering time mid- to late spring
flower colour varied – often red + yellow
height 10-15cm (4-6in)

Primulas of many sorts are among the most cheerful of spring flowers and the lovely markings of the Gold Laced Group make them especially attractive. Here they are growing in dappled shade with one of the yellow-leaved forms of *Spiraea japonica*, so that the whole picture gleams gently. Both these plants can be grown in sunnier positions, but then the polyanthus' need for moisture as well as good drainage is particularly important.

The spiraea will grow in a wide variety of soils. Its dense, slightly arching branches are most strongly coloured before flowering time and in sunny sites. In full sun, yellow-leaved spiraeas can make excellent, bright backgrounds for hot-coloured tulips. However, some gardeners find that the softer, greener foliage colour produced in some shade is more appealing, especially when the insistent pink of the flowers arrives. Removing the flowers in bud not only prevents a combination of yellow and strong pink but also keeps the plant neat and tidy.

Newer yellow-leaved forms of *Spiraea japonica*, such as 'Gold Mound', have a brighter, longer-lasting foliage colour than 'Goldflame'. In all forms the early growths are coppery or red, and in some autumns orangey tones can return before the leaves fall.

6.15 Lysimachia & Euonymus

Lysimachia nummularia 'Aurea'

(creeping Jenny)
sun/shade ○ ◖
type of plant hardy perennial
zonal range 3-8 (C-WT)
flowering time early to mid-summer
flower colour bright yellow
height 2.5-5cm (1-2in)
special characteristics evergreen, yellow foliage, suitable for damp soils

Euonymus fortunei 'Emerald Gaiety'

sun/shade ○ ◖
type of plant hardy shrub/climber
zonal range 5-9 (C-WT)
height 60-90cm (2-3ft) as a shrub
special characteristics evergreen, variegated foliage

This combination looks good both when the euonymus is very young and low-growing, as here, and later when it takes on its mature, bushy and more upright shape. Eventually, the leaves of the creeping Jenny will form a pool of cheerful yellow around the euonymus. In size and shape of leaf the two plants are very similar, preventing the planting as a whole from being too fussy.

The euonymus is fairly slow-growing. Its foliage is an especially smart, crisp association of white and grey-green; in the colder months the leaves can become tinged with pink.

Both plants will grow in sun or partial shade but, especially in sunnier positions, the creeping Jenny must be kept moist. In the damp, partial shade it prefers, this vigorous plant will produce long trailing stems. In some sun, its growth will be denser and it will form a mat of weed-suppressing stems. In this yellow-leaved form, creeping Jenny is not very free-flowering.

Like many of the variegated euonymuses, 'Emerald Gaiety' mixes flatteringly with a wide range of plants. The cool shades of its leaves are especially good with hotter colours (see 3.31). This plant occasionally produces climbing shoots – with rather longer, more oval leaves – which will grow up to 3m (10ft) high (see 2.27).

6.16 Tolmiea & Viola

Tolmiea menziesii 'Taff's Gold'

(piggyback plant)
sun/shade ◖
type of plant hardy perennial
zonal range 6-9 (C-WT)
flowering time late spring to early summer
flower colour coppery brown
height 20cm (8in) (leaves)
special characteristics semi-evergreen, yellow/yellow-variegated foliage

Viola 'Violacea'

(violet)
sun/shade ○ ◖
type of plant hardy perennial
zonal range 5-8 (C-CT)
flowering time mainly late spring to midsummer
flower colour rich mauve
height 15-23cm (6-9in)
special characteristics evergreen

Tolmiea menziesii 'Taff's Gold' grows best in cool, partially shaded sites, but it will also perform well in some sun. In sunnier positions, as here, an overall creamy yellowness tends to predominate. In shadier sites, the leaves are more distinctly mottled and freckled in green and yellow. The plant is fairly vigorous, but easily uprooted, and the shapely foliage makes good ground cover.

Viola 'Violacea' also produces weed-suppressing clumps of leaves from which longer, lazier growths emerge to entwine attractively with other plants. A similarly coloured but more readily available violet is *V.* 'Gustav Wermig'. However, any of the excellent blue, purple or even white forms of *Viola cornuta* would look well in this combination.

All these violets need a fertile, moist soil. They can be encouraged to produce a second crop of flowers if the plants are cut back hard at the end of summer. The tolmiea's long, thin spires of brown flowers are not particularly decorative.

For an earlier-flowering combination which includes *Tolmiea menziesii* 'Taff's Gold', see 9.35.

6.17 Philadelphus & Hosta

Philadelphus coronarius '**Aureus**'

(mock orange)
sun/shade ◐
type of plant hardy shrub
zonal range 5-8 (C-WT)
flowering time early to mid-summer
flower colour creamy white
height 1.5-2.1m (5-7ft)
special characteristics yellow-green foliage, fragrant flowers

Hosta sieboldiana var. *elegans*

(plantain lily)
sun/shade ◐
type of plant hardy perennial
zonal range 3-9 (C-WT)
flowering time early to mid-summer
flower colour palest lilac
height 75-90cm (2½-3ft)
special characteristics blue-grey foliage, suitable for damp soils

Although the ingredients of this combination and the following one seem so similar, the effect is quite different. In each there are good contrasts in leaf shape and general habit of growth, but here the contrast is heightened, first by the largeness of the hosta's wonderful puckered and cupped leaves and secondly by the unusually intense blue-grey of this foliage. Here, in early summer, the foliage has yet to extend fully. In ideal conditions of some shade and a damp, rich soil, individual leaves can be well over 30cm (12in) wide. Even in ordinarily moisture-retentive soil this plant can form a large, dense clump. The philadelphus' appearance is less solid, but it is quite thickly twiggy.

For both these plants, some shade and moisture will give the best, longest-lasting leaf colour. The philadelphus will be a brighter yellow for a shorter time in full sun and drier soil, but then its relatively thin-textured leaves may become scorched.

As added attractions, the philadelphus' simple, single flowers are very sweetly scented, and the hosta produces flowers of a pleasing solidity and paleness. In autumn, the hosta's foliage briefly turns a good, rich yellow. The seedheads are also attractive.

For a midwinter combination featuring blue-grey leaves with yellow foliage, see 6.1.

6.18 Philadelphus & Hosta

Philadelphus coronarius '**Aureus**'

(mock orange)
sun/shade ◐
type of plant hardy shrub
zonal range 5-8 (C-WT)
flowering time early to mid-summer
flower colour creamy white
height 1.5-2.1m (5-7ft)
special characteristics yellow-green foliage, fragrant flowers

Hosta undulata var. *albomarginata*

(syn *H.* 'Thomas Hogg')
(plantain lily)
sun/shade ◐
type of plant hardy perennial
zonal range 3-9 (C-WT)
flowering time early to mid-summer
flower colour pale lilac
height 60-90cm (2-3ft)
special characteristics variegated foliage, suitable for damp soils

Dappled shade and some moisture will produce the best specimens of these two plants. These conditions will also ensure that, in both cases, the foliage remains fresh and attractive for many months. The leaves of the philadelphus will keep their lime-yellow colour for longest – usually throughout the summer – in some shade. In sun, the foliage of this fairly dense and twiggy shrub will be a much more insistent yellow and it will fade to an ordinary green more quickly; there may be some browning of the leaf edges, too. In full shade the foliage will always be greener and there will be no opportunity for sunlight to filter through the leaves as it does so attractively here. Indeed, the gentle, golden glow cast by the philadelphus has transformed the markings on this hosta from white into soft greeny yellow.

Although the leaves of both these plants are so appealing, this is by no means a foliage-only combination. Not only are the cup-shaped flowers of the philadelphus pretty and simple, but they are also very sweetly scented and the plant flowers well in shade. The hosta's slightly later spires of little flared bells are held well clear of the plant's foliage. In fertile soils, and especially in those that are always moist or damp, the hosta will form great mounds of ground-covering leaves.

6.19 Ligularia & Hosta

Ligularia dentata 'Desdemona'
(syn *L. clivorum* 'Desdemona')
sun/shade ○ ◐
type of plant hardy perennial
zonal range 4-8 (C-WT)
flowering time mid- to late summer
flower colour yellow-orange
height 1.2m (4ft)
special characteristics purple foliage, suitable for damp soils

Hosta fortunei var. albopicta f. aurea
(syn *H. f. aurea*)
(plantain lily)
sun/shade ◐
type of plant hardy perennial
zonal range 3-9 (C-WT)
flowering time midsummer
flower colour lilac
height 45-60cm (1½-2ft)
special characteristics yellow young foliage, suitable for damp soils

Not only is there a dramatic contrast in the foliage colour of these plants but the two leaf shapes are quite different as well. The overall effect of the combination is quite calm, however, and this is due mainly to the fact that both leaf shapes are bold and fairly simple. The dusky green, veined foliage of the ligularia is almost circular and this shape is a tranquil one. The hosta's ribbed, elegantly pointed leaves overlap one another in a dense mound which is, in essence, a bold block of delicate colour.

During midsummer the hosta's leaves slowly change to a light green. In midsummer, too, the great, purple-tinged, branching flower stems of the ligularia lengthen and become topped with big, brazen daisies. These tend to overshadow the hosta's much more modest spires of funnel-shaped flowers.

The planting conditions for this combination are mainly dictated by the hosta. The leaves of this plant are delicate in texture, and in dry conditions and sunny sites they can easily become browned at the edges. Cool shade and a moist, fertile soil ensure that the whole plant looks good. The clump-forming ligularia also appreciates moisture and fertile conditions, where its leaves can be up to 45cm (18in) wide.

6.20 Lamium & Viola

Lamium maculatum 'Aureum'
(spotted dead nettle)
sun/shade ◐
type of plant hardy perennial
zonal range 4-8 (C-WT)
flowering time mid-spring to early summer
flower colour mauve-pink
height 8-10cm (3-4in)
special characteristics evergreen/semi-evergreen, yellow/variegated foliage

Viola 'Molly Sanderson'
(violet)
sun/shade ○ ◐
type of plant hardy perennial
zonal range 5-7 (C-CT)
flowering time late spring to late summer
flower colour nearly black + yellow
height 10-15cm (4-6in)

Very dark flowers such as those of *V.* 'Molly Sanderson' have a special appeal but they can easily get lost amongst green foliage. However, if they are combined with a lighter and brighter companion their subtle darkness becomes more conspicuous. Not only does the light, acid yellow of this lamium's foliage emphasize the dark flowers of the viola, it also picks up the tiny yellow eye in each viola flower. Strictly speaking, the lamium, with its white central stripe on each leaf, has variegated foliage. However, the overall effect is one of sharp yellow.

Both plants grow well in moisture-retentive soil and partial shade. In these conditions, the lamium leaves will remain unscorched and they will form a dense, non-invasive carpet of growth. The leaves are most brightly coloured in spring and summer. The viola is perennial only in the cooler parts of countries in the Southern hemisphere. The leaves of this plant form a loose mat of foliage.

For other combinations featuring yellow or yellow-green foliage, see:
COOL-COLOURED FLOWERS 1.39   HOT-COLOURED FLOWERS 3.10, 3.19, 3.22   PURPLE FOLIAGE 4.1, 4.5, 4.14, 4.17   YELLOW FLOWERS 5.5, 5.9, 5.12, 5.14, 5.16, 5.19   GREEN FLOWERS 7.1, 7.4, 7.9,   VARIEGATED FOLIAGE 9.1, 9.13, 9.18, 9.19, 9.35   AUTUMN FOLIAGE 10.1   AROMATIC FOLIAGE 11.15, 11.17, 11.19   FRUIT 12.10   FRAGRANT FLOWERS 13.19, 13.20   CLIMBING PLANTS 15.2   DAMP AND WET SOILS 16.5, 16.6   GRASSES AND FERNS 17.5, 17.9, 17.12, 17.13, 17.18

7 Green Flowers

Flower arrangers love green flowers because the subtle shades of these blooms allow them to blend beautifully with a very wide range of other colours in a way that more strident hues cannot. Outdoors and at a distance in the garden, green flowers may lack the visual impact they have at closer quarters in indoor arrangements. With careful positioning, however, their unusual colouring and their ability to create sophisticated harmonies with other plants can be made conspicuous.

In any case, not all green flowers are unobtrusive. One of the most useful plants for creating attractive combinations is *Alchemilla mollis*. Though its flower colour is a yellowish-green, the acidity of this colouring and the generous size of the foamy flowerheads ensure that the flowers are eye-catching even from some distance. Still more striking are the very large, cylindrical flowerheads of *Euphorbia characias wulfenii* and its near relations (see, for example, 7.5). Even the gentle, silvery green of the midwinter catkins of *Garrya elliptica* looks striking when a mass of these long, slender flowers are seen dangling among the shrub's foliage.

In all-green plantings in which foliage is the principal ingredient, green flowers add extra, distinctly different textures and forms without disrupting the elegant tranquillity of a monochrome composition. As a bonus, several green-flowered plants – including *Alchemilla mollis* and some hellebores, such as *Helleborus foetidus* and *H. argutifolius* – can also contribute attractive green foliage to these and other planting schemes.

COOL TONES

The various effects produced when green flowers are combined with other colours depend to some extent on how soft or sharp the shade of green is. Very often, however, the effect is quiet and fairly low-key. The classic pairing of purple and yellow becomes softer and more delicate when green rather than yellow flowers are used (compare, for instance, the combination in 7.2 with that in 4.2). In the same way, partnerships of yellow and pure mid-blue or of yellow and brilliant red become less boisterous when green is used instead of yellow. (For combinations in which green flowers appear with bright blue flowers and with glowing red leaves, see 7.15 and 4.23, respectively.) Green flowers have a similar calming effect on orange flowers or orange-tinted leaves. However, they should not be regarded simply as coolers and calmers of vibrant colours. While they do indeed make combinations that include intense or harsh colours seem softer, they also have the ability to point up the clarity and freshness of many pure colours.

With leaves which are themselves as gently and subtly coloured as most green flowers, particularly harmonious effects can be produced. For instance, the yellow-green flowers of *Alchemilla mollis* can echo most agreeably both the green and the yellow parts of yellow-variegated leaves (see 9.23). Like green flowers, grey foliage often acts as a softener of contrasts and a creator of harmonies in gardens. When grey leaves and green flowers are combined, the green flowers add interesting texture and an additional neutral colour to the partnership without upsetting the subtle, low-key balance of the composition. Touches of white, another neutral colour, either from flowers or from variegated leaves, will usually add sparkle to green flowers. The general impression will be quite sharp and clean, especially if the green flowers are of a rather citrus colour.

The range of flowers that are both decorative and green is not large. Apart from the plants shown in this section, the main sources of green floral colour are some bulbs and tubers. Viridiflora tulips like 'Spring Green' have conspicuous green markings on their petals. There are also the green-marked flowers of irises such as 'Green Spot', the flamboyant, top-knotted green spires of the pineapple plant (*Eucomis bicolor*) and the much more modest green flowers of some fritillaries, including *Fritillaria acmopetala*.

EXTENDING THE LIMITS

The range of green flowers can be extended if some immature flowers are admitted to the category. Certain sedums are striking even when their large flowerheads are still pale green (see 1.6), and the viburnum in 17.17 looks especially fresh in its pale green state. In addition, the flowering panicles of many grasses are almost as attractive when they are green as when they ripen into more mellow colours. Later in the gardening year, there are the fading blooms of some varieties of hydrangea, such as *H. macrophylla* 'Madame Emile Mouillère', which become distinctly green-tinged during autumn.

Finally, a certain amount of manipulation of our perception of flower colour can be employed to make flowers that are really more yellow than green appear distinctly green. The principal method of emphasizing green tones in flowers is to give them a background either of more or less pure yellow or of warm, orange-tinged yellow. Against a contrastingly warm background of this sort, the cooler green tones of greenish yellows will predominate.

7.1 Garrya & Chamaecyparis

Garrya elliptica

sun/shade ○ ◐
type of plant slightly tender shrub
zonal range 9-10 (CT-WT)
flowering time late autumn to late winter
flower colour silvery green
height 2.4-4.5m (8-15ft)
special characteristics evergreen

Chamaecyparis lawsoniana 'Stewartii'

(Lawson cypress)
sun/shade ○
type of plant hardy conifer
zonal range 6-7 (CT-WT)
height 9-12m (30-40ft)
special characteristics evergreen, yellow foliage

In midwinter *Garrya elliptica* drips with pale green tassels (see 14.5). Here, in mid-autumn, they are already making their mark. On male plants these tassels may be about 23cm (9in) long; female flowers are shorter, but ripen into purplish berries. Though many gardeners are attracted by the unusual colour of these winter catkins, the rather leaden leaf colour of this fast-growing plant is often seen as a drawback. Here the foliage has been most successfully enlivened by layers of feathery yellow foliage. Indeed, the particular conifer shown here is even more richly coloured in spring and summer when, apart from the tattered remains of its catkins, the garrya is simply a mass of dark greenery.

The conifer emphasizes the good points of the garrya's foliage, its bold fans of matt yellow pointing up the soft gleam and the gently undulating margins of these smooth, dark leaves. At the same time, the garrya acts as a suitably sedate counterpoint to the flamboyant conifer. The outlines of the two plants combine pleasingly, too: the garrya is rather upright but dense and bushy, whereas the conifer forms a distinct cone of growth.

Each of these plants likes a well-drained soil that is also moisture-retentive. Cold or drying winds can burn the leaves of the garrya and the plant should therefore be given a sheltered position.

7.2 Cotinus & Alchemilla

Cotinus coggygria 'Royal Purple'

(smoke tree, Venetian sumach)
sun/shade ○
type of plant hardy shrub/tree
zonal range 5-9 (CT-WT)
fruiting time mid- to late summer
fruit colour pink purple
height 2.4-3m (8-10ft)
special characteristics purple foliage, autumn foliage, fruit

Alchemilla mollis

(lady's mantle)
sun/shade ○ ◐
type of plant hardy perennial
zonal range 4-8 (C-WT)
flowering time early to mid-summer
flower colour yellow-green
height 45cm (18in)
special characteristics decorative green foliage, suitable for damp soils

It seems sometimes as if there is hardly a plant that is not enhanced by the pretty scalloped leaves and the acid green flowers of *Alchemilla mollis*. However, a particularly dramatic effect is produced when the alchemilla's tangy pastels are combined with rich, dark foliage.

Along with the colour contrast in the partnership illustrated here, there are several attractive differences in texture. The rounded, red-purple leaves of the cotinus feel like smooth silk, whereas the alchemilla's lime-green foliage is softly hairy (and especially lovely after rain; see 1.32).

A gentle haziness is added to the combination by the alchemilla's froth of little flowers and by the cotinus's clouds of fruiting heads. These fruits ripen from the plant's tiny, early summer flowers. Some gardeners like to prune the cotinus to get plenty of large-leaved foliage, but then few, if any, flowers – and, therefore, fruits – appear. This treatment also tends to make the plant more upright and less rounded in its habit of growth.

The cotinus is late into leaf. In mid-autumn its leaves start to turn red (see 10.5). The colour is especially vivid on light, poor soils, but in any case the plant needs good drainage. The alchemilla will grow in almost any soil and is a prolific self-seeder.

7.3 Acer & Euphorbia

Acer negundo 'Elegans'
(syn A. n. 'Elegantissimum')
(box elder)
sun/shade ○ ◐
type of plant hardy shrub/tree
zonal range 3-9 (C-WT)
height 1.5-2.4m (5-8ft) when pruned and grown as a shrub; 4.5-6m (15-20ft) as a tree
special characteristics variegated foliage

Euphorbia characias ssp. characias 'Humpty Dumpty'
(spurge)
sun/shade ○
type of plant slightly tender/hardy shrub/perennial
zonal range 7-10 (C-ST)
flowering time mid-spring to early summer
flower colour yellow-green
height 60-75cm (2-2½ft)
special characteristics evergreen, blue-green foliage

For gardeners who like the green flowers and the bottle-brushes of foliage produced by *Euphorbia characias* and its relations but who find these plants too large for their purpose, there is the option of the smaller variety shown here. As with all euphorbias of this type, the rather restrained colouring enables gentle harmonies to be created. At the same time, however, the striking, upright shapes of the cylindrical flowerheads and the boldly arranged glaucous foliage mean that this euphorbia will never simply merge with surrounding plants.

In the combination illustrated here, the apple-green flower colour of *E. c. c.* 'Humpty Dumpty' is a calm counterpoint to the dappled, almost flickering effect produced by the irregular yellow margins of the accompanying acer's leaves. The boldness of the euphorbia's erect clump of growth also steadies the acer's busy, bowl-shaped mass of foliage – which is, contrastingly, somewhat pendent.

This euphorbia has a long flowering season; it is interesting even when it consists of leaves alone. Delicate touches of extra colour are added when the new leaves of the acer emerge pink-tinged.

Although *Acer negundo* will grow in almost any site, this variegated form merits a position that is not too dry or windy. In any case, the euphorbia needs shelter; it also requires good drainage.

7.4 Chamaecyparis & Euphorbia

Chamaecyparis pisifera 'Golden Mop'
(Sawara cypress)
sun/shade ○
type of plant hardy conifer
zonal range 5-8 (C-CT)
height 90-150cm (3-5ft)
special characteristics evergreen, yellow foliage

Euphorbia amygdaloides 'Purpurea'
(syn E. a. 'Rubra')
(spurge)
sun/shade ○ ◐
type of plant hardy perennial
zonal range 7-9 (C-WT)
flowering time mid-spring to early summer
flower colour yellow-green
height 45-60cm (1½-2ft)
special characteristics evergreen, purple foliage

There are relatively few green-flowered plants that have coloured foliage (though see the tellima in 7.14). Here, in mid-spring, *Euphorbia amygdaloides* 'Purpurea' is a particularly striking mixture of bright, yellow-green flowers and beetroot-maroon leaves and stems. By the middle of summer, the foliage colour will have softened to shady red-purples and dark greens and the long-lasting flowers will be less acidic in tone (see 4.25). The plant will, however, still be very attractive.

In the combination shown here, the erect stems and the dark, distinctly whorled foliage of this euphorbia have been dramatically emphasized by a curtain of pendent, yellow, thread-like foliage. Linking the two plants, which differ so much in habit of growth and in the texture, form and colour of their leaves, are the yellowish-green flowers of the euphorbia.

Chamaecyparis pisifera 'Golden Mop' is similar to *C. p.* 'Filifera Aurea' (see 6.1), though its foliage is a slightly brighter yellow and its wide cone of weeping growth tends to be much smaller. It is very slow-growing. In contrast, the euphorbia may spread quite rapidly, particularly in rich, moist soils. Both plants like well-drained soils but they will not do well in dry conditions. A lack of moisture makes it likely that the euphorbia will suffer from mildew.

7.5 Euphorbia & Bergenia

Euphorbia characias ssp. *wulfenii* × *E. characias* seedling
(spurge)
sun/shade ○
type of plant slightly tender/hardy shrub/perennial
zonal range 7-10 (WT-ST)
flowering time mid-spring to early summer
flower colour yellow-green
height 90-120cm (3-4ft)
special characteristics evergreen, blue-green foliage

Bergenia hybrid
sun/shade ○ ◖
type of plant hardy perennial
zonal range 3-8 (C-ST)
flowering time mid- to late spring
flower colour pink
height 30-45cm (12-18in)
special characteristics evergreen, decorative green foliage

Any idea that all green flowers are modest and unassuming is soon dispelled by seeing the great, thickset, cylindrical heads of *E. characias* and its forms. These plants tend to interbreed (the specimen shown here is a hybrid). They all have bold, upright bottle-brushes of glaucous foliage (see 6.1).

All this drama needs a steadying influence of some sort and here the calm, rounded shapes of leathery bergenia leaves anchor – and at the same time emphasize – the exuberant assertiveness of the euphorbia.

Other forms of bergenia with leaves of approximately the same size as those of the specimen shown here include 'Abendglut' and 'Morgenröte'. These plants have purplish-crimson and deep pink flowers respectively.

Good drainage is essential for *E. characias* and its relations and shelter from cold winds is also important. In general, bergenias are tough, easily grown plants that prosper in most soils.

The flowerheads of these euphorbias are notably long-lasting, and indeed the plants are decorative even in bud. For a plant combination in which an unusually small variety of *E. characias characias* has been used, see 7.3.

7.6 Astrantia & Erigeron

Astrantia major ssp. *involucrata* 'Shaggy' seedling
(syn *A. m.* ssp. *i.* 'Margery Fish' seedling)
(masterwort)
sun/shade ○ ◖
type of plant hardy perennial
zonal range 4-8 (C-WT)
flowering time early to late summer
flower colour white + green
height 75cm (2½ft)

Erigeron 'Rosa Juwel'
(syn *E.* 'Pink Jewel')
(fleabane)
sun/shade ○
type of plant hardy perennial
zonal range 5-8 (C-WT)
flowering time early to late summer
flower colour bright, light pink
height 60cm (2ft)

Many astrantias have flowers of modest size and colouring, but the form shown here produces large blooms with bracts that are longer than normal and tipped with bright green. Equipped in this way, *A. m. i.* 'Shaggy' and its offspring can act as foils to stronger colours without ever becoming completely dominated by them. This astrantia self-seeds generously, but the seedlings are variable. Though the specimen shown here has flowers nearly 5cm (2in) wide, its green-tipped bracts are not as long as those of the best forms.

The papery texture of the astrantia's strong-stemmed flowers enables them to remain decorative over a long period, and since the erigeron is another plant with a long flowering season this is a combination that looks good for a substantial part of the summer. As well as a successful juxtaposition of cool green-and-white and strong, sweet pink, this partnership also features an interesting contrast in flower texture. The crispness of the astrantia's flowers looks – and feels – quite different from the fluffiness of the erigeron's semi-double daisies.

Both these clump-forming plants grow best in fertile, well-drained soils that retain moisture during the warmer months. The erigeron's thin leaves are rather sparsely produced, but the astrantia creates a leafy mound of deeply lobed foliage.

7.7 Salvia & Helleborus

Salvia officinalis Purpurascens Group

(purple sage)

sun/shade ○

type of plant slightly tender shrub/perennial (herb)

zonal range 7-9 (C-ST)

flowering time early to mid-summer

flower colour violet-purple

height 60-75cm (2-2½ft)

special characteristics evergreen/semi-evergreen, aromatic, purple foliage

Helleborus argutifolius

(syn *H. lividus* ssp. *corsicus*)

(Corsican hellebore)

sun/shade ○ ◐

type of plant hardy perennial

zonal range 7-9 (C-WT)

flowering time late winter to late spring

flower colour pale green

height 60cm (2ft)

special characteristics evergreen, decorative green foliage

Purple and yellow is a favourite colour combination in gardens; purple and green, though rather less dramatic, has its own attractions. The richness of tone still remains, but if the green is pale there is freshness, too. The combination used here, shown in late spring, consists of a particularly attractive pairing of smoky purple and beautiful, clean apple-green. The soft, greyish-green tones in the leaves of the sage provide an important link between the two plants.

At this point in the year the Corsican hellebore's old foliage and large heads of cup-shaped flowers are falling forwards among the veined, velvety leaves of the purple sage. Soon the new foliage will have matured into a shrubby, lax-stemmed clump of very handsome, curving leaflets (see 8.7). The sage's mound of upright stems and purple growths is in conspicuous contrast to the hellebore's more openly branched mass of deep, soft green.

A well-drained soil and a sheltered, sunny site provide the ideal conditions for this combination. The hellebore needs a soil that is reasonably moisture-retentive. The sage grows neatly if clipped, but then there are few flowers. The leaves are warmly and pungently aromatic.

Other green-flowered hellebores appear in 7.12 and 7.15.

7.8 Erysimum & Alchemilla

Erysimum 'Bowles' Mauve'

(perennial wallflower)

sun/shade ○

type of plant slightly tender perennial/shrub

zonal range 8-9 (CT-WT)

flowering time late spring to late summer

flower colour mauve

height 75cm (2½ft)

special characteristics evergreen/semi-evergreen, grey-green foliage

Alchemilla conjuncta

sun/shade ○ ◐

type of plant hardy perennial

zonal range 3-7 (C-WT)

flowering time early to late summer

flower colour acid green

height 30-40cm (12-15in)

special characteristics decorative green foliage

The smaller species of *Alchemilla* tend to get overlooked in favour of their highly popular and very versatile relation, *A. mollis*. However, there are circumstances in which a lower-growing green-flowered plant of this sort is appropriate. In this combination the neat little flowerheads of *A. conjuncta* flatter the bright wallflowers in just the same way as the flowers of *A. mollis* would, but because there is quite a marked difference in height between this little alchemilla and the wallflower, the upright stems and the dark, grey-green foliage of the latter are shown to particular advantage.

In contrast to the darkness of the wallflower's pointed leaves, the alchemilla's clump of rounded leaflets is a rather bright green. Each of these leaflets is edged with the silken, silvery hairs that cover the undersides of the foliage. This pale, narrow edging does much to endow the whole plant with its beautifully precise appearance.

Like its larger relative, *A. conjuncta* will grow well in almost any soil. It does not, however, self-seed with the same abandonment as *A. mollis*. The wallflower is a quick-growing but fairly short-lived plant with an exceptionally long flowering season. *Erysimum* 'Bowles' Mauve' needs good drainage and is hardiest, densest and most floriferous in light, rather poor soils.

123

7.9 Origanum & Ornithogalum

Origanum vulgare 'Aureum'
(golden marjoram)
sun/shade ◌
type of plant hardy perennial (herb)
zonal range 4-8 (C-WT)
height 23cm (9in)
special characteristics evergreen/semi-evergreen, aromatic, yellow foliage

Ornithogalum umbellatum
(star-of-Bethlehem)
sun/shade ◌ ◑
type of plant hardy bulb
zone 5 (CT-ST)
flowering time late spring
flower colour white + green
height 12-20cm (5-8in)

Star-of-Bethlehem wears two different costumes: on sunny days the flowerheads are a mass of glistening, white stars; on cloudy days, and in shaded places, the flowers stay neatly closed and reveal the beautiful, fresh, soft green markings on the backs of their petals. Whether open or shut, the flowers look very fetching against the tidy carpet of cheerful yellow leaves produced by this marjoram. When the combination consists of white stars and yellow leaves the whole effect is particularly bright and lively, but the quieter, gentler-looking picture created in shaded conditions has its own charm.

Star-of-Bethlehem's long, centrally white-striped leaves die back by flowering time. The plant is vigorous and increases quickly.

Any well-drained soil will suit this combination. However, if conditions are very hot and dry, the leaves of the marjoram may become scorched and unsightly. During the summer months the pungently scented foliage of this herb becomes progressively less yellow, but the whole plant continues to grow neatly and densely as a very satisfactory mass of little leaves and upright stems. This yellow-leaved form of marjoram tends to flower sparsely.

For a much larger-scale combination of green flowers and yellow foliage, see 7.1.

7.10 Aucuba & Euphorbia

Aucuba japonica 'Variegata'
(syn *A. j.* 'Maculata')
(spotted laurel)
sun/shade ◌ ◑
type of plant hardy/slightly tender shrub
zonal range 7-10 (WT-ST)
height 1.5-2.4m (5-8ft)
special characteristics evergreen, variegated foliage

Euphorbia amygdaloides var. *robbiae*
(syn *E. robbiae*)
(spurge)
sun/shade ◌ ◑
type of plant hardy perennial
zonal range 8-9 (CT-WT)
flowering time late spring to early summer
flower colour yellow-green
height 45-60cm (1½-2ft)
special characteristics evergreen, decorative green foliage

The variegated forms of *Aucuba japonica* are outstandingly tolerant and much-maligned plants which are often positioned alone in the driest, most densely shaded parts of gardens. However, giving them other plants as companions can do much to enhance the underrated attractions of their generous mounds of large, glossy leaves.

Euphorbia amygdaloides robbiae makes an ideal partner for spotted laurel. Its open heads of tangy yellow-green flowers provide a rather stylish link with the yellow markings on this shrub's leaves. And it too is a tolerant and very easily grown plant which copes well with dry, shady conditions. The flowers of this euphorbia are long-lasting; they look good in bud (see 8.20) and, often, as seedheads as well (see 8.18). At all times the plant's leathery rosettes of foliage are strikingly shaped and of a gleaming dark green. They therefore provide an interesting contrast to the very different leaves of the aucuba.

Where growing conditions are reasonably moist and fertile, both the plants shown here will look particularly shiny and healthy – and the euphorbia's spreading roots may become a nuisance.

The genus *Euphorbia* is a very good source of green or yellow-green flowers – see also 4.25, 4.10, 7.3 and 7.5.

7.11 Alchemilla & Weigela

Alchemilla mollis
(lady's mantle)
sun/shade ○ ◖
type of plant hardy perennial
zonal range 4-8 (C-WT)
flowering time early to mid-summer
flower colour yellow-green
height 45cm (18in)
special characteristics decorative green foliage, suitable for damp soils

Weigela 'Florida Variegata'
sun/shade ○ ◖
type of plant hardy shrub
zonal range 5-8 (C-WT)
flowering time late spring to early summer
flower colour pink
height 1.2-1.5m (4-5ft)
special characteristics variegated foliage

The foamy heads of yellow-green flowers borne by *Alchemilla mollis* complement a very wide range of plants. They are perhaps at their most attractive in midsummer, as shown here. Later, the whole plant can become quite untidy. However, if at this stage the weed-smothering mound of growth is cut right back, the plant soon produces another crop of beautifully scalloped, velvety, lime-green leaves and usually a few more flowers, too.

In the combination shown here, the shapely, pointed leaves of *Weigela* 'Florida Variegata' are in marked contrast to the alchemilla's rounded flower-heads and almost circular leaves. The variegation of the weigela's foliage also introduces a crisper element into the composition, though the various colours in the leaves harmonize very prettily with the alchemilla. As temperatures drop in the autumn, some of the yellowish to pale cream leaf edges may become tinged with pink. Though decid-uous, the foliage remains in remarkably good con-dition until late autumn or early winter.

The weigela's funnel-shaped flowers are borne fairly close to the main, upright stems of the shrub.

Each of these plants is very easy to grow. Indeed, the alchemilla and its numerous seedlings seem to thrive in virtually any soil anywhere.

7.12 Helleborus & Euonymus

Helleborus foetidus
(stinking hellebore)
sun/shade ○ ◖
type of plant hardy perennial
zonal range 6-9 (CT-WT)
flowering time late winter to mid-spring
flower colour pale green, often maroon-rimmed
height 45-60cm (1½-2ft)
special characteristics evergreen, decorative green foliage

Euonymus fortunei 'Emerald Gaiety'
sun/shade ○ ◖
type of plant hardy shrub/climber
zonal range 5-9 (C-WT)
height 60-90cm (2-3ft) as a shrub
special characteristics evergreen, variegated foliage

Here, in late winter, the beautiful, delicate green bells of this hellebore are just emerging. Even at this stage the contrast between the plant's dark leaves and its long-lasting, pale flowers is very strik-ing. The spidery foliage is, however, of a rather som-bre tone and it benefits from being combined with lighter, brighter colours. In this partnership, the lit-tle rounded leaves of a variegated euonymus are dis-tributed among the hellebore's long, dark leaflets. Each of these grey-green leaves is edged in white and some of these margins usually become tinged with pink during the colder months, as can be seen in this photograph.

In time, this slow-growing euonymus will form a dense hummock of growth. Mature specimens sometimes produce longer-leaved, climbing shoots which will grow up to 3m (10ft) high. The helle-bore's stems are basically quite upright, but the spreading shapes of the leaves create a substantial, rather rounded clump of growth.

Both these plants are easily grown. The euony-mus is particularly accommodating and will do well in almost any soil. Ideally, the hellebore should be given a moist, fertile soil and a shady site. The com-mon name of this poisonous plant alludes to the unattractive smell emitted by the leaves and roots when they are bruised.

7.13 Euphorbia & Hedera

Euphorbia amygdaloides var. *robbiae*
(syn *E. robbiae*)
(spurge)
sun/shade ○ ●
type of plant hardy perennial
zonal range 8-9 (CT-WT)
flowering time late spring to early summer
flower colour yellow-green
height 45-60cm (1½-2ft)
special characteristics evergreen, decorative green foliage

Hedera helix
(common ivy)
sun/shade ○ ●
type of plant hardy climber
zonal range 5-9 (C-ST)
height 10-15cm (4-6in) when creeping horizontally
special characteristics evergreen, decorative green foliage

For such an adaptable and easily grown plant, this euphorbia has flowers of very sophisticated colouring. Both in shape and in colour these loosely arranged, citrus-coloured flowerheads contrast most effectively with the plant's own rosettes of deep green foliage and with the accompanying ivy's dark, neatly lobed leaves. Even before the euphorbia flowers, this association of two evergreen plants has considerable charm (see 8.20, where this combination is described more fully).

Climbing specimens of *Hedera helix* which produce shrubby growth when they reach maturity also bear green flowers. The flowers form drumstick-like heads (see 8.1).

For other combinations using *Euphorbia amygdaloides robbiae*, see 7.10, 8.18 and 14.12.

7.14 Tellima & Geranium

Tellima grandiflora Rubra Group
(syn *T. g.* 'Purpurea')
sun/shade ○ ●
type of plant hardy perennial
zonal range 4-9 (C-WT)
flowering time late spring to early summer
flower colour green + purple-pink
height 45-60cm (1½-2ft)
special characteristics evergreen, decorative green foliage, autumn/winter foliage

Geranium himalayense 'Gravetye'
(syn *G. grandiflorum* var. *alpinum*,
G. himalayense alpinum)
(cranesbill)
sun/shade ○ ●
type of plant hardy perennial
zonal range 4-8 (C-WT)
flowering time early to mid-summer
flower colour violet-blue + red
height 30cm (12in)
special characteristics decorative green foliage

The tiny flowers of this tellima are a particularly delicate shade of creamy green, yet the arrangement of the flowers in long, slender wands, the edging of soft pink at the mouth of each bell and the darkness of the plant's stems all add up to an impression of quiet emphasis. Normally the stems are erect and the repeated upright shapes they create also draw attention to the flowers; here, in early summer, they are tangled after a heavy shower of rain.

As demonstrated in this combination, these wands of gentle green can increase the vividness and clarity of stronger hues. In addition to this interesting association of colours, there are several other attractive contrasts between the two plants here. *Geranium himalayense* 'Gravetye' carries its flowers just above its delicately lobed and divided foliage, while the tellima's flowers are of quite different shape and arrangement, and its leaves are scalloped and almost circular. As the summer progresses, the tellima's foliage takes on pinkish-bronze tones (see 8.12). In winter the foliage is a striking, burnished purple-maroon.

Both of these easily grown perennials will spread fairly quickly, especially in well-drained, moisture-retentive soils. They make good ground cover. The tellima is very adaptable and it self-seeds.

7.15 Pulmonaria & Helleborus

Pulmonaria angustifolia 'Munstead Blue'

(blue cowslip, lungwort)

sun/shade ◖
type of plant hardy perennial
zonal range 3-8 (C-CT)
flowering time early to late spring
flower colour bright blue
height 15-23cm (6-9in)

Helleborus orientalis hybrid

(Lenten rose)

sun/shade ◖
type of plant hardy perennial
zonal range 4-9 (C-WT)
flowering time late winter to mid-spring
flower colour pale green
height 45cm (18in)
special characteristics evergreen/semi-evergreen

Among the many, very variable forms of Lenten rose there are plants with pale flowers, some of which, though they are often described as white, are in fact pale green. In the combination shown here, the sculpted, hanging cups of this particular green form create a spring picture of delicate freshness beside the beautiful blue of a lungwort. (When the lungwort's flowers are combined with sharp yellow, the effect is more one of bursting cheerfulness – see 17.13.)

Woodland conditions of partial or full shade and an open but moisture-retentive soil are ideal for both these plants. When well-suited, they will form good, ground-covering clumps of growth. Both plants will self-seed. In time, the lungwort in particular is likely to cover sizeable areas with its simple, smoothly shaped leaves. The deeply lobed foliage of many Lenten rose hybrids lasts well into winter.

For other combinations involving green-flowered hellebores see, for instance, 7.12 and 14.8.

For other combinations featuring green flowers, see:
COOL-COLOURED FLOWERS 1.14, 1.32 PURPLE FOLIAGE 4.10, 4.23, 4.25, 4.26 GREEN FOLIAGE 8.1, 8.21
VARIEGATED FOLIAGE 9.23 AUTUMN FOLIAGE 10.12 FRUIT 12.13 FRAGRANT FLOWERS 13.8 WINTER FLOWERS 14.5, 14.8, 14.12 DAMP AND WET SOILS 16.7, 16.10, 16.14, 16.17

8 DECORATIVE GREEN FOLIAGE

The tranquillity of green makes it a wonderful foil for other colours. This does not mean, however, that green is always just an unobtrusive background for more exciting events. There are green flowers – such as the great cylindrical heads of some euphorbias and the clouds of tangy, pastel lime blooms of *Alchemilla mollis* – that are far from inconspicuous, and there are green leaves too that are very striking.

Some green foliage is eye-catching because it is so large: few plants can begin to match the 1.8m (6ft) wide leaves of *Gunnera manicata* (see 16.4) but, especially among moisture-loving plants, there are plenty of big, bold leaves (see pages 235-245). Some large-leaved plants for drier situations appear in this Green Foliage section and they include *Vitis coignetiae* (a most impressive ornamental vine) and the ever-useful bergenias.

Big, plain green shapes such as these look well combined with a contrasting multiplicity of much smaller green forms – with, for example, the fronds of ferns or the neat rows of small, shining leaves produced by *Cotoneaster horizontalis*. They are also attractive when set beside jagged-edged or deeply lobed leaves, or beside leaves that are conspicuously veined, such as those of *Viburnum rhytidophyllum*.

MIXING TEXTURE, TONE AND HABIT

As well as a huge range of sizes and shapes, plants with green foliage provide the gardener with numerous different textures and a surprisingly complex palette of colours. In this section alone there are, for example, the very dark green, deeply channelled and glossy leaves of *Viburnum davidii* and the smooth, apple-green foliage of *Hebe rakaiensis*, the vivid green, dry-textured needles of *Juniperus communis* 'Green Carpet', the fleshy leaves of *Saxifraga × urbium* and the velvety, lime-green leaves of *Alchemilla mollis*.

In some cases it is the arrangement of the leaves as much as the leaves themselves that makes the foliage especially decorative: *Cotoneaster horizontalis*, for example, has distinctive, fishbone branches and twigs, and the leaves of *Saxifraga × urbium* are gathered into pretty rosettes. All these different sizes, shapes, textures and colours mean that it is not difficult to devise interesting all-green compositions (see, for example, 8.12).

INTRODUCING OTHER COLOURS

How green foliage behaves with other colours depends on many factors, but some broad generalizations may be made. With red, its complementary colour, green creates combinations of vibrant contrast. With the closer colours of orange and yellow the effect is less exciting, though still pleasing; yellow and green in particular make harmonious partners. Pretty, visually unassertive combinations can be created with blues and greens, but when blues deepen and redden into violets and purples there is a tendency for a merging of colours to occur (though distinct differences in habit of growth and in leaf form can help to differentiate the plants involved).

When partnered with variegated leaves, plain green foliage comes into its own as a restful, uncomplicated foil to elaborateness and intricacy. White foliage markings – and white flowers, too – look cool and calm with greens; yellow variegation harmonizes more closely. Partnerships of grey and green foliage can be gentle, subdued affairs with interesting contrasts in texture (see 8.7) or, when the grey is glaucous and the green is yellowish, they can be bright and colourful (see 8.23).

Many of the plants featured in this section have flowers that are just as attractive as their handsome leaves. Indeed, hardy geraniums, daylilies, euphorbias and hellebores, as well as larger plants such as mahonias, would be regarded primarily as flowering plants by most gardeners. As an additional attraction, there are a number of plants which have good-looking green foliage that colours well in autumn and winter. Various maples, for example, are outstanding for vivid autumn colour and, among smaller plants, the leaves of some bergenias turn burnished bronze, red or purple in the coldest months.

Gardeners all too often take green for granted or treat it simply as a backdrop for floral dramas, yet it is – in all its diversity – an interesting ingredient in its own right. And, in combination with other colours or in all-green plantings, it can create a wide range of effects from cool, elegant harmonies to bright, dynamic contrasts.

8.1 Vitis & Hedera

Vitis vinifera 'Purpurea'

(claret vine, Teinturier grape, grape vine)
sun/shade ○
type of plant hardy climber
zonal range 6-9 (C-WT)
height 3-4.5m (10-15ft)
special characteristics purple foliage, autumn foliage, fruit

Hedera helix

(common ivy)
sun/shade ○ ◑
type of plant hardy climber
zonal range 5-9 (C-ST)
flowering time early to late autumn
flower colour green
height 20-30m (60-90ft)
special characteristics evergreen, decorative green foliage

In its juvenile, close-clinging and small-leaved state common ivy is certainly attractive. When, as here, a mature specimen also produces shrubby growth, the effect is altogether more luxuriant and relaxed. Some of these arching arborescent shoots can billow dramatically 60-90cm (2-3ft) away from the tops of walls, bearing foliage that is larger and more smoothly shaped than normal. As a bonus, these shoots also produce flowerheads like bobbled drumsticks, which ripen into black fruits in spring.

In this particular combination, a purple-leaved vine is providing not only another colour but also a larger leaf – up to 15cm (6in) wide – with a much more precise outline. Over the growing season, the leaf colour of this twining climber changes considerably. The newest growths are greyish, but they soon mature to a deep, matt purple with which the ivy's shiny green manages to look both opulent and lively. During autumn, the vine leaves become redder (see 5.1) and often turn bright crimson. Often, too, there are small bunches of black, bitter grapes (see 12.1).

During its first years especially, this vine is slow-growing. To do well, it needs a fertile, moisture-retentive soil with good drainage and a position that receives plenty of sun. The ivy is a very tolerant plant that can be grown almost anywhere.

8.2 Cortaderia, Bergenia, Hosta & Ruta

Cortaderia selloana

(syn *C. argentea*) (pampas grass)
sun/shade ○
type of plant hardy/slightly tender perennial (grass)
zonal range 7-10 (CT-ST)
flowering time late summer to mid-autumn
flower colour cream
height 1.8-2.7m (6-9ft)
special characteristics evergreen, suitable for damp soils

Bergenia cordifolia

sun/shade ○ ◑
type of plant hardy perennial
zonal range 3-8 (C-ST)
flowering time early to mid-spring
flower colour mauve-pink
height 30-40cm (12-15in)
special characteristics evergreen, decorative green foliage, autumn/winter foliage

Hosta fortunei var. *albopicta*

(plantain lily)
sun/shade ○ ◑
type of plant hardy perennial
zonal range 3-9 (C-WT)
flowering time midsummer
flower colour pale lilac
height 45-60cm (1½-2ft)
special characteristics variegated young foliage, suitable for damp soils

Ruta graveolens 'Jackman's Blue'

(rue)
sun/shade ○
type of plant hardy shrub
zonal range 6-8 (C-WT)
flowering time mid- to late summer
flower colour yellow
height 45-60cm (1½-2ft)
special characteristics evergreen, aromatic, blue-grey foliage

There are variegated leaves here and bright blue-grey foliage, too, but the undoubted linchpin of the group is the great, firm, gleaming mass of plain greenery produced by *Bergenia cordifolia*. The solidity of these almost circular leaves makes the bergenia a very useful foil for plants of more complex outline and colouring. It is principally because the bergenia is such a calming influence that the glaucous laciness of the rue, the slender, arching leaves of the pampas grass and the two-toned, bunched foliage of the hosta in this combination do not look just a jumble of different shapes and colours.

Between them, these four plants produce flowers from early spring to mid-autumn. In autumn the tall, feathery plumes of the pampas grass create a silvery cloud.

The sharp leaves of the pampas grass can damage nearby plants in windy places. A sheltered site, therefore, and a fertile, well-drained, moisture-retaining soil would suit this combination best. In hot climates the pampas grass can be an invasive weed. For further details of the bergenia, the hosta and the rue, see 8.19, 8.16 and 5.4 respectively.

8.3 Weigela & Hebe

Weigela 'Praecox Variegata'
sun/shade ○ ◖
type of plant hardy shrub
zonal range 5-8 (C-WT)
flowering time late spring to early summer
flower colour pink
height 1.5-1.8m (5-6ft)
special characteristics variegated foliage

Hebe rakaiensis
sun/shade ○
type of plant hardy/slightly tender shrub
zonal range 8-10 (CT-WT)
flowering time early to mid-summer
flower colour white
height 60cm (2ft)
special characteristics evergreen, decorative green foliage

Hebe rakaiensis is one of the most versatile of all green-leaved plants. Its dense dome of light, rather yellow, green leaves looks good with a range of other colours (see, for example, 4.14, 5.6 and 8.5).

Here the leaf colour picks up the pretty, fresh green in the foliage of *Weigela* 'Praecox Variegata'. At the same time, the smallness and tidiness of the hebe's leaves, closely set upon their stems, emphasize the more open arrangement and elegant tapering of the weigela's foliage. The edges of these leaves are at first cream, then white (as here, in early summer) and finally, yellow-green. The foliage is notably long-lasting and often remains in good condition well into winter. In cold weather some of the leaf edges may become tinged with pink.

The flowers of these plants give a rather shorter-lived display, but both sets of blooms are pretty. The weigela's main stems are fairly upright, but the subsidiary, rather twiggy branches arch becomingly and are generously decorated with slightly fragrant, funnel-shaped flowers. The hebe's little flower spikes are usually sprinkled rather unevenly over the plant. Neither of these shrubs is difficult to grow, and when combined they need only sunshine and good drainage to do well. However, a really dry position would not be ideal.

8.4 Hebe & Euphorbia

Hebe rakaiensis
sun/shade ○
type of plant hardy/slightly tender shrub
zonal range 8-10 (CT-WT)
flowering time early to mid-summer
flower colour white
height 60cm (2ft)
special characteristics evergreen, decorative green foliage

Euphorbia griffithii 'Fireglow'
(spurge)
sun/shade ○ ◖
type of plant hardy perennial
zonal range 4-9 (C-WT)
flowering time late spring to early summer
flower colour bright orange-red
height 60-90cm (2-3ft)
special characteristics autumn foliage

Orange is reputedly the least popular flower colour. Gardeners who appreciate its warmth and vivacity, but who feel uncertain about combining it with other hot colours, might like to contemplate the partnership shown here. *Hebe rakaiensis* has light, apple-green foliage, and while this colour cools the orange of the euphorbia it also allows it to stay sharp and lively.

Illustrated here in early summer, the euphorbia's blooms have lost some of their most vibrant colouring. They are, however, still conspicuously orange and the flowers of this plant remain interesting over many weeks. The hebe's fluffy flower spikes are altogether more restrained in colouring. They usually appear in broad patches across the exceptionally neat, dome-shaped surface of this shrub.

The euphorbia consists of a series of fairly upright, bushy stems with foliage of a much darker green than that of the hebe. There are, therefore, distinct contrasts, both in habit of growth and in leaf colour, between these two plants. In mid-autumn, the euphorbia's foliage often turns orange and yellow (see 10.17).

Ideally, this combination should be planted in a soil that is well-drained but not too dry. Full sun produces the densest specimens of hebe and also encourages good autumn colour on the euphorbia.

8.5 Hebe & Viburnum

Hebe rakaiensis

sun/shade ○
type of plant hardy/slightly tender shrub
zonal range 8-10 (CT-WT)
flowering time early to mid-summer
flower colour white
height 60cm (2ft)
special characteristics evergreen, decorative green foliage

Viburnum davidii

sun/shade ○ ◖
type of plant hardy shrub
zonal range 8-9 (CT-WT)
flowering time early summer
flower colour white
height 60-90cm (2-3ft)
special characteristics evergreen, decorative green foliage, fruit

These two shrubs are so similar in outline and in density of growth that the eye is concentrated upon the striking differences in their leaves. Whereas the hebe's neat dome consists of little ovals of light yellowish green, the viburnum's slightly more flat-topped hummock is made up of much larger-scale, deeply veined, dark green leaves. Both sets of handsome, gleaming foliage are versatile enhancers of many different types of planting. The hebe is especially useful for enlivening groups of plants, but if a calm, deep note is needed the viburnum is particularly valuable.

The flowers of these shrubs are not, perhaps, quite so attractive as their leaves. However, the hebe's irregular sprinkling of fluffy little flower spikes certainly has some charm, while the red-stalked heads produced by the viburnum emphasize the attractive way in which the leaves of this plant are arranged.

Where there is enough space for several specimens of the viburnum, female plants of this shrub will, if pollinated by a male, bear bunches of long-lasting, very bright blue berries.

Viburnum davidii, though hardy, grows slowly and benefits from a little shelter. Both plants must have a reasonable supply of moisture. The hebe is neatest and most dense in full sun.

8.6 Berberis & Hebe

Berberis buxifolia 'Pygmaea'

(syn B. b. 'Nana') (barberry)
sun/shade ○ ◖
type of plant hardy shrub
zonal range 6-9 (C-WT)
flowering time mid-spring
flower colour rich yellow
height 60cm (2ft)
special characteristics evergreen/semi-evergreen, decorative green foliage

Hebe 'Edinensis'

sun/shade ○ ◖ type of plant hardy shrub
zonal range 6-10 (CT-ST)
height 30-45cm (12-18in)
special characteristics evergreen, decorative green foliage

Hebe 'Youngii'

(syn H. 'Carl Teschner')
sun/shade ○
type of plant slightly tender shrub
zonal range 8-11 (CT-ST)
flowering time midsummer
flower colour violet-blue
height 23cm (9in)
special characteristics evergreen

This satisfying assemblage of three dense, small-leaved shrubs relies almost entirely upon subtle differences in habit of growth and leaf colour for its success. Differences in height also play a part, of course. *Hebe* 'Youngii' forms a wide-spreading hummock of slightly grey foliage and this low shape is important to the balance of the whole arrangement. The taller plants differ considerably in the colour and arrangement of their leaves: the upright stems of *Hebe* 'Edinensis' are covered so closely in overlapping, bright green leaves that the whole plant looks like a conifer; in contrast the berberis foliage is very dark and the leaves are held almost at right angles to the distinctly red, slightly arching stems.

Flowers play a relatively minor role here. Indeed, *Hebe* 'Edinensis' rarely flowers and the same is true of some forms of the berberis. *Hebe* 'Youngii' is, however, a notably floriferous plant – see 1.16.

In order to ensure that all these plants grow neatly and densely, a sunny site is needed. In addition, good drainage and some shelter will protect the hebes from possible winter damage in colder areas.

8.7 Helleborus & Ballota

Helleborus argutifolius

(syn *H. lividus* ssp. *corsicus*)
(Corsican hellebore)
sun/shade ○ ◑
type of plant hardy perennial
zonal range 7-9 (CT-WT)
flowering time late winter to late spring
flower colour pale green
height 60cm (2ft)
special characteristics evergreen, decorative green foliage

Ballota pseudodictamnus

sun/shade ○
type of plant slightly tender perennial/shrub
zonal range 7-9 (CT-WT)
flowering time early to mid-summer
flower colour mauve
height 45-60cm (1½-2ft)
special characteristics evergreen/semi-evergreen, grey foliage

Of all the readily available hellebores, *Helleborus argutifolius* has the boldest and most handsome foliage. Its thick, pale-stalked leaves are made up of three elegantly pointed, slightly curving leaflets of a soft, rich green. Here these leaves have been contrasted, most successfully, with the much paler, grey and woolly foliage of *Ballota pseudodictamnus*. The interesting differences in leaf texture, colour and size are heightened by dissimilarities in habit of growth. The ballota's white-felted stems are very conspicuously upright, while the hellebore's clump of thick, rather lax stems is topped with much more widely branching foliage, so that the overall shape of the plant is quite rounded and shrubby.

Every bit as decorative as its foliage are the beautiful and long-lasting flowers of this hellebore (see 7.7 and 14.8). The ballota's flowers – in bud here, in early summer – are very small, but they add attractive pinpoints of subdued colour to the grey foliage.

Both these plants need good drainage and some shelter. The hellebore will thrive in partial and even full shade but, particularly in colder regions, a sheltered site in a sunny position will probably give better results. The ballota must have sun. For the sake of the hellebore, this combination should be planted in a reasonably moisture-retentive soil.

8.8 Berberis & Dicentra

Berberis thunbergii 'Atropurpurea Nana'

(barberry)
sun/shade ○
type of plant hardy shrub
zonal range 5-8 (C-WT)
flowering time mid- to late spring
flower colour pale yellow + red
height 30-60cm (1-2ft)
special characteristics purple foliage, autumn foliage, fruit

Dicentra 'Bacchanal'

sun/shade ◑
type of plant hardy perennial
zonal range 4-8 (C-CT)
flowering time mid-spring to midsummer
flower colour dark crimson
height 30-40cm (12-15in)
special characteristics decorative green foliage

The lovely, pale, ferny foliage of *Dicentra* 'Bacchanal' has been partnered here, most satisfactorily, with neat little oval leaves of a rich, purplish red-bronze. Just as successful as this flattering contrast between different leaves is the complementing of the dicentra's dusky flower colour by the dark foliage of the berberis.

All the popular dicentras are noted for the abundant clumps of foliage they produce from mid-spring onwards, and *D.* 'Bacchanal' is no exception. The slight tinge of blue present in this plant's leaves and the charming way in which the flowers are poised above the foliage add to the general impression of light laciness. In contrast, the slow-growing, rather prickly hummock of the berberis is dense and firm.

Given a moist, humus-rich soil and some shade, *D.* 'Bacchanal' is an exceptionally long-flowering plant; in ideal conditions there may still be flowers at the beginning of autumn. As a late-season bonus, the berberis leaves turn dark purple-mahogany in autumn and accompany the plant's ripened scarlet fruits.

The berberis needs sun for its shiny foliage to colour well. As long as conditions are not too alkaline, this shrub can be grown in a wide variety of soils.

133

8.9 Geranium & Erica

Geranium macrorrhizum
(cranesbill)
sun/shade ○ ◖
type of plant hardy perennial
zonal range 4-8 (C-WT)
flowering time late spring to midsummer
flower colour magenta-pink
height 30-40cm (12-15in)
special characteristics semi-evergreen, aromatic, decorative green foliage, autumn foliage

Erica carnea 'December Red'
(heath, heather)
sun/shade ○
type of plant hardy shrub
zonal range 5-7 (C-CT)
flowering time midwinter to late spring
flower colour pale pink changing to pink-purple
height 15-23cm (6-9in)
special characteristics evergreen

Geranium macrorrhizum and its forms are some of the most effective of all carpeting weed-smotherers. The richly aromatic foliage of these plants always looks fresh and sprightly. In winter the lobed, almost circular, deciduous leaves, evident here in late spring, die back to a low mat of smaller, darker, evergreen leaves. As they die, the deciduous leaves become tinged with reds, oranges and yellows (see 8.15).

Here *Geranium macrorrhizum* has been combined with a winter-flowering heather. Heaths and heathers are usually given rather dry-textured partners, such as conifers, and this partnership is an interesting illustration of how a lusher companion can produce equally effective results. As well as contrasts in leaf size, shape and colour, there is a highly successful echoing of flower colour between these two plants.

Like many varieties of *Erica carnea*, 'December Red' is in flower for several months. If clipped after flowering, it forms a dense carpet of growth.

For the sake of the heather, this combination should be given an open, sunny position and a well-drained but moisture-retentive soil. The soil need not be lime-free. The geranium is a vigorous, unfussy plant that will thrive in most soils and sites.

8.10 Juniperus & Ajuga

Juniperus communis 'Green Carpet'
(juniper)
sun/shade ○
type of plant hardy conifer
zonal range 3-7 (C-WT)
height 8-10cm (3-4in)
special characteristics evergreen, decorative green foliage

Ajuga reptans 'Atropurpurea'
(bugle)
sun/shade ○ ◖
type of plant hardy perennial
zonal range 3-9 (C-ST)
flowering time late spring to early summer
flower colour deep blue
height 15-20cm (6-8in)
special characteristics evergreen/semi-evergreen, purple foliage

This conifer's foliage is not so decorative as, for example, the curvaceous fans of *Chamaecyparis obtusa* 'Nana Gracilis' (see 10.16). However, in colour, the close-knit carpet of tiny, neatly arranged needles is wonderfully fresh and vivid. This colouring is shown off to perfection by another carpeting plant, a dark-leaved form of bugle, with much larger and more rounded leaves of a very deep, glossy purple. The contrast in texture – between the shiny lushness of the bugle and the prickly aridity of the juniper – also adds greatly to the appeal of the combination.

During the greater part of the year there is little change in the appearance of these two sets of foliage, apart from a darkening and a slight bronzing of the juniper's leaves in winter. In late spring, however, the flowers of the bugle appear. These introduce a bright, rich colour and a quite different, upright shape into the partnership (see 1.39).

Juniperus communis and its forms are particularly at home in soils with good drainage, including those that are limy and chalky. However, here, conditions must be reasonably moisture-retentive, since the bugle's foliage will not be at its best in hot, dry situations. The juniper grows fairly slowly, but will eventually have a spread of about 90cm (3ft). The bugle is a fast-growing plant.

8.11 Vitis & Athyrium

Vitis coignetiae
(ornamental vine)
sun/shade ○ ☾
type of plant hardy climber
zonal range 5-9 (C-WT)
height 15-24m (50-80ft)
special characteristics decorative green foliage, autumn foliage

Athyrium filix-femina
(lady fern)
sun/shade ☾
type of plant hardy fern
zonal range 4-9 (C-WT)
height 75cm (2½ft)
special characteristics decorative green foliage, suitable for damp soils

Vitis coignetiae has some of the most exuberant foliage of any hardy climber – individual leaves may be up to 30cm (12in) wide. The lady fern which accompanies it here is constructed on a completely different scale, with erect and then arching fronds decorated in a particularly clear-cut, filigreed pattern of tiny leaflets. The combination has an especially cool and graceful air about it, principally because the colour palette, in spring and summer at least, is very restricted.

In autumn, the vine's great, rough-textured, brown-backed leaves turn rich, caramelized tones of yellow, orange and purple-crimson. The most striking colours are produced in light soils and sunny sites. However, this climber needs a reasonably moisture-retentive soil, and one that is quite fertile, too, to encourage it to grow well, particularly when young. Once established, the plant can put on several metres/yards of growth in a season. Winter pruning can limit the increase in restricted areas.

The fern does especially well in moist soils; it is not a plant for dry places. Here, though the site receives plenty of light, the fern is shaded and kept cool by the long, tendrilled growths and large leaves of the vine. As long as they have some shade and moisture, the fronds of this fern keep their lovely, fresh, light green colour over a long period.

8.12 Acer, Tellima & Hosta

Acer palmatum
(Japanese maple)
sun/shade ○ ☾ **type of plant** hardy shrub/tree
zonal range 6-8 (C-WT)
height 4.5-6m (15-20ft)
special characteristics decorative green foliage, autumn foliage

Tellima grandiflora Rubra Group
(syn *T. g.* 'Purpurea')
sun/shade ○ ☾ **type of plant** hardy perennial
zonal range 4-9 (C-WT)
flowering time late spring to early summer
flower colour green + purple-pink
height 45-60cm (1½-2ft)
special characteristics evergreen, decorative green foliage, autumn/winter foliage

Hosta plantaginea
(plantain lily)
sun/shade ○ ☾ **type of plant** hardy perennial
zonal range 3-9 (C-WT)
flowering time late summer to early autumn
flower colour white
height 60cm (2ft)
special characteristics decorative green foliage, fragrant flowers, suitable for damp soils

The cool elegance of this combination shows just what sophisticated results can be achieved when only green foliage is used in plantings. The plants are shown here in midsummer and, even though at other times in the year there are flowers and colourful autumn leaves, the group is probably at its most beautifully graceful at this period.

Acer palmatum varies somewhat even in its plain, green-leaved form, but it is always a plant with great poise. It often grows as a spreading shrub but, over time and in the right conditions, it will form a round-headed tree with open, airy layers of lobed and pointed foliage. In flattering contrast to the maple, the tellima creates a dense carpet of scalloped greenery, and the hosta's broad, ribbed leaves rise and arch in thick clumps of pale, yellowish green. In winter, the tellima's foliage becomes conspicuously burnished with bronze and maroon tones. In mid-autumn, the maple's leaves turn red and orange before falling (though some specimens can be rather disappointing in their autumn colouring). Earlier still, there are the long, very sweetly scented, trumpet-shaped flowers of the hosta. The tellima's spring and early summer flower spikes add slender, upright shapes to this composition (see 7.14).

A sheltered, very lightly shaded site and a moist, rather acid, well-drained soil create the ideal conditions for the most demanding of the plants in this combination – the maple. The hosta will also grow well in these sort of surroundings but, in cold areas, it needs sun for good flower production. The tellima is a tough, self-seeding perennial.

8.13 Viburnum & Vinca

Viburnum rhytidophyllum
sun/shade ○ ●
type of plant hardy shrub
zonal range 6-8 (C-WT)
flowering time late spring to early summer
flower colour creamy white
height 3-3.6m (10-12ft)
special characteristics evergreen, decorative green foliage, fruit

Vinca minor 'Argenteovariegata'
(syn *V. m.* 'Variegata')
(lesser periwinkle)
sun/shade ○ ●
type of plant hardy shrub/perennial
zonal range 4-9 (C-WT)
flowering time mid-spring to early summer
flower colour pale violet-blue
height 10-15cm (4-6in)
special characteristics evergreen, variegated foliage

With a prettily coloured, small-leaved partner at its feet, all the good points of this viburnum are enhanced and the tendency for its long, dark foliage to appear rather lugubrious is counteracted. Each of the viburnum's lower leaves stands out handsomely against the periwinkle's tight-knit carpet of greyish-green and white.

Though neither plant is in flower here, in mid-autumn, the viburnum's beige-felted flower-buds are already conspicuous. They have the effect of drawing attention to the almost radial arrangement of the plant's gleaming, deeply veined leaves. When several specimens of this fast-growing, erect viburnum are grown together, good crops of berries appear in large bunches, ripening from red to black. The periwinkle will flower best on those shoots which are not too shaded.

Although *Vinca minor* is a very tolerant plant that will grow almost anywhere, the foliage of this variegated form is at its best in not too dark or too dry a position. In any case, the viburnum needs a moisture-retentive soil, and some shelter too. *Vinca minor* 'Argenteovariegata' is not as vigorous as the green-leaved species, but it can still be expected to have a spread of about 60cm (2ft). For a combination of *Viburnum rhytidophyllum* and a larger variegated plant, see 9.17.

8.14 Mahonia & Euonymus

Mahonia japonica
sun/shade ○ ●
type of plant hardy shrub
zonal range 7-9 (CT-WT)
flowering time late autumn to early spring
flower colour pale yellow
height 1.8-2.4m (6-8ft)
special characteristics evergreen, decorative green foliage, fragrant flowers

Euonymus fortunei 'Emerald 'n' Gold'
sun/shade ○ ●
type of plant hardy shrub/climber
zonal range 5-9 (C-WT)
height 60cm (2ft) as a shrub
special characteristics evergreen, variegated foliage

As well as its strings of fragrant winter flowers – so deliciously redolent of lily-of-the-valley – *Mahonia japonica* has very handsome foliage. The leaves are arranged in large whorls on rather upright stems, the individual stalks within these whorls often being 30-45cm (12-18in) long. This bold greenery is accompanied here by a variegated euonymus, and the density and smaller scale of the variegated foliage emphasize the mahonia's impressive simplicity.

The mahonia's newer foliage has a distinctly yellow cast to it, and it combines pleasingly with the gold- and cream-edged foliage of the euonymus. When the mahonia's yellow flowers begin to open, they too are complemented by the yellow markings on the euonymus leaves.

The mahonia's mature foliage is a gleaming dark green (see 3.25). In open sites and poor soils particularly, it can turn rich shades of red and bronze in winter, though the best quality foliage is produced in moisture-retentive soils and sheltered, lightly shaded places. Shelter also protects the winter flowers of the shrub. The euonymus is an easily grown plant that is suitable for most soils and sites. The plant slowly forms a bushy clump of growth. Really mature specimens may produce climbing shoots and grow up to 2.4m (8ft) tall.

8.15 Acer & Geranium

Acer palmatum var. *dissectum*
Dissectum Viride Group
(Japanese maple)
sun/shade ○ ◐
type of plant hardy shrub
zonal range 5-8 (C-WT)
height 1.5-2.4m (5-8ft)
special characteristics decorative green foliage, autumn foliage

Geranium macrorrhizum
(cranesbill)
sun/shade ○ ◐
type of plant hardy perennial
zonal range 4-8 (C-WT)
flowering time late spring to midsummer
flower colour magenta-pink
height 30-40cm (12-15in)
special characteristics semi-evergreen, aromatic, decorative green foliage, autumn foliage

Each of the leaves of this maple is divided into at least seven leaflets which themselves are deeply cut and lobed. Since the arching branches of this plant are heaped up into a rounded mound, the overall effect is a cascade of floating featheriness. Here, in early autumn, the basic, light, bright green leaf colour (see 1.33) is just beginning to assume the golds and oranges of autumn (see 10.16). The accompanying geranium also has light green leaves for most of the year and it too is starting to take on brighter autumn tones.

The colouring of these two plants is quite similar, but they differ markedly in leaf shape: the maple's foliage hangs in ferny fronds, while the geranium's lobed leaves, with their almost circular shape, create an altogether firmer impression. These leaves form a really efficient, weed-smothering carpet of foliage. They are strongly aromatic. In winter, the taller, deciduous leaves, which are beginning to colour here, die back and a lower, smaller-leaved mat of foliage remains. The branched heads of pretty flowers are held on dusky red stems (see 8.9).

Geranium macrorrhizum is an undemanding plant that is happy in almost any soil. The maple needs a site that is sheltered from winds, and an acid or neutral soil that is both well-drained and moisture-retentive. It is a very slow-growing plant.

8.16 Rodgersia & Hosta

Rodgersia podophylla
sun/shade ○ ◐
type of plant hardy perennial
zonal range 5-8 (C-CT)
flowering time early to mid-summer
flower colour cream
height 90-120cm (3-4ft)
special characteristics bronze foliage, decorative green foliage, autumn foliage, suitable for damp and wet soils

Hosta fortunei var. *albopicta*
(plantain lily)
sun/shade ○ ◐
type of plant hardy perennial
zonal range 3-9 (C-WT)
flowering time midsummer
flower colour pale lilac
height 45-60cm (1½-2ft)
special characteristics variegated young foliage, suitable for damp soils

Illustrated here in early summer, the rodgersia's leaves are at this stage a lively mid-green. When they are combined with the pale-centred foliage of the hosta, the overall impression is one of exuberant freshness. Even when the hosta's pretty variegation becomes much more subdued, after the plant's spires of trumpet-shaped flowers have faded, this is an interesting partnership of differing shapes and textures. The big, jagged leaves of the rodgersia, with their long stalks and network of veins, are always quite distinct from the clump of pointed and ribbed leaves produced by the hosta.

The contrast between these two plants is strongest in spring, when the hosta's leaves are particularly pale and the rodgersia's newest foliage is a deep maroon-bronze. As summer progresses, and especially in sunnier positions, the rodgersia's leaves again take on bronze tones (see 8.17 and 4.25). The foliage becomes redder still during autumn. The flowers of the rodgersia, seen here in bud, open out into broad-based spires. This is not, however, a very free-flowering plant.

All rodgersias grow vigorously in damp and marshy soils and sheltered places. These conditions also suit the hosta. In ordinary, moisture-retentive soil both plants will be smaller and less wide-spreading.

8.17 **Rodgersia & Viola**

Rodgersia podophylla

sun/shade ○ ◐

type of plant hardy perennial

zonal range 5-8 (C-CT)

flowering time early to mid-summer

flower colour cream

height 90-120cm (3-4ft)

special characteristics bronze foliage, decorative green foliage, autumn foliage, suitable for damp and wet soils

Viola cornuta Alba Group

(horned violet)

sun/shade ○ ◐

type of plant hardy perennial

zonal range 5-8 (C-CT)

flowering time mainly late spring to midsummer

flower colour white

height 15-23cm (6-9in)

special characteristics evergreen

With a cloud of small, white petals beside it, the forcefully shaped foliage of *Rodgersia podophylla* looks particularly bold and handsome. Each of the long-stemmed leaves is made up of five jagged and veined leaflets, some of which may well be over 30cm (12in) long. In comparison, the whole demeanour of the viola is lighter and less substantial.

Violas in this group are vigorous, clump-forming plants with a long flowering season. They can be encouraged to produce a second crop of flowers if they are cut right back in late summer. Prolific flowering, both early and late, is most likely in fertile, moisture-retentive soils.

These conditions, along with some shelter from drying winds, also suit the rodgersia. In addition, this plant thrives in damp and boggy soils and its clumps of imposing foliage look well beside water. If conditions are slightly dry, at least some shade is advisable.

In a sunny position, as they are here, the rodgersia's leaves are a rich, bronzed green from midsummer until autumn, when they become distinctly redder. The newest foliage is a maroon-bronze. The tiny flowers of this plant, though often rather sparsely produced, are carried in broad, spire-shaped clusters.

8.18 **Euphorbia & Hemerocallis**

Euphorbia amygdaloides var. *robbiae*

(syn *E. robbiae*)

(spurge)

sun/shade ○ ◐

type of plant hardy perennial

zonal range 8-9 (CT-WT)

flowering time late spring to early summer

flower colour yellow-green

height 45-60cm (1½-2ft)

special characteristics evergreen, decorative green foliage

Hemerocallis fulva

(daylily)

sun/shade ○ ◐

type of plant hardy perennial

zonal range 3-9 (C-ST)

flowering time mid- to late summer

flower colour soft orange

height 90-105cm (3-3½ft)

special characteristics semi-evergreen, decorative green foliage, suitable for damp soils

Almost all daylilies produce very handsome clumps of arching leaves. These cascades of green are a long-lasting complement to many other plants (see 3.14 and 5.17).

Here daylily leaves are accompanying a softly shaped and subtly ginger-tinted cloud of fading euphorbia flowerheads. When these flowerheads finally need to be removed, the daylily's leaves look just as good with the euphorbia's very definitely shaped foliage, which takes the form of gleaming, dark green, leathery rosettes (see 7.13). Especially in spring, when the daylily's foliage emerges a beautiful lime-green, the contrast in colour between these two sets of leaves is very striking.

Each shapely, elegant bloom of the daylily lasts only one day, but the numerous buds, held on erect stems, open over a period of several weeks. *Hemerocallis fulva* is an exceptionally vigorous, spreading species, but the daylilies in general are robust and very easily grown plants. Particularly luxuriant growth is produced in damp conditions. The euphorbia grows quite satisfactorily in dry, shady places and sometimes becomes invasive in more hospitable surroundings. The coppery colouring of the flowerheads seems to occur most reliably when this euphorbia is grown in light soils and sunny positions.

8.19 Cotoneaster & Bergenia

Cotoneaster horizontalis

(fishbone cotoneaster)

sun/shade ○ ◖
type of plant hardy shrub
zonal range 5-8 (C-WT)
flowering time early summer
flower colour pinkish white
height 60cm (2ft), up to 2.4m (8ft) against a wall
special characteristics decorative green foliage, autumn foliage, fruit, ornamental twigs

Bergenia cordifolia

sun/shade ○ ◖
type of plant hardy perennial
zonal range 3-8 (C-ST)
flowering time early to mid-spring
flower colour mauve-pink
height 30-40cm (12-15in)
special characteristics evergreen, decorative green foliage, autumn/winter foliage

Cotoneaster horizontalis has several decorative features: even when leafless, its fishbone fans of stiff, dark twigs are distinctive and striking; its neat little rows of flowers are followed in early autumn by very attractive, bright red berries; and its autumn foliage is an unusually rich mixture of deep crimsons and dark oranges. With all these attractions, it is sometimes easy to overlook just how very pleasing the neat, shining green leaves look in spring and summer.

Bergenia cordifolia has leathery, mid-green leaves which are almost circular in shape and may be over 20cm (8in) in diameter. Their solid, squat shape steadies the intricate pattern of the cotoneaster and their sheer size points up the small scale of its foliage.

Both of these plants are easy to grow in almost any soil and are quite happy in some shade. In exposed sites the bergenia's leaves may become tinged with purple during cold weather, as they have here, in mid-autumn. This additional colour looks well with the berries and with the autumn foliage of the cotoneaster. The bergenia is also colourful in spring when its rather short-stalked but prominently coloured flowerheads coincide with the very fresh green of the cotoneaster's emerging foliage.

8.20 Euphorbia & Hedera

Euphorbia amygdaloides var. robbiae

(syn *E. robbiae*)
(spurge)

sun/shade ○ ◖
type of plant hardy perennial
zonal range 8-9 (CT-WT)
flowering time late spring to early summer
flower colour yellow-green
height 45-60cm (1½-2ft)
special characteristics evergreen, decorative green foliage

Hedera helix

(common ivy)

sun/shade ○ ◖
type of plant hardy climber
zonal range 5-9 (C-ST)
height 10-15cm (4-6in) when creeping horizontally
special characteristics evergreen, decorative green foliage

Each of these plants grows well in dry, shady places and each of them has attractive, softly gleaming foliage of a good deep green. Although rooty areas beneath trees often feature one or other of these plants, the photograph shows how interesting a combination of the two can look together.

The common ivy is so familiar and so easily grown that its virtues tend to be overlooked. It is a very variable plant but the precise, lobed shape of its leaves and the lovely contrast between pale veining and dark leaf colour are consistent features. Many forms will, like the specimen here, take on particularly dark tones during cold weather.

In contrast to the ivy's gentle pattern of overlapping leaves, the euphorbia's leathery foliage is arranged in large, boldly shaped rosettes. Here, in earliest spring, the centre of each rosette contains a dusky maroon flower bud. The subsequent heads of flowers are long-lasting, and the seedheads are often attractively coppery (see 8.18).

The ivy's ground-covering capabilities vary: there are likely to be areas of open, trailing stems as well as patches of much denser growth. The euphorbia is a very vigorous plant with roots that can spread widely, especially in what are probably the ideal conditions for this combination – partial shade and a moisture-retentive, open-textured soil.

8.21 Alchemilla & Ajuga

Alchemilla mollis
(lady's mantle)
sun/shade ○ ◐
type of plant hardy perennial
zonal range 4-8 (C-WT)
flowering time early to mid-summer
flower colour yellow-green
height 45cm (1½ft)
special characteristics decorative green foliage, suitable for damp soils

Ajuga reptans 'Atropurpurea'
(bugle)
sun/shade ○ ◐
type of plant hardy perennial
zonal range 3-9 (C-ST)
flowering time late spring to early summer
flower colour deep blue
height 15-20cm (6-8in)
special characteristics evergreen/semi-evergreen, purple foliage

The beautifully sueded and scalloped leaves of *Alchemilla mollis* are among the most versatile of all leaves for combining with other plants. Here their lime-green colouring contrasts strikingly with the rich, dark purple leaves and the intense blue flowers of a bugle.

The most conspicuous difference between the two plants in this combination is one of colour. However, other differences, in texture and in overall habit of growth, are just as important to the success of the partnership. The alchemilla's leaves are velvety (and at their most lovely, perhaps, when decorated with raindrops – see 1.32), whereas the bugle's foliage is smooth and glossy. The alchemilla forms a dense mound of growth topped by tiny flowers which expand into a froth of yellow-green, while the bugle consists of a close mat of overlapping leaves and very upright flower spikes.

Neither of these plants is difficult to grow. Indeed, the alchemilla is a very prolific self-seeder that will thrive almost anywhere, including damp soils. The bugle grows most densely and luxuriously in moisture-retentive soils and a little shade. For especially well-coloured foliage, however, this purple-leaved form of *Ajuga reptans* needs a reasonably sunny site. In rich, moist soils this plant will spread widely.

8.22 Bergenia, Saxifraga & Viola

Bergenia crassifolia
sun/shade ○ ◐ **type of plant** hardy perennial
zonal range 3-8 (C-WT)
flowering time early to mid-spring
flower colour mauve-pink
height 30-40cm (12-15in)
special characteristics evergreen, decorative green foliage, autumn/winter foliage

Saxifraga × urbium
(London pride)
sun/shade ◐ **type of plant** hardy perennial
zonal range 6-7 (CT)
flowering time late spring to early summer
flower colour pale pink
height 23-30cm (9-12in)
special characteristics evergreen, decorative green foliage

Viola riviniana Purpurea Group
(syn *V. labradorica*, *V. l. purpurea*) (Labrador violet)
sun/shade ○ ◐ **type of plant** hardy perennial
zonal range 3-8 (C-WT)
flowering time mid- to late spring
flower colour purple-violet
height 10-15cm (4-6in)
special characteristics evergreen, purple foliage

Even when none of these plants is in flower, this is still an interesting combination of differing shapes and sizes. All three sets of leaves are evergreen, and so the association of large, relatively smooth shapes, more elaborate, crinkle-edged rosettes and little heart-shaped leaves is one that looks well almost all year long. London pride and the bergenia have leathery, green leaves, but the violet's mat of trailing stems is decorated with daintier, thinner-textured foliage. This foliage adds an important area of dark, concentrated purple to the composition.

The photograph shows the combination in late summer, when all three plants have flowered. In sheltered sites, the bergenia's long-stalked sprays may well begin to open during the last weeks of winter. Although the violet's blooms (see 3.27) are small, they have great charm. London pride also has small flowers, but they appear in large numbers above the plant's tight-knit carpet of foliage (see 3.33), with which the shining solidity of the bergenia's foliage contrasts markedly.

None of these plants is difficult to grow and all of them will create good ground cover in most soils and sites. London pride and the violet are, however, particularly well-suited to shade. In sunnier positions, the violet and London pride could be kept

relatively cool by careful positioning of the bergenia's substantial clump of leaves. In sun, the leaves of the violet will be a particularly deep purple and the bergenia's leaves will take on reddish, livery tones during the colder months. This violet is a prolific self-seeder, but the seedlings are very easily uprooted.

8.23 Tiarella & Acaena

Tiarella cordifolia
(foam flower)

sun/shade ◐

type of plant hardy perennial

zonal range 3-8 (C-WT)

flowering time late spring to early summer

flower colour pale cream

height 23-30cm (9-12in)

special characteristics evergreen, decorative green foliage, autumn/winter foliage

Acaena saccaticupula 'Blue Haze'
(syn *A.* 'Pewter')

sun/shade ○

type of plant hardy perennial

zonal range 6-8 (C-WT)

height 10-15cm (4-6in)

special characteristics semi-evergreen, blue-grey foliage, fruit

Handsomely lobed and interestingly coloured, the leaves of this tiarella make efficient and decorative ground cover in shady places. In this particular planting, the necessary shade has been provided by medium-sized shrubs nearby. In a rather lighter position in the foreground, there are the smoky, blue-grey leaves of an acaena. This vigorous, carpeting plant is particularly dense and well-coloured in full sun, but even when it is slightly shaded the tiny leaflets are sufficiently blue to look attractive with pale, yellowish greens – such as the lime-green of this tiarella's foliage.

Photographed here in late spring, the flower spikes of the tiarella are not yet fully expanded but they will open to form a soft froth of pale cream. The veins of the plant's leaves are stained bronze, and in late autumn and winter this colouring spreads over the whole leaf surface. From late summer, the acaena bears attractive, red-brown burrs. The preceding flowers are not generally regarded as decorative.

Both the acaena and the tiarella like well-drained soils but, though the acaena will thrive in quite dry places, the tiarella must have moisture to do well. In places where the whole site is shaded, the tiarella could be combined with, for instance, the purple-leaved violet in 3.27 and 8.22.

9 VARIEGATED FOLIAGE

Many of the most versatile plants for creating successful combinations have leaves that are a mixture of colours. The mixture can take the form of subtle colour blends – the neither-quite-grey-nor-quite-purple foliage of *Rosa glauca* is a case in point – or it can be made up of more or less clearly demarcated constituent colours, as it is in the case of variegated foliage.

The most familiar form of variegation among garden plants is that where a central, usually green, area of leaf is surrounded by a margin of different colouring. The ever-increasing number of white- or yellow-edged hostas conform to this pattern (see 9.19, 9.27, and 9.30). So too do plants like the variegated form of *Ilex aquifolium* in 9.14, and the variegated form of *Pachysandra terminalis* in 9.36.

Sometimes the centre of the leaf is yellow or white and the margin is green (see, for example, *Elaeagnus pungens* 'Maculata' in 9.17 and *Hosta undulata undulata* in 9.32). This second, 'reversed' kind of variegation tends to be rather unstable and wholly green leaves may be produced. Any of these all-green growths should be removed promptly before the entire plant becomes overwhelmed by more vigorous, plain green foliage.

Some of the plants mentioned above have foliage that is very neatly edged in a contrasting colour and the general effect is quite formal and precise. A much bolder and more flamboyant effect can be produced if the margins are wide and irregular (see *Hedera colchica* 'Sulphur Heart' in 14.4). Both these kinds of variegation are useful, though usually in different styles of plantings.

When long, slender leaves are edged in a contrasting colour they appear as stripes. Striping emphasizes the slenderness of long leaves and this can be exploited in combinations of contrasting plants. A different effect again is created if the variegation takes the form of marbling, veining, splashing or spotting. These more diffuse kinds of markings often create quite a gentle and restrained impression, but they can be bold and dashing.

DESIGNING WITH VARIEGATION

Just how conspicuous any variegated leaf appears to be and, therefore, how it combines with the leaves and flowers of other plants, depends on several factors. First, there is the pattern of variegation itself. Secondly, there is the relationship of the colours in a variegated leaf: a dark green leaf edged in white will be more noticeable than a yellow-green leaf with a yellow margin.

Then there is the effect of sun and shade: in shaded sites particularly, white gleams so strikingly that it can outshine everything around it, to the extent that it unbalances a group of plants. Sun and shade also have a direct influence on the intensity of the colours in variegated leaves. Individual plants vary but, as a broad generalization, most white-variegated plants appreciate shade. Where plants do well in either sun or shade, the brightness of the variegation tends to be greatest in sunshine, whatever the colour. In sun, however, there may be some unsightly browning of white- or yellow-edged leaves that are also thin in texture. Shelter from the damaging effects of strong sun, cold winds and very low temperatures is important for some variegated plants.

In the case of some variegated plants, the intensity of the leaf colours changes with the seasons. The variegation of several popular plants is brightest in spring. It then fades after the plants have flowered and becomes much more muted (see *Hosta fortunei albopicta* in 8.16 and *Iris pseudacorus* 'Variegata' in 16.12).

Finally, the appearance of any sort of variegation is affected by the distance from which it is viewed. Individually and at close quarters, the variegated leaves of some trees and larger shrubs can seem too bold, but at the boundary of a garden or at the back of a border the colours and markings of the leaves merge and the general effect is simply a lively lightness and airiness. At the other end of the scale, very small leaves with delicate markings need to be brought nearer to eye level in a raised bed or container in order to be appreciated.

Variegated foliage is a complex material, and a certain amount of forethought is essential if it is to be used effectively in gardens; but it is its complexity and variability that makes it so versatile. It is frequently regarded as difficult to place. But, in certain circumstances, the very presence of two or more colours in foliage makes those leaves fit in with other plants more readily than any plain green foliage might.

CREATING SUCCESSFUL PARTNERSHIPS

The extra colours of variegated leaves can echo the colours of nearby flowers, fruits and leaves and this creates very satisfying harmonies among groups of plants – see, for example, 1.36, 9.23 and 15.8. In each case, the two plants in each pair are clearly partners rather than just neighbours. And, of course, the great advantage of using leaves rather than flowers to establish these echoes and links is that the former tend to be decorative over a much longer period than the latter.

Variegated foliage can also be used as a source of contrasting rather than matching colour. White-variegated leaves combined with hot colours such as red and orange produce a bright, spruce effect; a calmer, clean look emerges when they are associated with blues and violets. The warmer colouring of much yellow-variegated foliage means that it is particularly compatible with reds and oranges. With cooler colours – and especially with its opposite or complementary colour, violet – it can produce surprisingly intense contrasts (see 1.39).

Combinations of variegated leaves and plain green foliage require careful balancing acts. Very starkly variegated foliage can outshine plain green leaves to the extent that the plain greens appear insignificant. However, integrated carefully into a group of plants, with flowers or fruits to repeat its extra colour if necessary, variegated foliage can be the most elegant enlivener of plain greenery. For its part, plain greenery calms variegation by providing a serene contrast to the beguiling vivacity of patterned leaves. Grey foliage finds its most compatible variegated partners among those leaves that are themselves basically grey or blue-grey. For those who enjoy variegated plants, there is fun – and much aesthetic pleasure – to be had in creating combinations involving more than one set of variegated leaves (see 1.39 and 9.34).

So wide is the range of patterns, sizes and colours in variegated foliage that, somewhere among the hostas and hollies and ivies, the thymes and mints, there will be a leaf pattern to suit every style of garden and gardener.

9.1 Elaeagnus & Juniperus

Elaeagnus × *ebbingei* 'Gilt Edge'
sun/shade ○ ◐
type of plant hardy shrub
zonal range 6-9 (C-WT)
height 1.5-1.8m (5-6ft)
special characteristics evergreen, variegated foliage, fragrant flowers

Juniperus chinensis 'Plumosa Aurea'
(juniper)
sun/shade ○
type of plant hardy conifer
zonal range 5-9 (C-WT)
height 3-3.6m (10-12ft)
special characteristics evergreen, yellow-green foliage, autumn/winter foliage

Both these plants are slow-growing at first, but they eventually make quite large specimens and can contribute substantially to the colour and texture of a winter border as well as looking good at other times of the year. The elaeagnus has smooth, leathery foliage, mistily olive-grey at first, and then broadly edged in bright, rich cream. In really open, sunny sites the edging is yellow. The juniper's tiny, scale-like leaves have a quite different, prickly look; they are suffused with yellow-green. In winter this conifer becomes bronzed and more gold in colour.

These two plants differ markedly in habit of growth: the elaeagnus makes a rather upright, fairly loose bush, whereas the juniper's branches splay upwards and outwards to create a much more striking shape. Although there are so many differences between these plants, they still look good together because of the immediately obvious link in their colouring.

The tiny cream blooms of the elaeagnus, which appear in autumn, are very sweetly fragrant but are so small as to be more or less invisible.

As long as the drainage is reasonably good, the juniper is happy in a wide range of soil types. The elaeagnus likes a moisture-retentive, well-drained soil. In cold winters it may shed some of its leaves.

9.2 Cornus & Meconopsis

Cornus alternifolia 'Argentea'
(syn *C. a.* 'Variegata')
(pagoda dogwood)
sun/shade ○
type of plant hardy shrub/tree
zonal range 5-7 (C-CT)
height 2.4-3m (8-10ft)
special characteristics variegated foliage

Meconopsis cambrica
(Welsh poppy)
sun/shade ○ ◐
type of plant hardy perennial
zonal range 6-8 (C-WT)
flowering time late spring to late summer
flower colour yellow or orange
height 30-45cm (12-18in)

The impression of lightness and delicacy created by this variegated dogwood is due partly to the broad edging of white on each of its grey-green leaves and partly to the way in which its branches are arranged in a series of horizontal layers. This distinctive structure makes the foliage seem as if it is almost floating.

Underplanting this edifice with the translucent, silky blooms of Welsh poppies heightens this airy effect still further. In a border or rockery these prolifically self-seeding poppies can be a nuisance, but in a relatively informal area and, importantly, with the competition of some grass, their loveliness can be appreciated without their fertility being resented. The sunshine colours of their flowers contrast pleasingly not only with the dogwood's rather cool foliage colour but also with their own pale green leaves. The dogwood's flowers appear in late spring or early summer, but the cream-white clusters tend to be lost among the variegated leaves.

The Welsh poppies will thrive almost anywhere, though they seem to appreciate some shade (which they are provided with here underneath the dogwood's branches). The dogwood will not grow well unless it is given both shelter and sun. It needs a well-drained soil.

9.3 Sambucus & Berberis

Sambucus nigra 'Marginata'
(syn *S. n.* 'Albomarginata')
(elder)
sun/shade ○ ◑
type of plant hardy shrub
zonal range 6-8 (C-CT)
flowering time early summer
flower colour creamy white
height 2.4-3m (8-10ft)
special characteristics variegated foliage, fruit, suitable for damp soils

Berberis × *ottawensis* 'Superba'
(syn *B. thunbergii* 'Atropurpurea Superba')
(barberry)
sun/shade ○
type of plant hardy shrub
zonal range 5-9 (C-WT)
flowering time late spring
flower colour yellow + red
height 1.8-2.4m (6-8ft)
Special characteristics purple foliage, autumn foliage

Particularly when it is in full, foamy flower, this variegated form of elder is a lovely mixture of bright green and creamy white. The freshness and liveliness of this colouring is emphasized here by an accompaniment of exceptionally deep red-purple berberis foliage which, much later in the year, turns radiant red and orange before falling. In autumn the elder also takes on some purplish tones, and from late summer onwards its generous bunches of black berries are conspicuous among its pale leaves. The berberis's clusters of little flowers are followed by red berries, but some specimens do not seem to fruit as reliably as others.

Both shrubs have a more or less rounded outline, but the berberis's prickly branches are of a more markedly upright and then arching habit of growth. For the best leaf colour, the berberis needs sun. However, a very exposed position is not suitable for this combination since this may lead to the elder's foliage becoming scorched.

Almost any soil will produce satisfactory results with these shrubs, but if plenty of good foliage is wanted the conditions must be reasonably moist. The elder's flowers have a heavy, fruity scent that is not to everyone's taste.

9.4 Cornus & Aster

Cornus alba 'Spaethii'
(red-barked dogwood)
sun/shade ○ ◑
type of plant hardy shrub
zonal range 3-9 (C-CT)
height 1.8m (6ft)
special characteristics variegated foliage, autumn foliage, ornamental twigs, suitable for damp and wet soils

Aster × *frikartii* 'Mönch'
sun/shade ○
type of plant hardy perennial
zonal range 5-8 (C-WT)
flowering time late summer to mid-autumn
flower colour lavender-blue
height 90cm (3ft)

This cheerful, late summer combination of yellow and blue could have been achieved with flowers alone, but by using a shrub to contribute the yellow of the scheme the season of interest has been greatly extended and a firmer structure added to the whole area of planting. Throughout spring and summer the cornus's shapely green and yellow foliage is vividly coloured, while the aster produces a succession of finely petalled flowers over an exceptionally long period.

As the last of the aster's blooms appear, the foliage of the cornus starts to take on soft orange tints. Later still, when these leaves have fallen, the upright, deep red stems are revealed. For a good display of well-coloured stems, this shrub must have at least some of its older growth cut right back each year in spring.

Aster × *frikartii* and its varieties are unusually mildew-free relations of the Michaelmas daisy. They will grow well in a variety of soils, but will produce the greatest number of flowers on their well-branched stems if they are given a fertile, moisture-retentive soil with good drainage. The name 'Mönch' tends to be applied to several different varieties of this aster, but they are all attractive plants. The cornus is a vigorous plant that thrives in most soils and sites, including damp and wet areas.

9.5 Griselinia & Ballota

Griselinia littoralis 'Variegata'
sun/shade ○
type of plant slightly tender shrub
zonal range 9-10 (WT-ST)
height 1.8m (6ft)
special characteristics evergreen, variegated foliage

Ballota pseudodictamnus
sun/shade ○
type of plant slightly tender perennial/shrub
zonal range 7-9 (CT-WT)
flowering time early to mid-summer
flower colour mauve
height 45-60cm (1½-2ft)
special characteristics evergreen/semi-evergreen, grey foliage

This griselinia's gleaming leaves are at first a combination of bright green and yellow, but as they mature the colouring becomes a rather softer mixture of greyish-green and cream. Both the earlier, sharper colouring and the later, more subdued tones associate pleasingly with the gentle grey of *Ballota pseudodictamnus*. There are also interesting contrasts in texture and in habit of growth in this combination: the ballota's leaves are woolly, whereas the griselinia's are very smooth and leathery, and the ballota's felted stems are distinctly erect against the griselinia's more rounded mass of foliage.

Although *Griselinia littoralis* itself can withstand salty, seaside winds, this variegated and more expensive form should be planted in less exposed positions. Sun and shelter are important and in all but the mildest districts really good drainage is essential, too, since the plant is likely to suffer if the roots are cold and wet in winter. The ballota enjoys the same sunny, well-drained conditions as the griselinia. Its flowers are small, but at close range they are very becoming to the overall prettiness of the plant. It consorts well with many different flowers and leaves, including those of *Carpenteria californica* (see 13.3) and *Salvia officinalis* Purpurascens Group (see 4.15).

9.6 Berberis & Weigela

Berberis thunbergii
f. atropurpurea
(barberry)
sun/shade ○
type of plant hardy shrub
zonal range 5-8 (C-WT)
flowering time mid- to late spring
flower colour pale yellow + red
height 1.2-1.8m (4-6ft)
special characteristics purple foliage, autumn foliage, fruit

Weigela 'Praecox Variegata'
sun/shade ○ ◖
type of plant hardy shrub
zonal range 5-8 (C-WT)
flowering time late spring to early summer
flower colour pink
height 1.5-1.8m (5-6ft)
special characteristics variegated foliage

The habit of growth of these two shrubs is not so very dissimilar and therefore all attention is focused on the difference between the light, soft colouring of the weigela's variegated foliage and the rich red-brown of the berberis's little leaves. The overall effect of this combination – of dense, arching, dark-leaved branches and more upright main growths of paler foliage – is gentle and informal.

Both sets of leaves are still relatively new here in late spring. During early summer they broaden and elongate somewhat, and later in summer the weigela's leaf margins change from white to light yellow-green. In mid-autumn the berberis's foliage turns fiery red and is accompanied by the shiny red berries of the plant, which begin to ripen in late summer. In autumn, too, the weigela's leaves, which remain fresh-looking well into winter, may become tinged with pink. There is usually a short period during which the berberis's clusters of little flowers overlap with the slightly scented pink blooms of the weigela.

These two plants are tolerant of a wide range of growing conditions. The prickly berberis will thrive in any soil that is neither very wet nor very alkaline. It needs sun for its foliage to colour well. The weigela will produce plenty of its pretty foliage in soils that retain moisture fairly easily.

9.7 Berberis & Anemone

Berberis thunbergii 'Rose Glow'

(barberry)

sun/shade ○
type of plant hardy shrub
zonal range 5-8 (C-WT)
flowering time mid- to late spring
flower colour pale yellow + red
height 1.2m (4ft)
special characteristics variegated foliage, autumn foliage, fruit

Anemone × hybrida 'Königin Charlotte'

(syn *A. × h.* 'Queen Charlotte', *A. japonica* 'Königin Charlotte', *A. j.* 'Queen Charlotte')
(Japanese anemone)

sun/shade ○ ◖
type of plant hardy perennial
zonal range 5-8 (C-WT)
flowering time late summer to mid-autumn
flower colour pink
height 75-90cm (2½-3ft)

As it matures, the foliage of *Berberis thunbergii* 'Rose Glow' gradually loses its pink and grey variegation and becomes a more or less uniform red-purple. Against such a rich leaf colour, the outline of each of these large, open-faced, Japanese anemone flowers is beautifully clear and precise. The numerous touches of subdued pink that remain on some of the berberis's younger leaves provide a pleasing link with these pale pink flowers.

To encourage plenty of lighter, variegated foliage, this prickly, arching shrub should be given a sunny position, pruned in spring and lightly clipped from time to time during the summer months. The conspicuously variegated summer leaves also look good with pale foliage (see 9.8) and with leaves even darker than themselves (see 15.8).

The berberis's flower clusters are followed, from late summer onwards, by shining, rich red, droplet-shaped berries. There is a final burst of colour – usually in mid-autumn – from this plant, when its leaves turn crimson and orange-red before they fall.

The anemone's fairly large, lobed foliage creates usefully dense ground cover. Particularly in heavy-ish soils, this plant may eventually spread widely. It can be grown in a variety of soils. Apart from a dislike of wet and very alkaline soils, the berberis is easily pleased.

9.8 Berberis & Acaena

Berberis thunbergii 'Rose Glow'

(barberry)

sun/shade ○
type of plant hardy shrub
zonal range 5-8 (C-WT)
flowering time mid- to late spring
flower colour pale yellow + red
height 1.2m (4ft)
special characteristics variegated foliage, autumn foliage, fruit

Acaena saccaticupula 'Blue Haze'

(syn *A.* 'Pewter')

sun/shade ○
type of plant hardy perennial
zonal range 6-8 (C-WT)
height 10-15cm (4-6in)
special characteristics semi-evergreen, blue-grey foliage, fruit

The pink and grey mottling of this berberis's foliage is pretty, but it can look rather too busy unless combined with plants of more straightforward colouring. Here the plain, blue-grey leaves and dense growth of an acaena create a low carpet which contrasts attractively with the looser, slightly arching growth and more elaborate foliage of the berberis.

When they first emerge the berberis's leaves are briefly plain red-purple, but they soon become variegated. Mature foliage, and foliage produced in shady sites, is almost entirely purple; if plenty of pink, well-marked leaves are wanted, a sunny position must be chosen and at least some pruning should be carried out each year in spring, followed by periodic light clipping during the summer. In autumn, the foliage of this prickly shrub turns a mixture of crimson and orange-red and there are also shiny, rich red berries. The acaena also bears fruit, in the form of red-brown burrs, from late summer. Its preceding flowers are not very decorative.

Like the typical species, 'Rose Glow' will grow in almost any soil as long as it is neither very alkaline nor wet. The acaena needs good drainage to remain dense and neat. It is a vigorous plant that can spread widely, or even become invasive, when well-suited.

9.9 Hebe & Vinca

Hebe rakaiensis

sun/shade ○
type of plant hardy/slightly tender shrub
zonal range 8-10 (WT-ST)
flowering time early to mid-summer
flower colour white
height 60cm (2ft)
special characteristics evergreen, decorative green foliage

Vinca minor 'Argenteovariegata'

(syn V. m. 'Variegata')
(lesser periwinkle)
sun/shade ○ ◐
type of plant hardy shrub/perennial
zonal range 4-9 (C-WT)
flowering time mid-spring to early summer
flower colour pale violet-blue
height 10-15cm (4-6in)
special characteristics evergreen, variegated foliage

The variegated forms of *Vinca minor* all produce close carpets of trailing, rooting stems and prettily marked leaves. *V. m.* 'Argenteovariegata' has foliage that is basically greyish-green, with leaf edges that are at first cream and later white. In the combination illustrated here, the plant is weaving around beneath a tidy bun of apple-green leaves. The resultant pale-on-pale partnership is prevented from being a muddle of light green by the marked difference in habit of growth of the two plants involved.

Both these plants have pretty flowers. The periwinkle often produces some blooms in late summer and autumn as well as earlier in the year. The hebe's flowers are fluffy little spikes that are sprinkled – usually rather unevenly – over the dense, domed surface of the plant.

Vinca minor and its varieties are frequently planted in dry, shady places. However, the variegated forms are worthy of better treatment, and in any case flowering is much more prolific when the plants are either in sun or only lightly shaded. Both flowers and leaves also respond well to having a soil that is reasonably moisture-retentive. The hebe does best in well-drained, but not very dry conditions.

For a combination that places this periwinkle beneath a shrub with dark foliage, see 8.13.

9.10 Yucca & Ophiopogon

Yucca filamentosa 'Variegata'

(Adam's needle)
sun/shade ○
type of plant hardy shrub
zonal range 5-9 (CT-ST)
flowering time mid- to late summer
flower colour pale cream
height 45-60cm (1½-2ft)
special characteristics evergreen, variegated foliage, fragrant flowers

Ophiopogon planiscapus 'Nigrescens'

sun/shade ○ ◐
type of plant hardy perennial
zonal range 6-10 (CT-ST)
flowering time mid- to late summer
flower colour pale pink-mauve
height 15cm (6in)
special characteristics evergreen, purple foliage, fruit

The dense clumps of foliage produced by yuccas are always dramatic, but especially so when the sword-shaped leaves are variegated, as they are in this form of *Yucca filamentosa*. Planting this bold variegated foliage with an exceptionally dark-leaved plant emphasizes both the yucca's stripiness and the thin, almost black leaves of the ophiopogon. Since both plants are evergreen, this a combination that looks interesting all year long.

There are flowers, too, but this form of yucca is a good deal less free-flowering than its green-leaved counterpart, and the ophiopogon's blooms, visible here in late summer, are attractive in a fairly subdued way. This slow-growing yucca is most likely to flower in the really warm, sheltered sites and fertile, well-drained soils it likes best. When they do appear, the bell-shaped blooms are carried 90-120cm (3-4ft) high in sumptuous heads. They release a fresh, clean fragrance in the evening. The ophiopogon's flowers are followed by long-lasting, black berries. For this plant's wonderful, spidery heaps of foliage to grow thickly, conditions should not be too dry.

The colour and markings of plants sold under the name *Y. f.* 'Variegata' will vary somewhat, but there is also a distinct form with thin, yellow margins called 'Bright Edge'.

9.11 Anaphalis & Lamium

Anaphalis triplinervis
(pearly everlasting)
sun/shade ○
type of plant hardy perennial
zonal range 4-9 (C-WT)
flowering time late summer to early autumn
flower colour white
height 30-45cm (12-18in)
special characteristics grey foliage

Lamium maculatum 'White Nancy'
(spotted dead nettle)
sun/shade ◑
type of plant hardy perennial
zonal range 4-8 (C-WT)
flowering time mid-spring to early summer
flower colour white
height 12-20cm (5-8in)
special characteristics evergreen, variegated foliage

Although the light requirements of these two perennials seem to be incompatible, both plants can in fact be grown together. Unusually for a grey-leaved plant, *Anaphalis triplinervis* needs a moisture-retentive soil, and as long as the lamium has moisture at its roots it too will grow well in some sun. In this particular pairing, the anaphalis's taller, curving stems mingle with the lamium's carpet of loose-stemmed foliage and thereby provide the smaller plant with some shade.

Considering that the plants are shown here in mid-autumn, this white and grey composition is looking remarkably fresh. The lamium's flowers will have finished many weeks before, although a few later blooms are often produced intermittently. However, the papery texture of the anaphalis bracts means that the flowers dry on the plant and are therefore decorative long after their official flowering period is over.

Just as decorative as these flowers are the two sets of leaves. Each silvery, heart-shaped leaf of the lamium has a thin margin of green that gives the whole plant a very precise appearance. The felted foliage of the anaphalis has a rather firmer, more solid look to it.

For another late season association featuring *Lamium maculatum* 'White Nancy', see 9.22.

9.12 Geranium & Vinca

Geranium cinereum 'Lawrence Flatman'
(cranesbill)
sun/shade ○
type of plant hardy perennial
zonal range 5-8 (C-WT)
flowering time late spring to early autumn
flower colour pink + dark crimson
height 10cm (4in)
special characteristics semi-evergreen/evergreen

Vinca minor 'Argenteovariegata'
(syn *V. m.* 'Variegata')
(lesser periwinkle)
sun/shade ○ ◑
type of plant hardy shrub/perennial
zonal range 4-9 (C-WT)
flowering time mid-spring to early summer
flower colour pale violet-blue
height 10-15cm (4-6in)
special characteristics evergreen, variegated foliage

The lovely veined and dark-eyed flowers of this geranium are produced over many weeks. As an accompaniment, they have here not only the plant's own neat, lobed greenery but also pale and pretty periwinkle foliage. The foliage is basically grey-green with margins that are at first cream and then white. Because both these sets of leaves are of a similar size and the main contrast is one of leaf colour, the foliage does not detract from the flowers.

The periwinkle has just finished flowering here, in early summer, though it will often produce some blooms later, too. At all stages the combination of pink geraniums and blue periwinkles has great charm, and the intermingling of the geranium's rather loose and tangled clump of leaves and the periwinkle's variegated carpet is attractive over an even longer period.

Though the very vigorous, plain-leaved varieties of *Vinca minor* are often relegated to rooty, shaded places, the less rampageous variegated forms benefit from better treatment. This particular combination requires sun for the sake of the geranium, and sun will also enhance the variegation and stimulate the flowering of the periwinkle. While the geranium needs a well-drained soil, conditions must not be hot and dry if the periwinkle is to grow densely and produce plenty of good-looking foliage.

149

9.13 Aucuba & Cedrus

Aucuba japonica 'Crotonifolia'
(spotted laurel)
sun/shade ○ ◑
type of plant hardy/slightly tender shrub
zonal range 7-10 (CT-ST)
height 1.5-2.4m (5-8ft)
special characteristics evergreen, variegated foliage

Cedrus deodara 'Aurea'
(golden Deodar cedar)
sun/shade ○ ◑
type of plant hardy conifer
zonal range 7-8 (CT-WT)
height 4.5-6m (15-20ft)
special characteristics evergreen, yellow-green foliage

The spotted laurels are among the most despised of all shrubs, and gardeners who take over established specimens often plan to get rid of them as soon as possible. However, another approach to the problem is to keep the shrubs and to enhance their good points by the addition of other, flattering plants. In their favour the spotted laurels have big, glossy leaves, they almost invariably form large mounds of healthy foliage, and they are tolerant of all sorts of difficult growing conditions.

The yellow-leaved conifer shown here makes a successful partner for this variegated aucuba partly because, in a suitably low-key way, it echoes the aucuba's colouring. In addition, its arching, pendulous habit of growth contrasts elegantly with the aucuba's much denser, rounded shape and its needles are radically different from the aucuba's large, broad leaves. These contrasts in habit and leaf size will be attractive even when, during the colder months, the cedar's youngest foliage changes from yellow to green.

Both these plants are initially slow-growing. The aucuba is outstandingly easy to please. The cedar, however, needs a fertile, well-drained soil and some shelter when young.

For another combination featuring a spotted laurel, see 7.10.

9.14 Ilex & Cornus

Ilex aquifolium yellow-margined form
(holly)
sun/shade ○ ◑
type of plant hardy shrub
zonal range 7-9 (CT-WT)
height 4.5-5.4m (15-18ft)
special characteristics evergreen, variegated foliage, fruit

Cornus alba 'Sibirica'
(red-barked dogwood)
sun/shade ○ ◑
type of plant hardy shrub
zonal range 3-8 (C-CT)
height 1.5-2.4m (5-8ft)
special characteristics autumn foliage, ornamental twigs, suitable for damp and wet soils

Good, yellow-margined forms of *Ilex aquifolium* include 'Golden van Tol' and 'Madame Briot'. (The yellow edging on the leaves of the variety shown here appears paler than normal in low winter sunshine.) The foliage of these plants makes a colourful, often contrastingly prickly accompaniment to the smooth, brilliant red stems of *Cornus alba* 'Sibirica'. Partnering these stems with white- or very pale cream-variegated holly leaves, such as those shown in 9.15 gives a somewhat cooler, crisper effect. Variegated hollies will also enliven this cornus in summer, when its tapering leaves are an unremarkable plain green until they assume their orange and red autumn tints.

For plenty of very brightly coloured stems to be produced, this cornus needs to be cut right back each spring, or at least every other spring. A sunny position shows off the colour best.

Both of these plants are easily grown. *Ilex aquifolium* and its forms have a preference for well-drained soils. The cornus will thrive near water and in drier places, too. It is a vigorous, upright, quick-growing plant, while the hollies slowly form bushy cones or broad columns of growth. When fertilized, female yellow-variegated hollies bear clusters of red berries.

9.15 **Ilex & Arum**

Ilex aquifolium 'Silver Queen'

(holly)

sun/shade ○ ◖
type of plant hardy shrub
zonal range 7-9 (C-CT)
height 4.5-5.4m (15-18ft)
special characteristics evergreen, variegated foliage

Arum italicum ssp. *italicum* 'Marmoratum'

(syn *A. i.* 'Pictum')

sun/shade ○ ◖
type of plant hardy tuber
zonal range 6-9 (C-ST)
flowering time late spring
flower colour greenish cream
height 30-45cm (12-18in)
special characteristics variegated foliage, fruit

For those who particularly like variegated foliage, this sort of association, where two similarly coloured but differently marked plants are combined, has special appeal. The partnership here has the added attraction of looking its best all through the coldest months of the year: even if the arum's marbled spearheads of foliage become frozen they revive undamaged after thawing, while the broad, pale-edged, prickly leaves of the holly are remarkably tough and frost-resistant. In spring, the youngest growths on *I. a.* 'Silver Queen' are attractively pink-tinged.

The arum's leaves first appear in mid-autumn, after the bare-stemmed heads of poisonous, orange-red berries, which will have begun to ripen in late summer. The leaves finally die down in early summer. The flowers of this plant are less striking than either its leaves or its berries.

On both plants, the most distinct markings occur in positions that are not too shady. However, dry, sunny places are not suitable, since the arum needs a cool, moisture-retentive soil to produce good clumps of growth. Here light shade is provided at the edges of the holly's bushy cone of branches. Well-drained soils of all sorts suit the holly best, but it is a very robust and tolerant, if slow-growing, plant that will prosper almost anywhere.

9.16 **Hedera & Camellia**

Hedera canariensis 'Gloire de Marengo'

(syn *H.c.* 'Variegata')
(ivy)

sun/shade ○ ◖
type of plant slightly tender climber
zonal range 9-10 (WT)
height 3-4.5m (10-15ft)
special characteristics evergreen, variegated foliage

Camellia × *williamsii* 'Donation'

sun/shade ○ ◖
type of plant hardy shrub
zonal range 7-9 (CT-WT)
flowering time early to mid-spring
flower colour pink
height 1.8-3m (6-10ft)
special characteristics evergreen, decorative green foliage, needs acid soil

Especially if their flowers are big and either double or semi-double, camellias tend to be simultaneously formal and flamboyant and this can make them difficult to mix with other plants. Here the 12cm (5in) flowers of this vigorous, rather upright camellia have been given a backdrop of large ivy leaves which are irregularly variegated in grey-green and creamy white. There are no flowers that might outshine the camellia's blooms, but the rather cool colouring of the ivy foliage is very flattering to the pretty pink of the camellia. It also provides an excellent, relatively light background for the camellia's good-looking, leathery leaves of a deep, polished green.

Both plants here need shelter from severe frosts and cold winds. In really favourable positions and in certain years the camellia begins to flower in late winter. The numerous flowers are normally fairly robust but they are still liable to damage if they thaw too quickly after a frost. An east-facing position is therefore unsuitable. The edges of the ivy's maroon-stemmed leaves often become pink-tinged in winter. The camellia must have an acid soil and, ideally, this should be both well-drained and moisture-retentive. The ivy, which clings to supports by means of stem-roots, will grow in most soils.

9.17 Elaeagnus & Viburnum

Elaeagnus pungens 'Maculata'
(syn *E. p.* 'Aureovariegata')
sun/shade ○ ◑
type of plant hardy shrub
zonal range 7-10 (WT-ST)
height 2.4-3m (8-10ft)
special characteristics evergreen, variegated foliage, fragrant flowers

Viburnum rhytidophyllum
sun/shade ○ ◑
type of plant hardy shrub
zonal range 6-8 (C-WT)
flowering time late spring to early summer
flower colour creamy white
height 3-3.6m (10-12ft)
special characteristics evergreen, decorative green foliage, fruit

*E*laeagnus pungens 'Maculata' has characteristically broad, central areas of yellow on each of its glossy leaves. This colouring is at its brightest in winter (the photograph shows the plant in midspring; see 12.2 for the leaves in mid-autumn).

The foliage is borne on angular shoots and overall the shrub has a spreading, rather disorganized habit of growth. In contrast, the accompanying viburnum has a much more dignified appearance, with its rounded, spreading shape and long, deeply crinkled leaves of a somewhat sombre green.

The elaeagnus does flower, in mid- and late autumn, though in colder gardens particularly its tiny, very sweetly scented cream blooms may not appear every year. The viburnum blooms reliably, and even in brown-felted bud, as here, the flowers are striking. If several plants are grown together, good crops of berries are produced. The fruits ripen from red to black in early autumn.

Most soils, as long as they are fairly moisture-retentive, are suitable for both these shrubs. The viburnum is a fast-growing plant that flourishes in sheltered sites. The elaeagnus grows slowly when young. It has a tendency to produce shoots with plain green leaves, and unless these are completely removed, plain green foliage will soon predominate.

9.18 Ligustrum & Lonicera

Ligustrum ovalifolium 'Aureum'
(golden privet)
sun/shade ○ ◑
type of plant hardy shrub
zonal range 6-11 (CT-ST)
flowering time midsummer
flower colour white
height 2.7-3.6m (9-12ft)
special characteristics evergreen/semi-evergreen, yellow foliage/variegated foliage

Lonicera nitida 'Baggesen's Gold'
(shrubby honeysuckle)
sun/shade ○ ◑
type of plant hardy shrub
zonal range 7-9 (CT-ST)
height 1.2-1.8m (4-6ft)
special characteristics evergreen, yellow foliage

*I*n a position of partial shade, as here, the foliage of both these plants is yellow-green in colouring. In sun, the lonicera's tiny leaves are much yellower (see 6.4) and sunshine makes the privet's foliage altogether more stridently coloured and more conspicuously variegated. Often, however, the gentle, shade-induced lime-green marries more easily with other colours than the harsher yellows produced by sun. This particular partnership could, for instance, be used as a background for plants of stronger yellows, as it would enhance their colour.

Left unclipped, both these plants have attractive, contrasting habits of growth: the privet produces a fairly loose, bushy structure of upright, splaying branches, whereas the lonicera has a dense but rather spiky outline. There are pleasing contrasts in leaf shape and size, too. Flowers are very much of secondary importance here, and the privet's blooms have the drawback of smelling offensively heavy to many people. As compensation, both sets of foliage look good almost all year round.

The privet is easily accommodated in most soils, including those that are dry and poor. In hot climates it may self-seed very prolifically. However, if these shrubs are to produce good quality foliage they both need a reasonably fertile, well-drained soil that is not too dry.

9.19 Ligustrum & Hosta

Ligustrum ovalifolium 'Aureum'
(golden privet)
sun/shade ○ ◐
type of plant hardy shrub
zonal range 6-11 (CT-ST)
flowering time midsummer
flower colour white
height 2.7-3.6m (9-12ft)
special characteristics evergreen/semi-evergreen, yellow foliage/variegated foliage

Hosta fortunei var. aureomarginata
(syn *H.* 'Obscura Marginata', *H.* 'Yellow Edge')
(plantain lily)
sun/shade ○ ◐
type of plant hardy perennial
zonal range 3-9 (C-WT)
flowering time midsummer
flower colour violet
height 90cm (3ft)
special characteristics variegated foliage, suitable for damp soils

White-variegated hostas can enhance the white flowers of other plants (see 16.18). In the same way, yellow-variegated hostas can flatter yellowish flowers (see 9.23) or – as here – yellow leaves. *Hosta fortunei aureomarginata* is a particularly valuable variety since its light yellowish-green margins remain colourful well into autumn.

In the combination shown here, this hosta has been paired with a clipped specimen of golden privet. In sunny sites the variegation of this shrub tends to be sharply defined and some leaves are entirely yellow. In shadier sites the leaf margins are greener and the colouring is altogether gentler (see 9.18). Left untrimmed, the plant forms a bushy mass of upright, splaying branches. Its small, smooth leaves will always contrast interestingly with clumps of bigger, bolder leaves like those of the hosta. The hosta produces good heads of trumpet-shaped flowers. Most people find the scent of the privet's flowers heavy and unpleasant.

Though it can be grown in a wide variety of soil types, golden privet will produce much better quality foliage in the fertile, moisture-retentive conditions enjoyed by the hosta. In rich, damp soils the hosta grows very luxuriantly. Self-sown seedlings of the privet may be a nuisance in hot climates.

9.20 Iris, Cornus & Bergenia

Iris pseudacorus 'Variegata'
(yellow flag)
sun/shade ○ ◐ **type of plant** hardy perennial
zonal range 5-9 (C-WT)
flowering time early summer
flower colour yellow + brown
height 90cm (3ft)
special characteristics variegated foliage, suitable for water gardens, and damp and wet soils

Cornus alba 'Elegantissima'
(red-barked dogwood)
sun/shade ○ ◐ **type of plant** hardy shrub
zonal range 3-8 (C-CT) **height** 1.8-2.7m (6-9ft)
special characteristics variegated foliage, autumn foliage, ornamental twigs, suitable for damp and wet soils

Bergenia 'Bressingham Ruby'
sun/shade ○ ◐ **type of plant** hardy perennial
zonal range 3-8 (C-ST)
flowering time mid- to late spring
flower colour deep pink
height 30-40cm (12-15in)
special characteristics evergreen, decorative green foliage, autumn/winter foliage

The splendid, striped exclamation marks of this iris are given firm full stops in the form of solid, rounded bergenia leaves. A contrasting softness of shape and colour is added by the cornus, with its relatively small, grey-green, white-edged foliage. Even when the variegation of the iris has faded, as it does gradually after flowering, the sword-like shape of the plant's leaves continues to look striking.

Though this is predominantly a group of spring and summer foliage contrasts, these three plants between them have plenty of other interesting features. In spring, the bergenia's strongly coloured flower clusters appear on top of maroon stems. Later, in early summer, the flowers of the iris appear, tending to mingle with the plant's striped leaves. As the weather becomes colder, the bergenia's leaves can take on purple-maroon tones and the cornus's foliage will turn soft shades of orange and pink.

Later still, when the leaves of the cornus have fallen, the upright, maroon stems of this shrub become visible. These stems are most colourful when young. Some gardeners cut back all the stems each year to encourage the maximum amount of new growth. Others remove only a proportion of stems, so that an unsightly gap is not left.

Both the cornus and the iris will grow well in damp or wet soils. The iris is also suitable for plant-

ing in shallow water. However, these are adaptable plants that will thrive in ordinary, moisture-retentive soils. In such conditions the iris may be nearer 60cm (2ft) in height. The bergenia is not a plant for wet or very damp soils, but will grow almost anywhere else.

9.21 Astrantia & Cornus

Astrantia major rubra
(masterwort)
sun/shade ○ ◐
type of plant hardy perennial
zonal range 4-8 (C-WT)
flowering time early to late summer
flower colour dusky wine-red
height 60cm (2ft)

Cornus alba 'Spaethii'
(red-barked dogwood)
sun/shade ○ ◐
type of plant hardy shrub
zonal range 3-9 (C-CT)
height 1.8m (6ft)
special characteristics variegated foliage, autumn foliage, ornamental twigs, suitable for damp and wet soils

Each fresh green, elegantly tapered leaf of *Cornus alba* 'Spaethii' has a bright yellow edge. In full sun this colouring may be too dazzling for some gardeners, but it can be tamed somewhat by partial shade. Even if the plant is grown in sun, the foliage does not scorch as is sometimes the case with yellow-variegated plants.

Here these leaves are combined with a form of *Astrantia major* which has the usual long-lasting, papery flowers but unusual deep colouring. The clumps of divided foliage are also darker than those of the typical species.

This combination of bright variegated leaves and richly coloured blooms looks good throughout the summer months. In mid-autumn the leaves of the cornus begin to turn attractive shades of soft orange, and the astrantia's foliage quite often becomes a rich yellow. Later still, after leaf fall, the deep red of the cornus's youngest stems is revealed. Since the brightest colouring is on the newest growths, hard pruning of at least some of the stems is needed each spring.

All the varieties of *Cornus alba* are vigorous, upright plants. They thrive in damp and wet ground, but they also do very well in drier soils. A drier soil is required here as although the astrantia appreciates moisture, it needs good drainage, too.

9.22 Fuchsia & Lamium

Fuchsia magellanica var. *gracilis*
sun/shade ○ ◐
type of plant slightly tender shrub
zonal range 8-9 (WT-ST)
flowering time midsummer to mid-autumn
flower colour red + violet
height 90-120cm (3-4ft)

Lamium maculatum 'White Nancy'
(spotted dead nettle)
sun/shade ◐
type of plant hardy perennial
zonal range 4-8 (C-WT)
flowering time mid-spring to early summer
flower colour white
height 12-20cm (5-8in)
special characteristics evergreen, variegated foliage

After a few early autumn frosts – and a recent downpour – the silvery-white, green-rimmed leaves of the lamium shown here are not at their crispest and cleanest. Nevertheless, these leaves make an excellent background for the arching growths and brilliant, hanging bells of a fuchsia, and the whole combination is bright and vivacious. (See 9.11 for a photograph of the lamium in mid-autumn when a more sheltered site has protected the foliage.)

Much earlier in the year, the lamium will have produced its upright little clusters of white, hooded blooms. Even in the absence of any fuchsia flowers, these white blooms contrast pleasingly with the shrub's rich green foliage and its red-stemmed, downward-curving growths. In mild areas the fuchsia does not die back to ground level each year and therefore eventually grows quite tall. In such places, the fuchsia begins to flower in late spring and the flowering seasons of the fuchsia and the lamium overlap.

Both the plants in this combination like a soil that is moist and also well-drained. Provided the lamium's carpet of growth can receive some shade, either from the fuchsia or from other nearby plants, this combination can be placed in a sunny position.

9.23 Hosta & Alchemilla

Hosta fortunei var. aureomarginata

(syn H. 'Obscura Marginata', H. 'Yellow Edge')
(plantain lily)
sun/shade ○ ◖
type of plant hardy perennial
zonal range 3-9 (C-WT)
flowering time midsummer
flower colour violet
height 90cm (3ft)
special characteristics variegated foliage, suitable for damp soils

Alchemilla mollis

(lady's mantle)
sun/shade ○ ◖
type of plant hardy perennial
zonal range 4-8 (C-WT)
flowering time early to mid-summer
flower colour yellow-green
height 45cm (18in)
special characteristics decorative green foliage, suitable for damp soils

While the foamy flowers of *Alchemilla mollis* would look good with the smoothly shaped leaves of almost any hosta, a yellow-edged variety such as the one shown here makes a particularly good partner. As well as creating good contrasts in shape, this hosta echoes very pleasingly the flower colour of the alchemilla.

The pale, greenish-yellow margins of this hosta retain their colouring well into autumn. If the untidy late-summer growths of the alchemilla are cut right back and a small second crop of flowers results, this is an especially long-lasting combination. The alchemilla is in any case very attractive over a period of many months, since its velvety, lime-green leaves are of such a pretty scalloped shape. The alchemilla produces a mound of leaves, while the hosta quite quickly creates a layered clump of foliage about 45-60cm (1½-2ft) high, above which its trumpet-shaped flowers are borne in generous heads.

Alchemilla mollis will grow vigorously and produce copious quantities of self-sown seedlings in almost any soil. It will even do well by streams and in other areas of damp but not waterlogged soil. The hosta must have moisture and a fairly cool position in order to thrive. Both plants are very efficient suppressors of weeds once established.

9.24 Symphytum & Tanacetum

Symphytum × uplandicum 'Variegatum'

(syn S. peregrinum 'Variegatum')
(comfrey)
sun/shade ○ ◖
type of plant hardy perennial
zonal range 5-9 (C-WT)
flowering time late spring to early summer
flower colour lilac-pink changing to blue
height 90cm (3ft)
special characteristics evergreen/semi-evergreen, variegated foliage, suitable for damp soils

Tanacetum vulgare var. crispum

(tansy)
sun/shade ○ ◖
type of plant hardy perennial
zonal range 4-9 (C-WT)
height 60cm (2ft)
special characteristics aromatic, decorative green foliage

Almost as striking as the difference in colouring between the leaves of these two plants is their marked contrast in texture: the comfrey's foliage is large and simple in shape, whereas the tansy's leaves are intricate and the individual leaflets are tiny. The comfrey's bolder foliage is a mixture of soft grey-green and pale cream, contrasting with the plain, rich green of the tansy leaves.

The tansy's feathery leaves are carried on upright stems and the comfrey's flowering stems are erect, too. However, the general effect of the tansy is one of a densely frilled mass. Because this mass is so finely textured, the plant provides a surprisingly unfussy background for the comfrey.

If the comfrey's flowering stems are cut right back after the flowers have faded, a second, 30cm (12in) crop of large basal leaves emerges. This second show of bold foliage looks good well into autumn, particularly if the plant is given fairly moist growing conditions. Where a drier position is chosen, the foliage benefits from some shade.

Almost any reasonably well-drained soil and most sites will suit the tansy. Though less energetic than the typical species, the variety shown here is vigorous. Like the species, its foliage is strongly and rather sweetly aromatic. However, there are usually few, if any, flowers (though see 11.4).

155

9.25 Liriope & Euonymus

Liriope muscari
(lily turf)
sun/shade ○ ◐
type of plant hardy perennial
zonal range 6-10 (CT-ST)
flowering time late summer to late autumn
flower colour violet
height 30-45cm (12-18in)
special characteristics evergreen, decorative
green foliage

Euonymus fortunei 'Emerald Gaiety'
sun/shade ○ ◐
type of plant hardy shrub/climber
zonal range 5-9 (C-ST)
height 60-90cm (2-3ft) as a shrub
special characteristics evergreen, variegated
foliage

Liriope muscari is often used as ground cover for dry soils, particularly in areas of dry shade. Though it has an obliging nature and its cylinders of bead-like flowers are valuable so late in the year, its arching foliage can sometimes look slightly lacklustre. Paired with this sprucely variegated shrub, however, everything is enlivened and both the flowers and the foliage of the liriope are complemented. The liriope's fountain of leaves looks especially attractive surrounded by and intermingling with the small, rounded leaves of the euonymus. The upright flowers of the liriope also look well with the grey-green of the euonymus. In winter, the euonymus foliage can become tinged with pink.

Both these plants are slow-growing, but in time they produce dense growth. The euonymus will prosper in most soils. It is usually hummock-shaped but, given suitable support, mature specimens sometimes put forth climbing shoots which may be as much as 3m (10ft) tall (see 2.27). In common with many of the variegated plants of its genus, *Euonymus fortunei* 'Emerald Gaiety' is a versatile shrub for creating attractive plant combinations (see, for example, 6.15 and 3.31).

9.26 Arum & Ajuga

Arum italicum ssp. *italicum* 'Marmoratum'
(syn *A. i.* 'Pictum')
sun/shade ○ ◐
type of plant hardy tuber
zonal range 6-9 (C-ST)
flowering time late spring
flower colour greenish cream
height 30-45cm (12-18in)
special characteristics variegated foliage, fruit

Ajuga reptans 'Atropurpurea'
(bugle)
sun/shade ○ ◐
type of plant hardy perennial
zonal range 3-9 (C-ST)
flowering time late spring to early summer
flower colour deep blue
height 15-20cm (6-8in)
special characteristics evergreen/semi-
evergreen, purple foliage

This attractive mingling of light and dark, plain and marbled shows off each of the plants admirably. The arum's spear-shaped leaves, with their pale veins, stand out well among the bugle's glossy purple foliage, and the exceptional darkness of the latter is not lost, as it sometimes can be when surrounded by plain greenery.

The bugle's leafy flower stems can be seen lengthening here, in mid-spring. (For an illustration of the flowers in early summer, see 1.39.) The arum's flowers are not particularly decorative, but they are followed, in late summer and autumn, by heads of bright, orange-red berries. These poisonous fruits are carried on bare stalks with little or no accompanying foliage. The arum's beautiful leaves die down in early summer and only begin to emerge again in mid-autumn. The new leaves are a remarkable addition to any garden in winter (see 9.15). In frosty weather the foliage will collapse but it will revive unscathed once temperatures rise.

Once established, the arum will self-seed and its clumps of growth will spread. The bugle is an even more vigorous, carpeting plant. Both plants need moisture and some shade to produce good quantities of foliage, but as in each case the leaf colour is best when the position is quite light, a cool soil and a spot with only a little shade should be chosen.

9.27 Acer & Hosta

Acer palmatum var. *dissectum* Dissectum Atropurpureum Group

(Japanese maple)
sun/shade ○ ◗
type of plant hardy shrub
zonal range 5-8 (C-WT)
height 1.5-2.4m (5-8ft)
special characteristics purple foliage, autumn foliage

Hosta Fortunei Albomarginata Group

(plantain lily)
sun/shade ◗
type of plant hardy perennial
zonal range 3-9 (C-WT)
flowering time early to mid-summer
flower colour usually pale lilac
height 60-90cm (2-3ft)
special characteristics variegated foliage, suitable for damp soils

Maples sold under this or a similar name vary somewhat, but they all have foliage which combines a very delicate shape with really deep colouring. Both features look their best against plants with relatively large, bright, smoothly shaped leaves, such as the hosta shown here.

In this particular combination there is an interesting difference in the overall habit of growth, as well as contrasts in leaf shape and colour. In spring the new leaves of hostas in this cultivar group usually stand upright. Later they open out into dense, arching clumps. In contrast, the maple has a rounded, hummocky outline and its feathery leaves hang down from its branches. Before they fall, during mid-autumn, these leaves turn red.

In time, the maple will grow large enough to make a good dark background for the pale, long-stalked flower spikes of the hosta. The cut-leaved forms of Japanese maple are, however, very slow-growing plants. They all need a sheltered site. However, in very shaded positions the purple-leaved forms become more green than purple. The soil should be acid or neutral as well as both well-drained and moisture-retentive. Hostas in the Fortunei Albomarginata group also appreciate these growing conditions, and they thrive in damp, rich soils.

9.28 Weigela & Hosta

Weigela 'Praecox Variegata'

sun/shade ○ ◗
type of plant hardy shrub
zonal range 5-8 (C-WT)
flowering time late spring to early summer
flower colour pink
height 1.5-1.8m (5-6ft)
special characteristics variegated foliage

Hosta fortunei

(plantain lily)
sun/shade ◗
type of plant hardy perennial
zonal range 3-9 (C-WT)
flowering time midsummer
flower colour pale lilac
height 60-75cm (2-2½ft)
special characteristics decorative green foliage, suitable for damp soils

Weigela 'Praecox Variegata' is one of the most attractive and easy-going of all variegated shrubs. Its slender leaves often last well into winter. The margins are, at first, cream, then white and finally yellow-green.

The name *Hosta fortunei* covers a number of slightly different forms of hosta, but they all have plain leaves of a soft green, often with a grey or bluish cast. Both the form and the colour of the large, heart-shaped leaves of the hosta shown here complement this weigela's foliage. In overall shape, too, these plants complement each other: the weigela a more or less rounded mass of curving twigs on relatively straight main growths, while the hosta forms a solid clump of long-stemmed leaves that arch gently outwards.

The photograph shows the weigela after its slightly scented flowers have faded and before the hosta's generous clusters of small trumpets have opened. At the first frosts many of the weigela's leaves may become tinged with pink.

Almost any soil is suitable for the weigela, though the best specimens will be produced on soils that do not dry out too rapidly. Sun encourages the production of flowers. The hosta needs a moisture-retentive soil. It thrives in damp, rich soils and can be grown in full shade.

9.29 **Iris & Hosta**

Iris foetidissima var. *citrina*

(stinking iris, gladdon, gladwyn iris)
sun/shade ○ ◐
type of plant hardy perennial
zonal range 5-9 (C-WT)
flowering time early summer
flower colour soft beige-yellow
height 45-60cm (1½-2ft)
special characteristics evergreen, decorative green foliage, fruit

Hosta 'Aureomarginata' (*ventricosa*)

(syn *H.* 'Variegata' (*ventricosa*))
(plantain lily)
sun/shade ◐
type of plant hardy perennial
zonal range 3-9 (C-WT)
flowering time mid- to late summer
flower colour rich violet
height 90cm-120cm (3-4ft)
special characteristics variegated foliage, suitable for damp soils

The variegation on this hosta's broad, handsome leaves lasts well into autumn, changing with age from pale yellow to white. Here, in early summer, its yellowness enhances the rather subdued buff and yellow of the iris flowers. Throughout the growing season there is also a very satisfactory contrast between the long, arching, strap-like leaves of the iris and the smooth outline and prominent veins of the hosta's foliage.

Though the iris flowers are not very conspicuous, they are followed by heavy pods of shining, red-orange berries. These ripen in autumn and often last until early spring (see 12.19). The hosta's flowers, carried well above the leaves, are an unusually deep colour for plants of this genus.

After a slow start, this hosta matures into a big, dense clump of growth. The foliage is usually about 45-60cm (1½-2ft) high. In fertile soils that are always moist or damp this plant will be especially large and lush. The iris is a very tolerant plant that will thrive in a wide range of soils and sites, including dry shade and dense shade. It will also grow in full sun as long as its roots are not too hot and dry. When cut, its leaves emit a distinct but not unpleasant smell of roast beef.

9.30 **Hosta & Viola**

Hosta undulata var. *albomarginata*

(syn *H.* 'Thomas Hogg')
(plantain lily)
sun/shade ◐
type of plant hardy perennial
zonal range 3-9 (C-WT)
flowering time early to mid-summer
flower colour pale lilac
height 60-90cm (2-3ft)
special characteristics variegated foliage, suitable for damp soils

Viola 'Desdemona'

(violet)
sun/shade ○ ◐
type of plant hardy perennial
zonal range 5-7 (C-CT)
flowering time late spring to mid-autumn
flower colour white + pale lilac
height 30cm (12in)

The two colours in the flowers of this viola have their counterparts in the white margins of the hosta's leaves and the lilac of its flowers. Since the viola has a long flowering season, there is a matching of colours over many weeks. In addition, the small scale of the viola's foliage and flowers is in pretty contrast to the dense clump of large-leaved growth produced by the hosta. Like many plants of its genus, this wide-spreading viola weaves and almost climbs among taller companions.

Though the foliage of *Hosta undulata albomarginata* is its chief feature and the most striking part of this planting, its flowers are attractive, too. Here, very early in summer, the flower buds are visible. When fully developed, the stalks stand well above the foliage and are topped with clusters of small, lilac trumpets. The viola can be persuaded to produce a second, autumn crop of flowers by being cut right back at the end of summer.

A fertile, moisture-retentive soil suits both these plants. The hosta luxuriates in damp, rich soils.

Other suitable violas with lilac flowers include some of the *V. cornuta* varieties, such as Lilacina Group, and *V.* 'Winona Cawthorne'.

For other combinations featuring this hosta, see 1.36, 9.31 and 16.20.

9.31 Hosta & Lamium

Hosta undulata var. *albomarginata*
(syn *H.* 'Thomas Hogg')
(plantain lily)
sun/shade ◑
type of plant hardy perennial
zonal range 3-9 (C-WT)
flowering time early to mid-summer
flower colour pale lilac
height 60-90cm (2-3ft)
special characteristics variegated foliage, suitable for damp soils

Lamium maculatum 'White Nancy'
(spotted dead nettle)
sun/shade ◑
type of plant hardy perennial
zonal range 4-8 (C-WT)
flowering time mid-spring to early summer
flower colour white
height 12-20cm (5-8in)
special characteristics evergreen, variegated foliage

Though white-edged hostas look good with dark foliage (see 9.27), they also combine very satisfactorily with pale leaves. *Lamium maculatum* 'White Nancy' has leaves which are almost entirely silver, except for a very thin green margin, and the overall effect of this particular combination is beautifully cool.

Two variegated plants together may sound rather fussy and complicated, but both sets of leaves here are very similar in colouring and shape, and this simplifies the appearance of the combination. In addition the flowers of *Lamium maculatum* 'White Nancy' are white, so only the hosta's long-stalked, pale flowers add an extra colour to this green-and-white scheme.

Partial shade and a moisture-retentive soil suit both of these plants. In such conditions, the hosta will grow into a large, dense clump and the lamium will form a ground-covering carpet of foliage. However, provided the soil remains cool and moist, both plants can also be grown successfully in some sun. The hosta is especially large and lush in rich, damp soils.

9.32 Helleborus, Hosta & Persicaria

Helleborus foetidus
(stinking hellebore)
sun/shade ○ ◑ **type of plant** hardy perennial
zonal range 6-9 (C-WT)
flowering time late winter to mid-spring
flower colour pale green, often maroon-rimmed
height 45-60cm (1½-2ft)
special characteristics evergreen, decorative green foliage

Hosta undulata var. *undulata*
(syn *H.* 'Mediovariegata')
(plantain lily)
sun/shade ◑ **type of plant** hardy perennial
zonal range 3-9 (C-WT)
flowering time mid- to late summer
flower colour pale violet
height 30-45cm (12-18in)
special characteristics variegated foliage, suitable for damp soils

Persicaria affinis 'Superba'
(syn *P. a.* 'Dimity', *Polygonum affine* 'Superbum')
(knotweed)
sun/shade ○ ◑ **type of plant** hardy perennial
zonal range 3-9 (C-ST)
flowering time midsummer to early autumn
flower colour pink changing to red
height 15cm (6in)
special characteristics autumn/winter foliage

The most striking component of this group of plants is the hosta, with its broad splashes of white on twisted, deep green leaves. As a necessary calming influence there is the sturdy clump of exceptionally dark green foliage produced by *Helleborus foetidus*, while the knotweed's contribution consists of long-lasting, prettily coloured flowers and a contrastingly low mat of small leaves that turn vivid russet in autumn and winter. The hosta produces flowers, too, but not very prolifically.

Even in the colder months, when the hosta's leaves have disappeared, this is a combination that works well. The hellebore's very deeply cut foliage always looks interesting, and especially so against the knotweed's russet carpet. The flowers of the hellebore (see 7.12) are attractive both in bud and when seed has set; indeed, they often look good from as early as midwinter until the end of spring. When bruised, the leaves and roots of this poisonous hellebore emit an unpleasant smell.

A partially shaded site is best for this combination, since the hosta's leaves are inclined to scorch in too much sun. Although the hellebore is a very accommodating plant, it will appreciate the moisture-retentive soil that both the hosta and the knotweed require to do well. *H. undulata undulata* is not a vigorous plant. Similar, rather more vigorous hostas with narrower areas of cream or white and less twisted leaves are usually sold under the name *H. undulata univittata*. There is a good deal of variation in both forms.

9.33 Iris & Saxifraga

Iris foetidissima 'Variegata'
(stinking iris, gladdon, gladwyn iris)
sun/shade ◖
type of plant hardy perennial
zonal range 5-9 (C-WT)
height 45-60cm (1½-2ft)
special characteristics evergreen, variegated foliage

Saxifraga 'Aureopunctata' (× *urbium*)
(syn S. 'Variegata' (*umbrosa*))
(London pride)
sun/shade ◖
type of plant hardy perennial
zonal range 6-7 (CT-WT)
flowering time late spring to early summer
flower colour pink
height 30cm (12in)
special characteristics evergreen, variegated foliage

Each of this iris's long, pointed leaves has a cream stripe down one side. The foliage and its distinctive patterning remain unusually clean and crisp-looking throughout the year (the photograph shows the plant in frosty midwinter). Surrounding these conspicuously upright leaves is a dense, neat carpet of leathery foliage which is arranged in tight rosettes. These rosettes are also variegated, with flecks of yellow. Though the variegated form of *Iris foetidissima* seldom flowers or, therefore, fruits, this variety of London pride produces a cloud of tiny flowers well above its low-growing foliage.

Those gardeners who would find this combination of two different variegations too fussy should bear in mind that there are plain green-leaved versions of both these plants. If a green-leaved form of the iris was substituted here, the splendid red or orange berries (see 12.19) would be a bonus in the colder months.

Ideally, both these plants should be given a cool position in either partial or full shade, and a well-drained but moisture-retentive soil. However, both plants are very easy to please and they will grow well in some sun and in dense shade. Despite one of its common names, this iris does not stink, but its cut leaves do emit a smell of roast beef.

9.34 Pulmonaria & Lamium

Pulmonaria officinalis
(spotted dog, soldiers and sailors, lungwort)
sun/shade ◖ **type of plant** hardy perennial
zonal range 4-8 (C-WT)
flowering time early to late spring
flower colour pink changing to blue
height 25cm (10in)
special characteristics evergreen, variegated foliage

Lamium maculatum 'Album'
(spotted dead nettle)
sun/shade ◖ **type of plant** hardy perennial
zonal range 4-8 (C-WT)
flowering time mid-spring to midsummer
flower colour white
height 15cm (6in)
special characteristics evergreen, variegated foliage

This charming mixture of stripes and spots works so well because the shape and colouring of the two sets of leaves are roughly similar; the only major differences are in leaf size and in the pattern of the variegation. The two plants appear therefore as variations on a theme rather than completely distinct entities.

The lamium forms a spreading but not invasive carpet of white-striped foliage and lax stems. Its hooded flowers are a lovely, clean white, which some gardeners may prefer to the rather indeterminate magenta of the species. The lungwort has little sprays of funnel-shaped flowers above its clumps of foliage (see 1.34). The leaves are generously mottled and splashed with very pale, silvery green.

In cool, moisture-retentive soils and shady places both these plants will grow densely and create good ground cover. Their leaves are likely to remain in excellent condition almost all year long.

For other combinations featuring variegated leaves, see:
COOL-COLOURED FLOWERS 1.22, 1.24, 1.34, 1.36, 1.39   GREY FOLIAGE 2.15, 2.22, 2.26, 2.27 HOT-COLOURED FLOWERS 3.15, 3.28, 3.31, 3.32, 3.34
PURPLE FOLIAGE 4.5, 4.6, 4.16, 4.24, 4.27, 4.28   YELLOW FOLIAGE 6.7, 6.10, 6.12, 6.13, 6.15, 6.16, 6.18, 6.20   GREEN FLOWERS 7.3, 7.10, 7.11, 7.12
DECORATIVE GREEN FOLIAGE 8.2, 8.3, 8.13, 8.14, 8.16   AUTUMN FOLIAGE 10.10, 10.11, 10.14   AROMATIC FOLIAGE 11.2, 11.3, 11.7, 11.9, 11.10, 11.11,
11.12, 11.13, 11.14, 11.16, 11.20   FRUIT 12.2, 12.10, 12.15, 12.18   FRAGRANT FLOWERS 13.1, 13.4, 13.15   WINTER FLOWERS 14.4, 14.6, 14.7, 14.11, 14.13
CLIMBING PLANTS 15.6, 15.8, 15.15, 15.18, 15.19   WATER GARDENS AND DAMP AND WET SOILS 16.1, 16.2, 16.3, 16.6, 16.11, 16.12, 16.13, 16.18, 16.20
GRASSES AND FERNS 17.4, 17.6, 17.7, 17.8, 17.10, 17.12, 17.14, 17.20

9.35 Tolmiea & Omphalodes

Tolmiea menziesii 'Taff's Gold'

(piggyback plant)

sun/shade ◖

type of plant hardy perennial

zonal range 6-9 (CT-ST)

flowering time late spring to early summer

flower colour coppery brown

height 20cm (8in) (leaves)

special characteristics semi-evergreen, yellow/yellow-variegated foliage

Omphalodes cappadocica

sun/shade ◖

type of plant hardy perennial

zonal range 6-9 (CT-WT)

flowering time early to late spring

flower colour bright, clear blue

height 15-23cm (6-9in)

special characteristics semi-evergreen

The wonderful, concentrated blue of the flowers of *Omphalodes cappadocica* is intensified still further by the yellow markings on the foliage of this tolmiea. Even when these flowers are finished (and they are produced over a long period), the neat, veined leaves of the omphalodes continue to provide a good background for the more intricate shapes and colours of the tolmiea's foliage.

In the cool, moist shadiness that both these plants prefer, their leaves form dense, spreading carpets of growth. In sunnier positions, both plants may be less vigorous. In some sun, the tolmiea's foliage will be yellower and less variegated (see 6.16). If either of these easily grown and unfussy plants seems to be spreading too quickly, it is a simple matter to uproot and remove parts of them. Some gardeners also like to remove the spires of sparsely arranged, brown flowers that are produced by the tolmiea.

9.36 Cornus & Pachysandra

Cornus canadensis

(creeping dogwood)

sun/shade ◖

type of plant hardy perennial/shrub

zonal range 2-6 (C-CT)

flowering time late spring to early summer

flower colour white + greenish purple

height 10-15cm (4-6in)

special characteristics autumn foliage, needs acid soil

Pachysandra terminalis 'Variegata'

(Japanese spurge)

sun/shade ◖

type of plant hardy perennial/shrub

zonal range 4-8 (C-CT)

height 15cm (6in)

special characteristics evergreen, variegated foliage, fragrant flowers, needs acid soil

Pachysandra terminalis, with its plain leaves, is an all-too-familiar ingredient of large-scale ground-cover schemes. This slower-growing variety is an excellent brightener of dull foliage, even in densely shaded places. Here, in late spring, its creamy-white leaf edges emphasize the white bracts of *Cornus canadensis* most engagingly. When these bracts have faded, the plain, yellower green and the smoother outline of the cornus's ribbed foliage mean that there are still clear differences between the two plants. The pachysandra's contrastingly busy foliage consists of whorls of rather twisted, toothed leaves that are basically a greyish-green.

As long as the plant has not been grown in too shady a position, the cornus leaves will become tinged with wine colours in autumn. There may also be red berries in some years. The pachysandra's spires of tiny flowers are easy to overlook but they are sweetly fragrant. Of the two plants, the pachysandra is the less vigorous and it is probably advisable to establish it for a year or two before adding the cornus.

This combination can be grown in quite inhospitable places, including areas of dry shade. The carpet of growth will establish more quickly, however, if some moisture is available.

In autumn, one of the most theatrical events in the gardening year takes place when placid greens turn into smouldering reds, oranges and yellows. The display is often fairly short-lived and is followed by a period of almost complete inactivity, which serves to heighten the sense of drama.

Setting bright red autumn leaves in a smooth sea of green grass is the classic way of emphasizing the vibrancy of their colour, but there are various other methods of maximizing the impact of autumn foliage. One popular way is to contrast it with cool colours. Foliage that is palely variegated or of an inert, ashen grey or of a still chillier blue-grey heightens fiery reds and oranges, and similar effects can be achieved using cool-coloured autumn flowers such as gentians (see 10.18) or some of the asters.

An altogether different approach is to turn up the heat by adding yet more hot colours. These can be supplied by flame-coloured fruits or flowers. Alternatively, quite large-scale 'bonfires' can be constructed out of several different plants all with brilliantly coloured autumn foliage. To these can be added clashing purples and deep pinks – for example from Michaelmas daisies and colchicums – for extra excitement and fizz.

When you are creating autumn foliage groups there is a range of possible leaf colours to draw upon. As well as the blistering reds and oranges of maples and deciduous azaleas, there are the rich wine-purples of some viburnum leaves and the gentler golds and yellows of the climbing hydrangea *Hydrangea anomala petiolaris* (see 17.19) and of many birches. Russet autumn colours are produced by some beeches and certain species and forms of sorbus.

Either as additions to large-scale groups or where space is restricted, smaller plants with colourful autumn foliage are useful. The leaves of certain cranesbills, a few peonies and some euphorbias all colour interestingly before falling. Some grasses turn beautiful shades of parchment and ivory in autumn and, unless they are flattened by snow, remain attractive during most of winter. There are also some small evergreen plants that take on bronze, purplish or maroon tones in cold weather. These include a number of bergenias, epimediums, tellimas and tiarellas, as well as some heaths and heathers and some dwarf and prostrate conifers. Because the colouring of these plants lasts through winter, it can provide a good background for winter flowers such as snowdrops and other early bulbs.

No matter how spectacular its autumn foliage is, any plant grown for this feature should ideally be attractive at other times of the year, too. Autumn foliage plants that earn their keep at other seasons include the elegantly shaped maples such as *Acer palmatum* and its forms and purple-leaved shrubs and trees such as *Cotinus coggygria* 'Royal Purple'. Some autumn foliage plants have fragrant flowers, including *Fothergilla major* and the winter-flowering *Hamamelis mollis* (Chinese witch hazel). Autumn foliage plants with additional decorative features will give pleasure in the garden even if, as happens sometimes, a particular year is disappointing for autumn leaf colour.

CHOOSING A SITE

Any autumn foliage plant, large or small, benefits greatly from being positioned so that it can be lit, for a part of the day at least, by the low, soft sun of autumn. Though the scarlets of maples and the buttery yellows of birches can look attractive even on dull autumn days or in shade, with sun shining through them they appear almost magically translucent and ethereal.

As a broad generalization, some sunshine is also needed to produce good autumn colour. For this reason, plants that are happy both in sun and in partial shade should be positioned in sun for the best colours to develop. A poor soil also tends to encourage the production of bright autumn colouring. Finally, shelter is an important consideration when you are choosing a site for autumn foliage plants. Many deciduous plants are really colourful for only a brief period in autumn, and in a windy position dying leaves are particularly likely to be blown away quickly.

10.1 Acer & Cedrus

Acer palmatum 'Aureum'
(Japanese maple)
sun/shade ○ ◖
type of plant hardy shrub/tree
zonal range 5-8 (C-WT)
height 6m (20ft)
special characteristics yellow foliage, autumn foliage

Cedrus libani ssp. atlantica Glauca Group
(syn *C. atlantica glauca*)
(blue cedar)
sun/shade ○
type of plant hardy conifer
zonal range 7-8 (C-CT)
height 18-24m (60-80ft)
special characteristics evergreen, blue-grey foliage, fruit

Few gardens can easily accommodate the great height and majestic, sweeping branches of the blue cedar. However, the idea of combining very blue foliage with golden-yellow autumn leaves is one that could be copied in many situations. Compared with the more familiar association of grey foliage and red or orange autumn colour (see 10.3 and 10.7), a blue and yellow partnership has an almost springlike freshness and delicacy.

Acer palmatum 'Aureum' is faster-growing than many Japanese maples. It is initially a fairly upright shrub, spreading more widely in maturity and forming an elegant tree with branches that fork fairly near ground level. Its precisely lobed leaves are greenish-yellow in shade and brighter and yellower in sun. The young leaves are rimmed in light red. In autumn the foliage turns a beautiful golden yellow.

Smaller evergreens with intensely blue foliage include several blue spruces, such as *Picea pungens* 'Hoopsii' and 'Koster', which are about 9m (30ft) high.

Japanese maples are happiest in acid to neutral soils that are well-drained and moisture-retentive. They need shelter from cold winds. Most well-drained soils will suit the blue cedar.

Some of the cedar's squat, blue-grey cones are visible in this photograph.

10.2 Acer & Euphorbia

Acer palmatum 'Sango-kaku'
(syn *A. p.* 'Senkaki')
(coral-bark maple)
sun/shade ○ ◖
type of plant hardy tree
zonal range 5-8 (C-WT)
height 6m (20ft)
special characteristics decorative green foliage, autumn foliage, ornamental twigs

Euphorbia dulcis 'Chameleon'
(spurge)
sun/shade ○
type of plant hardy perennial
zonal range 4-9 (C-WT)
flowering time late spring to early summer
flower colour lime green
height 45-60cm (1½-2ft)
special characteristics purple foliage, autumn foliage

Placing dark leaves beneath this maple's effervescent mass of ascending branches and airy, lobed foliage emphasizes not only the vivacious appearance of this small tree but also its glorious, bright yellow autumn colouring. In addition, the red-purple of the euphorbia's dark foliage draws attention to the maple's twigs, which at this stage in the year are red. In late winter and early spring the twigs and youngest branches are a vivid and very striking orange-pink.

During most of spring and summer the maple's foliage is light green. Here, in mid-autumn, are the beginnings of what later, before leaf-fall, will be a beautiful apricot-gold. The accompanying euphorbia often puts on a late autumn display, too, when its willowy, slim-stemmed clump of rounded leaves turns a mixture of pinks and apricots. Earlier in the year, there are numerous, small but sharply acidic green flowers.

Each of these plants likes well-drained, moisture-retentive soils; the maple will grow most satisfactorily in acid or neutral conditions. It needs shelter from cold and drying winds. The specimen of *Acer palmatum* 'Sango-kaku' shown here is fairly young. In maturity, plants are more distinctly tree-like.

For other combinations using plants with ornamental bark and twigs, see 17.1, 9.14 and 10.13.

10.3 Abies & Euonymus

Abies magnifica 'Nana'
(Californian red fir)

sun/shade ○
type of plant hardy conifer
zonal range 5-8 (C-CT)
height 3.6-4.5m (12-15ft)
special characteristics evergreen, blue-grey foliage

Euonymus oxyphyllus

sun/shade ○ ◗
type of plant hardy shrub/tree
zonal range 6-9 (CT-WT)
height 2.4-3.6m (8-12ft)
special characteristics autumn foliage, fruit

The blue-grey conifer shown here is not readily available but the popular blue spruces (for an example of which see 2.1) would make good substitutes, providing a crisp, cool background against which the euonymus could glow conspicuously in autumn. As with any combination of evergreen conifer and deciduous autumn-colouring shrub, there is an interesting contrast here between one plant that looks more or less the same throughout the year and another that changes considerably with the seasons.

The euonymus leaves are an unremarkable green in spring and summer, but in mid-autumn the foliage turns a mixture of rich crimson and purplish-red. At the same time, the dangling fruits of the plant open to reveal scarlet seeds. At all stages this upright shrub's airy arrangement of pendent, tapered leaves will contrast strikingly with the closely packed, needle-like foliage and general rigidity of conifers such as the firs and spruces.

Almost all well-drained soils will suit the euonymus. It is a fairly slow-growing plant, especially when young. This is also true of its relation *Euonymus alatus* (see 10.18), which would also look attractive in the company of grey-blue conifers. Firs and spruces like deep, moist, well-drained soils. Firs prefer acid to neutral conditions.

10.4 Helleborus & Acer

Helleborus orientalis hybrid
(Lenten rose)

sun/shade ◗
type of plant hardy perennial
zonal range 4-9 (C-WT)
flowering time late winter to mid-spring
flower colour various shades of pink, purple, white
height 45cm (18in)
special characteristics evergreen/semi-evergreen

Acer palmatum
f. atropurpureum
(Japanese maple)

sun/shade ○
type of plant hardy shrub/tree
zonal range 6-8 (C-WT)
height 3.6-4.5m (12-15ft)
special characteristics purple foliage, autumn foliage

These glossy, rich green hellebore leaves provide just the right sort of background for showing off the elegant, fingered foliage of the maple. This is true both when the maple's leaves are a rich maroon in summer and when they turn scarlet in autumn. Here, in mid-autumn, they are mainly a subdued version of their summer colour and the glorious bright scarlet of autumn is just appearing.

When the spectacular autumn display is over, there are the early flowers of the hellebore to look forward to. These blooms are of a beautiful, sculptural shape and notably long-lasting. The flower colour of *Helleborus orientalis* varies considerably (see, for example, 7.15 and 14.12). The ground-covering clumps of foliage produced by these plants remain in good condition well into winter.

Though the maple needs sun to colour well, the hellebore thrives in shade, provided here by the maple's spreading branches. As well as sun, the maple needs a moist, preferably acid soil, good drainage and some shelter. The hellebore likes to grow undisturbed in well-drained, leaf-mould soil.

It is advisable to choose specimens of this maple in leaf, since some forms may be less colourful – both in summer and in autumn – than others. All forms are, however, slow-growing, taking many years to form bushy-headed, small trees.

10.5 Cotinus & Cotoneaster

Cotinus coggygria 'Royal Purple'
(smoke tree, Venetian sumach)
sun/shade ○
type of plant hardy shrub/tree
zonal range 5-9 (C-WT)
fruiting time mid- to late summer
fruit colour pink-purple
height 2.4-3m (8-10ft)
special characteristics purple foliage, autumn foliage, fruit

Cotoneaster franchetii
sun/shade ○ ◖
type of plant hardy shrub
zonal range 7-9 (C-WT)
flowering time early summer
flower colour white tinged pink
height 1.8-2.4m (6-8ft)
special characteristics semi-evergreen/evergreen, fruit

The silky, rounded leaves of this cotinus are just turning here, in mid-autumn, from dark red-purple to translucent red. Accompanying this bushy head of rich colour are the graceful, arching branches of *Cotoneaster franchetii*, clothed with sage-green leaves and numerous orange-red berries. Though the combination is shown here at its most colourful, the cotoneaster contrasts beautifully with the cotinus throughout the summer too.

This particular specimen of *Cotinus coggygria* 'Royal Purple' has been allowed to develop as a small tree. If the plant is pruned hard each year it will be shrubby, smaller and more upright. Treated in this way it will also bear few flowers and, therefore, few of the characteristic, smoky clouds of seed-heads. It will, however, produce plenty of large, well-coloured leaves. Pruned or unpruned, this plant is late into leaf. It will not usually be well-clothed in foliage until the little flower clusters of the cotoneaster open.

Light, rather poor soils produce the most vivid autumn colour on the cotinus. The cotoneaster is a tolerant plant that will prosper in a wide range of soil types.

10.6 Crocosmia & Viburnum

Crocosmia paniculata
(syn *Curtonus paniculatus*)
sun/shade ○
type of plant hardy corm
zonal range 6-9 (CT-ST)
flowering time late summer to early autumn
flower colour orange-red + orange
height 1.2m (4ft)
special characteristics decorative green foliage

Viburnum plicatum 'Mariesii'
(syn *V. tomentosum* 'Mariesii')
sun/shade ○ ◖
type of plant hardy shrub
zonal range 6-8 (C-WT)
flowering time late spring
flower colour white
height 1.8-2.4m (6-8ft)
special characteristics autumn foliage

The fiery flowers and bright green foliage of *Crocosmia paniculata* are joined here, in late summer, by the first signs of vinous autumn colour on a viburnum. The colour of these viburnum leaves will deepen considerably in the following two months. The chief attractions of this particular shrub are, however, its markedly horizontal habit of growth (its width is always greater than its height) and its lovely, lace-cap flowers. Since these are features which are attractive in spring and summer and the colouring shown here is basically autumnal, this is a combination with a long period of interest. Throughout this period the very upright sheaves of pleated and pointed foliage produced by the crocosmia contrast strikingly with the viburnum's tiered branches.

Both of these plants are easy to grow: the viburnum likes moisture-retentive soils and alkaline conditions; the crocosmia is at its very best in moisture-retentive soils that are also fertile and well-drained.

'Lanarth' is another variety of *Viburnum plicatum* very similar to 'Mariesii' (see 1.20).

10.7 Fothergilla & Santolina

Fothergilla major

sun/shade ○ ◑
type of plant hardy shrub
zonal range 5-9 (C-CT)
flowering time late spring
flower colour greenish white
height 1.8-2.4m (6-8ft)
special characteristics autumn foliage, fragrant flowers, needs acid soil

Santolina chamaecyparissus

(syn *S. incana*)
(cotton lavender)
sun/shade ○
type of plant hardy shrub
zonal range 6-9 (C-WT)
flowering time midsummer
flower colour bright yellow
height 45-60cm (1½-2ft)
special characteristics evergreen, aromatic, silver foliage

Sandwiched between two hummocks of silvery-grey foliage, the crimsons, reds and yellows of this fothergilla's autumn foliage blaze with special clarity and intensity. *Fothergilla major* is a fairly upright, slow-growing plant which will usually be about 90-120cm (3-4ft) high after 10 years. As well as its spectacular and long-lasting colour in mid- and late autumn, there are conspicuous, sweetly scented, bottle-brush flowers which begin to open just before the rather rounded leaves unfurl.

Both the plants in this combination need well-drained soil. For the fothergilla, conditions must also be lime-free and moisture-retentive; in a sunny site, the autumn foliage will be particularly well-coloured. Although the santolina thrives in dry soils, it will be quite satisfactory in moister places provided the drainage is good and there is plenty of sun. If it is to remain neat and dense, this pungently aromatic little shrub needs to be clipped closely in spring. This treatment means that few of the rather strongly coloured, button-shaped flowers develop.

Grey or blue-grey, close-textured foliage plants that would be more appreciative of the moisture needed by this fothergilla include forms of spruce such as *Picea pungens* 'Globosa' and the very slow-growing *P. mariana* 'Nana'.

10.8 Paeonia & Ruta

Paeonia lactiflora hybrid

(peony)
sun/shade ○ ◑
type of plant hardy perennial
zonal range 3-9 (CT-C)
flowering time early summer
flower colour various shades of pink, red, white
height 75-105cm (2½-3½ft)
special characteristics decorative green foliage; some hybrids have colourful autumn foliage and fragrant flowers

Ruta graveolens 'Jackman's Blue'

(rue)
sun/shade ○
type of plant hardy shrub
zonal range 6-8 (C-WT)
flowering time mid- to late summer
flower colour yellow
height 45-60cm (1½-2ft)
special characteristics evergreen, aromatic, blue-grey foliage

As well as their glorious flowers, the hybrids from *P. lactiflora* have handsome foliage with slim, smoothly shaped leaflets. In autumn, the leaves of some of these hybrids turn rich shades of maroon and wine-purple. Examples of varieties with good autumn foliage include the single-flowered *P. l.* 'White Wings' and the deep red, double-flowered *P. l.* 'President Franklin D. Roosevelt'. Here the soft, warm colour and smooth shape of peony leaves have been set against the cool, blue-grey laciness of a particularly well-coloured form of rue.

Full sun enhances the colour of the rue's leaves. Although this is a plant that will tolerate hot, dry conditions, it will be happy to share the well-drained, moisture-retentive and at least reasonably fertile soil required by the peony. Should the rue become lanky, it can be cut back hard in spring to ensure a dense, rounded shape. Many gardeners like to pinch out this plant's clusters of bright yellow flowers before they develop fully, and this too encourages bushiness. However, the pungently aromatic leaves of this rue can be an irritant, and some protection should be worn by those with sensitive skin. The lactiflora peonies are very long-lived plants, but they usually take a year or two to become established and flower well.

10.9 Bergenia & Acaena

Bergenia cordifolia 'Purpurea'

sun/shade ○ ◐
type of plant hardy perennial
zonal range 3-8 (C-WT)
flowering time early to mid-spring
flower colour bright magenta
height 45-60cm (1½-2ft)
special characteristics evergreen, decorative green foliage, autumn/winter foliage

Acaena saccaticupula 'Blue Haze'

(syn *A.* 'Pewter')
sun/shade ○
type of plant hardy perennial
zonal range 6-8 (C-WT)
height 10-15cm (4-6in)
special characteristics semi-evergreen, blue-grey foliage, fruit

Bergenias are useful plants, but those species and varieties that take on red or purple tones in autumn and winter are especially valuable. The variety illustrated here produces dense clumps of large, rounded, mid-green leaves which become tinged with reddish-purple in cold weather.

In this combination, these warm tones are contrasted with the icy blue-grey of *Acaena saccaticupula* 'Blue Haze'. There is also a striking difference in foliage size: the leaves of the bergenia are about 20cm (8in) wide, whereas each little acaena leaflet is less than 1cm (½in) long. The acaena, shown here in midwinter, is not entirely evergreen, but even the light tan of its dying leaves is attractive.

Like the leaves, the flowers of the bergenia are conspicuous and bold. They appear in large heads on eye-catching, rhubarb-like stalks. The acaena's less decorative flowers develop into spiky burrs of a rich red-brown from late summer (see 17.5).

Almost any soil and site suits the bergenia, but the best autumn and winter colour occurs on plants grown in open positions and in well-drained, rather infertile soils. Other bergenias with foliage that becomes particularly well coloured include *B.* 'Sunningdale' (see 12.12). Full sun and good drainage suit this vigorous, carpeting acaena, too, but it can be invasive in warm climates.

10.10 Nerine & Cotoneaster

Nerine bowdenii

sun/shade ○
type of plant slightly tender bulb
zonal range 8-10 (CT-ST)
flowering time early to late autumn
flower colour pink
height 45-60cm (1½-2ft)

Cotoneaster atropurpureus 'Variegatus'

(syn *C. horizontalis* 'Variegatus')
sun/shade ○ ◐
type of plant hardy shrub
zonal range 5-8 (C-WT)
flowering time early summer
flower colour pink
height 45-60cm (1½-2ft), 1.2-1.8m (4-6ft) against a wall
special characteristics variegated foliage, autumn foliage, ornamental twigs

Relatively few plants have foliage that turns pink in autumn, but the tiny, grey-green, white-edged leaves of this cotoneaster take on deep pink tones and tinges of rusty orange and purple in the middle and later part of the season. The nerine's blooms, borne in long succession, are also unusual, as flowers of this lovely, curled shape and fresh colour seem to belong to the summer months. Not only the pink autumn foliage of the cotoneaster but also the conspicuous, fan-like arrangement of its twigs make an interesting background for these pretty flowers, and they in their turn enhance the cotoneaster's colouring.

Until recently, this variegated cotoneaster was considered to be a variety of the fishbone cotoneaster, *Cotoneaster horizontalis*. Although very similar to it in many respects, and equally easy to grow in a wide range of soils, this plant is much less vigorous and its little flowers are followed by very few red berries. Like the fishbone cotoneaster, however, it can be trained against a wall.

The nerine is rather more demanding about the growing conditions it requires. It must have a really well-drained soil and full sun for substantial numbers of flowers to appear. Its strap-shaped leaves are produced after flowering and die back in summer.

10.11 Parthenocissus & Hedera

Parthenocissus tricuspidata
(syn *Vitis inconstans*)
(Boston ivy)
sun/shade ○ ◐
type of plant hardy climber
zonal range 5-8 (C-WT/ST)
height 21m (70ft)
special characteristics autumn foliage

Hedera helix 'Marginata Major'
(ivy)
sun/shade ○ ◐
type of plant hardy climber
zonal range 5-9 (C-ST)
height 4.5m (15ft)
special characteristics evergreen, variegated foliage

Parthenocissus tricuspidata is a very vigorous, self-clinging climber, and tall structures swathed in its glossy foliage will turn completely crimson-red in early autumn. Adding a cool, greyish-green, cream-variegated ivy to this dense mass of red not only emphasizes the brilliance and heat of the autumn colour, but also sharpens the whole picture. (Using a green-leaved ivy in similar circumstances creates a richer effect – see 10.12.) Earlier in the year the parthenocissus leaves are a deep but bright green and at this stage, too, the ivy's variegated foliage is an attractive, enlivening accompaniment.

Hedera helix 'Marginata Major' makes a particularly good partner for this parthenocissus because it is vigorous enough not to be completely dwarfed by the larger plant. However, it is an old variety that is not very readily available nowadays. Vigorous, bold-leaved, variegated ivies that could be used as substitutes here include the slightly tender (zones 9-10) *H. canariensis* 'Gloire de Marengo' (see 9.16).

The parthenocissus takes a year or two to become established, but it then climbs rapidly. Both it and the self-clinging ivy shown here are suitable for walls of all aspects. The parthenocissus is robust enough to grow in a wide range of soils. The ivy is a very tolerant and easily grown plant.

10.12 Parthenocissus & Hedera

Parthenocissus quinquefolia
(syn *Vitis quinquefolia*)
(Virginia creeper)
sun/shade ○ ◐
type of plant hardy climber
zonal range 4-8 (C-WT)
height 15-21m (50-70ft)
special characteristics decorative green foliage, autumn foliage

Hedera helix
(common ivy)
sun/shade ○ ◐
type of plant hardy climber
zonal range 5-9 (C-WT/ST)
flowering time early to late autumn
flower colour green
height 20-30m (60-90ft)
special characteristics evergreen, decorative green foliage

The wonderful, glowing reds of Virginia creeper are just appearing here in early autumn. When the whole plant turns from soft green to a sheet of vivid scarlets and crimsons, the ivy that accompanies it will make these autumn colours seem more radiant still.

Mature specimens of common ivy, like the one shown here, often produce great masses of shrubby, large-leaved growth and globular flowerheads in addition to their clinging, flowerless, smaller-leaved shoots (see also 8.1). All the foliage is a rich, dark, glossy green with which the intense reds of the Virginia creeper contrast spectacularly. The pale bobbles of the ivy flowers add another cool note to the combination and a quite different texture, too. In spring these ripen into black berries.

Both of the climbers in this combination are vigorous, large-scale plants that will easily cover very substantial areas of wall. Virginia creeper becomes established most quickly in fertile soils. Once established, it will attach itself to surfaces by means of adhesive tendrils. The ivy is an outstandingly tolerant plant which will grow almost anywhere. However, shrubby growth seems to be produced most readily on specimens grown in regions of high rainfall. Both plants are suitable for walls of all aspects.

169

10.13 Acer & Acer

Acer palmatum var. *dissectum*
Dissectum Viride Group
(Japanese maple)
sun/shade ○ ◑
type of plant hardy shrub
zonal range 5-8 (C-WT)
height 1.5-2.4m (5-8ft)
special characteristics decorative green foliage, autumn foliage

Acer griseum
(paper-bark maple)
sun/shade ○ ◑
type of plant hardy tree
zonal range 6-8 (C-CT)
height 10.5-12m (35-40ft)
special characteristics decorative green foliage, autumn foliage, ornamental bark

The ingredients of this mid-autumn concoction of cinnamon and glowing orange look good at other times of the year, too. In spring and summer the much-divided foliage of the smaller maple is an especially fresh green (see 1.33), and both in its green state and when it turns orange or red this rounded hummock of feathery leaves makes a close-textured and very decorative background for the peeling bark of *Acer griseum*. In addition to the bark, which always looks intriguing, this rather upright, dome-headed tree has attractive dark green leaves consisting of three leaflets. The tree is late into leaf and it is not until late autumn that the leaves turn red and orange before falling.

A. griseum is one of the quicker-growing maples, whereas all the cut-leaved maples increase in size very slowly. Both the plants in this combination appreciate shelter and a soil that is well-drained and moisture-retentive. *A. griseum* is tolerant of a wide range of soil types, but its companion needs a neutral to acid soil. In positioning the former it is important to remember that the peeling bark will be most conspicuous if it is lit by low winter sun.

Smaller plants that would look interesting with these two maples include several epimediums. The spring and autumn foliage of these perennials is attractively copper- and russet-toned, see 17.21.

10.14 Betula & Hosta

Betula alleghaniensis
(syn *B. lutea*)
(yellow birch)
sun/shade ○ ◑
type of plant hardy tree
zonal range 3-6 (C-CT)
flowering time late spring
flower colour greenish yellow
height 9-13.5m (30-45ft)
special characteristics autumn foliage, ornamental bark and twigs

Hosta 'Frances Williams'
(*sieboldiana*)
(plantain lily)
sun/shade ◑
type of plant hardy perennial
zonal range 3-9 (C-WT)
flowering time mid- to late summer
flower colour off-white
height 75-90cm (2½-3ft)
special characteristics variegated foliage, suitable for damp soils

This mid-autumn combination will have given pleasure long before both sets of leaves turn to shades of butter and toffee. The birch is a pretty, upright tree, often with several stems. In winter and early spring its pale yellow-green twigs and lovely, glossy, golden-brown bark are particularly conspicuous. In spring it produces catkins. The hosta, too, is decorative well before its rather brief – but still striking – display of autumn colour. In spring and summer each of its large, puckered, blue-green leaves is edged in lime-yellow. The dense flowerheads of the plant are carried just above the leaves.

In partial shade and moist soils the hosta produces very substantial clumps of growth. In sun its leaf margins tend to become scorched, although this is less likely if its roots are permanently damp. Here the birch's lower branches provide the necessary shade for the hosta, but as the birch is competing with the hosta for moisture the latter will not reach its full potential.

The birch grows well in moisture-retentive soils. A sheltered position is advisable to protect its earliest leaves from frost damage in spring and its autumn leaves from blowing away too quickly.

10.15 Acer & Hamamelis

Acer palmatum 'Osakazuki'

(Japanese maple)
sun/shade ○ ◐
type of plant hardy tree
zonal range 6-8 (C-WT)
height 3.6-4.5m (12-15ft)
special characteristics decorative green foliage, autumn foliage

Hamamelis mollis

(Chinese witch hazel)
sun/shade ○ ◐
type of plant hardy shrub/tree
zonal range 5-9 (C-WT)
flowering time early to late winter
flower colour yellow + red
height 2.4-3.6m (8-12ft)
special characteristics autumn foliage, fragrant flowers

The intense flame-crimson of this maple would look spectacular in almost any setting – including a swathe of green grass. However, combining it with other, paler autumn leaves makes it seem particularly deep and rich and brilliant. A paler colour also helps to outline the elegant arrangement of the tree's low-forking branches. Using a witch hazel to provide the lighter background ensures that this partnership is of interest beyond a fairly brief period in autumn.

Towards the end of the first month of winter the witch hazel's clusters of frost-resistant flowers start to open, emitting a pervasive, sweet-and-spicy fragrance. Each flower consists of tiny, ribbon-like petals. The flowers are borne close to the dark grey, bare branches of the plant.

The veined and rounded leaves of this witch hazel are large (up to 15cm/6in long). With the plant's open network of rather upright branches they help to create a generous, bowl-shaped head of growth. The maple's leaves are striking even in their green state, being very deeply lobed and up to 12cm (5in) long.

Both these plants are slow-growing and both need an acid or neutral soil in order to thrive. They also require good drainage and moisture, and the maple needs shelter.

10.16 Acer & Chamaecyparis

Acer palmatum var. *dissectum* Dissectum Viride Group

(Japanese maple)
sun/shade ○ ◐
type of plant hardy shrub
zonal range 5-8 (C-WT)
height 1.5-2.4m (5-8ft)
special characteristics decorative green foliage, autumn foliage

Chamaecyparis obtusa 'Nana Gracilis'

(Hinoki cypress)
sun/shade ○ ◐
type of plant hardy conifer
zonal range 5-8 (C-CT)
height 3.6-4.5m (12-15ft)
special characteristics evergreen, aromatic, decorative green foliage

From a distance, the golds and oranges of this maple's autumn foliage merge to create a delectable burnt orange. Here this caramelized colouring and the feathery shapes of the very finely divided leaves have been provided with a dramatic backdrop of frilled, deep green foliage. Even when the maple's leaves are light green (see 1.33), these two sets of foliage enhance each other beautifully. The combination is therefore attractive for at least six months of the year.

In addition to the conspicuous dissimilarities in the colour and texture of these two plants' leaves, there is a very pleasing contrast in habit. The conifer forms a generous pyramid of growth, whereas the maple's wide-spreading, arching branches create a comparatively low, rounded shape.

Both of these plants are very slow-growing; neither of them will be much more than 90cm (3ft) in ten years. They both have a preference for acid or neutral soils and thrive in well-drained, moisture-retentive conditions. The maple should be sheltered from cold and drying winds. When crushed, the cypress foliage emits a sweet, resinous scent.

10.17 Viburnum & Euphorbia

Viburnum plicatum
(syn *V. tomentosum*)
sun/shade ○ ◑
type of plant hardy shrub
zonal range 6-8 (C-WT)
flowering time late spring
flower colour white
height 2.4-3m (8-10ft)
special characteristics autumn foliage, fruit

Euphorbia griffithii 'Fireglow'
(spurge)
sun/shade ○ ◑
type of plant hardy perennial
zonal range 4-9 (C-WT)
flowering time late spring to early summer
flower colour bright orange-red
height 60-90cm (2-3ft)
special characteristics autumn foliage

Viburnum plicatum is less commonly grown now than its varieties, but all these plants have autumn foliage that turns rich shades of maroon, plum and wine. Here, in mid-autumn, these colours provide an interesting background for the brighter oranges and yellows of *Euphorbia griffithii* 'Fireglow'. The euphorbia does not always colour so well in autumn, and in very wet and windy weather its stems may become battered. However, this is, in any case, a good combination at other seasons.

The long-lasting and brilliantly coloured flowers of the euphorbia coincide with the viburnum's pretty lace-cap blooms, and together they create a sparkling association of colours. The viburnum has branches of a more or less horizontal habit of growth, particularly pronounced in 'Mariesii' and also evident in 'Lanarth' (see 1.20). These tiers of growth contrast well with the euphorbia's upright, red-stemmed, bushy growths.

Most soils are suitable for both these plants, though the viburnum grows particularly well in moisture-retentive, alkaline conditions. In rich, moist ground the euphorbia may become invasive, and for the best autumn colour ordinary, well-drained soil and sun are most suitable. Where several viburnums are grown together, they will produce crops of berries which ripen from red to black.

10.18 Euonymus & Gentiana

Euonymus alatus
sun/shade ○ ◑
type of plant hardy shrub
zonal range 5-9 (C-WT)
height 1.8-2.4m (6-8ft)
special characteristics autumn foliage, ornamental twigs

Gentiana, various, including *G. sino-ornata* and forms
(gentian)
sun/shade ○ ◑
type of plant hardy perennial
zonal range 5-7 (C-CT)
flowering time early to mid-autumn
flower colour shades of blue
height 8-10cm (3-4in)
special characteristics semi-evergreen, needs acid soil

During mid-autumn, the dark green, pendent leaves of *Euonymus alatus* turn a remarkable rosy red. The intensity of this colouring is given extra impact if there are bright blues nearby. Here this very broad-headed shrub is beginning to glow above a pool of brilliant blue, trumpeted-shaped gentian flowers.

Many gentians are rather difficult to grow. However, *Gentiana sino-ornata* and its forms are vigorous plants, creating wide mats of grassy leaves in most acid soils that remain reliably moisture-retentive. The plants thrive in areas of high rainfall and cool summers. In warmer, drier regions they need some shade. Blue asters would be possible substitutes in alkaline soils.

The euonymus is a very easily grown plant that will prosper in any well-drained soil. It is usually a good deal wider than it is tall and, where space is limited, the very dense, slightly smaller variety known as 'Compactus' would be more suitable. Both are slow-growing plants.

After leaf-fall, the euonymus's strange, corky 'wings' are revealed along the younger growths of the plant. Together with the stiff branches, they give the shrub a striking, angular appearance in winter. *Euonymus alatus* may also produce red-seeded fruits.

10.19 Cotoneaster & Geranium

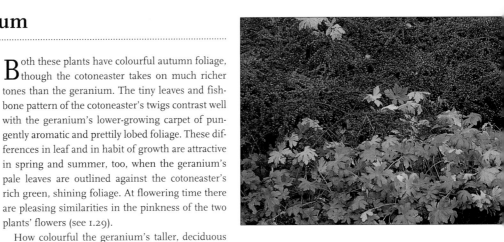

Cotoneaster horizontalis
(fishbone cotoneaster)
sun/shade ○ ◐
type of plant hardy shrub
zonal range 5-8 (C-WT)
flowering time early summer
flower colour pinkish white
height 60cm (2ft), up to 2.4m (8ft) against a wall
special characteristics decorative green foliage, autumn foliage, fruit, ornamental twigs

Geranium macrorrhizum 'Album'
(cranesbill)
sun/shade ○ ◐
type of plant hardy perennial
zonal range 4-8 (C-WT)
flowering time late spring to midsummer
flower colour pinkish white
height 30-40cm (12-15in)
special characteristics semi-evergreen, aromatic, decorative green foliage, autumn foliage

Both these plants have colourful autumn foliage, though the cotoneaster takes on much richer tones than the geranium. The tiny leaves and fishbone pattern of the cotoneaster's twigs contrast well with the geranium's lower-growing carpet of pungently aromatic and prettily lobed foliage. These differences in leaf and in habit of growth are attractive in spring and summer, too, when the geranium's pale leaves are outlined against the cotoneaster's rich green, shining foliage. At flowering time there are pleasing similarities in the pinkness of the two plants' flowers (see 1.29).

How colourful the geranium's taller, deciduous leaves will be in autumn depends partly on soil and site. The plant grows well in all soils with reasonable drainage and in almost all positions. However, the best autumn colour is produced when the site is quite sunny and there is not a great deal of moisture. The particular specimen shown here receives little sun, and its autumn colours are consequently soft rather than bright.

Almost all soils suit the cotoneaster. The bright red berries of this shrub ripen early in autumn. Its fans of growth can be trained up vertical surfaces, or it can be allowed to create mounds of 'fishbones' over low walls or on banks.

10.20 Viburnum & Rhododendron

Viburnum furcatum
sun/shade ◐ **type of plant** hardy shrub
zonal range 4-7 (C-CT)
flowering time late spring to early summer
flower colour creamy white
height 1.8-2.4m (6-8ft)
special characteristics decorative green foliage, autumn foliage, fruit, needs acid soil

Rhododendron cinnabarinum ssp. xanthocodon Concatenans Group
(syn R. concatenans)
sun/shade ◐ **type of plant** hardy shrub
zonal range 6-7 (C-CT)
flowering time mid-spring to early summer
flower colour soft yellow-orange
height 1.2-1.5m (4-5ft) **special characteristics** evergreen, blue-grey foliage, needs acid soil

The rounded leaves of *Viburnum furcatum* are large (about 15cm/6in long) and basically quite a deep green. In late summer they assume the wine-purple tones evident here. By mid-autumn they are deep red. At all stages they provide an excellent background for the much smaller-scale, almost turquoise-blue foliage of the accompanying rhododendron's youngest growths.

Both plants here have attractive flowers. The viburnum's dainty lace-cap blooms are followed in mid-autumn by berries which are at first red and then black. The best crops of fruits are produced if several specimens of the plant are grown together. The rhododendron's elegant, bell-shaped flowers are softly and subtly coloured.

Each of the shrubs in this combination is neat, dense and fairly upright in its habit of growth. *Viburnum furcatum* is not readily available.

However, *V. plicatum* and its varieties, which are easily obtained, also have wine-coloured foliage in late summer and autumn (see 10.17).

Light, dappled shade – from high trees, for instance – suits both the plants in this partnership. They both thrive in moist, acid soils.

11 AROMATIC FOLIAGE

Aromatic plants are reminiscent of medieval herb gardens, sun-baked Mediterranean hillsides and irresistibly delicious herb-flavoured food. They therefore seem to be simultaneously mysterious, alluring and useful. As with fragrant flowers, most of us would find planning combinations of plants on the basis of harmonizing or contrasting leaf scents too complicated. Fortunately, however, many of the aromatic plants that we find so beguiling not only smell delightful but also look attractive. This means that they can easily be incorporated into mixed planting schemes rather than being confined to special herb gardens, which can look rather tired and miserable by early spring – particularly in districts with cold, damp winters.

DECORATIVE AND AROMATIC FOLIAGE

Throughout this book there are numerous plants with leaves that are both decorative and aromatic. For example, the grey foliage of several pungently scented artemisias and santolinas and some minty-leaved nepetas (catmints) can be seen partnering many different leaves and flowers. From a distance, some white- or cream-variegated leaves also appear grey – for example the variegated form of lemon-scented thyme shown in 2.22.

Aromatic plants with rather more conspicuously variegated leaves include some mints, such as *Mentha × gracilis* 'Variegata' and *M. suaveolens* 'Variegata' (see 11.7 and 11.9, respectively). The first of these plants has yellow-variegated foliage. Other aromatic plants with foliage that is yellow-variegated or entirely yellow include the popular golden marjoram (see 11.15) and thymes such as *T. × citriodorus* 'Bertram Anderson' (see 11.17). There are also aromatic plants that have good-looking green foliage (see, for example, *Choisya ternata*, 11.19, and *Tanacetum vulgare crispum*, 9.24). The best known purple-leaved plants with aromatic foliage are purple sage (see 11.7 and 11.8) and the dark-leaved form of common fennel (see 11.1 and 11.2). A few mints, such as *Mentha × piperita citrata*, also have purplish foliage.

Although many aromatic plants have ornamental foliage – and are, therefore, very useful for combining with other plants – their flowers are often not particularly decorative. There are exceptions, however.

These include the lavenders and *Choisya ternata* in this section and the monardas in 1.19 and 3.26. And, of course, there are many non-aromatic plants with flowers that are both decorative and fragrant. This means that doubly scented combinations of aromatic leaves and fragrant flowers can be devised (see, for example, 13.6 and 13.9).

SITING AROMATIC PLANTS

By and large, aromatic leaves do not release their scent freely upon the air in the way that most fragrant flowers do, though there are a few exceptions. The simmering, spicy scent of the curry plant (*Helichrysum italicum serotinum*), for example, will drift pervasively around a garden on a warm day. The majority of aromatic leaves, however, must be bruised or at least brushed against before their fragrance can be perceived. For this reason, these plants need to be sited beside garden seats or main paths or close to the house if their aromatic properties are to be fully appreciated. If evergreen herbs such as thyme and rosemary are to be used in the kitchen during the colder months, they too need to be within easy reach.

The fragrant oils in aromatic leaves are often there for the purpose of protecting the plants against the desiccating effects of hot winds and scorching sun. It is not surprising, therefore, that many aromatic plants grow well in full sun and really well-drained soils. Those that actually enjoy some shade and a moisture-retentive soil are to be found principally among the mints, but other examples of shade-tolerant aromatic plants include *Geranium macrorrhizum* and its forms, *Choisya ternata* and some rhododendrons.

Specialist nurseries list many aromatic plants with distinctive leaves and flowers. Thymes in particular are a rich source of decorative foliage and unusual scents: there are, for example, thymes that smell of lemon, orange, caraway and pine. Other foliage aromas include the very resinous fragrances of some conifers, the cool scents of mints and the warm, musk-like scents of certain olearias. As with floral fragrance, the perception of the scents of aromatic leaves is a highly personal matter, so ideally the buying of these plants should be preceded by some squeezing and sniffing.

11.1 Digitalis & Foeniculum

Digitalis lutea
(syn *D. eriostachya*)
(foxglove)
sun/shade ○ ◗
type of plant hardy perennial
zonal range 4-8 (C-CT)
flowering time early to mid-summer
flower colour light, creamy yellow
height 60-75cm (2-2½ft)

Foeniculum vulgare 'Purpureum'
(syn *F. v.* 'Bronze')
(fennel)
sun/shade ○
type of plant hardy perennial (herb)
zonal range 4-9 (C-WT)
flowering time midsummer to early autumn
flower colour yellow
height 1.5-1.8m (5-6ft)
special characteristics aromatic, purple foliage

Clouds of gossamer-fine, dusky purple foliage and slim spires of softest yellow combine here to create a picture that is both gentle and elegant. The fennel's leaves, which are darkest and most colourful when young, emit the characteristic aniseed scent and flavour of common fennel. Though the general impression here is one of wispiness and airiness, both plants have features that contribute a certain firmness of structure to the partnership: the fennel's haze of foliage is interspersed with stout, glaucous, upright stems, while the foxglove has clumps of firmly shaped, glossy leaves as well as conspicuously erect flower stems.

Neither of these perennials is very long-lived. However, the fennel is a prolific self-seeder – to such an extent that some gardeners like to pinch out the cow parsley-shaped flowers before they set seed. This treatment also has the effect of lengthening the life of the plant. The fennel thrives in light, well-drained soils. The foxglove is easily pleased, but it is not at its best in really hot, dry conditions.

The dusky purple of this fennel can be very attractively echoed in the leaf colour of purple sage (for this sage, see 11.7).

11.2 Foeniculum & Mentha

Foeniculum vulgare 'Purpureum'
(syn *F. v.* 'Bronze')
(fennel)
sun/shade ○
type of plant hardy perennial (herb)
zonal range 4-9 (C-WT)
flowering time midsummer to early autumn
flower colour yellow
height 1.5-1.8m (5-6ft)
special characteristics aromatic, purple foliage

Mentha × gracilis 'Variegata'
(syn *M. × g.* 'Aurea', *M. × gentilis* 'Variegata', *M. × g.* 'Aurea')
(ginger mint)
sun/shade ○
type of plant hardy perennial (herb)
zonal range 4-9 (C-WT/ST)
flowering time midsummer to early autumn
flower colour lilac
height 30-45cm (12-18in)
special characteristics aromatic, variegated foliage

Compared with the gentle creaminess of the foxglove flowers in the preceding combination, the yellow markings of these mint leaves are far brighter and jazzier looking. Setting the fennel's dark purplish gauze beside a very flamboyant partner creates a partnership of strong contrasts rather than soft harmonies.

Both plants here are aromatic. The fennel's thread-like foliage is aniseed-scented, whereas the mint's pointed leaves emit a fresh smell with peppery, gingery undertones. The dusky colouring of the fennel is strongest on young growths.

Both sets of leaves are punctuated by upright stems. The fennel has thick, glaucous stalks; the mint's stems are dark red. The foliage of the mint tends to form a clump of overlapping ovals. This creates just the right sort of lower, more solidly constructed anchor that works well with airy plants like the fennel.

The fennel is such a prolific self-seeder that many gardeners prefer to pinch out the cow parsley-shaped flowers while they are still in bud. The mint's modestly coloured blooms are shown in 11.7.

The mint too is a vigorous colonizer, especially if it is grown in rich, moist soils. It will do well in most conditions, but it will not thrive in hot, dry places. The fennel likes a light soil with good drainage.

11.3 Euonymus & Rosmarinus

Euonymus fortunei 'Variegatus'
(syn *E. f.* 'Silver Gem')
sun/shade ○ ◑
type of plant hardy shrub/climber
zonal range 5-9 (C-WT)
height 45-60cm (1½-2ft as a shrub)
special characteristics evergreen, variegated foliage

Rosmarinus officinalis
(rosemary)
sun/shade ○
type of plant slightly tender shrub (herb)
zonal range 8-9 (CT-WT)
flowering time late spring to early summer
flower colour lavender-blue
height 1.2-1.8m (4-6ft)
special characteristics evergreen, aromatic foliage

The very narrow, leathery leaves of rosemary emit a heady scent that is both fresh and warm, and the plant is as popular in gardens as it is in kitchens. The curving nature of its stems is accentuated by the paleness of the young shoots and the white undersides of the leaves. Overall, however, the plant usually has a distinctly upright habit of growth.

This erectness contrasts well with bushier, more hummocky plants such as the euonymus shown here. In this instance there is also a lively contrast between relatively large, variegated leaves and dark, plain, almost conifer-like foliage. At first, the leaf edges of the euonymus are buttery yellow. Mature leaves are dark-centred with almost white edges. Here this deep greyish green echoes the foliage colour of the rosemary. In cold weather the euonymus's leaf edges may become flushed with pink.

Though leaves are obviously the main attraction here, the rosemary is normally covered in little lipped flowers as spring turns into summer.

Most soils suit the euonymus but the rosemary will be happiest – and hardiest – in a well-drained, rather light soil. Established specimens of this slow-growing euonymus may produce self-clinging, climbing shoots that will reach up to 3m (10ft) high.

11.4 Tanacetum & Agapanthus

Tanacetum vulgare var. crispum
(tansy)
sun/shade ○ ◑
type of plant hardy perennial
zonal range 4-9 (C-WT)
height 60cm (2ft)
special characteristics aromatic, decorative green foliage

Agapanthus Headbourne Hybrid
(African blue lily)
sun/shade ○
type of plant slightly tender perennial
zonal range 8-11 (CT-ST)
flowering time midsummer to early autumn
flower colour pale blue to deep blue
height 60-120cm (2-4ft)
special characteristics evergreen

The cut-leaved tansy's green frills provide a vibrantly coloured setting for the beautiful blue of these agapanthus flowers. The name Headbourne Hybrids covers a number of different seedlings which vary in height and flower colour. Some of these plants are available as named varieties. They all bloom late in the gardening year and carry their loose flowerheads on strong stalks above bold clumps of strap-shaped leaves. Here, this loose arrangement of the rounded flowerheads is in marked contrast to the very dense, finely textured foliage and erect stems of the tansy. Even before the agapanthus comes into flower, there are interesting differences in foliage between the two plants in this combination.

Like the species, this cut-leaved form of tansy is powerfully and rather sweetly aromatic. It is a vigorous plant that is likely to grow strongly in the rich, well-drained soil that suits the agapanthus best. This form of tansy is not generally free-flowering, but in this instance there are some bright buttons of yellow adding to the general impression of freshness and liveliness.

177

11.5 Caryopteris & Helichrysum

Caryopteris × *clandonensis*
sun/shade ○
type of plant hardy shrub
zonal range 6-9 (C-WT)
flowering time late summer to early autumn
flower colour bright blue
height 60-90cm (2-3ft)
special characteristics aromatic, grey-green foliage

Helichrysum italicum ssp. *serotinum*
(syn *H. angustifolium* ssp. *serotinum*, *H. serotinum*)
(curry plant)
sun/shade ○
type of plant slightly tender shrub/perennial
zonal range 8-10 (CT-ST)
flowering time early to late summer
flower colour yellow
height 23-40cm (9-15in)
special characteristics evergreen/semi-evergreen, aromatic, silver foliage

The curry plant has one of the strongest and most distinctive scents of all garden plants, and a warm wind will waft its culinary aroma considerable distances. This subshrubby little plant also has silvery-grey, needle-like leaves and very pale, upright stems which give it a bright appearance overall. In the combination illustrated here, this attractive, close-textured silveriness intensifies still further the lovely strong blue of the caryopteris's late-season blooms.

Caryopteris × *clandonensis* also has greyish leaves, though they are larger and darker than those of the curry plant. This darker, rather sprawling, bushy mass makes a good background for the very pale grey of the smaller plant and also shows off nicely the latter's little button-like flowers, the last of which are visible here, in early autumn.

The caryopteris may not be quite as exotically scented as the curry plant, but it too is aromatic. When bruised, the leaves emit a smell which has been likened to varnish, though there are also refreshing undertones of rosemary and mint.

Light, well-drained soils suit both these plants. Fairly hard pruning in spring makes the caryopteris flower freely and discourages too open a growth habit. There are various named forms of this plant, some of them with especially dark blue flowers.

11.6 Lavandula & Lychnis

Lavandula angustifolia 'Hidcote'
(lavender)
sun/shade ○
type of plant hardy shrub
zonal range 6-9 (C-WT)
flowering time mid- to late summer
flower colour deep violet
height 60cm (2ft)
special characteristics evergreen, aromatic, grey foliage, fragrant flowers

Lychnis coronaria Atrosanguinea Group
(rose campion)
sun/shade ○
type of plant hardy perennial
zonal range 4-8 (C-WT)
flowering time mid- to late summer
flower colour crimson
height 60-75cm (2-2½ft)
special characteristics grey foliage

The silvery-grey foliage of this dark-flowered form of common lavender has the same refreshing 'clean laundry' scent as that of the typical species. In this combination the plant has been paired with a perennial of an even paler grey. As well as woolly, pointed leaves, *Lychnis coronaria* and its varieties produce clumps of pale-felted, branched flower stems. These leaves and stems contrast conspicuously with the denser, finer-textured growth of the lavender.

Still more eye-catching, however, is the association of two strong, rich flower colours. The use of the crimson-flowered form of *Lychnis coronaria*, with its deep hue and blue tones, makes for an especially successful harmonizing of the two colours. However, the sizzling magenta-pink of the species (see 3.1) would also work well here. The lavender is normally a very free-flowering plant and its 5cm (2in), heavily scented spikes are decorative from the bud stage onwards.

Each of these plants thrives in light, rather dry soils and sunny places. The lychnis is short-lived, but good drainage extends its lifespan. The lavender needs to be clipped, preferably twice a year in early spring and after flowering, if it is to form a good, dense hummock of growth.

11.7 Salvia & Mentha

Salvia officinalis Purpurascens Group
(purple sage)
sun/shade ○
type of plant slightly tender shrub/perennial (herb)
zonal range 7-9 (CT-WT)
flowering time early to mid-summer
flower colour violet-purple
height 60-75cm (2-2½ft)
special characteristics evergreen/semi-evergreen, aromatic, purple foliage

Mentha × gracilis 'Variegata'
(syn *M. × g.* 'Aurea', *M. × gentilis* 'Variegata', *M. × g.* 'Aurea')
(ginger mint)
sun/shade ○
type of plant hardy perennial (herb)
zonal range 4-9 (C-WT/ST)
flowering time midsummer to early autumn
flower colour lilac
height 30-45cm (12-18in)
special characteristics aromatic, variegated foliage

The soft greyish-purple of this sage mixes well with many other colours. It blends beautifully with, for example, grey leaves (see 4.15) and flowers that are mauve, purple or pink (see the following combination). It also contrasts effectively with yellows and yellow-greens – as it does here, where its subtle, smoky colouring is a calm counterpoint to the bright green and yellow leaves of variegated ginger mint. At the same time, the mint's bold splashes and stripes enliven the sage's restrained duskiness.

The mint's veined foliage has a fresh, gingery smell and, though they are not as pungently aromatic as the green-leaved species, the velvety leaves of the purple sage emit the same characteristic warm scent. The mint's little leaves are carried on numerous, erect, dark red stems. Especially if it is clipped each spring, the stems of the sage will also be rather upright and the plant will form a dense hummock of growth. If clipped there will be few of the small lipped flowers, but in any case the purple sage is not usually a free-flowering plant. The flowers of the mint are small and quietly coloured.

A well-drained, dryish soil and plenty of sun also encourage the sage to grow neatly. The mint prefers a moist soil, but it is a very vigorous plant which is basically unfussy. However, it will not produce good quality foliage in a soil that is very dry in summer.

11.8 Salvia & Thymus

Salvia officinalis Purpurascens Group
(purple sage)
sun/shade ○
type of plant slightly tender shrub/perennial (herb)
zonal range 7-9 (CT-WT)
flowering time early to mid-summer
flower colour violet-purple
height 60-75cm (2-2½ft)
special characteristics evergreen/semi-evergreen, aromatic, purple foliage

Thymus serpyllum 'Annie Hall'
(thyme)
sun/shade ○
type of plant hardy shrub/perennial
zonal range 4-8 (C-WT)
flowering time early to mid-summer
flower colour purplish-pink
height 5-8cm (2-3in)
special characteristics evergreen/semi-evergreen, aromatic foliage

Both pink and purple flowers and those that are a mixture of these colours blend very pleasingly with the subtly coloured foliage of the purple sage. In the combination illustrated here, the charming blooms of a subshrubby thyme brighten the more subdued grey-greens and purples of the sage.

Both of the plants in this combination are aromatic: though the purple sage is not quite so strongly scented as the green-leaved species, *Thymus serpyllum* 'Annie Hall' has the refreshing, pungent smell of most thymes. Its little leaves form a closely woven carpet of greenery, contrasting well with the sage's rounded hummock of upright stems and slender, velvety, comparatively large leaves. Specialist nurseries will list numerous low-growing thymes, many of which would look attractive with this sage. While some have the characteristic thyme scent, there are forms with other aromas such as caraway, lemon and pine.

Most well-drained, rather light soils will suit these two plants. They will perform well in hot, dry positions. Both benefit from a spring clipping, which results in dense, neat growth but, in the case of the sage, lessens the likelihood of any flowers. However, the purple sage is not generally a very free-flowering plant.

11.9 Mentha & Santolina

Mentha suaveolens 'Variegata'

(syn *M. rotundifolia* 'Variegata')
(pineapple mint)
sun/shade ○ ◖
type of plant hardy perennial (herb)
zonal range 5-9 (C-ST)
height 30-45cm (12-18in)
special characteristics aromatic, variegated foliage

Santolina pinnata ssp. *neapolitana*

sun/shade ○
type of plant slightly tender shrub
zonal range 7-9 (CT-WT)
flowering time midsummer
flower colour bright lemon-yellow
height 60-75cm (2-2½ft)
special characteristics evergreen, aromatic, grey-green foliage

Where the pineapple mint is all bright, crisp variegation on neat little wrinkly leaves, this santolina is cool, grey-green uniformity and graceful wispiness. The general impression is one of cheerful audacity alongside restrained elegance.

Each of the plants in this combination is aromatic. The pineapple mint has leaves that emit a rather dry, fruity smell when bruised, while the santolina's fragrance is less strong but sharper. The mint's foliage is disposed around rather curving but basically upright stems. As the leaves mature, their very pale margins become almost white, as they are here, in early autumn. The santolina's foliage is also carried on erect stems, but it is much finer in texture and the overall effect is dense and hummocky.

To achieve this effect of neatness and density, however, the santolina needs to be clipped at least once a year. Some gardeners like to remove the very bright flowers of this plant while they are still in bud, and this treatment too discourages any tendency to lank, loose growth. The mint's flowers are an unassertive pink.

In rich, moist soils the mint can be invasive. Giving it the well-drained conditions that the santolina demands will curb its vigour somewhat. The mint's bright variegation looks attractive with hot as well as with cool colours (see 11.16).

11.10 Salvia & Ballota

Salvia officinalis 'Icterina'

(syn *S. o.* 'Variegata')
(golden sage)
sun/shade ○
type of plant slightly tender shrub/perennial (herb)
zonal range 7-9 (C-WT)
height 60cm (2ft)
special characteristics semi-evergreen, aromatic, variegated foliage

Ballota acetabulosa

sun/shade ○
type of plant slightly tender perennial/shrub
zonal range 7-9 (C-WT)
flowering time mid- to late summer
flower colour white + purple
height 60cm (2ft)
special characteristics evergreen/semi-evergreen, grey foliage

The softly variegated leaves of golden sage, with their muted grey-greens and yellows, harmonize beautifully with many other plants (see 6.7 and 11.11). Here they are enhancing the large but very subtly coloured green calyces of *Ballota acetabulosa*. Such an understated colour scheme also allows the lovely textural differences between these two plants to be seen to advantage. The sage's mound of rather slim, overlapping leaves contrasts very pleasingly with the ballota's clump of pale, upright stems and rounded, grey-green leaves. Flowers play a minor role here: the golden sage rarely blooms and the ballota's flowers are tiny points of colour in the much more prominent calyces of the plant.

Both these plants thrive in light soils with good drainage. They are ideally suited to hot, dry situations, where the warmly pungent foliage of the sage will be especially aromatic. In mild areas the leaves of both these plants will look good almost all year long; in districts with cold winters they are, however, likely to appear rather tired and battered until the new growth appears. Wherever it is grown, the sage will be particularly neat and dense if it is clipped each spring.

For another sage and ballota combination, this time using purple sage, see 4.15.

11.11 Lavandula & Salvia

Lavandula stoechas
(French lavender)
sun/shade ○
type of plant slightly tender shrub
zonal range 8-9 (C-WT/ST)
flowering time early to late summer
flower colour dark blue-purple + violet
height 45cm (18in)
special characteristics evergreen, aromatic, grey foliage, fragrant flowers

Salvia officinalis 'Icterina'
(syn *S. o.* 'Variegata')
(golden sage)
sun/shade ○
type of plant slightly tender shrub/perennial (herb)
zonal range 7-9 (CT-WT)
height 60cm (2ft)
special characteristics semi-evergreen, aromatic, variegated foliage

French lavender's wispy, pale grey foliage is powerfully aromatic, with undertones of the scent of rosemary. Here this foliage has been combined with the very decoratively variegated leaves of the golden sage. The much larger and broader leaves of this second plant contrast nicely with the thin little leaves of the lavender. However, it is the soft yellows and greyish-greens of the sage, combined with the deep purple flower spikes and the flamboyant, violet topknots of the lavender, that make this partnership of plants particularly appealing.

Although the sage rarely flowers, the lavender usually does so prolifically and over a long period; it is shown here in early autumn. In the subspecies *Lavandula stoechas pedunculata* the topknots are even longer and more eye-catching. The flowers of both the species and subspecies have a fragrance similar to that of the plant's foliage. The leaves of the golden sage have the characteristic, warm pungency of the typical species.

Both these plants benefit from a warm site and really good drainage. They will grow especially well in hot, dry places. Clipping the plants each spring ensures that they grow neatly and densely. Treated in this way, the sage forms a close mound of overlapping leaves and the lavender creates a little forest of upright stems.

11.12 Cotoneaster, Calamintha & Rhododendron

Cotoneaster atropurpureus 'Variegatus'
(syn *C. horizontalis* 'Variegatus')
sun/shade ○ ◑ **type of plant** hardy shrub
zonal range 5-8 (C-CT)
flowering time early summer
flower colour pink **height** 45-60cm (1½-2ft), 1.2-1.8m (4-6ft) against a wall
special characteristics variegated foliage, autumn foliage, ornamental twigs

Calamintha nepeta ssp. nepeta
(syn *C. nepetoides*)
sun/shade ○ **type of plant** hardy perennial
zonal range 5-9 (C-WT)
flowering time late summer to early autumn
flower colour blue + white
height 30-40cm (12-15in)
special characteristics aromatic foliage

Rhododendron impeditum
sun/shade ○ ◑ **type of plant** hardy shrub
zonal range 6-8 (C-CT)
flowering time mid- to late spring
flower colour purplish blue **height** 30cm (12in)
special characteristics evergreen, aromatic foliage, needs acid soil

All the plants here have small leaves and the overall effect of the combination is soft and gentle. There are, however, marked differences in habits of growth and these differences prevent the combination from being either fussy or too indeterminate. The cotoneaster's grey-green, white-edged leaves are borne on branches that fan and arch conspicuously in much the same way as the branches of *Cotoneaster horizontalis* (fishbone cotoneaster) do. In contrast, the numerous, bushy stems of the calamintha, with their spearmint-scented leaves, are distinctly erect. Finally, the dark, dense, dome shape of the rhododendron acts as an anchor to the whole arrangement. The fruitily scented leaves of the latter have a greyish caste.

Illustrated here in late summer, the calamintha is, characteristically, covered in flowers. The spring blooms of the rhododendron appear in similarly generous quantities. The flowers of both the calamintha and the cotoneaster are very attractive to bees. As a late-season bonus, the cotoneaster's leaves turn pink and soft red in mid- and late autumn (see 10.10), but there are rarely more than a few scarlet berries on the plant.

Provided conditions are lime-free for the sake of the rhododendron, most well-drained, reasonably moisture-retentive soils will suit these plants. Like

Cotoneaster horizontalis, the cotoneaster can be grown upright against high walls or allowed to scramble over lower structures. It may also be used as freestanding ground cover. Both it and the rhododendron are very slow-growing plants.

11.13 Ruta & Mentha

Ruta graveolens 'Jackman's Blue'
(rue)
sun/shade ○
type of plant hardy shrub
zonal range 6-8 (C-WT)
flowering time mid- to late summer
flower colour yellow
height 45-60cm (1½-2ft)
special characteristics evergreen, aromatic, blue-grey foliage

Mentha × gracilis 'Variegata'
(syn *M. × g.* 'Aurea', *M. × gentilis* 'Variegata', *M. × g.* 'Aurea')
(ginger mint)
sun/shade ○
type of plant hardy perennial (herb)
zonal range 4-9 (C-WT/ST)
flowering time midsummer to early autumn
flower colour lilac
height 30-45cm (12-18in)
special characteristics aromatic, variegated foliage

The association of yellow and blue is usually a happy one, and when the colours are supplied by foliage rather than flowers the combination is also long-lasting. The variety of rue shown here has leaves of a strikingly intense blue-grey. This shrub forms a neat and elegant mound of foliage, especially if it is clipped each spring and any of the rather strong yellow flowers that begin to appear are pinched out when still in bud. Its partner here, a form of the ginger-scented mint, is altogether brighter and bolder and more flamboyant in appearance. Its pointed leaves, with their cheerful streaks of yellow and bright green, and its dark red, upright stems are in marked contrast to the cool blue laciness of the rue.

Good drainage and plenty of sun produce the best specimens of the rue. The mint is a vigorous and basically easy-going plant that can be grown in a variety of soils. It is often invasive in rich, moist conditions. For an illustration of the rather modestly coloured flowers of this plant, see 11.7. The rue should be handled carefully by gardeners with sensitive skin, since the sharply, drily aromatic foliage can be an irritant.

11.14 Ruta, Lamium & Stachys

Ruta graveolens 'Jackman's Blue'
(rue)
sun/shade ○ **type of plant** hardy shrub
zonal range 6-8 (C-WT)
flowering time mid- to late summer
flower colour yellow
height 45-60cm (1½-2ft)
special characteristics evergreen, aromatic, blue-grey foliage

Lamium maculatum 'Chequers'
(spotted dead nettle)
sun/shade ◖ **type of plant** hardy perennial
zonal range 4-8 (C-WT)
flowering time mid-spring to midsummer
flower colour bright pink
height 15cm (6in)
special characteristics evergreen, variegated foliage

Stachys byzantina 'Silver Carpet'
(syn *S. lanata* 'Silver Carpet', *S. olympica* 'Silver Carpet') (lamb's tongue, lamb's ear, lamb's lug)
sun/shade ○ **type of plant** hardy perennial
zonal range 4-9 (C-WT)
height 10-15cm (4-6in)
special characteristics evergreen, silver foliage

Intensely blue-grey and immaculately lacy, this variety of rue is also very aromatic, with a sharp, strong scent. Its smooth little leaflets have been partnered here with *Stachys byzantina* 'Silver Carpet', another grey plant but one that has bold, softly furred foliage. Its large, broad leaves, on their long stems, cover the ground densely and provide a pleasing contrast to the rounded outline of the rue. Weaving their way through these two plants are the small, burgundy-blotched leaves and bright flowers of a vigorous variety of lamium. The small touches of colour supplied by this lax-stemmed carpeter are very decorative, yet they never distract attention from the lovely textural differences between the rue and the lamb's tongue.

A light, well-drained soil would suit this combination best. In cool, moist soils the lamium can be invasive; in drier conditions some of the energy of this tolerant and very easily grown plant will be curbed, but positioning it between two other plants, as here, does provide it with some shade and coolness. The variety 'Beacon Silver' is somewhat similar to 'Chequers', though its leaves are more completely silvered and less heavily blotched with red-purple. It is less likely to be invasive.

Many gardeners like to pinch out the flower buds of the rue, since they feel that the strong yellow

blooms detract from the appearance of the plant's foliage. This treatment – along with clipping in spring – also ensures that the rue grows neatly and densely. Any handling of the plant must be undertaken with care as the growths can irritate skin.

11.15 Santolina & Origanum

Santolina pinnata ssp. *neapolitana* 'Edward Bowles'

sun/shade ○
type of plant slightly tender shrub
zonal range 7-9 (CT-WT)
flowering time midsummer
flower colour cream
height 45cm (18in)
special characteristics evergreen, aromatic, grey-green foliage

Origanum vulgare 'Aureum'

(golden marjoram)
sun/shade ○
type of plant hardy perennial (herb)
zonal range 4-8 (C-WT)
height 23cm (9in)
special characteristics evergreen/semi-evergreen, aromatic, yellow foliage

The feathery, grey-green foliage of this santolina is pungently aromatic, while the neat yellow leaves of the accompanying marjoram have a warmer and stronger scent. Uniting these two sets of leaves, with their most attractive contrasts in size, texture, colour and scent, is the santolina's mass of slender-stalked, yellow buttons. When fully open these flowers are a gentle, pale cream, which some gardeners prefer to the brighter flower colour of *S. p. neapolitana* itself. The flowers of the marjoram are quite modestly coloured, and they tend to appear only in small numbers on this yellow-leaved variety.

Each of these plants grows densely. As long as the santolina's numerous flowers are removed promptly once they have faded, the plant forms a mound of finely textured foliage. The new leaves are green. The marjoram's foliage gradually becomes less yellow as the summer progresses, but the plant remains a thick, weed-suppressing mass of stems and leaves throughout the growing season. In very hot, dry places the leaf edges of this marjoram may become scorched. Ideally, therefore, this combination should be given a well-drained, rather light soil but one that never dries out completely.

11.16 Geranium & Mentha

Geranium sanguineum

(bloody cranesbill)
sun/shade ○
type of plant hardy perennial
zonal range 4-8 (C-WT)
flowering time early summer to early autumn
flower colour magenta-pink
height 23cm (9in)
special characteristics decorative green foliage, autumn foliage

Mentha suaveolens 'Variegata'

(syn *M. rotundifolia* 'Variegata')
(pineapple mint)
sun/shade ○ ◑
type of plant hardy perennial (herb)
zonal range 5-9 (C-WT)
height 30-45cm (12-18in)
special characteristics aromatic, variegated foliage

In this combination it is the crisp appearance of the pineapple mint's very pale cream leaf margins combined with the really hot pink flowers of *Geranium sanguineum* that give the partnership such freshness and brilliance. Since the geranium flowers prolifically over several months, this is a combination with an especially long season of interest. Indeed, even when the geranium has finally stopped flowering, there is the bonus of bright autumn foliage colour from its very deeply lobed leaves.

The geranium's leaves are attractive in their green state, too, and they make good companions for the mint's rounded, undivided foliage. Both plants will grow densely in most soils that are reasonably well-drained and moisture-retentive. The geranium forms a spreading hummock of greenery, while the mint's curving stems expand fairly rapidly into wide clumps of growth, especially in moist, rich soils. The mint's wrinkled leaves emit a fruity, slightly musty scent when bruised.

There are several readily available varieties of *Geranium sanguineum* with flowers that are paler and gentler in colour than those of the typical species. They too would look attractive with the pineapple mint. The mint usually produces only a very few modestly coloured flowers (see 11.9).

11.17 Bergenia & Thymus

Bergenia 'Abendglut'
(syn *B.* 'Evening Glow')

sun/shade ○ ◐
type of plant hardy perennial
zonal range 3-8 (C-WT)
flowering time mid- to late spring
flower colour bright rose-crimson
height 20-30cm (8-12in)
special characteristics evergreen, decorative green foliage, autumn/winter foliage

Thymus × citriodorus 'Bertram Anderson'
(syn *T.* 'Anderson's Gold', *T.* 'E. B. Anderson')
(lemon-scented thyme)

sun/shade ○
type of plant hardy shrub (herb)
zonal range 6-8 (C-WT)
height 8-10cm (3-4in)
special characteristics evergreen, aromatic, yellow foliage

The tiny, citrus-scented leaves of this thyme are most brightly coloured in spring and summer but are still distinctly yellow even in early winter, as shown here. Planting these leaves beside foliage of a strikingly dark wine-maroon successfully maximizes their yellowness, and also emphasizes the neat, dense habit of growth of this thyme and the close, rather dry texture of its foliage. The accompanying bergenia grows densely too but its leaves are big (about 15cm/6in long) and bold. They are also contrastingly lustrous and fleshy.

These contrasts make for an interesting partnership almost all year long. These evergreen plants are not at their best in late winter and early spring, but by the time the bergenia's red-stemmed flowerheads appear they will both be producing attractive new leaves. The bergenia's spring and summer foliage colour is a good rich green. Its winter foliage colour is deepest if the plant is given an open, sunny position and a dryish, not too fertile soil. These conditions are ideal for the thyme, which will form an especially neat carpet of growth when given a springtime trimming each year. This particular variety of lemon-scented thyme produces only a few, pale mauve flowers.

For another combination featuring a bergenia with colourful winter leaves, see 12.12.

11.18 Artemisia & Ajuga

Artemisia schmidtiana 'Nana'

sun/shade ○
type of plant hardy perennial/shrub
zonal range 3-7 (C-CT)
height 10-15cm (4-6in)
special characteristics evergreen/semi-evergreen, aromatic, silver foliage

Ajuga reptans 'Atropurpurea'
(bugle)

sun/shade ○ ◐
type of plant hardy perennial
zonal range 3-9 (C-WT)
flowering time late spring to early summer
flower colour deep blue
height 15-20cm (6-8in)
special characteristics evergreen/semi-evergreen, purple foliage

There are a number of popular artemisias with deeply divided silver leaves, all of which are pungently aromatic plants (see 2.12 and 2.13). Most of them are, however, much larger than the silvery-grey perennial shown here. This plant too has sharply aromatic foliage. Its paleness and featheriness are beautifully set off by a carpet of the smoothly shaped, shiny, dark purple leaves of *Ajuga reptans* 'Atropurpurea'.

As well as very richly coloured foliage, the bugle contributes lovely bright blue flowers to this combination. Here, in late spring, these flowers are just opening. (For an illustration of them at a later stage, see 5.8.) Because they are conspicuously upright, these flower spikes add interesting vertical shapes to this partnership of two ground-hugging plants. The yellowish, summer flowers of the artemisia are produced in summer. They are not particularly decorative and the plant is neater if they are removed. (In this photograph the lengthening flower stalks have been flattened by a heavy shower of rain.)

This combination will grow best in a well-drained soil that does not become too dry. Although the bugle spreads widely and grows vigorously in moist soils, it is important that, in winter especially, the roots of the artemisia are not wet. In heavy, moist soils the artemisia is likely to be very short-lived.

For other combinations with aromatic foliage, see:
COOL-COLOURED FLOWERS 1.10, 1.11, 1.12, 1.19, 1.23, 1.29 GREY FOLIAGE 2.4, 2.5, 2.12, 2.13, 2.14, 2.15, 2.16, 2.19, 2.22, 2.26 HOT-COLOURED FLOWERS 3.6, 3.8, 3.19, 3.26 PURPLE FOLIAGE 4.9, 4.15, 4.17, 4.26 YELLOW FLOWERS 5.4, 5.10, 5.14 YELLOW FOLIAGE 6.2, 6.7, 6.8, 6.9 GREEN FLOWERS 7.7, 7.9 GREEN FOLIAGE 8.2, 8.9, 8.15 VARIEGATED FOLIAGE 9.24 AUTUMN FOLIAGE 10.7, 10.8, 10.16, 10.19 FRAGRANT FLOWERS 13.6, 13.7, 13.9, 13.10, 13.11, 13.14 WINTER FLOWERS 14.7 CLIMBING PLANTS 15.13, 15.14 GRASSES AND FERNS 17.4, 17.22

11.19 Spiraea & Choisya

Spiraea japonica 'Goldflame'
sun/shade ○ ◖
type of plant hardy shrub
zonal range 4-9 (C-WT)
flowering time early to mid-summer
flower colour crimson-pink
height 75-90cm (2½-3ft)
special characteristics yellow foliage, orange when young

Choisya ternata
(Mexican orange blossom)
sun/shade ○ ◖
type of plant slightly tender shrub
zonal range 7-9 (CT-WT)
flowering time mainly late spring to early summer, some flowers early autumn
flower colour white
height 1.8-2.4m (6-8ft)
special characteristics evergreen, aromatic, decorative green foliage, fragrant flowers

As the very sweetly scented flowers of *Choisya ternata* start to fade, the newer, lime-green leaves of this fast-growing shrub emerge. Both this yellow-green, young foliage and the older, rich green leaves are glossy and strongly orange-scented. The two shrubs are basically rounded in outline and, though the spiraea is twiggier and slightly more arching, both grow densely. The size and shape of the leaves of these plants show some similarities, too. Altogether these likenesses simplify the combination into a rather gentle and informal weaving together of differently coloured leaves.

The spiraea's foliage is at its brightest before its flowers appear. Later the leaves are less yellow. Here, in earliest summer, the spiraea's youngest growths are a coppery red and this makes the flowers of the choisya look particularly fresh and clean. Some gardeners object to the spiraea's vividly coloured flowers and pinch them out in bud. This makes the plant grow especially neatly and densely.

Most soils suit this spiraea. The choisya needs good drainage and, in areas with cold winters, a sunny site. In full sun the spiraea's foliage is particularly bright, but if conditions are rather dry some scorching of the leaf edges may occur.

11.20 Choisya & Pulmonaria

Choisya ternata
(Mexican orange blossom)
sun/shade ○ ◖
type of plant slightly tender shrub
zonal range 7-9 (CT-WT)
flowering time mainly late spring to early summer, some flowers early autumn
flower colour white
height 1.8-2.4m (6-8ft)
special characteristics evergreen, aromatic, decorative green foliage, fragrant flowers

Pulmonaria officinalis 'Sissinghurst White'
(spotted dog, soldiers and sailors, lungwort)
sun/shade ◖
type of plant hardy perennial
zonal range 4-8 (C-CT)
flowering time early to mid-spring
flower colour white
height 20-30cm (8-12in)
special characteristics evergreen/semi-evergreen, variegated foliage

Aromatic foliage is just one of the attractions of *Choisya ternata*. As well as emitting a rich, citrus scent when bruised, the leaves of this shrub are a beautiful, deep, glossy green and elegantly smooth in shape. There are very sweetly fragrant flowers to enjoy, too, and these sparkle against the good-looking foliage (see 13.14).

An underplanting of lungwort leaves, splashed with pale, silvery-green markings, adds a pretty touch of lightness to the choisya's rounded mass of plain green. When the choisya is in flower this pale variegation echoes the larger plant's white blossom very decoratively, and when the lungwort blooms its long-stemmed sprays of white stand out especially well against the choisya's foliage.

In mild areas *Choisya ternata* can be grown in quite shady places; a sunny position is safer in cold districts. Most well-drained soils suit this fast-growing plant. The lungwort is particularly at home in moist, cool soils, and in these conditions its clumps of foliage are especially dense. It is, however, an easily pleased plant which is quite happy, as it is here, in light shade cast by larger plants. It will tolerate dry shade.

The preceding combination shows *Choisya ternata* combined with a larger, more warmly coloured foliage plant.

12 ORNAMENTAL FRUITS & SEEDHEADS

For gardeners who enjoy combining plants, ornamental fruits have two main attractions. First, many of them appear late in the season and they therefore provide material for combinations at a time when flowers are becoming scarcer in the garden. Secondly, most of them have a distinctively dense consistency and a firmness of form that is not normally found among flowers and leaves.

Ornamental fruits come in a wide assortment of shapes and colours. Not all fruits are berry-like and, indeed, not all berries are red or orange. This chapter does include illustrations of orange-red rose hips and the red berries of several familiar cotoneasters, but there are also pale, silky clematis seedheads and purple-black grapes. Other less usual fruits in this section include the mauve berries of *Callicarpa bodinieri giraldii* 'Profusion', pink sorbus berries, yellow pyracantha berries and the rich russet seedheads of *Sedum* 'Herbstfreude'.

In addition to the fruits illustrated in the following combinations, there are seedpods and conifer cones. Both these types of fruit tend to create bigger and usually bolder shapes than berries. *Decaisnea fargesii*, for example, has eye-catching, frosty blue pods, and the beans of *Catalpa bignonioides* (the Indian bean tree) are exceptionally long and slender. The distinctive fruits of conifers introduce yet more shapes and colours. Among the more decorative cones are those of the Korean fir (*Abies koreana*), which are neat and cylindrical and of a remarkable, violet-tinged, navy blue.

USING FRUIT IN PLANT COMBINATIONS

All these different shapes and colours mean that ornamental fruits are a rich source of material with which to create interesting combinations. The large numbers of red and orange berries have obvious autumnal partners among the glowing colours of much autumn foliage (see 10.5) and they also look well with late-season flowers of warm colours. However, 12.15 and 12.17 show how the contrasting coolness of blue-grey foliage or palely variegated leaves can intensify the warmth of red berries. Cool blue flowers can have a similar effect on orange berries (see 12.19).

Perhaps the most cheerful combination of all consists of red or orange-red berries with green leaves. This is conveniently illustrated by certain red-berried plants, such as hollies and pyracanthas, which supply their own, excellent, glossy greenery. The resultant intense contrast between the two complementary colours creates an effect of almost aggressive jollity. Yellow fruits, on the other hand, being closer on the colour spectrum to green, sometimes merge too readily with green foliage. However, combining yellow fruits with touches of yellow, either from leaves or from flowers (see 12.9), can do much to give the fruits extra impact.

We may yearn for hot colours in some form or other as the days become colder, but the softer light of autumn often gives cool colours a special luminosity. In slanting autumn sun, the ghostly chill of very pale or blue-tinged fruits can be almost as conspicuous as the loud cheerfulness of red and orange berries. Some gardeners will enjoy contrasting cool-coloured fruits with hot oranges and reds and warm yellows, but the lavender-blue flowers of some asters (see 1.1 and 1.22), the violet spikes of *Liriope muscari* (see 9.25) and the blues and mauves of certain autumn-flowering crocuses can all emphasize cool-coloured fruits very effectively.

ORNAMENTAL FRUIT FOR SMALL GARDENS

Even in quite limited spaces, there is room for some plants with ornamental fruit. Small or medium-sized plants illustrated in this section include *Acaena microphylla* (see 12.7) with spiky, crimson burrs, *Iris foetidissima citrina* (12.19), which has fat pods of bright orange berries, and *Pulsatilla vulgaris* (see 12.6), which produces charming, frizzy seedheads.

The fruit-bearing plants least suitable for small gardens are those that bear fruit – or fruit really well – only if several specimens are grown together. Most plants are self-fertile, but the majority of hollies and skimmias, for example, have male and female flowers on separate plants. This means that plants of both sexes must be grown for fruits to appear. Few gardeners with very limited space would be prepared to relinquish precious ground to more than one holly or skimmia.

Some plants with attractive fruit have other decorative features, too. These plants are particularly valuable and especially so in small gardens. Many roses bear richly coloured hips, but these plants will have very often been grown principally for their flowers. As a bonus, some roses with good hips have flowers that are fragrant (see 13.15). Fragrant flowers and richly coloured fruits are also produced by some honeysuckles (see 12.10 and 12.11). The flowers of certain plants ripen into seedheads, rather than fleshy fruits, and various combinations in this section include alliums, sedums and small-flowered clematis, all of which have attractive flowers and, later, very decorative seedheads.

ORNAMENTAL FOLIAGE

Several plants have colourful autumn foliage as well as ornamental fruit, including *Vitis vinifera* 'Purpurea', *Cotoneaster horizontalis* and *Sorbus reducta*, all of which are illustrated in this section. Each of these three plants has foliage which is also attractive in its summer state. Hollies are the principal source of variegated foliage and ornamental fruit; there are very few small variegated plants with good fruit, though *Arum italicum italicum* 'Marmoratum' has beautiful, veined and marbled leaves (see 4.28) and spectacular orange berries. There are also grey-leaved, yellow-leaved and purple-leaved plants with ornamental fruit, and berrying plants with handsome green foliage. Ornamental fruit, in all its diversity, has many special attractions. The delights of berries, seed-pods, seed-heads and cones do not, however, preclude the pleasures of fragrant flowers, glowing autumn leaves and beautiful, coloured foliage.

12.1 Vitis & Hydrangea

Vitis vinifera 'Purpurea'

(claret vine, Teinturier grape, grape vine)
sun/shade ○
type of plant hardy climber
zonal range 6-9 (C-WT)
height 3-4.5m (10-15ft)
special characteristics purple foliage, autumn foliage, fruit

Hydrangea anomala ssp. *petiolaris*

(syn *H. petiolaris*)
(climbing hydrangea)
sun/shade ○ ◑
type of plant hardy climber
zonal range 5-8 (C-WT)
flowering time early summer
flower colour white
height 15-18m (50-60ft)
special characteristics autumn foliage

This vine's gleaming bunches of purple-black grapes are very much less luscious than they look, but accompanied by crimson and yellow mid-autumn leaves they certainly create a picture of mellow autumnal abundance. For there to be plenty of fruit and for its dying leaves to turn a good crimson, this twining plant needs to be grown against a warm, sheltered wall. This will also ensure that the shapely foliage is a deep, dusky purple earlier in the year (see 15.8). At all stages it contrasts attractively with the smaller and more simply shaped leaves of the hydrangea, which themselves change in colour from a lively mid-green in spring and summer to a clear, buttery yellow in autumn.

This combination is perhaps at its most decorative in mid-autumn. However, the large, lacy flowers of the hydrangea (see 15.20) and the purple leaves of the vine – which emerge a lovely soft grey – are very handsome in the preceding months.

Both of these climbers are slow-growing, at least when young. Once established, the hydrangea becomes completely self-supporting by means of aerial roots. The vine needs full sun and a fertile, moisture-retentive and well-drained soil. The hydrangea will also thrive in this sort of soil, but it can be planted in cool, shady positions as well as sunnier places.

12.2 Elaeagnus & Callicarpa

Elaeagnus pungens 'Maculata'

(syn *E. p.* 'Aureovariegata')
sun/shade ○ ◑
type of plant hardy shrub
zonal range 7-10 (C-WT/ST)
height 2.4-3m (8-10ft)
special characteristics evergreen, variegated foliage, fragrant flowers

Callicarpa bodinieri var. *giraldii* 'Profusion'

sun/shade ○
type of plant hardy shrub
zonal range 6-8 (C-CT)
height 1.5-1.8m (5-6ft)
special characteristics autumn foliage, fruit

When seen for the first time, the berries of this callicarpa never fail to astonish. Their highly unusual, almost eerie violet-mauve colour would be surprising at any time of the year, but in autumn it seems extraordinary. To make the most of this colouring, this rather upright shrub needs a sunny site, in which the clustered fruits can glisten conspicuously, and a suitably contrasting background.

Here the berries have been given a background of glossy leaves which have very broad, central areas of warm yellow. These broad leaf markings and the dense, if slightly muddled system of growth create a good, solid backdrop of contrasting colour for the callicarpa berries.

The elaeagnus's markings are especially bright in winter but it is a striking plant at other seasons, too, and it will help to enliven the callicarpa's rather lacklustre foliage in spring and summer. In mid-autumn the callicarpa's pointed leaves often take on mauve, yellow and orange tints. The flowers of both plants are tiny, and only in warm districts will the elaeagnus bear its sweetly scented, autumn blooms.

Most well-drained soils are suitable for these two shrubs, though the elaeagnus resents very dry conditions. Any plain, green-leaved shoots on the elaeagnus should be removed before the whole plant reverts.

12.3 Cotoneaster & Euphorbia

Cotoneaster horizontalis
(fishbone cotoneaster)
sun/shade ○ ◐
type of plant hardy shrub
zonal range 5-8 (C-WT)
flowering time early summer
flower colour pinkish white
height 60cm (2ft), up to 2.4m (8ft) against a wall
special characteristics decorative green foliage, autumn foliage, fruit, ornamental twigs

Euphorbia characias ssp. *wulfenii*
(spurge)
sun/shade ○
type of plant slightly tender/hardy shrub/perennial
zonal range 7-10 (CT-WT/ST)
flowering time mid-spring to early summer
flower colour yellow-green
height 90-120cm (3-4ft)
special characteristics evergreen, blue-green foliage

There are various differences in foliage, habit and colour between these two plants which make them stand out as separate but complementary entities throughout the year. In early autumn, the blueness in the euphorbia's bottle-brush leaves sets off the bright red of the cotoneaster's berries. Three or four weeks later this same foliage colour will enhance the deep crimson and rusty oranges of the cotoneaster's dying leaves (see 10.19), and later still it will show the dark, fishbone pattern of the cotoneaster's bare twigs to advantage. Early in the following spring, the euphorbia's large, long-lasting, cylindrical flowerheads will begin to emerge. (For very similar flowers, see 7.5.) When these impressive flowers are fully open, the rich, shining green foliage of the cotoneaster provides them with a very flattering background.

The cotoneaster is a tough and tolerant plant which will grow in almost all soils. However, the euphorbia needs good drainage, shelter from winds and some warmth to do well. To obtain large, dense bottle-brushes of foliage, the faded flowers of the euphorbia should be removed promptly – but care must be taken, since the milky juices from the cut stems can irritate eyes and skin.

Cotoneaster horizontalis is often used to cover low walls, but it can be grown up taller structures.

12.4 Sedum & Euphorbia

Sedum 'Herbstfreude'
(syn *S.* 'Autumn Joy')
(stonecrop)
sun/shade ○
type of plant hardy perennial
zonal range 3-10 (C-WT)
flowering time late summer to mid-autumn
flower colour rose changing to salmon-pink, then bronze
height 45-60cm (1½-2ft)
special characteristics blue-green foliage, fruit

Euphorbia characias ssp. *wulfenii* 'Lambrook Gold'
(spurge)
sun/shade ○
type of plant slightly tender/hardy shrub/perennial
zonal range 7-10 (CT-WT/ST)
flowering time mid-spring to early summer
flower colour yellow
height 90-120cm (3-4ft)
special characteristics evergreen, blue-grey foliage

The strong shapes and contrasting colours of these two perennials make an exceptionally striking winter combination. The great, flat seedheads of this popular sedum are of a splendid, rich red-brown, a colouring that is intensified by the icy blue-grey of the euphorbia's shaggy foliage.

This is a pairing of plants that is of interest throughout the year. The large, cylindrical flowerheads of this and other, related euphorbias elongate in mid-spring, but they are conspicuous several weeks beforehand. During spring the sedum's solid clumps of fleshy, blue-green leaves emerge. Even in foliage-only combinations these leaves look very attractive. The sedum's flowers are at their most colourful in autumn, but they are good-looking even when green (see 1.6).

As long as the euphorbia has warmth, some shelter and a well-drained or even dry soil, there are usually plenty of long, upright stems covered with very handsome foliage. Prompt removal of the faded flowerheads also helps to produce plenty of leafy growth, but the juices from the cut stems can severely irritate some people's skin and eyes.

The sedum, too, thrives in well-drained soils. However, if conditions are poor as well as rather dry, the growth will be thin and the flowerheads small.

12.5 Allium & Sidalcea

Allium cristophii

(syn *A. albopilosum*)
sun/shade ○
type of plant hardy bulb
zonal range 4-8 (C-CT)
flowering time early summer
flower colour pale mauve
height 45cm (18in)
special characteristics fruit

Sidalcea 'Rose Queen'

sun/shade ○ ◖
type of plant hardy perennial
zonal range 5-8 (C-WT)
flowering time early to late summer
flower colour rose-pink
height 75-90cm (2½-3ft)

Both of the plants in this pairing look good over many weeks: the sidalcea has a long flowering season, especially if it is grown in fertile soil and a sunny position, and the allium is attractive both when fresh and, as here, in late summer, when at the seedhead stage. Even when the allium flowers have faded, the stalks of the tiny, star-like flowers remain colourful. In this combination, they harmonize beautifully with the sidalcea's deep pink blooms. There are interesting contrasts here, too: the sidalcea's flowers are softly shaped, whereas the allium has an almost prickly appearance; and the allium's globe-shaped flowerhead is quite different from the upright spires of the sidalcea.

Though it performs best in fertile soils, the sidalcea is basically an easily grown plant. The allium needs good drainage. Many gardeners like to place *Allium cristophii* among other plants in order to disguise its stems, which are usually devoid of foliage by flowering time. The sidalcea's rounded leaves form a clump of basal growth.

12.6 Pulsatilla & Veronica

Pulsatilla vulgaris

(syn *Anemone pulsatilla*)
(pasque flower)
sun/shade ○
type of plant hardy perennial
zonal range 5-7 (C-CT)
flowering time mid- to late spring
flower colour violet-purple + yellow
height 23-30cm (9-12in) (approx 10-15cm/4-6in at flowering time)
special characteristics decorative green foliage, fruit

Veronica prostrata 'Spode Blue'

(syn *V. rupestris* 'Spode Blue')
(creeping speedwell)
sun/shade ○
type of plant hardy perennial
zonal range 5-8 (C-WT)
flowering time late spring to early summer
flower colour lilac-tinged blue
height 10-15cm (4-6in)

The large, bell-shaped, yellow-centred blooms of *Pulsatilla vulgaris* are some of the most beautiful flowers of the spring garden. After flowering, the plant's soft, feathery leaves and flower stalks lengthen considerably, and the flowers gradually turn into delightful seedheads with an idiosyncratic, slightly frizzled appearance. Here the insubstantiality of these seedheads is most decoratively complemented by a mass of erect flower spikes of a particularly pretty blue. The pasque flower's seedheads would be charming even in isolation, but the presence of a flattering plant close by ensures their delicate wispiness is not overlooked.

Good drainage is essential for both the plants in this combination. However, for the sake of the pasque flower in particular, conditions must not be too dry. Both plants thrive in alkaline soils. The veronica is a fairly vigorous plant and in time its mats of foliage may spread up to 45cm (18in) wide. The pasque flower is happiest when its clumps of growth are left undisturbed.

There are colour variants of the pasque flower, including varieties with white, red and pink flowers. White- and pink-flowered varieties of the veronica can be obtained, but the most readily available forms of this plant have blue flowers.

12.7 Hebe & Acaena

Hebe pinguifolia 'Pagei'
sun/shade ○ ●
type of plant hardy/slightly tender shrub
zonal range 8-10 (C-WT/ST)
flowering time late spring to early summer
flower colour white
height 15-30cm (6-12in)
special characteristics evergreen, blue-grey foliage

Acaena microphylla
sun/shade ○
type of plant hardy perennial
zonal range 5-8 (C-CT)
height 2.5-5cm (1-2in)
special characteristics semi-evergreen, bronze foliage, fruit

The suffusion of bronze over the tiny leaves of this acaena, though more conspicuous in spring, definitely adds to the success of this mid-autumn combination. As well as differentiating the two sets of leaves here, this bronzing also flatters the spiky crimson fruits that are the acaena's main attraction, its flowers being small and barely noticeable. Both the burrs and the leaves of this plant contrast very pleasingly with the smooth, glaucous foliage of the hebe. The latter's stems, each of which is tipped with one or more small, pretty flower spikes, spray outwards and will root at some points.

In full sun and well-drained soils, the acaena will form wide mats of dense foliage. The hebe appreciates good drainage, too, and in cold districts this will prevent it from succumbing to the damaging effects of wetness combined with low temperatures.

Combination 12.17 demonstrates how the blue-grey leaves of *Hebe pinguifolia* 'Pagei' can show off bright red berries as well as deeper crimson fruits, such as those of *A. microphylla*.

12.8 Parthenocissus & Rosa

Parthenocissus quinquefolia
(syn *Vitis quinquefolia*)
(Virginia creeper)
sun/shade ○ ●
type of plant hardy climber
zonal range 4-8 (C-WT)
height 15-21m (50-70ft)
special characteristics decorative green foliage, autumn foliage

Rosa 'Geranium'
(syn *R. moyesii* 'Geranium')
(rose)
sun/shade ○ ●
type of plant hardy shrub
zonal range 6-8 (C-WT)
flowering time early summer
flower colour scarlet
height 2.1-2.4m (7-8ft)
special characteristics fruit

Virginia creeper is an excellent background plant, for in spring and summer the soft green of its leaflets makes a good foil for many flowers, while in autumn its crimson and scarlet foliage picks up the fruit colours of many trees and shrubs. Here its autumn leaf colour is enhancing the orange-red of some shapely, 5cm (2in) long rose hips.

The preceding flowers of this popular rose are single and not long-lived, but they are of a wonderful bright scarlet (see 3.23). The whole plant arches attractively. It is sufficiently vigorous not to require an especially rich soil, but the Virginia creeper establishes itself most rapidly in fertile conditions. After a few years the Virginia creeper will start to cling to surfaces by means of adhesive tendrils. This robust plant is eventually very large and can be expected to reach about 4.5m (15ft) high in ten years. It is suitable for walls of all aspects.

12.9 Sorbus & Clematis

Sorbus 'Sunshine'
(rowan, mountain ash)
sun/shade ○ ◐
type of plant hardy tree
zonal range 5-8 (C-CT)
flowering time late spring
flower colour creamy white
height 7.5-9m (25-30ft)
special characteristics decorative green foliage, autumn foliage, fruit

Clematis 'Bill MacKenzie'
(syn *C. orientalis* 'Bill MacKenzie')
sun/shade ○ ◐
type of plant hardy climber
zonal range 6-8 (C-CT)
flowering time midsummer to mid-autumn
flower colour yellow + dark red
height 4.5-6m (15-20ft)
special characteristics fruit

In general, yellow fruits seem to be less attractive to birds than fruits that are red or orange. However, they are often less immediately eye-catching, especially at some distance. One way in which they can be made more conspicuous is to team them with other yellows. Here, in late summer, there are already generous bunches of berries on *Sorbus* 'Sunshine'. Quite soon the fruits will become a deeper, more definitely orange colour, when they will stand out among the sumptuous reds, oranges and dark purples of the tree's autumn foliage. While the leaves of the sorbus are still a glossy green, however, the numerous, thick-sepalled, 8cm (3in) flowers of this clematis give valuable extra impact to the berries.

Sorbus 'Sunshine' is a seedling of the well-known, yellow-berried form called *S.* 'Joseph Rock'. Both plants have very attractive, ferny foliage and large heads of tiny flowers. Their rather upright branches create good supporting frameworks for climbers. The clematis produces silky, silvery seedheads. (For similar seedheads, see 5.1.)

The roots of this vigorous clematis should be positioned on the shady side of the sorbus in, ideally, a fertile, moisture-retentive and well-drained soil. The sorbus has a preference for neutral or slightly acid loams, but it is happy in most soils.

12.10 Lonicera & Ligustrum

Lonicera periclymenum
(common honeysuckle, woodbine)
sun/shade ○ ◐
type of plant hardy climber
zonal range 5-9 (C-WT)
flowering time early to late summer
flower colour cream + purplish pink or yellow
height 4.5-6m (15-20ft)
special characteristics fruit, fragrant flowers

Ligustrum ovalifolium 'Aureum'
(golden privet)
sun/shade ○ ◐
type of plant hardy shrub
zonal range 6-11 (C-ST)
flowering time midsummer
flower colour white
height 2.7-3.6m (9-12ft)
special characteristics evergreen/semi-evergreen, yellow foliage/variegated foliage

The fragrant summer flowers of honeysuckles are their main attraction, but several of the species and their forms bear colourful berries, especially in cool regions. Honeysuckle berries and the bright foliage of golden privet produce a cheerful autumn combination. During the main growing season, the dark green foliage of the honeysuckle makes a good background for the more elaborately patterned leaves of the privet.

Just how brightly the privet's leaves will be coloured depends upon the amount of light they receive. In full sun they are a vivid yellow and conspicuously variegated. In partial shade the colouring is gentler because the colour of the leaf markings is greener, while in full shade the foliage may be wholly yellow-green.

Golden privet will grow almost anywhere. In hot climates there may be numerous self-sown seedlings. Left untrimmed, this shrub creates a generous bunch of outwardly splaying branches. The honeysuckle likes a moisture-retentive soil and also appreciates some shade, at least at its roots. Its twining growths can be used to cover shaded walls.

In contrast to the honeysuckle's delicious, full fragrance (which is particularly strong in the evening), the flowers of the privet have a heavy, almost aromatic scent which most people dislike.

12.11 Geranium & Lonicera

Geranium wallichianum 'Buxton's Variety'
(syn *G.* 'Buxton's Blue')
(cranesbill)
sun/shade ○ ◖
type of plant hardy perennial
zonal range 4-8 (C-WT)
flowering time midsummer to mid-autumn
flower colour lavender-blue + white
height 30cm (12in)
special characteristics decorative green foliage

Lonicera periclymenum 'Serotina'
(late Dutch honeysuckle)
sun/shade ○ ◖
type of plant hardy climber
zonal range 5-9 (C-WT)
flowering time midsummer to mid-autumn
flower colour cream + red or red-purple
height 4.5-6m (15-20ft)
special characteristics fruit, fragrant flowers

The richly coloured and very sweetly fragrant flowers of this honeysuckle are followed by shiny crimson fruits. Climates with cooler summers tend to encourage the production of larger crops of these berries. In this instance, the honeysuckle's twining growths have been trained along a low wall and the accompanying geranium, which has a trailing habit of growth, has been placed in a nearby raised bed. The two plants are therefore able to mingle attractively. However, if the honeysuckle is used in a more conventional way to cover a much higher wall, the geranium will look almost as good at its base.

Whichever arrangement is chosen, this geranium will be an excellent companion for the honeysuckle. Its 3cm (1¹/₂in), cheerful flowers are produced over such a long period that they coincide with both the flowers and the fruits of the honeysuckle. In addition, the soft red markings on the geranium's flower stalks (and on its pretty leaves in colder weather) repeat the redness in the flowers and fruits of the honeysuckle.

Neither of these plants enjoys hot, dry conditions. They are most at home in well-drained, moisture-retentive soils. The honeysuckle will grow quite happily on a shaded wall. In a sunnier position, it is important that its roots are shaded.

12.12 Cotoneaster & Bergenia

Cotoneaster lacteus
sun/shade ○ ◖
type of plant hardy shrub
zonal range 6-8 (C-WT)
flowering time early to mid-summer
flower colour pale cream
height 3-4.5m (10-15ft)
special characteristics evergreen, fruit

Bergenia 'Sunningdale'
sun/shade ○ ◖
type of plant hardy perennial
zonal range 3-8 (C-WT)
flowering time early to mid-spring
flower colour bright rose-pink
height 30-45cm (12-18in)
special characteristics evergreen, decorative green foliage, autumn/winter foliage

The large, handsome leaves of this bergenia turn bronze-red in colder weather. For this reason they make particularly good companions for the red fruits of this cotoneaster, and vice versa. The bergenia's solid clump of foliage also acts as an anchor for the arching growths of the cotoneaster. The latter's main attraction is its fruit, which begins to ripen in late autumn and lasts well into winter (the photograph shows the plant in midwinter). Its heads of cream-white flowers are also attractive, though not as striking as the bergenia's bright blooms on their red stalks.

For the best leaf colour, the bergenia should be grown in well-drained soil and in an open, sunny site. The cotoneaster is an easily pleased plant which will prosper in most soils.

Other bergenias with leaves that colour well in autumn and winter include *B. purpurascens*, *B.* 'Eric Smith' and *B.* 'Bressingham Ruby'. The flowers of these plants are various shades of deep pink.

12.13 Itea & Viburnum

Itea ilicifolia

sun/shade ○ ◐
type of plant slightly tender shrub
zonal range 8-10 (C-WT/ST)
flowering time late summer to early autumn
flower colour pale green
height 2.4-3m (8-10ft)
special characteristics evergreen, decorative green foliage, fragrant flowers

Viburnum plicatum 'Rowallane'

(syn *V. tomentosum* 'Rowallane')
sun/shade ○ ◐
type of plant hardy shrub
zonal range 7-9 (C-WT)
flowering time late spring
flower colour white
height 1.5-1.8m (5-6ft)
special characteristics autumn foliage, fruit

The free-fruiting forms of *Viburnum plicatum* are highly attractive plants, though they are less readily available than varieties such as 'Lanarth'. 'Rowallane', 'Dart's Red Robin' and 'Cascade' all have the usual distinctive, horizontal habit of growth and pretty lace-cap flowers (see 1.20) as well as the characteristic wine-red, autumn leaf colour. In addition, however, they are bejewelled with ruby fruits which turn jet-black.

Here, in mid-autumn, the leaves and berries of 'Rowallane' have an especially lavish and opulent look to them beside the much brighter, green foliage and pale, dangling tassels of *Itea ilicifolia*. However, all through the growing season there are interesting contrasts between these two plants: the itea's decorative foliage is glossy and holly-like while the viburnum's pointed leaves are deeply veined, and the latter's dense layers of growth create a quite different impression to the itea's more upright and much looser collection of long, arching shoots. Although in this illustration most of the itea's long, sweetly scented tassels are disintegrating, their distinctly vertical lines are still a conspicuous feature of the combination.

Both these plants appreciate a soil that is well-drained but also reliably moisture-retentive. In most gardens, the itea needs shelter.

12.14 Pyracantha & Cotoneaster

Pyracantha rogersiana 'Flava'

(firethorn)
sun/shade ○ ◐
type of plant hardy shrub
zonal range 7-9 (CT-WT)
flowering time early summer
flower colour white
height 2.4-3m (8-10ft)
special characteristics semi-evergreen/evergreen, fruit, fragrant flowers

Cotoneaster horizontalis

(fishbone cotoneaster)
sun/shade ○ ◐
type of plant hardy shrub
zonal range 5-8 C-WT)
flowering time early summer
flower colour pinkish white
height 60cm (2ft), up to 2.4m (8ft) against a wall
special characteristics decorative green foliage, autumn foliage, fruit, ornamental twigs

As well as the numerous orange- and red-fruited forms of pyracantha, there are several varieties with yellow berries. In this planting, the bright red, shiny berries and crimson-and-rust autumn foliage of *Cotoneaster horizontalis* create a close-textured, richly coloured background for *Pyracantha rogersiana* 'Flava' and emphasize the relative paleness of its fruits. At the same time, the two sets of berries produce a remarkably cheerful combination of colours with winter not far away.

Both plants look attractive at other times of the year, too. In particular, the pyracantha looks beautifully pale and frothy when covered in its 5cm (2in) clusters of flowers. These flowers emit a clean, sweet fragrance.

The cotoneaster's rows of little flowers are less decorative than its berries, but they do look pretty against the plant's glossy, deep green foliage. Throughout spring and summer these tiny, neatly arranged cotoneaster leaves, on their dark, fishbone fans of twigs, contrast pleasingly with the pyracantha's larger, brighter green foliage. The pyracantha's growths are rather wayward, but mainly upright.

Both plants here are suitable for shaded walls. The cotoneaster can be grown in almost any soil; the pyracantha is best where drainage is good.

12.15 Cotoneaster & Euonymus

Cotoneaster horizontalis
(fishbone cotoneaster)

sun/shade ○ ◖
type of plant hardy shrub
zonal range 5-8 (C-WT)
flowering time early summer
flower colour pinkish white
height 60cm (2ft), up to 2.4m (8ft) against a wall
special characteristics decorative green foliage, autumn foliage, fruit, ornamental twigs

Euonymus fortunei 'Variegatus'
(syn *E. f.* 'Silver Gem')

sun/shade ○ ◖
type of plant hardy shrub/climber
zonal range 5-9 (C-WT)
height 45-60cm (1½-2ft as a shrub)
special characteristics evergreen, variegated foliage

The rather cool-coloured foliage of this euonymus sets off the shining, red berries of *Cotoneaster horizontalis* most successfully. Even when the berries have been eaten by birds and the autumn leaves have fallen, the fishbone pattern of the cotoneaster's dark twigs looks well with the euonymus.

This distinctive pattern also shows all the cotoneaster's other features to advantage, giving a striking structure to its rows of little flowers, its glossy green summer foliage and its lovely rusty orange and crimson autumn leaves. With each of these features, as well as with the bright fruits, the leaves of the euonymus look crisp and fresh.

Cotoneaster horizontalis will grow in a wide range of soil types. With the support of a tall, vertical structure of any aspect the 'fishbones' rise upwards in a series of fans. They also look well heaped up on low walls or covering banks. The euonymus too will grow in most soils. Although normally a bushy shrub, it sometimes produces climbing shoots and then it may reach up to 3m (10ft) high. The very pale cream edges of this plant's greyish-green leaves can become tinged with pink in cold weather.

12.16 Sorbus & Persicaria

Sorbus reducta
(rowan, mountain ash)

sun/shade ○ ◖
type of plant hardy shrub
zonal range 5-7 (C-CT)
flowering time late spring to early summer
flower colour white or palest pink
height 45-75cm (1½-2½ft)
special characteristics decorative green foliage, autumn foliage, fruit

Persicaria affinis
(syn *Polygonum affine*)
(knotweed)

sun/shade ○ ◖
type of plant hardy perennial
zonal range 3-9 (C-WT)
flowering time early spring to mid-autumn
flower colour rose-pink turning russet
height 15-23cm (6-9in)
special characteristics autumn/winter foliage

Here is a combination with ingredients that look interesting long before the sorbus berries turn their unusual, eye-catching pink. Throughout the growing season, the leaves of this erect little shrub are attractively shaped and of a shining, rich green with hints of blue. In early summer the foamy flowers of the sorbus appear, followed by the upright pink spikes of the knotweed. The exact flowering season of *Persicaria affinis* varies somewhat and some forms may begin flowering earlier than others. The flowers of all forms will eventually turn a rich red-brown.

The sorbus berries are decorative from late summer until mid-autumn. During autumn, the knotweed's foliage turns a deep crimson-russet and this colouring is retained throughout the winter months. The leaves of the sorbus become a mixture of red, bronze and purplish-maroon in mid-autumn.

These two plants both appreciate a leaf mould-rich, moisture-retentive soil, although they will tolerate rather drier conditions, too. When well-suited, the knotweed forms a dense, wide-spreading mat of foliage, in marked contrast to the upright stems of the sorbus. Most specimens of the sorbus form small thickets and the shrub suckers. However, it is not usually an invasive plant.

195

12.17 Hebe & Cotoneaster

Hebe pinguifolia 'Pagei'
sun/shade ○ ◐
type of plant hardy/slightly tender shrub
zonal range 8-10 (C-WT)
flowering time late spring to early summer
flower colour white
height 15-30cm (6-12in)
special characteristics evergreen, blue-grey foliage

Cotoneaster cochleatus
sun/shade ○ ◐
type of plant hardy shrub
zonal range 6-8 (C-WT)
flowering time late spring to early summer
flower colour white
height 23-30cm (9-12in)
special characteristics evergreen, fruit

The fruit colour of this vigorous, carpeting cotoneaster may vary a little, but there are always large crops of brilliantly coloured, shiny berries. These ripen in early autumn and may remain on the plant until well into spring or even later.

Here their lovely bright red is intensified both by the crisp blue-grey of the hebe's neat foliage and by the cotoneaster's own glossy, rich green leaves. The hebe's stems spray outwards and slightly upwards, in contrast to the more downward arching growths of the cotoneaster. Both these shrubs have white flowers, the hebe's neat little spikes being produced towards the ends of the plant's shoots, while the numerous blooms of the cotoneaster appear all along its stems.

The cotoneaster is tolerant of a wide range of soils and growing conditions. However, a sunny site will ensure particularly large crops of flowers and, subsequently, fruits. The hebe needs well-drained soil. Especially in very cold areas, the plant may not survive periods of severe weather if its roots are wet as well as cold.

In time, the cotoneaster will spread about 1.8m (6ft) wide. It may therefore need some restraining if it is not to overwhelm specimens of the hebe.

12.18 Parthenocissus & Clematis

Parthenocissus henryana
(syn *Vitis henryana*)
sun/shade ◐
type of plant hardy climber
zonal range 7-8 (C-WT)
height 6-7.5m (20-25ft)
special characteristics variegated foliage, autumn foliage

Clematis alpina
sun/shade ○ ◐
type of plant hardy climber
zonal range 5-8 (C-CT)
flowering time mid- to late spring
flower colour violet-blue
height 1.5-2.4m (5-8ft)
special characteristics fruit

The very pretty small flowers of *Clematis alpina* (see 15.19) are followed by long-lasting, silvery seedheads. Here this silveriness is echoed in the pale mid-ribs of the purplish leaves of *Parthenocissus henryana*. Between them, these plants have a long season of interest. Just after the clematis produces its flowers the new foliage of the parthenocissus, which is an attractive, deep red-bronze colour, begins to expand; then, in early summer, the first clematis seedheads develop and the variegated leaves of the parthenocissus mature. As the summer progresses the clematis seedheads become silky and fluffy and finally, in autumn, the parthenocissus foliage turns red.

Both these climbers like fertile, moisture-retentive soils. They can both be grown on shaded walls. The clematis climbs by twining its leaf-stalks around suitable supports, which include other plants. The parthenocissus clings to surfaces by means of adhesive tendrils, but it can be several years before this plant starts to climb vigorously. A partially shaded position is best for this combination, since the clematis likes its roots to be shaded and the variegation of the parthenocissus is much more conspicuous in partial shade.

12.19 Iris & Brunnera

Iris foetidissima var. *citrina*
(stinking iris, gladdon, gladwyn iris)

sun/shade ○ ◖
type of plant hardy perennial
zonal range 5-9 (C-WT)
flowering time early summer
flower colour soft beige-yellow
height 45-60cm (1½-2ft)
special characteristics evergreen, decorative green foliage, fruit

Brunnera macrophylla

sun/shade ◖
type of plant hardy perennial
zonal range 4-8 (C-WT)
flowering time early to late spring
flower colour bright blue
height 45cm (18in)

The rich orange-red berries of this iris ripen in autumn and are so long-lasting that they can coincide with some spring flowers; they are shown here in mid-spring. Later the brunnera's piercing blue flower sprays will be looser and more expansive. The iris's flowers (see 9.29) are much less conspicuous than its fruit. As compensation, the plant's handsome, strap-like foliage forms a fountain of green which looks very attractive beside the crinkled, heart-shaped leaves of the brunnera. As summer progresses, the brunnera's leaves become quite large and rather dry and shabby. Some gardeners like to cut the whole plant back to encourage the production of fresher, tidier foliage.

The especially good and readily available form of *Iris foetidissima* shown here is, like the typical species, a very tolerant plant which will grow well in dry shade, dense shade and other inhospitable conditions. It will prosper in sun, too, as long as the soil is not very dry. The brunnera is also easy to grow. It too may be planted in dense shade, but it does not like dry places. This combination is, then, one for light shade and reasonably moisture-retentive soils. In these conditions both plants will produce good, ground-covering clumps of foliage.

The leaves of this iris emit an intriguing aroma of roast beef when cut.

For other combinations featuring ornamental fruit and seedheads, see:
HOT-COLOURED FLOWERS 3.2 YELLOW FLOWERS 5.1 VARIEGATED FOLIAGE 9.7 AUTUMN FOLIAGE 10.1, 10.3, 10.5, 10.19 WINTER FLOWERS 14.10 CLIMBING PLANTS 15.18 GRASSES AND FERNS 17.15

13 FRAGRANT FLOWERS

Not many of us have a sense of smell sophisticated enough to devise plant partnerships on the basis of scent. We can all appreciate that very sweet, heavy scents might overpower nearby fragrances that are fresher and lighter, but even so, relatively few of us would, for instance, be too concerned about the compatibility of the floral fragrances of the plants shown in 13.18. Most people would simply enjoy the two different scents and take pleasure in the visual attractions of the combination.

In many cases, the fact that a plant is fragrant merely makes it more than usually attractive for inclusion in a particular combination. For example, various pale double peonies could have been used to accompany the neat pink flowers of *Astrantia maxima*, shown in 13.16; they would all have looked well, but the variety 'Sarah Bernhardt' was chosen because of the delicious fragrance of its flowers.

However, in some cases, fragrance is undoubtedly the most important consideration. Fragrant climbers and aromatic plants are nearly always the first choice for areas beside garden seats, and for some gardeners flowers that are fragrant have such an irresistible allure that no matter what the site or situation, scent will always be the primary consideration for selecting a plant.

The range of floral scents is so large that there is surely a fragrance – or group of fragrances – to suit every nose. In this section alone there are flowers that give off headily rich and sweet scents, fresh citrus scents, spicy scents and warm, fruity scents. In a few cases, a single genus will encompass a remarkable range of floral fragrances. The scents of roses in particular vary widely from lemon-fresh to richly musk- and tea-scented, with all sorts of clove, apple and violet fragrances in between.

The perception of a particular fragrance does, however, vary considerably from person to person. For example, *Narcissus poeticus* (see 13.21) is generally regarded as having flowers of a wonderfully rich and intense sweetness, but some people find this scent nauseatingly heavy; and while the majority view of the scent of privet flowers is that it is an odd blend of aromatic and fishy smells, there are a few people who actually relish it. As a further complication there are flowers that seem wonderfully fragrant to some people, though they have little or no scent for others.

CHOOSING A SITE

To maximize the perception of fragrance, in cool climates particularly, a fairly sheltered planting site should be chosen if possible. Placing a scented rose or honeysuckle in some protected corner will do much to trap and intensify the fragrance of its flowers. Positioning fragrant flowers near a seat or where they will often be walked past also makes sense. The latter siting is particularly important in the case of winter-flowering fragrant plants, as few people linger in their gardens in winter. Therefore mahonias, witch hazels and scented snowdrops such as *Galanthus* 'S. Arnott', for example, should be planted close to the house where their fragrance can be easily appreciated.

It should also be remembered that some flowers are at their most fragrant when temperatures begin to drop in the evening. This is true of the flowers of many honeysuckles, some yuccas and a few daylilies. These flowers need to be placed where their fragrance is most likely to be noticed – beside garden seats that are positioned to catch the last of the day's sun, perhaps, or beneath windows that will be opened on summer evenings.

FRAGRANCE AND COLOUR

From the combinations in this chapter, it is clear that many fragrant flowers are either pale or of rather cool colouring. Yellow flowers do feature, but there are relatively few plants of a perennial nature that have flowers that are both fragrant and of a deep or warm colouring. The best sources of good scent with rich flower colour are the crimson, wine-coloured and magenta roses, possible examples of which include *Rosa* 'Roseraie de l'Haÿ', *R.* 'Charles de Mills' and *R.* 'Guinée'.

As well as their enticing scents, plants with fragrant flowers often have other attractive features. There are sweetly scented plants with variegated foliage (see 13.1), yellow foliage (see 13.19) and elegant green foliage (see 13.18). Many azaleas with fragrant flowers are noted for the excellence of their autumn foliage colour, and the blooms of a number of roses are followed by shapely, colourful hips. There are even some plants that manage to perform a double act and produce aromatic foliage as well as fragrant flowers (see 13.14 and 13.10). It is not difficult, therefore, to have combinations of plants that look interesting, often over several seasons, and at the same time smell delectable.

13.1 **Trachelospermum & Lonicera**

Trachelospermum jasminoides '*Variegatum*'
(Confederate jasmine, star jasmine, Chinese jasmine)
sun/shade ○
type of plant slightly tender climber
zonal range 8-10 (CT-WT/ST)
flowering time mid- to late summer
flower colour white
height 3-4.5m (10-15ft)
special characteristics evergreen, variegated foliage, fragrant flowers

Lonicera × *americana*
(syn *L. grata*)
(honeysuckle)
sun/shade ○ ◖
type of plant hardy climber
zonal range 6-9 (C-WT)
flowering time early summer to early autumn
flower colour deep purple-pink + cream
height 7.5-9m (25-30ft)
special characteristics semi-evergreen/deciduous, fragrant flowers

Once established, both these twining climbers produce quantities of richly and sweetly scented blooms. As with many honeysuckles, *Lonicera* × *americana* is at its most fragrant in the evening. Without the trachelospermum's variegated foliage, however, this combination of plants might be rather too large a mass of plain leaves; the white leaf edges do much to enliven the honeysuckle's exuberant tangle of glossy greenery. They also amplify the pale cream parts of the honeysuckle's sinuously fingered flowers. Since the honeysuckle blooms very freely over many weeks, this matching of pale colour is a long-lasting feature.

The photograph shows the trachelospermum at the end of its flowering period, and only a very few of its tiny white stars are visible. However, they too look well with the white-edged foliage and with the quite differently shaped flowers of the honeysuckle. When temperatures are low, the grey-green and white of the trachelospermum's foliage becomes flushed with russet-crimson and pink.

A sheltered site is needed for both these plants. In sun it is important that at least the roots of the honeysuckle are cool. *Lonicera* × *americana* is quite shrubby and needs plenty of support. Though the trachelospermum prefers neutral or acid soils, both plants do well in a variety of fertile soils.

13.2 **Syringa & Philadelphus**

Syringa × *prestoniae* hybrid
(lilac)
sun/shade ○
type of plant hardy shrub
zonal range 4-7 (C-CT)
flowering time early summer
flower colour rose-pink
height 3-3.6m (10-12ft)
special characteristics fragrant flowers

Philadelphus coronarius
(mock orange)
sun/shade ○ ◖
type of plant hardy shrub
zonal range 5-9 (C-WT)
flowering time early summer
flower colour creamy white
height 1.8-3m (6-10ft)
special characteristics fragrant flowers

Neither the habit of growth nor the foliage of either of these shrubs could be described as particularly decorative. However, both plants have flowers which are deeply fragrant: the philadelphus exudes a wonderfully sweet and fruity scent from its creamy clusters of single flowers, while the elegantly loose panicles of the lilac give off a heavy, almost spicy perfume. These two sets of flowers are also sufficiently different in form to look interesting together. At the same time, their colouring is gentle enough not to interfere with the plants' general air of undemanding informality.

Partnerships of two large shrubs of this sort are probably best planted either at the back of deep borders or in less manicured parts of the garden. Each of the shrubs in this combination is fairly upright in growth, and the philadelphus is also dense and bushy. Both plants thrive in light, fertile soils and are especially good in alkaline conditions.

In the British Isles, *S.* × *p.* 'Elinor' is the most readily available of the Preston hybrid lilacs. Its flowers are purplish-red in bud and pale lilac when fully open. All the Preston lilacs are vigorous plants. Their scent is less fresh than that of *Syringa vulgaris* and its varieties, and some people find it unpleasant.

13.3 Carpenteria & Ballota

Carpenteria californica

sun/shade ○
type of plant slightly tender shrub
zonal range 8-9 (CT-WT)
flowering time early to mid-summer
flower colour white
height 1.8-3m (6-10ft)
special characteristics evergreen, fragrant flowers

Ballota pseudodictamnus

sun/shade ○
type of plant slightly tender perennial/shrub
zonal range 7-9 (CT)
flowering time early to mid-summer
flower colour mauve
height 45-60cm (1½-2ft)
special characteristics evergreen/semi-evergreen, grey foliage

The gleaming, anemone-like flowers of *Carpenteria californica* have a light, sweet scent. The clarity of their colouring is enhanced both by the presence of yellow stamens and by the rather sombre green of the plant's glossy leaves. The ballota's neat, grey woolliness lifts this sombre greenery, and the paleness of its newest leaves also provides a link to the white of the carpenteria's flowers. The ballota has only very small flowers and its lovely soft foliage is its main decorative feature.

The carpenteria has a rounded, bushy habit of growth; older specimens can become rather thinner and more awkward. The ballota's stems sprawl somewhat, but are basically upright.

Both these plants need full sun and good drainage, though the carpenteria does not do well in very dry soils. The ballota will not survive in cold, wet conditions, and the carpenteria will suffer considerable superficial damage in severe frosts unless it is given a really sheltered site.

13.4 Ceanothus & Cornus

Ceanothus 'Concha'

(Californian lilac)
sun/shade ○
type of plant slightly tender shrub
zonal range 8-10 (CT-WT)
flowering time early to mid-summer
flower colour bright blue
height 1.8-3m (6-10ft)
special characteristics evergreen, fragrant flowers

Cornus alba 'Variegata'

(red-barked dogwood)
sun/shade ○ ◖
type of plant hardy shrub
zonal range 3-8 (C-CT)
height 1.5-2.4m (5-8ft)
special characteristics variegated foliage, autumn foliage, ornamental twigs, suitable for damp and wet soils

Sweetly fragrant and usually humming with bees, the beautifully coloured flowers of this ceanothus seem even bluer with fresh, light foliage beside them. The variegated forms of *Cornus alba* are very versatile plants. Here the white-edged, greyish leaves of *C. a.* 'Variegata' provide a lively, pale display against the relatively dense, wide-spreading growth of the ceanothus.

In this photograph the flowerheads of the ceanothus have not yet quite fully expanded. In full bloom the shrub looks spectacular, but even when flowering has finished, it acts as a suitably close-textured background of glossy, rich green for the various decorative features of the cornus. As well as looking attractive in spring and summer, the foliage of the cornus turns gentle shades of pink and orange in autumn. Later still, when the leaves have fallen, the erect and shiny, maroon-barked twigs form striking embellishments to the winter garden.

All forms of *Cornus alba* thrive in heavy clays and in wet places beside water. However, they are vigorous plants that also do well in the light, well-drained soils and sheltered positions that the ceanothus must have. In order to produce plenty of maroon-coloured twigs, the cornus needs at least some of its stems to be cut back hard each year in spring.

13.5 Osmanthus & Brunnera

Osmanthus delavayi

sun/shade ○

type of plant slightly tender shrub
zonal range 8-10 (CT-WT/ST)
flowering time mid- to late spring
flower colour white
height 1.8-2.4m (6-8ft)
special characteristics evergreen, fragrant flowers

Brunnera macrophylla

sun/shade ◑

type of plant hardy perennial
zonal range 4-8 (C-WT)
flowering time early to late spring
flower colour bright blue
height 45cm (18in)

The pale, very sweetly scented flowers of *Osmanthus delavayi* shine out from among neat, dark green foliage. The addition of the brunnera's tiny, penetrating blue flowers and clumps of light green leaves creates a particularly fresh-looking spring combination.

Here these two plants have been placed against a west-facing wall at the back of a deep border. This arrangement has the advantage of giving the osmanthus some shelter, which it appreciates, and also means that later-maturing herbaceous material shades the brunnera and obscures its rather coarse summer foliage. In more prominent positions, the plant can be cut right back in summer and tidier, fresher leaves will soon emerge.

The dark, glossy foliage of the osmanthus remains orderly throughout the year, and it makes an excellent background for many other plants. In mild areas particularly, the stiff, arching growths of this slow-growing shrub will eventually form a wide mound of dense greenery. However, these growths respond well to being cut back.

Almost all well-drained soils, as long as they are not too shallow, suit the osmanthus. The brunnera must have a reasonably moisture-retentive soil and light shade to do well. Here some shade is afforded by the osmanthus.

13.6 Rosa & Artemisia

Rosa 'Constance Spry'

(rose)

sun/shade ○

type of plant hardy shrub/climber
zonal range 4-9 (C-WT)
flowering time early to mid-summer
flower colour pink
height 1.8-2.4m (6-8ft)
special characteristics fragrant flowers

Artemisia 'Powis Castle'

sun/shade ○

type of plant slightly tender perennial/shrub
zonal range 5-8 (C-WT)
height 60-90cm (2-3ft)
special characteristics evergreen/semi-evergreen, aromatic, silver foliage

The large, generously shaped and richly fragrant flowers of this rose are at their best for only two weeks or so. They are, however, produced in large numbers and together with the big, well-formed leaves of the plant the whole effect is one of luscious profusion. Here the exceptionally pretty colouring of the flowers is made still prettier and more delicate by the addition of feathery, pale grey leaves.

Since this particular form of artemisia flowers only rarely, its mound of sharply aromatic foliage remains neat and its stems stay tidy. It is an evergreen or, more usually, a semi-evergreen plant, depending on climate. It is most likely to survive in colder gardens if it is given really well-drained soil. It tolerates hot, dry conditions. In the planting shown here, it is growing right at the edge of a bed beside warm paving stones.

The rose will prosper in all fertile, reasonably well-drained soils. It can be grown as a shrub, but more often its long stems are trained upwards. Treated as a climber, it may well reach over 3m (10ft) in height and be at least as wide as it is high.

13.7 Rosa & Nepeta

Rosa 'Chianti'

(rose)
sun/shade ○
type of plant hardy shrub
zonal range 4-9 (C-WT)
flowering time early to mid-summer
flower colour purple-crimson
height 1.2-1.8m (4-6ft)
special characteristics fragrant flowers

Nepeta × faassenii

(catmint)
sun/shade ○
type of plant hardy perennial
zonal range 4-8 (C-WT)
flowering time early summer to early autumn
flower colour lavender-blue
height 30-45cm (12-18in)
special characteristics semi-evergreen, aromatic, grey-green foliage

Most perennial and shrubby plants with fragrant flowers have blooms that are pale in colour. However, roses are generally excellent sources of deep colour combined with good scent. The free-flowering shrub rose shown here has richly vinous, velvety blooms that exude a delightful 'old rose' scent. (A more readily available fragrant rose of similar shape and colour is the Gallica cultivar 'Cardinal de Richelieu'.)

Catmint is a classic partner for roses of many colours, flattering them but never competing with their lavish flowers. In this particular partnership, the catmint's gentle haze of minty-scented, grey-green leaves and slender flower sprays looks, as usual, most becoming. However, the combination of flower colours here is especially successful, since the cool blue of the catmint accentuates the purplish tones of the rose. *Rosa* 'Chianti' is a leafy, rounded shrub; with a leggier rose, the flowers of the two plants would not be so attractively close to each other.

Rosa 'Chianti' is vigorous enough to do well in not particularly fertile conditions. The catmint thrives in all well-drained soils. If the stems carrying the first flush of blooms are removed, then this plant will grow densely and will flower over many weeks.

13.8 Philadelphus & Euphorbia

Philadelphus 'Manteau d'Hermine'

(mock orange)
sun/shade ○ ◑
type of plant hardy shrub
zonal range 5-9 (C-WT)
flowering time early to mid-summer
flower colour white
height 90-120cm (3-4ft)
special characteristics fragrant flowers

Euphorbia dulcis 'Chameleon'

(spurge)
sun/shade ○
type of plant hardy perennial
zonal range 4-9 (C-WT)
flowering time late spring to early summer
flower colour lime green
height 45-60cm (1½-2ft)
special characteristics purple foliage, autumn foliage

Many of the popular mock oranges make shrubs which are too big for small gardens, but the densely twiggy, rounded variety shown here is much lower-growing than usual. Its double flowers have the sweet, slightly fruity fragrance characteristic of the genus. Its leaves are a conspicuous light green which here provides a good background for the dark purple foliage of a euphorbia. This light green colouring also echoes, and thereby emphasizes, the euphorbia's little acid green flowers.

In a sunny position the philadelphus will flower well and the euphorbia's foliage will be a good, rich colour. Neither plant is fussy about soil type as long as the drainage is reasonable. The philadelphus is particularly good on light and chalky soils.

This purple-leaved euphorbia hardly ever gets mildew, which can be a problem with the more familiar *Euphorbia amygdaloides* 'Purpurea' (see 7.4). Like all spurges, however, its cut stems exude a juice which can irritate skin and eyes. In autumn, the leaves of this bushy, slim-stemmed plant take on very pretty pink and orange tones.

The red spikes and glossy leaves in front of the philadelphus in this illustration are those of *Persicaria milletti*. This species of knotweed is not very readily available. It tends to be a rather patchy flowerer, except in consistently moist conditions.

13.9 Iris & Artemisia

Iris 'Jane Phillips'

sun/shade ○
type of plant hardy perennial
zonal range 4-9 (C-WT)
flowering time early summer
flower colour pale blue
height 90-105cm (3-3½ft)
special characteristics fragrant flowers

Artemisia ludoviciana var. *latiloba*

(syn *A. palmeri* var. *latiloba*)
(white sage)
sun/shade ○
type of plant hardy perennial
zonal range 4-8 (C-CT)
height 60cm (2ft)
special characteristics aromatic, grey foliage

Everything about this pair of plants is soft and pretty, including the gentle, sweet fragrance of the iris. The particular form of artemisia shown here has broader, more jagged foliage than the typical species. It is a versatile, pale grey plant that looks good with flowers and foliage of rich, warm colours as well as harmonizing attractively with cooler pastels. In this combination, its forest of leafy, upright stems has a pleasingly delicate, almost insubstantial air. The iris is, in contrast, a much more solidly constructed plant. Its glaucous stems are much thicker and its sword-shaped leaves far longer and broader. In addition, its elegantly arranged petals are wide and generous beside the artemisia's modest grey bobbles. For a while, the iris' grey leaves also contribute to this partnership. However, the foliage begins to look tired and shabby soon after the blooms have faded. If you are unable to find 'Jane Phillips', other similar varieties may be easily substituted.

Light, well-drained soils suit both these plants. The iris must have plenty of sun to flower well. A sunny site will also intensify the paleness and the clean, fresh fragrance of the artemisia's leaves. The roots of the artemisia have a tendency to wander, but they are not usually invasive. Should the whole plant become rather floppy during the summer, it can be cut back and new, fresh growth will appear.

13.10 Ozothamnus & Ceanothus

Ozothamnus ledifolius

(syn *Helichrysum ledifolium*)
sun/shade ○
type of plant slightly tender shrub
zonal range 9-10 (CT-WT)
flowering time early summer
flower colour cream
height 90cm (3ft)
special characteristics evergreen, aromatic foliage, fragrant flowers

Ceanothus 'Blue Cushion'

(Californian lilac)
sun/shade ○
type of plant slightly tender shrub
zonal range 8-10 (CT-WT)
flowering time early to mid-summer
flower colour light blue
height 60-90cm (2-3ft)
special characteristics evergreen

No shrub smells quite like *Ozothamnus ledifolius*, with its predominant scent of lusciously sweet, cooked fruit. Resinous undertones are present, too, emanating mainly from the foliage. The numerous fragrant flowers and the accompanying dark, yellow-stemmed, yellow-budded leaves are all arranged densely on the plant.

This arrangement is echoed here to some extent in the more wide-spreading but similarly flower-covered hummock of growth produced by *Ceanothus* 'Blue Cushion'. Since there is relatively little difference between these plants in terms of shape, the eye is drawn to contrasts in colour. In this combination, the result is a block of blue set against a block of cream. Out of flower, the differences in foliage become more evident, with the leaves of the ceanothus clearly a brighter and glossier green than those of the ozothamnus. Even as two sets of foliage, these two comfortably shaped shrubs are useful for providing the kind of soothing, undemanding background that busier, bolder plants need.

Really mature specimens of *Ozothamnus ledifolius* can become slightly leggy. Both plants need shelter and good drainage, although for the ceanothus the soil must be reasonably moisture-retentive, too.

13.11 Dianthus, Viola & Nepeta

Dianthus 'Doris'

(pink)

sun/shade ○ **type of plant** hardy perennial
zonal range 4-8 (C-WT)
flowering time early to mid-summer
flower colour pink **height** 30cm (12in)
special characteristics evergreen, grey foliage,
fragrant flowers

Viola 'Maggie Mott'

(violet)

sun/shade ○ ◐ **type of plant** hardy perennial
zonal range 5-7 (C-CT)
flowering time late spring to late summer
flower colour pale mauve-blue
height 10-15cm (4-6in)
special characteristics fragrant flowers

Nepeta 'Six Hills Giant'

(catmint)

sun/shade ○ **type of plant** hardy perennial
zonal range 4-8 (C-WT)
flowering time early summer to early autumn
flower colour lavender-blue
height 60-75cm (2-2½ft)
special characteristics semi-evergreen,
aromatic, grey-green foliage

All three plants here are scented: the dianthus is sweetly spicy, the viola has a light, fresh fragrance and the leaves of the catmint emit a slightly fusty, minty smell when crushed. All three plants also share a silveriness in colouring, whether it is in their flowers or their foliage.

Since two of the plants here – the viola and the catmint – flower over many weeks, this is a soft, gentle grouping of colours that remains good-looking almost all summer long. The catmint's haze of flower spikes contrasts pleasingly with the tighter, neater shapes of the dianthus and viola flowers, and the low mats of foliage produced by these two smaller plants do much to emphasize and enhance the catmint's crowded mass of curving stems.

Good drainage is appreciated by all the plants here. The dianthus and the catmint will thrive in light and chalky soils, but if the viola is to do well the conditions must not be too hot and dry.

Though they are not particularly colourful, the larger leaves of a peony, visible here among the viola, add firm shapes to this combination and stop the whole group from being too small-scale and fussy.

13.12 Erysimum & Acaena

Erysimum 'Bredon'

(perennial wallflower)

sun/shade ○
type of plant slightly tender perennial
zonal range 8-9 (C-WT)
flowering time mid-spring to early summer
flower colour mustard yellow
height 30-45cm (12-18in)
special characteristics semi-evergreen, fragrant
flowers

Acaena saccaticupula 'Blue Haze'

(syn *A.* 'Pewter')

sun/shade ○
type of plant hardy perennial
zonal range 6-8 (C-WT)
height 10-15cm (4-6in)
special characteristics semi-evergreen, blue-grey foliage, fruit

Few of the perennial wallflowers are quite as fragrant as the familiar biennial forms used for spring bedding. However, the bright flowers of the variety shown here do emit the warm, spicy scent associated with all wallflowers. In this instance, a lively blue-and-yellow partnership has been created by underplanting the rounded mass of neat, dark-budded flowerheads with an attractive, tangled carpet of distinctly blue foliage. Though the acaena's flowers are dull compared to the wallflower's, they ripen in late summer into decorative, red-brown burrs (see 17.15).

Good drainage and plenty of sunshine suit both these plants. However, even under ideal conditions, the erysimum is a short-lived plant. It forms a rounded though not particularly dense clump of fairly upright stems and slightly glaucous leaves. The acaena is neatest and densest in open positions. Full sun encourages an especially blue foliage colour. This ground-covering, rooting plant usually grows vigorously and may need restraining in some situations.

When looking for *Erysimum* 'Bredon' in catalogues, it is as well to remember that it is sometimes regarded as a shrub. In addition, it may appear under the name *Cheiranthus* rather than *Erysimum*.

13.13 Muscari & Sedum

Muscari neglectum
(syn *M. racemosum*)
(grape hyacinth)
sun/shade ○ ●
type of plant hardy bulb
zonal range 4-9 (C-WT)
flowering time mid-spring
flower colour deep blue
height 15cm (6in)
special characteristics fragrant flowers

Sedum spathulifolium 'Purpureum'
(stonecrop)
sun/shade ○
type of plant hardy perennial
zonal range 4-8 (C-WT)
flowering time early to mid-summer
flower colour golden yellow
height 8-10cm (3-4in)
special characteristics evergreen, purple foliage

This variable species of grape hyacinth is easy to grow in most reasonably well-drained soils and it may increase quite rapidly. Its leaves are not as prolific nor as untidy as those of the well-known *Muscari armeniacum*, but they do appear early and die back after flowering. This, therefore, is not a plant for a prominent position on a very tidy rockery. In most forms of *M. neglectum* the top flowers on each spike are pale blue and sweetly fragrant.

Here the stronger blue of these upright flower spikes is most attractively set off by the sedum's tight mat of succulent, red-purple leaf rosettes. During the summer months the centres of these rosettes become whiter. The habit of growth and colouring of this sedum are complementary to many plants (see, for example, 17.16, where it is shown with a small fern). The flowers of this plant consist of little, rich yellow clusters on short stalks.

13.14 Choisya & Acer

Choisya ternata
(Mexican orange blossom)
sun/shade ○ ●
type of plant slightly tender shrub
zonal range 7-9 (C-WT)
flowering time mainly late spring to early summer, some flowers early autumn
flower colour white
height 1.8-2.4m (6-8ft)
special characteristics evergreen, aromatic, decorative green foliage, fragrant flowers

Acer palmatum var. *dissectum* Dissectum Atropurpureum Group
(Japanese maple)
sun/shade ○ ●
type of plant hardy shrub
zonal range 5-8 (C-WT)
height 1.5-2.4m (5-8ft)
special characteristics purple foliage, autumn foliage

Even if *Choisya ternata* did not have such very sweetly scented flowers, this would be an attractive combination. The laciness and the sombre purple colouring of this maple's foliage are set off beautifully by the rich green glossiness and smooth shapes of the choisya's leaves, while the choisya's bright white flowers add further sparkle.

This is a pairing of plants with a long season of interest. In spring and summer there are fragrant flowers and two sets of elegant leaves. In autumn the maple's leaves turn red before falling, and the choisya's citrus-scented foliage always looks good.

Both these plants need a sheltered site. The maple leaves are prone to wind and frost damage in exposed positions, though too much shade leads to a rather murky, green-purple foliage colour. The maple also requires a neutral to acid soil that is well-drained and moisture-retentive. Even in ideal conditions this is a very slow-growing plant. The choisya grows much faster, and in sheltered sites in mild districts it can be almost twice the size given here. Most well-drained soils are suitable. Both these plants are rounded in outline.

Plants sold under the name *Acer palmatum* var. *dissectum* Dissectum Atropurpureum Group will vary in foliage colour somewhat and individual specimens should be chosen when in leaf.

13.15 Rosa & Pulmonaria

Rosa 'Sarah van Fleet'

(rose)

sun/shade ○ ◐

type of plant hardy shrub

zonal range 5-8 (C-WT)

flowering time early summer to early autumn

flower colour clear pink

height 1.2-1.8m (4-6ft)

special characteristics fruit, fragrant flowers

Pulmonaria saccharata Argentea Group

(lungwort)

sun/shade ◐

type of plant hardy perennial

zonal range 4-8 (C-CT)

flowering time early to late spring

flower colour pink changing to blue

height 25-30cm (10-12in)

special characteristics variegated foliage

Like many Rugosa hybrids, 'Sarah van Fleet' has flowers that are beautifully scented. In this case, the fragrance is light and sweet with warm, clove-like undertones. As a charming change from the usual catmints and lavenders, this rose has been underplanted here with an especially silvery form of lungwort. Indeed, most of these large, smoothly shaped leaves are so heavily marked with palest, silvery green that the overall effect is almost grey. With its bold outlines and delicate colouring, this foliage makes an especially flattering companion for the rose's very clear pink flowers.

Established specimens of this rose form substantial masses of arching branches and very thorny, upright main stems. There is always plenty of healthy, attractively wrinkled foliage. Even in partial shade, *Rosa* 'Sarah van Fleet' is a notably free-flowering variety. In autumn there are pumpkin-shaped hips which ripen to a bright red.

Rosa 'Sarah van Fleet' does not require a particularly fertile soil. The lungwort grows best in cool, well-drained conditions. Here its overlapping leaves are shaded by the rose. Its dainty sprays of flowers appear early in the year.

13.16 Paeonia & Astrantia

Paeonia lactiflora 'Sarah Bernhardt'

(peony)

sun/shade ○ ◐

type of plant hardy perennial

zonal range 3-9 (C-CT)

flowering time early summer

flower colour pale pink

height 90cm (3ft)

special characteristics decorative green foliage, fragrant flowers

Astrantia maxima

(syn *A. helleborifolia*)

(masterwort)

sun/shade ○ ◐

type of plant hardy perennial

zonal range 4-8 (C-CT)

flowering time early to late summer

flower colour pink

height 60cm (2ft)

'Sarah Bernhardt' is one of the most popular of all peonies. Its big, frothy blooms have a delightful scent which is sweet but at the same time fresh and delicate. The flowers of the accompanying astrantia are in contrast quite small and demure; their more restrained shape and their stronger, less sugary colouring prevent the whole arrangement from being too cloying.

The peony's flowering period is fairly short. However, in the absence of flowers, its clump of handsome, boldly lobed foliage is an effective foil for other plants over many months (see 13.11). The astrantia's papery blooms are very long-lasting and make good material for dried flower arrangements.

Both of these plants need a moisture-retentive soil to grow well. The peony will only flower really generously in fertile soils. When well-suited, the astrantia spreads quite widely and its moderately attractive, three-lobed foliage makes good groundcover. Like all lactiflora peonies 'Sarah Bernhardt' is a notably long-lived perennial, but it may take several years to settle down and flower well.

13.17 Hemerocallis & Dryopteris

Hemerocallis lilioasphodelus
(syn *H. flava*)
(daylily)
sun/shade ○ ◐
type of plant hardy perennial
zonal range 3-9 (C-WT)
flowering time early to mid-summer
flower colour yellow
height 75cm (2½ft)
special characteristics decorative green foliage, fragrant flowers, suitable for damp soils

Dryopteris filix-mas
(male fern)
sun/shade ○ ◐
type of plant hardy fern
zonal range 4-8 (C-CT)
height 60-120cm (2-4ft)
special characteristics decorative green foliage

The sweet, rather heavily scented flowers of this daylily are individually short-lived, but there are plenty of flowers in succession over several weeks, especially when the plant is divided from time to time and the site is not too shady. Both the delicate, tubular shape of these flowers and the smoothness of the plant's arching, strap-shaped leaves are shown to advantage by fern fronds. (For a photograph of the daylily's leaves, see 5.17.)

The laciness of the male fern, its rich green colouring and its rather erect habit of growth all add considerably to the success of this planting. The male fern will grow almost anywhere, including dry shade, although its height will vary substantially according to growing conditions. Its foliage remains green almost until the end of the year.

Both the fern and the daylily are at their best in moist, partial shade, where they will produce dense, ground-covering growth. Both plants are suitable for heavy clay soils. The daylily will also thrive in permanently damp places.

13.18 Rhododendron & Smilacina

Rhododendron luteum
(syn *Azalea pontica*)
(azalea)
sun/shade ○ ◐
type of plant hardy shrub
zonal range 5-8 (C-CT)
flowering time late spring to early summer
flower colour yellow
height 1.8-3m (6-10ft)
special characteristics autumn foliage, fragrant flowers, needs acid soil

Smilacina racemosa
(false spikenard, false Solomon's seal)
sun/shade ◐
type of plant hardy perennial
zonal range 4-9 (C-CT)
flowering time late spring to early summer
flower colour creamy white
height 60-90cm (2-3ft)
special characteristics decorative green foliage, fragrant flowers

Both plants in this combination are fragrant. The scent of the yellow azalea, which is perceptible at some considerable distance from the plant, is very rich and sweet. The smilacina's scent, though sweet too, is altogether fresher and lighter.

In both this combination and 13.20, the smilacina has been given a yellow partner. Here it is flowers rather than leaves that provide the colour, and they have the effect of emphasizing the light, rather yellowish green of the smilacina's elegantly arranged foliage and the creaminess of its flowers. There is an interesting contrast between the smilacina's soft, fluffy blooms and the azalea's wide, more firmly outlined funnels. (In hot climates the smilacina is shy-flowering.)

After both sets of flowers have faded, the slim, rich green leaves of the azalea continue to provide a good background for the smilacina's upright stems of lighter, broader foliage. In autumn, however, when its erectly held leaves turn deep shades of red and orange, the azalea becomes the star of the show.

Both of these plants thrive in cool, moisture-retentive soils. The azalea must have lime-free conditions and the smilacina is also happiest in acid or neutral soils. *Rhododendron luteum* is a tough, self-seeding plant. It often produces suckers alongside its open framework of rather upright branches.

13.19 Rosa & Philadelphus

Rosa glauca
(syn *R. rubrifolia*)
(rose)
sun/shade ○ ◖
type of plant hardy shrub
zonal range 4-8 (C-WT)
flowering time early summer
flower colour pink + white
height 1.8-2.4m (6-8ft)
special characteristics grey/purple foliage, fruit

Philadelphus coronarius 'Aureus'
(mock orange)
sun/shade ◖
type of plant hardy shrub
zonal range 5-8 (C-WT)
flowering time early to mid-summer
flower colour creamy white
height 1.5-2.1m (5-7ft)
special characteristics yellow-green foliage, fragrant flowers

Like the green-leaved species (see 13.2), *Philadelphus coronarius* 'Aureus' has simple, single flowers that emit a deeply sweet and fruity fragrance. However, the added attraction of yellow foliage makes this dense, upright plant considerably more decorative than the species. The colour of the leaves varies according to the amount of light received: partial shade ensures a long-lasting, lime-yellow colour, while in sun the leaves are a harsher, brighter yellow and scorching of the leaf edges can occur. In full shade, the foliage is a rather nondescript, light green. At their best, the leaves blend beautifully with many different plants (see 6.11, 6.17 and 6.18). The same is true of the subtly coloured leaves of *Rosa glauca*, which in this instance make such a flattering, plummy blue-grey partner for the philadelphus.

Enlivening this attractive mingling of leaves are the rose's arching, almost thornless, maroon stems and its clean pink flowers. From late summer there are hips of a soft orange-red, and in mid-autumn the leaves turn briefly yellow.

Plenty of good quality foliage will be produced on both of these shrubs if they are given a moisture-retentive, fertile and reasonably well-drained soil. The colouring of the rose foliage benefits from fairly hard pruning each year.

13.20 Smilacina & Lysimachia

Smilacina racemosa
(false spikenard, false Solomon's seal)
sun/shade ◖
type of plant hardy perennial
zonal range 4-9 (C-CT)
flowering time late spring to early summer
flower colour creamy white
height 60-90cm (2-3ft)
special characteristics decorative green foliage, fragrant flowers

Lysimachia nummularia 'Aurea'
(creeping Jenny)
sun/shade ○ ◖
type of plant hardy perennial
zonal range 3-8 (C-WT)
flowering time early to mid-summer
flower colour bright yellow
height 2.5-5cm (1-2in)
special characteristics evergreen, yellow foliage, suitable for damp soils

The arching, fluffy flower spikes of *Smilacina racemosa* have a delightful fragrance that is both sweet and fresh. However, this partnership's attractive contrasts in foliage shape and colour and in habit of growth last well beyond the flowering time of the smilacina.

Throughout spring and summer the smilacina's erect stems, with their smooth, light green leaves, are poised elegantly above the mat of little yellow leaves produced by the creeping Jenny. In this yellow-leaved form creeping Jenny produces few flowers, but the leaf colour is very conspicuous. Here this colour emphasizes the slight yellowness present in the buds and, to a lesser extent, the expanding flowers of the smilacina. (For an illustration of the fully expanded flowers, see 13.18.)

Both of these plants grow well in cool, shady positions and moisture-retentive soils. In hot climates the smilacina does not flower freely. It is happiest in acid or neutral soils. In shade the creeping Jenny produces trailing stems; sun encourages denser growth. In all circumstances, but particularly in damp soils, this is a wide-spreading, vigorous plant.

For a larger-scale combination using *Smilacina racemosa*, again see 13.18.

13.21 Narcissus & Erythronium

Narcissus poeticus
(poet's narcissus, daffodil)
sun/shade ○ ◑
type of plant hardy bulb
zonal range 4-8 (C-CT)
flowering time mid- to late spring
flower colour white + yellow + red
height 40cm (15in)
special characteristics fragrant flowers

Erythronium tuolumnense
sun/shade ◑
type of plant hardy bulb
zone 5 (C-CT)
flowering time early to mid-spring
flower colour yellow
height 25-30cm (10-12in)

The fragrance of *Narcissus poeticus* is so rich and sweet that some people find it overwhelming, especially indoors. Outdoors, where some of the cloying undertones can be dispersed, the scent is usually perceived as wonderfully deep and spicy.

In this combination, the bright eye of each graceful narcissus flower has been emphasized by the clear yellow of another bulbous plant. Though this partnership of plants looks good for a relatively short period, it has great charm and makes very decorative use of space among deciduous shrubs.

When the narcissus and erythronium are in flower, few deciduous shrubs are in full leaf. At this stage, therefore, the bulbous plants are easily visible and they can receive plenty of light. As the weather becomes warmer the foliage of shrubs will expand, so masking the dying leaves of the narcissus and the erythronium and maintaining the cool, rather moist growing conditions that they like best.

The erythronium in particular appreciates a leaf mould-rich soil and thrives in a woodland setting. Its broad, gleaming leaves create an excellent background for the pretty, lily-like flowers of the plant. Once established, *Narcissus poeticus* grows well in grass. *N.* 'Actaea' is a closely related and rather more vigorous daffodil which also has richly fragrant flowers.

13.22 Convallaria & Pachysandra

Convallaria majalis
(lily-of-the-valley)
sun/shade ◑
type of plant hardy perennial
zonal range 4-9 (C-CT)
flowering time late spring
flower colour white
height 15-23cm (6-9in)
special characteristics fragrant flowers

Pachysandra terminalis
(Japanese spurge)
sun/shade ◑
type of plant hardy perennial/shrub
zonal range 5-8 (C-WT)
flowering time mid-spring
flower colour off white
height 23-30cm (9-12in)
special characteristics evergreen, decorative green foliage, fragrant flowers, needs acid soil

Few gardeners would deny that lily-of-the-valley is one of the most beautifully scented of all plants; the fragrance emitted from its sprays of tiny bells is deliciously sweet and clean. Understandably, the broad, pointed, erectly held foliage of this plant tends to get overlooked, but it remains an excellent fresh green for many months and, combined with other leaves of contrasting shape and texture, can create attractive ground cover in awkward areas of dry or dense shade.

Pachysandra terminalis is a rather mundane plant, but its whorls of glossy, toothed leaves are attractive in a low-key way and this ensures that the lily-of-the-valley's elegant simplicity is not eclipsed. Its off white, tassel-shaped spikes are not very conspicuous, though they do have a light, sweet scent. It too will grow in dry, shady places. Provided conditions are acid, this sub-shrub does well in a wide range of soils and will thrive in the moist, leafy soil that is often recommended as ideal for growing lily-of-the-valley. In heavily shaded sites, the tips of the pachysandra's shoots may need to be pinched out in order to prevent lankiness. When growing well this plant slowly forms a neat, dense carpet of foliage.

There is a variegated form of *Pachysandra terminalis* (see 9.36), but it would almost certainly be over-elaborate here.

In some of the illustrations the plants are either not in flower or the flowers are inconspicuous or not visible at all. Occasionally these flowers are pictured elsewhere in the book (for which, see index).

14 Winter-flowering Plants

Successful plant combinations give extra impact to individual plants by highlighting their decorative features. In winter more than at any other time of the year perhaps, it is especially important to make the most of what is available. The relative scarcity of winter flowers means they are much prized, and one way of ensuring that these precious blooms will not be overlooked is to combine them with flattering plants. For example, the sunny yellow blooms of winter jasmine can be accentuated by the addition of yellow-variegated leaves (see 14.4), and the rich flower colours of some winter-flowering heaths or heathers can be emphasized by being contrasted with the chilly grey-blues of certain conifers (see 14.3).

Year-round Interest

In each of the above combinations, the accompanying plants – the yellow-variegated ivy and the blue-leaved conifer – look good all the year round. Once their winter-flowering companions have finished flowering, the evergreens can be made to look particularly decorative by being given other companions which are at their best in spring, summer or autumn. The ivy would look especially attractive with, for example, the yellow leaves of Bowles' golden grass (see 17.12) planted at its base. The foliage of this grass is at its most colourful in spring but it forms a striking fountain of tangy green at other times, too. Plants to accompany blue conifers could include spring or summer-flowering perennials with purple leaves (see 2.17) and shrubs or trees with colourful autumn foliage (see 10.3).

Choosing partners for winter-flowering plants on the basis that these partners should be interesting at other seasons is prudent, especially when space is limited. It is also an advantage if the winter-flowering plants themselves have features which make them interesting over several seasons. The dramatic, whorled foliage of *Mahonia × media* 'Charity' (see 14.10) provides an excellent background for the shrub's fragrant winter flowers but is also good-looking throughout the year, while the long-lasting, late-winter flowers of many hellebores are also accompanied by very handsome, evergreen foliage (see 14.2). *Hamamelis mollis* (Chinese witch hazel) produces spicily scented flowers in winter, but the beautiful, glowing yellow of its autumn foliage (see 10.15) is almost as attractive as the flowers.

Evergreen foliage is particularly valuable for use in combinations that include winter flowers, and gardeners can choose from a huge range of leaves of many different shapes, colours and textures. The long-lasting fruits of some plants can also combine flatteringly with winter flowers. For example, some – but definitely not all – cotoneasters have berries that persist until late winter at least (see 12.17). Among perennials, *Iris foetidissima* and *I. f. citrina* (see 12.19) produce rows of berries that are decorative from autumn until spring, and there are the great, solid flowerheads of many sedums which turn a rich russet after flowering and remain intact throughout the winter months (see 12.4).

Using Bark, Twigs and Flowers

Ornamental bark and twigs, which are often at their most striking in winter, are another source of material for creating combinations with winter flowers. Varieties of the red-barked dogwood (*Cornus alba*) appear in several chapters of this book (see particularly 9.14 and 14.5), and the very decorative coral-bark maple (*Acer palmatum* 'Sango-kaku') is shown in the autumn combination 10.2. All these plants have brightly or richly coloured twigs that would look well with, for instance, the apple-green flowers of some hellebores. There are also several willows with unusually coloured twigs. Even the familiar fish-bone twigs of *Cotoneaster horizontalis* can provide a good background for some winter flowers, including the yellow trumpets of winter jasmine. Trees with ornamental bark include *Prunus serrula*, which has a shining, mahogany-coloured trunk (see 17.1), several pale-barked birches and the paper-bark maple (*Acer griseum*). The trunk of the latter is covered in eye-catching, peeling strips of gingery bark (see 10.13).

Any plant with ornamental bark or twigs needs careful positioning. A site which is never reached by the sun in winter should be avoided, since bark and twigs look much more striking when they are lit by the rays of the low winter sun than they do when they are in shade. A suitably contrasting background is important, too.

Some sun and an appropriate background will also enhance the appearance of many winter flowers, since these are predominantly pale in colour. Several well-known winter flowers are yellow but rich, deep colours are rare, the dusky, muted purples and maroons of some hellebores and the bright pinks and reds of winter-flowering heaths and heathers being notable exceptions. However, winter is not the season for a riot of colour; leafless branches and pale flowers match the mood of cold tranquillity. Big, bright blooms and a mass of lush foliage would disturb this special serenity.

The pale, even chilly colouring of some winter flowers is, however, often very subtly warmed by exceptional fragrance. Mahonia and witch hazel have already been mentioned, but there are also viburnums and shrubby honeysuckles that are warmly fragrant, daphnes and sarcococcas that have a sweet scent, and shrubs such as *Chimonanthus praecox* (winter sweet) that emit a spicy scent. Even on a chilly winter's day some of these scents will be surprisingly far-reaching – sufficiently enticing, perhaps, to encourage gardeners to get up from their cosy armchairs and venture out to see what brave flowers are newly opened in their winter gardens.

14.1 Erica & Mahonia

Erica carnea 'Springwood White'
(heath, heather)
sun/shade ○
type of plant hardy shrub
zonal range 6-7 (C-CT)
flowering time midwinter to early spring
flower colour white
height 20-30cm (8-12in)
special characteristics evergreen

Mahonia aquifolium
(Oregon grape)
sun/shade ○ ◑
type of plant hardy shrub
zonal range 5-8 (C-WT)
flowering time early to late spring
flower colour yellow
height 90-120cm (3-4ft)
special characteristics evergreen, decorative
green foliage, autumn/winter foliage, fruit

'Springwood White' is a vigorous, fast-growing heath with a long flowering season. This particular variety also looks attractive in bud, when the yellow-green of the long flower spikes combines with the bright emerald of the newest leaves to produce an overall impression of lime-green. This colouring looks especially striking beside darker-leaved plants, including those evergreens – such as the mahonia shown here – with foliage that becomes richly coloured in winter.

There are interesting differences in foliage and in habit of growth here, too. The mahonia has lustrous, prickly-edged leaves that are far bigger and broader than the tiny, dry-textured needles of the heath, and the latter's trailing, wide-spreading carpet of growth is much thicker than the mahonia's collection of upright, sometimes suckering stems. When the heath eventually stops flowering, the mahonia's bunched heads of blooms open fully (see 5.6). They are followed in summer by blue-black berries.

The mahonia will grow in most soils. This lime-tolerant heath is at its best in acid to neutral soils that are well-drained and moisture-retentive; it needs an open, sunny site. Sun produces good winter leaf colour on the mahonia. Here the heath is growing on top of a low retaining wall above the mahonia.

14.2 Helleborus & Erica

Helleborus × *sternii* 'Boughton Beauty'
(hellebore)
sun/shade ○
type of plant hardy perennial
zonal range 6-9 (C-WT)
flowering time late winter to mid-spring
flower colour pink-purple + green
height 45cm (18in)
special characteristics evergreen, decorative
green foliage

Erica carnea 'Praecox Rubra'
(heath, heather)
sun/shade ○
type of plant hardy shrub
zonal range 6-7 (C-CT)
flowering time early winter to mid-spring
flower colour rich pink
height 20-30cm (8-12in)
special characteristics evergreen

This combination shows how a familiar plant, carefully chosen, can very successfully enhance the appearance of a more distinguished and unusual companion. Both plants here – the comparatively commonplace heath, as well as the elegant hellebore – flower over a long period during the coldest months of the year. (The photograph shows the plants in mid-spring.)

The most striking feature of this planting is, perhaps, the interesting relationship between the colours of the flowers. However, the differences in form and texture of the plants also contribute to the success of the pairing. In contrast to the heath's busy mass of tiny flowers, the hellebore's sculpted, red-stemmed bowls look large and smooth. Similarly, the heath's dark, close-textured carpet of very small leaves sets off the imposing, almost shrubby growth and sizeable, shapely leaves of the hellebore. Leaves like these, with their soft, rich green colouring and slight marbling, look well in many groups of plants (see, for instance, 4.21).

Though most hellebores thrive in shade, *Helleborus* × *sternii* and its forms need sun and some shelter. The heath appreciates sun, too; it is lime-tolerant but will not do well on shallow, chalky soils. This combination should, ideally, have good drainage and a humus-rich, moisture-retentive soil.

14.3 Abies & Erica

Abies procera 'Glauca Prostrata'
(noble fir)
sun/shade ○
type of plant hardy conifer
zonal range 6-7 (C-CT)
height 30-45cm (12-18in)
special characteristics evergreen, blue-grey foliage, fruit, needs acid soil

Erica carnea 'Praecox Rubra'
(heath, heather)
sun/shade ○
type of plant hardy shrub
zonal range 6-7 (C-CT)
flowering time early winter to mid-spring
flower colour rich pink
height 20-30cm (8-12in)
special characteristics evergreen

The stiff, icy blue needles of *Abies procera* 'Glauca Prostrata' have the sort of biting colour and texture that look just right in winter. They appear particularly striking when set in a carpet of glowing, rich pink. Since the variety of heath shown here has such a long flowering season, this is a combination that looks good over several months.

Even when the flowers have faded, the heath creates a good background for the abies; against a dense mass of dark greenery the bold arrangement of the conifer's grey-blue needles and irregular, more or less prostrate branches is very conspicuous. From time to time, this slow-growing conifer may produce a vigorous, upright shoot. Any such shoot should be removed in order to preserve a fairly flat habit of growth. As well as striking foliage, this abies has large, upright, cylindrical cones that can be as much as 23cm (9in) long.

Although *Erica carnea* and its varieties are lime-tolerant, they are not suitable plants for shallow, chalky soils. In any case, the abies needs an acid soil. Both plants thrive where conditions are moist but well-drained. *Abies procera* 'Glauca Prostrata' may be expected to have a spread of about 90-120cm (3-4ft) after ten years.

14.4 Jasminum & Hedera

Jasminum nudiflorum
(winter jasmine)
sun/shade ○ ◐
type of plant hardy shrub
zonal range 6-10 (C-WT)
flowering time early to late winter
flower colour yellow
height 2.4-3m (8-10ft)

Hedera colchica 'Sulphur Heart'
(syn *H. c.* 'Paddy's Pride')
(Persian ivy)
sun/shade ○ ◐
type of plant hardy climber
zonal range 6-9 (C-WT/ST)
height 4.5m (15ft)
special characteristics evergreen, variegated foliage

Winter jasmine produces its little yellow trumpets in mild spells over a long period; in some years, flowering begins in late autumn. Although the dainty, tripartite leaves are absent in the colder months, the green shoots ensure that this plant never looks lifeless.

Winter jasmine is a scrambling shrub rather than a true climber and it can look rather angular and untidy, especially if it has been hoisted up and trained onto a wall. By using large, bold, yellow-variegated leaves as an accompaniment, a firmer pattern and some interesting contrasts in scale are introduced to the planting. At the same time, the jasmine's yellow colouring is reinforced.

Hedera colchica 'Sulphur Heart' is a vigorous ivy with heart-shaped leaves up to 23cm (9in) long. The specimen shown here is growing in a shady site. In sun, the central markings of pale yellow and light green cover a much larger proportion of each dark green leaf and the whole plant can look very bright and colourful indeed. In climates with hot summers, the leaves can scorch.

This particular ivy is not as close-clinging as some and it may need some support. Both plants will grow in almost any soil and both can be used as ground cover.

14.5 Cornus & Garrya

Cornus alba 'Sibirica'
(red-barked dogwood)
sun/shade ○ ◑
type of plant hardy shrub
zonal range 3-8 (C-CT)
height 1.5-2.4m (5-8ft)
special characteristics autumn foliage, ornamental twigs, suitable for damp and wet soils

Garrya elliptica
sun/shade ○ ◑
type of plant slightly tender shrub
zonal range 9-10 (WT)
flowering time late autumn to late spring
flower colour silvery green
height 2.4-4.5m (8-15ft)
special characteristics evergreen

The long, elegant and unusually coloured catkins of *Garrya elliptica* are probably at their very best in midwinter, as shown here, though they are conspicuous over many months (see 7.1). Indeed, their untidy remains can still be present on the plant in summer, which is something of a drawback.

Male plants produce the longest flowers – about 23cm (9in) or so in warm, sheltered gardens – but the shorter female catkins are followed by strings of purplish fruits. The plant itself is bushy and quick-growing; it needs some shelter if its leathery leaves are not to become burnt by cold winds. The foliage is of a rather sombre green, with a subdued sheen. Here, combined with a thicket of upright, crimson-red cornus stems, any gloominess is dispelled and the whole effect is one of quiet opulence.

As well as its striking stems, the cornus has foliage which takes on tinges of orange and red in most autumns. There are also variegated forms of *Cornus alba* (see 9.21 and 16.3). To obtain plenty of well-coloured stems, these plants need to be pruned hard at least every other spring.

The cornus is a tough and adaptable plant that flourishes in damp and wet soils but does well in drier conditions, too. In this instance a well-drained soil would be most suitable, since this is what the garrya requires for good growth.

14.6 Viburnum & Vinca

Viburnum tinus
(laurustinus)
sun/shade ○ ◑
type of plant slightly tender shrub
zonal range 8-10 (CT-WT)
flowering time late autumn to early spring
flower colour white
height 1.8-3m (6-10ft)
special characteristics evergreen

Vinca minor 'Argenteovariegata'
(syn *V. m.* 'Variegata')
(lesser periwinkle)
sun/shade ○ ◑
type of plant hardy shrub/perennial
zonal range 4-9 (C-WT)
flowering time mid- to early spring
flower colour pale violet-blue
height 10-15cm (4-6in)
special characteristics evergreen, variegated foliage

During mild spells of weather throughout winter and into spring, the pink flower buds of *Viburnum tinus* open to reveal pristine white petals. However, except in warmer districts or at the very end of the flowering period, only a sprinkling of blooms are likely to open at any one time. Some gardeners also feel that this quick-growing shrub's dense, bushy mass of softly gleaming foliage is a rather heavy green – and particularly so on dull days in winter. Here, in midwinter, the numerous red-stemmed heads of pink buds are doing much to enliven the appearance of the foliage, but a contrastingly low, trailing carpet of prettily variegated vinca leaves is lightening the scene considerably, too. At first the edges of these little grey-green leaves are cream; later they become white.

Both the viburnum and the vinca are easily-grown, shade-tolerant plants. However, their general growth and their flowering are much improved if they are planted in moisture-retentive soils and fairly sunny positions. Especially when it is given good growing conditions, the vinca is likely to produce a second flush of some flowers from late summer onwards.

If exposed to very cold winds, the viburnum's leaves are liable to become frost-damaged. In cold regions a sheltered site is advisable.

14.7 Buxus & Skimmia

Buxus sempervirens 'Elegantissima'

(box)
sun/shade ○ ◖
type of plant hardy shrub
zonal range 6-8 (C-WT)
height 90-120cm (3-4ft)
special characteristics evergreen, variegated foliage, fragrant flowers

Skimmia × confusa 'Kew Green'

sun/shade ○ ◖
type of plant hardy shrub
zonal range 7-9 (CT-WT)
flowering time late winter to mid-spring
flower colour greenish cream
height 90-120cm (3-4ft)
special characteristics evergreen, aromatic foliage, fragrant flowers

The very sweetly scented flowers of this vigorous skimmia open fully into large, dense heads in spring. However, as is evident here in midwinter, the flowers are conspicuous and decorative even when in bud. Apart from these attractive flowers, the plant has slim, pointed leaves of an excellent, bright, shiny green. They emit a sharp aroma when crushed.

Both the colour and shape of this foliage look particularly good against the much finer-textured mass of small, cream-edged, grey-green leaves of *Buxus sempervirens* 'Elegantissima'. This cream variegation also echoes the colouring of the skimmia's flower buds and in this way contributes to the satisfying unity of this combination. Because *Skimmia × confusa* 'Kew Green' is a male variety, its showy, scented flowers are not followed by berries. The box produces sweetly scented flowers, too, in mid-spring, but these are tiny and inconspicuous.

Both these plants grow very neatly. The box is a good deal denser and also much slower in growth than the skimmia. Any well-drained soil will suit it. However, the skimmia needs moisture as well as good drainage, particularly if it is grown in a sunny position.

14.8 Helleborus & Polypodium

Helleborus argutifolius

(syn *H. lividus* ssp. *corsicus*)
(Corsican hellebore)
sun/shade ○ ◖
type of plant hardy perennial
zonal range 7-9 (CT-WT)
flowering time late winter to late spring
flower colour pale green
height 60cm (2ft)
special characteristics evergreen, decorative green foliage

Polypodium cambricum

(syn *P. australe*)
(Welsh polypody)
sun/shade ○ ◖
type of plant hardy fern
zonal range 5-8 (C-CT)
height 25-30cm (10-12in)
special characteristics evergreen, decorative green foliage

The Corsican hellebore's beautiful bowls of pale green are among the most distinguished of all winter flowers and they are also very long-lasting. Just as good-looking are the plant's pale-stemmed leaves; each slightly curving, toothed leaflet is of a most attractive, soft, rich green, and the whole rounded mass of rather lax stems and firmly shaped foliage is handsome and imposing.

Against the relatively smooth, sculpted forms and soft colours of the hellebore, the brighter, yellower green and the much-divided leaves of a fern look especially lively. Even when the hellebore flowers eventually disintegrate, this combination still looks interesting since both sets of leaves are so attractive.

Ideally, both plants should be given a site with some shelter. The fern likes light, well-drained soils that are not too dry, and the hellebore will flourish under similar conditions.

Polypodium cambricum is a variable plant and there are a number of crested and plumed varieties. The new fronds of this species make a rather late appearance among the clump of older growths during the summer months.

14.9 Eranthis & Crocus

Eranthis hyemalis
(winter aconite)
sun/shade ○ ◐
type of plant hardy tuber
zonal range 5-8 (C-CT)
flowering time mid- to late winter
flower colour yellow
height 8cm (3in)

Crocus tommasinianus
sun/shade ○ ◐
type of plant hardy bulb
zonal range 5-8 (C-CT)
flowering time late winter to early spring
flower colour variable shades of pale lavender, lilac, purple
height 8-10cm (3-4in)

By late spring, both these plants will have died back completely. However, their lack of any decorative features for much of the year is amply compensated for by the fact that their flowering season often coincides with some of the coldest winter weather. Individually each of these charming plants would give pleasure, and together they create an especially attractive combination very early in the gardener's year. The lovely, delicate colours, the elegant flower shape and the slender, grassy leaves of the crocus are all enhanced by the aconite's richly coloured, rounder flowers with their delightfully jaunty ruffs of green.

Both of these plants may be naturalized in grass and beneath deciduous shrubs. The crocus will self-seed prolifically in rather gritty, alkaline soils and the aconite will form large colonies in fertile, moisture-retentive soils. However, though both plants will spread rapidly in ideal conditions, they are very accommodating and most garden soils will give good results.

Aconites are sometimes difficult to establish, but if their need for moisture is taken into account and they are planted immediately after flowering while still green, success is much more likely. Where conditions are not particularly moisture-retentive, the aconite should be given a partially shaded position.

14.10 Cotoneaster & Mahonia

Cotoneaster salicifolius 'Exburyensis'
sun/shade ○ ◐
type of plant hardy shrub/tree
zonal range 6-8 (C-WT)
flowering time early spring
flower colour white
height 2.4-3m (8-10ft)
special characteristics semi-evergreen/evergreen, fruit

Mahonia × *media* 'Charity'
sun/shade ◐
type of plant hardy/slightly tender shrub
zonal range 8-9 (C-WT)
flowering time late autumn to midwinter
flower colour yellow
height 2.4-3m (8-10ft)
special characteristics evergreen, decorative green foliage, fragrant flowers

With its masses of dark, scratchy foliage and its striking wands of flowers, this mahonia is one of the most imposing winter-flowering plants. To balance all this impressive solidity and these bold flowers and leaves, a small group of more slimly constructed, arching cotoneasters has been used in this combination. Since the cotoneasters produce generous bunches of long-lasting, apricot-tinged berries there is a very pleasing partnership of two yellows as well as an attractive contrast in habit of growth. The berries develop from wide heads of pale flowers. Similar cotoneasters (see 4.4) produce red berries which would create a particularly showy and festive effect when combined with this mahonia.

In early winter, as here, the mahonia's flower stems are still erect; later they become more spreading. Throughout the flowering season the globular blooms emit a delicious, lily-of-the-valley scent, though sadly it is not nearly so pronounced as the wonderful fragrance of *M. japonica*.

In time, this mahonia's rather upright stems and great whorls of foliage form a very substantial mass of growth, as wide as it is high. The cotoneaster is a vigorous plant which is happy in most well-drained soils. The mahonia appreciates a fertile, moisture-retentive soil and a sheltered, partially shaded site.

14.11 Euonymus & Skimmia

Euonymus fortunei 'Emerald 'n' Gold'

sun/shade ○ ◖
type of plant hardy shrub/climber
zonal range 5-9 (C-WT)
height 60cm (2ft) as a shrub
special characteristics evergreen, variegated foliage

Skimmia japonica 'Rubella'

sun/shade ◖
type of plant hardy shrub
zonal range 7-9 (C-WT)
flowering time early to mid-spring
flower colour white or pinkish
height 90-120cm (3-4ft)
special characteristics evergreen, fragrant flowers, needs acid soil

Strictly speaking, this skimmia is a spring-flowering plant. However, its red-stalked flower buds – which can be considerably larger than those shown here – are a highly decorative, glowing russet-pink from late autumn onwards. In early spring the buds open out into pale, very sweetly scented flowers. Since this is a male variety, there are no berries after the flowers.

By associating these colourful buds with brightly variegated foliage, a warm, lively and long-lasting combination has been created. Even in the absence of any flowers, the skimmia's dense, rounded mass of rich green leaves makes an excellent background for the yellow-variegated foliage of the euonymus.

Both these plants are slow-growing. In maturity, the euonymus may grow more quickly and it may also produce some self-clinging, climbing shoots up to 1.8-2.4m (6-8ft) high. Younger specimens of this plant form bushy hummocks of erect stems.

Almost any soil will suit the euonymus, but the skimmia is less accommodating. It needs a moist, open-textured, acid soil and a site that is sheltered from strong sun and cold winds.

In this photograph a few of the euonymus leaves are tinged with purplish-pink. This additional colouring occurs mainly on plants grown in sunny places.

14.12 Euphorbia & Helleborus

Euphorbia amygdaloides var. *robbiae*

(syn *E. robbiae*)
(spurge)
sun/shade ○ ◖
type of plant hardy perennial
zonal range 8-9 (C-WT)
flowering time late spring to early summer
flower colour yellow-green
height 45-60cm (1½-2ft)
special characteristics evergreen, decorative green foliage

Helleborus orientalis hybrid

(Lenten rose)
sun/shade ◖
type of plant hardy perennial
zonal range 4-9 (C-WT)
flowering time late winter to mid-spring
flower colour various shades of pink, purple, white
height 45cm (18in)
special characteristics evergreen/semi-evergreen

Photographed right at the beginning of spring, as the flowers of the euphorbia are just emerging from their dusky maroon buds, this combination will already have looked good for several weeks – and it will continue to look well, in its gentle, understated way, for many weeks to come.

At all times, the euphorbia's gleaming and boldly shaped rosettes of foliage and the hellebore's clumps of long-lobed, glossy leaves (see 10.4) create a rich green carpet of weed-suppressing growth. In this instance, a soft plum colour of Lenten rose has been used – a colour that is echoed in the stems of the euphorbia. However, some gardeners might prefer one of the very pale forms (see 7.15). Alternatively, the planting could be lightened by adding snowdrops to the group.

Whatever their colour, the flowers of this hellebore are notably long-lasting. This is also true of the acidic yellow-green flowerheads of the euphorbia (see 7.13). These will be sufficiently well-developed by mid-spring to combine attractively with the hellebore's nodding blooms.

Although the euphorbia is a vigorous and sometimes invasive plant that will tolerate dry shade, the hellebore prefers an open-textured, moisture-retentive soil. This combination is suitable for densely shaded positions.

219

14.13 Galanthus & Lamium

Galanthus nivalis 'Flore Pleno'
(snowdrop)
sun/shade ○ ◖
type of plant hardy bulb
zone 4 (C-CT)
flowering time mid- to late winter
flower colour white + green
height 10-20cm (4-8in)

Lamium galeobdolon 'Florentinum'
(syn *L. g.* 'Variegatum', *Galeobdolon luteum* 'Florentinum', *G. l.* 'Variegatum')
(yellow archangel)
sun/shade ◖
type of plant hardy perennial
zonal range 4-8 (C-WT)
flowering time early summer
flower colour yellow
height 30cm (12in)
special characteristics evergreen/semi-evergreen, variegated foliage

The first and the bravest of flowers in many gardens, snowdrops are also very tough and adaptable plants that will grow in a wide range of soils and situations. *Galanthus nivalis* and its forms are particularly at home in moist, woodland soils and partial shade. However, as in the combination shown here, they can survive in rather dry, shaded conditions and can compete successfully with very vigorous plants.

Lamium galeobdolon 'Florentinum' is an invasive thug that flowers patchily, but its ground-covering carpet of loose stems and attractively silvered leaves can be really valuable in the wild garden or in difficult areas under large trees. Elsewhere, its very rapid growth will soon be resented. In winter some of its growth dies back and this popular double-flowered snowdrop is able to rise prettily above the lamium's sea of silver and green. Combined in this way, the lovely, pure white of the snowdrop and the pale markings on the lamium's foliage are mutually enhanced.

Where the lamium would be much too vigorous, a similar effect could be achieved by planting snowdrops among white-variegated ivies such as *Hedera helix* 'Glacier' (see 15.18), or among non-invasive, white-variegated forms of *Lamium maculatum*, such as 'White Nancy' (see 9.31).

15 Climbing Plants

Most climbing plants take up take up surprisingly little ground space, considering their eventual height and spread. They are therefore quite often regarded as decorative surface-covers which are large enough in themselves to require no companions. It is common to find, for instance, a single, unaccompanied honeysuckle above a garden seat, a solitary rose upon a pergola and a lone clematis draped over a wall. But, especially where space is at a premium, it makes sense to create vertical as well as horizontal combinations of plants.

In addition to combinations of two or more climbers, partnerships of climbing and non-climbing plants can be devised: non-climbing companion plants can be placed at the base of climbers, and climbers can be encouraged to scramble over suitably sized shrubs or trees. Within a particular partnership, the plants can be chosen so that either their decorative periods coincide, or one plant takes over from another. If the first strategy is adopted, the overall effect may well be quite dramatic. However, the second strategy usually produces combinations with particularly long seasons of interest.

MAXIMIZING FOLIAGE DISPLAY

Choosing between the above strategies is not always easy. However, the use of evergreen foliage, which looks decorative over such an exceptionally long period, provides one solution to the problem. Climbers with handsome evergreen leaves include the enormous number of ivies with unusually coloured or variegated foliage. These plants look interesting all the year round, as do mature, climbing specimens of euonymus. Unlike plants that flower or fruit for only a brief period, they give a non-stop performance that simply reaches a crescendo when it is joined by the flowers or fruits of a neighbouring plant. For example, the big, boldly marked leaves of *Hedera colchica* 'Sulphur Heart' (see 14.4) are always eye-catching, but their yellow variegation looks particularly decorative with the yellow flowers of winter jasmine. At the same time, the yellow of these small flowers is considerably enhanced by the presence of the ivy's yellow-marked leaves.

A similar sort of pairing using a blue, spring-flowering clematis is shown in 15.19, and combinations 10.11 and 15.18 show variegated ivies with red autumn leaves and with shiny red berries respectively. Even green-leaved climbers can be useful in creating combinations that are interesting over a long period. *Vitis coignetiae* (see 8.11) has leaves that are plain green for much of the year, but they are also unusually large and handsome and they colour well in autumn.

COMBINING FLOWERS

Combinations that rely entirely upon flowers for their success have a much shorter period of interest, but part of the appeal of, for instance, a romantic intermingling of roses and clematis is its rather ephemeral nature. Though they may not last as long as evergreen leaves, these beautiful flowers can combine to produce outstandingly attractive colour associations (see 15.4 and 15.9).

Placing carefully chosen perennials, bulbs or small shrubs at the base of climbers produces a different effect from combinations where two climbers either weave among each other or form neighbouring blocks of contrasting colours. Plants placed at the base of climbers often act as interesting 'full stops', particularly when their habit of growth gives them a striking shape (see 15.20), but they can also be used more straightforwardly to create flattering colour harmonies with climbers (see 15.1).

USING TREES AND SHRUBS FOR SUPPORT

Another method of creating combinations with climbers is to use shrubs or trees as the means of support, which has the advantage of getting the maximum decorative value out of a single area of ground. Smaller trees, and especially those with fairly open, light canopies of branches, make the most suitable hosts for climbers (see 12.9). The most suitable shrubs for this purpose include those with a rather angular habit of growth (see, for instance, 15.14 and 15.2).

When choosing climbers to adorn trees and shrubs a certain amount of common sense and foresight have to be used. Very vigorous climbing plants will quickly smother and kill some shrubs and trees. Small to medium-sized climbers with relatively light, unobtrusive structures of stems and foliage make the best companions. Climbers of this type include many small-flowered clematis and their close relations (though not the very vigorous *C. montana* and its forms). Herbaceous rather than woody-stemmed climbers also work well with shrubs and small trees. These include *Tropaeolum speciosum* (see 15.16), *Clematis × durandii* (see 15.14), *Lathyrus latifolius* (the perennial or everlasting pea) and its varieties, and a climbing monkshood, *Aconitum volubile*.

In combinations where trees and shrubs are used to support climbers, it is nearly always advisable to give the host plant a head start of a few years before planting the climber. When a climber is added it is important to pay particular attention to feeding and watering, since there will obviously be competition for nutrients and moisture. Young plants especially need vigilance.

Climbers grown through or over smaller host plants will, in effect, be the same height as the host plants. However, to allow information about climbers to be used flexibly in other contexts, the heights given in the individual entries are the heights likely to be achieved in any circumstance.

DECORATIVE EFFECTS

Combinations of climbing plants appear throughout this book, which is an indication of the wide range of decorative effects they produce; as well as the wonderful fragrance of plants such as roses and honeysuckles, there are berries, seedheads and leaves of many different colours. Relatively few climbers bloom in winter. But before winter sets in, a number of the best-known climbers put on a spectacular display of autumn foliage. Especially in the case of those plants that turn burning red or bright orange at this season, it is important to bear in mind the background against which they will be seen.

This observation applies, to a greater or lesser extent, to all climbers that are grown against walls. Not only autumn leaves but flowers and fruits too can clash with their background. It is no pleasure to watch a carefully planned combination spread further and further across an expanse of strongly clashing bricks or stonework.

15.1 Wisteria & Allium

Wisteria sinensis
(Chinese wisteria)
sun/shade ○
type of plant hardy climber
zonal range 5-9 (C-ST)
flowering time late spring to early summer
flower colour mauve-lilac
height 9-15m (30-50ft)
special characteristics decorative green foliage, fragrant flowers

Allium hollandicum
(syn *A. aflatunense*)
sun/shade ○
type of plant hardy bulb
zonal range 4-8 (C-WT)
flowering time late spring to early summer
flower colour lilac-pink
height 90cm (3ft)
special characteristics fruit

The Chinese wisteria is extravagantly laden with sumptuous, sweetly scented blossom which cascades in racemes – each up to 30cm (12in) long – from stout, twining stems. The plant itself can grow 30m (100ft) high, although pruning and training will limit its growth. The sheer scale of this plant means that when it is in flower it outshines almost all other climbers. For this reason, much lower-growing, non-climbing plants usually make the most satisfactory companions.

In this particular combination, an ornamental onion with long, bare stems and dense, spherical, 8-10cm (3-4in) flowerheads is all neatness and composure beside the wisteria's languid abundance. The colour of these flowers is strong enough to punctuate the wisteria's mass of relatively cool, delicately coloured blossom. At the same time, the lilac tones present in both sets of flowers result in a beautiful harmonizing of two colours.

Once the flowers fade, the wisteria's leaflets expand into quantities of light, elegant greenery. The allium's strap-shaped leaves start to die back as its flowers expand.

Any soil with reasonable drainage will suit the allium. If the wisteria is to perform well it needs a rich, moisture-retentive soil.

15.2 Passiflora & Lonicera

Passiflora caerulea
(common passion flower)
sun/shade ○
type of plant slightly tender climber
zonal range 8-10 (CT-WT/ST)
flowering time early summer to early autumn
flower colour white + purple-blue
height 6-9m (20-30ft)
special characteristics semi-evergreen

Lonicera nitida 'Baggesen's Gold'
(shrubby honeysuckle)
sun/shade ○ ◑
type of plant hardy shrub
zonal range 7-9 (CT-WT/ST)
height 1.2-1.8m (4-6ft)
special characteristics evergreen, yellow foliage

The mixture of dense growth and spiky, longer branches produced by this lonicera makes it an ideal support for many climbing plants (see also 3.22). In addition, the smallness of its leaves and their greenish-yellow colouring create a flattering background for many different flowers.

In this instance, the close texture of these leaves sets off the exotic shapeliness of passion flowers to perfection. There is, too, a most successful harmonizing link between the green-tinged yellow of these leaves and the touches of green in the passion flowers. Although they appear in fairly limited numbers at any one time, these intricately structured blooms are borne over a long period.

The common passion flower is so vigorous that its partnership with this lonicera needs careful orchestration lest the latter is swamped. There should, ideally, be a small group or informal hedge of loniceras for the passion flower to twine across.

In order to thrive, the passion flower needs a warm, sheltered, sunny site. After hot summers, plum-shaped, yellow-orange fruits may ripen. The lonicera's leaves are yellowest in full sun. In areas with mild winters the passion flower's lobed leaves may be evergreen. A well-drained, reasonably moisture-retentive soil will suit this combination best.

15.3 Schizophragma & Vitis

Schizophragma integrifolium
sun/shade ○ ◖
type of plant hardy climber
zonal range 6-8 (C-CT)
flowering time midsummer to early autumn
flower colour creamy white
height 6-9m (20-30ft)

Vitis vinifera 'Purpurea'
(claret vine, Teinturier grape, grape vine)
sun/shade ○
type of plant hardy climber
zonal range 6-9 (C-WT)
height 3-4.5m (10-15ft)
special characteristics purple foliage, autumn foliage, fruit

Once it is established *Schizophragma integrifolium* is a magnificently floriferous plant, bearing flowerheads as much as 30cm (12in) wide for at least two months of the year. At the height of the flowering period its toothed leaves – which are a bright, rich green – are not very conspicuous and the impressive, but rather amorphous billowing mass of flowers is considerably enhanced by the presence of the clear-cut shapes of vine leaves. The presence of the vine also ensures that the end of schizophragma's flowering season does not mean an absence of any decorative interest.

Having emerged a greyish colour and then matured to a dusky purple (see 15.8), the vine's foliage starts to turn crimson in early autumn. Slightly later, bunches of bitter black grapes appear (see 12.1). Fruiting and autumn colour are both especially good in warm, sheltered gardens and sunny positions.

Like the schizophragma, the vine is slow-growing at first. Its twining growths are most likely to increase quickly when it has a really fertile, moisture-retentive soil and good drainage. The schizophragma also appreciates these conditions. In its early years, it may need support before its aerial roots start to cling efficiently to walls. It can be given a shady position, as long as it is not too exposed.

15.4 Rosa, Solanum & Clematis

Rosa 'Rambling Rector'
(rose)
sun/shade ○ **type of plant** hardy climber
zonal range 5-9 (C-WT)
flowering time early to mid-summer
flower colour creamy white, turning to white, + yellow
height 6m (20ft)
special characteristics fruit, fragrant flowers

Solanum crispum 'Glasnevin'
(syn *S. c.* 'Autumnale') (Chilean potato tree)
sun/shade ○
type of plant slightly tender shrub
zonal range 7-9 (C-WT)
flowering time early summer to mid-autumn
flower colour lilac-blue + yellow
height 4.5-6m (15-20ft)
special characteristics semi-evergreen, fragrant flowers

Clematis 'Hagley Hybrid'
sun/shade ○ ◖ **type of plant** hardy climber
zonal range 4-8 (C-CT)
flowering time early summer to late summer
flower colour pinkish mauve
height 1.8-2.4m (6-8ft)

For a brief but spectacular period beginning late in the first month of summer, *Rosa* 'Rambling Rector' covers its big, sprawling, exuberant mass of greyish-leaved growth with richly fragrant flowers. Here this blossom lends a special freshness to beautifully harmonized blue and mauve flowers.

Both the clematis and the solanum in this combination are very floriferous plants with exceptionally long flowering seasons. The solanum produces its very sweetly scented blossom especially freely in early summer and again in early autumn. At these times much of its pointed, veined foliage may be obscured by flowers. The clematis flowers are largest – about 15cm (6in) wide – early in the season. Three disparate flower shapes might seem a recipe for over-elaboration and disharmony, but the rather restricted range of colours and the wonderful blending of clematis mauve and solanum blue create a serenely elegant composition. The solanum's last burst of flower is accompanied by the small, red, long-lasting hips of the rose.

Each of these plants requires support. The clematis will hoist itself through the other two plants by means of twining leaf-stalks. Since the rose and the solanum are usually at least as wide as they are high, it may be advisable to plant at least two specimens of the smaller-growing clematis in this group.

The solanum and the rose thrive in warm, sunny places. The solanum will prosper in most well-drained soils; the rose and the clematis require conditions to be fertile and moisture-retentive as well. The clematis roots should be shaded and cool.

15.5 Clematis & Berberis

Clematis 'Abundance'
sun/shade ○ ◑
type of plant hardy climber
zonal range 5-9 (C-CT)
flowering time midsummer to mid-autumn
flower colour pink-crimson
height 3-4.5m (10-15ft)

Berberis × *ottawensis* 'Superba'
(syn *B. thunbergii* 'Atropurpurea Superba')
(barberry)
sun/shade ○
type of plant hardy shrub
zonal range 5-9 (C-WT)
flowering time late spring
flower colour yellow + red
height 1.8-2.4m (6-8ft)
special characteristics purple foliage, autumn foliage

In this combination, a bombardment of glorious flower colour glows against a background of dramatically dark and dusky foliage. *Berberis* × *ottawensis* 'Superba' is a bold and vigorous plant with quite large, very deep red-purple leaves. *Clematis* 'Abundance' is also vigorous and its colouring demands an assertive accompaniment. The berberis foliage has a bluish cast to it which echoes the blue tones in the 5cm (2in) blooms of the clematis.

The long flowering season of this clematis means that its last blooms may well coincide with the berberis's red and orange autumn foliage. There may also be red berries on the berberis but not all specimens of this shrub fruit reliably, though there are always plenty of the preceding clusters of little flowers.

The clematis needs to be cut right back each year in late winter or early spring. If the berberis's large, rounded head of arching, prickly branches is also pruned, the shrub produces particularly good quality foliage.

The berberis can be grown in most soils and will certainly appreciate the fertile, well-drained and moisture-retentive conditions that the clematis requires. The clematis likes a cool root run with its twining, leafy growth in the sun.

15.6 Clematis & Trachelospermum

Clematis 'Minuet'
sun/shade ○ ◑
type of plant hardy climber
zonal range 5-9 (C-CT)
flowering time midsummer to early autumn
flower colour white + mauve-purple
height 2.4-3m (8-10ft)

Trachelospermum jasminoides 'Variegatum'
(Confederate jasmine, star jasmine, Chinese jasmine)
sun/shade ○
type of plant slightly tender climber
zonal range 8-10 (CT-WT/ST)
flowering time mid- to late summer
flower colour white
height 3-4.5m (10-15ft)
special characteristics evergreen, variegated foliage, fragrant flowers

The very sweetly scented, starry flowers of this trachelospermum have just faded here, but the white edges of the plant's grey-green leaves look most attractive echoing the white parts of these little clematis flowers. During the period when both plants are in bloom the partnership looks particularly light and airy. Since the clematis is a late-flowering variety (indeed, there may be some flowers in mid-autumn), these two climbers look well together over a long period. As a very late-season, if minor, attraction, the trachelospermum's leaves become tinged with pinks and crimsons in cold weather.

Young specimens of the trachelospermum grow slowly and bloom sparsely, but mature plants usually produce plenty of flowers and sizeable tangles of twining stems. The clematis climbs by means of twining leaf stalks. Both plants must be provided with a framework such as trellis or wires in order to grow upright.

This is not a combination for cold, draughty places. The trachelospermum needs sun, shelter and a fertile soil to grow well. It has a preference for acid or neutral soils. The clematis is happy in most well-drained, fertile soils, as long as its roots are cool and moist.

226

15.7 Vitis & Clematis

Vitis vinifera 'Purpurea'
(claret vine, Teinturier grape, grape vine)
sun/shade ○
type of plant hardy climber
zonal range 6-9 (C-WT)
height 3-4.5m (10-15ft)
special characteristics purple foliage, autumn foliage, fruit

Clematis 'Perle d'Azur'
sun/shade ○ ◐
type of plant hardy climber
zonal range 4-9 (C-CT)
flowering time midsummer to early autumn
flower colour light blue
height 3-3.6m (10-12ft)

Like most plants with purple foliage, *Vitis vinifera* 'Purpurea' enhances flowers and leaves of many different colours, including blue flowers like those of the clematis shown here. In this instance, both these climbers have been planted in a site that, though warm and very sheltered, is not especially sunny, and this has affected their appearance: the clematis's 12cm (5in) flowers are a particularly rich shade of blue, and the lovely, precisely lobed leaves of the vine are greener than they might be. (See 15.8 for the vine's foliage later in the season, when grown in full sun.) However, the flower colour will lighten (see 15.17) and the vine's leaves will become darker as the summer progresses, making the combination more dramatic.

Between them the two plants here have a long season of interest. The clematis flowers very profusely over many weeks, while the vine's foliage emerges a soft grey, becomes purple and finally, in mid-autumn, turns crimson (see 12.1, where the bitter, black fruits of this vine are also visible). Autumn colour is richest and fruiting is most prolific in full sun in warm, sheltered gardens.

Both these twining climbers appreciate fertile, moisture-retentive soils and a sheltered site. The clematis should have a cool root run.

15.8 Vitis & Berberis

Vitis vinifera 'Purpurea'
(claret vine, Teinturier grape, grape vine)
sun/shade ○
type of plant hardy climber
zonal range 6-9 (C-WT)
height 3-4.5m (10-15ft)
special characteristics purple foliage, autumn foliage, fruit

Berberis thunbergii 'Harlequin'
(barberry)
sun/shade ○
type of plant hardy shrub
zonal range 5-8 (C-WT)
flowering time mid- to late spring
flower colour pale yellow + red
height 1.5m (5ft)
special characteristics variegated foliage, autumn foliage, fruit

On sunny, sheltered walls the summer leaves of this vine are a particularly dark purple, against which paler, more exuberant plants stand out beautifully. Here the vine has been combined with a berberis which is similar to the commonly grown *Berberis thunbergii* 'Rose Glow'. Compared with that variety, however, 'Harlequin' produces leaves that have more white in their pink-and-purple make-up. The overall impression is, therefore, of a rather creamier froth of pink. Though the contrasts of pale and dark and of large and small leaves are very striking here, the shared summer purpleness of these two plants is particularly appealing.

The berberis's variegation is brightest if the plant is grown in full sun and its arching, prickly branches are pruned in spring. From late summer onwards small red fruits appear, and in mid-autumn the foliage starts to turn a glowing red. The vine's lobed leaves usually colour slightly earlier in autumn and in a warm and sheltered position they can turn a wonderful rich crimson (see 12.1, where the bitter, black fruits are also visible). The younger leaves of this slow-growing, twining climber are greyish (see 15.3).

Provided the conditions are not very alkaline, the berberis will grow in most soils. The vine needs a fertile, moisture-retentive and well-drained soil.

15.9 Clematis & Rosa

Clematis 'Venosa Violacea'
sun/shade ○ ◐
type of plant hardy climber
zonal range 5-9 (C-CT)
flowering time midsummer to early autumn
flower colour violet-purple + white
height 2.4-3m (8-10ft)

Rosa 'Pink Perpétué'
(rose)
sun/shade ○
type of plant hardy climber
zonal range 6-9 (C-WT)
flowering time early to mid-summer and early autumn
flower colour pink
height 3-3.6m (10-12ft)
special characteristics fragrant flowers

Silvery-pink roses look pretty with other pale colours (see 15.10), but roses with flowers of a stronger pink associate particularly well with rich purples, violets and blues. Here, the freshly fragrant, rounded blooms of Rosa 'Pink Perpétué' almost glow among the lively, white-suffused, violet-purple stars of a viticella-type clematis.

Clematis 'Venosa Violacea' is especially useful for combining with other plants, mainly because, like all clematis of its type, it needs to be pruned very hard in spring each year. This means that it never builds up into a suffocating mass of old growth on any host plant. Secondly, compared with many viticella varieties, its 10cm (4in) flowers are relatively large and therefore make considerable impact. Lastly, its fine, divided foliage is not obtrusive.

'Pink Perpétué' is a dark-leaved, stiffly branched climbing rose that provides good support for other medium-sized climbing plants. In conjunction with a slim-stemmed, twining plant like this clematis, it looks less stiff and awkward than usual. Both these plants thrive in fertile soils that are also well-drained and moisture-retentive. The clematis is happiest when its roots are in cool shade and its top growth is in sun. The rose can tolerate a little shade, but it is most floriferous in sunny sites.

15.10 Rosa & Astrantia

Rosa 'Constance Spry'
(rose)
sun/shade ○
type of plant hardy shrub/climber
zonal range 4-9 (C-WT)
flowering time early to mid-summer
flower colour pink
height 3m (10ft), 1.8-2.4m (6-8ft) as a shrub
special characteristics fragrant flowers

Astrantia major
(masterwort)
sun/shade ○ ◐
type of plant hardy perennial
zonal range 4-8 (C-CT)
flowering time early to late summer
flower colour white + pale green, sometimes tinged pink
height 60cm (2ft)

Because it has long, arching stems, this shrub rose is often grown as a climber. Its big, voluptuously shaped and richly scented flowers appear in large numbers against a background of good-looking foliage. The flowering season is, however, only about two weeks long, and adding a flattering companion plant is one way of maximizing the impact of this glorious but short-lived display.

Since there is a distinct silveriness in the flower colour of this rose, it looks especially attractive with light grey foliage (see 13.6) and with other pale flowers. Some forms of Astrantia major are pinker than others; the specimen illustrated here has soft pink flowers in dense domes above the surrounding white bracts. So, crisp and prim though these flowers are, their colouring links them most attractively with the fuller, more languidly shaped blooms of the rose. After the rose has faded, the astrantia continues to look effective and later-flowering plants could be added to this combination to enhance the astrantia's long-lasting, papery-textured flowers.

Rosa 'Constance Spry' is tolerant of light shade, but ideally it should be given a position in full sun. It will thrive in any fertile, moisture-retentive soil that has good drainage. These conditions also suit the astrantia which, when growing well, will produce dense clumps of lobed foliage.

15.11 Ceanothus & Clematis

Ceanothus 'Autumnal Blue'
(Californian lilac)
sun/shade ○
type of plant slightly tender shrub
zonal range 8-10 (CT-WT)
flowering time late summer to mid-autumn
flower colour pale blue
height 1.5-2.4m (5-8ft)
special characteristics evergreen

Clematis viticella
sun/shade ○ ◑
type of plant hardy climber
zonal range 5-9 (C-CT)
flowering time midsummer to early autumn
flower colour variable – often violet-purple, also blue, rose-red
height 2.7-3.6m (9-12ft)

This basically upright but rather lax ceanothus has been used here to decorate a large pergola. Punctuating the fine texture of its powdery blue flowerheads and neat, glossy leaves are the numerous, nodding bells of *Clematis viticella*. The richer colour and the more emphatic shape of these clematis flowers add subtle emphasis to the relaxed, soft-focus appearance of the ceanothus. From a distance these two very attractive plants create a lovely blue-purple haze, while at close quarters their intricacies and details can be enjoyed.

The flowers of this vigorous, twining clematis are variable, though the colour shown here is a common one. Each bloom is usually about 3-5cm (1$^{1}/_{2}$-2in) wide. The leaves of the plant are small and deeply lobed and are therefore generally unobtrusive amid the foliage of companion plants. *Clematis viticella* must be cut right back in earliest spring each year. This means that the ceanothus's open structure of branches never becomes clogged with older, flowerless clematis stems.

In colder districts particularly, the ceanothus appreciates a warm, sheltered site – against a sunny wall, for example. The roots of the clematis should be cool, moist and shaded. Both plants here will prosper in fertile, well-drained soil.

15.12 Rosa & Clematis

Rosa 'Dublin Bay'
(rose)
sun/shade ○
type of plant hardy climber
zonal range 6-8 (C-WT)
flowering time midsummer to mid-autumn
flower colour rich red-crimson
height 1.8-2.4m (6-8ft)

Clematis 'Nelly Moser'
sun/shade ○ ◑
type of plant hardy climber
zonal range 4-9 (C-CT)
flowering time late spring to early summer and late summer to early autumn
flower colour palest mauve + deep carmine-pink
height 2.4-3.6m (8-12ft)

As with many rose and clematis combinations, there is here a striking contrast in flower form. The clematis's great, open-faced blooms and the cupped and closely petalled flowers of the rose are quite differently constructed, and this contrast in form is underlined by a marked dissimilarity in depth of colour.

The association of colours linking these flowers is unexpectedly successful. Crimson and pink sounds an unlikely recipe for harmony, but the bars on the clematis flowers are in fact a subtle mixture of colours, with crimson, lilac, pink and some blue tones all present. In this combination, the bluer and more crimson tints are made more prominent by the crimson of the rose. The flowers of this rose are only slightly fragrant, but they do appear over a very long period and the accompanying foliage is of an exceptionally rich and glossy green.

Rosa 'Dublin Bay' requires sun to grow and flower well. In really sunny positions, however, the clematis's flower colour will quickly fade and for this particular combination a site facing west would be more suitable. Both of these climbers need a rich, well-drained and moisture-retentive soil. The clematis climbs by means of twining leaf stalks. The rose needs artificial support.

229

15.13 Clematis & Santolina

Clematis 'H. F. Young'

sun/shade ○ ◐
type of plant hardy climber
zonal range 6-9 (C-CT)
flowering time late spring to early summer
flower colour mauve-tinged mid-blue
height 2.4-3m (8-10ft)

Santolina pinnata ssp. neapolitana

sun/shade ○
type of plant slightly tender shrub
zonal range 7-9 (C-WT)
flowering time midsummer
flower colour bright lemon-yellow
height 60-75cm (2-2½ft)
special characteristics evergreen, aromatic, grey-green foliage

The big, shapely blooms of this clematis are better accompanied by a mass of little flowers, rather than competing for attention with anything as large-scale as themselves. Illustrated here in early summer, the santolina's pale flower buds provide a lovely, low-key link with the cream stamens of the clematis. Indeed, the whole wispy, slender demeanour of this little shrub contrasts most flatteringly with the firmer structure of the clematis. Each of the santolina's numerous, button-like flowers is held on a slim stalk and the plant's grey-green leaves are fine and feathery.

In order to form a neat hummock of growth, the santolina must have good drainage, plenty of sun and at least one good cutting back each year. All parts of this quick-growing plant are pungently scented. The clematis is at its best in a west-facing position and a fertile, well-drained, moisture-retentive soil. Its roots should always be cool. In this combination the santolina shades the base of the clematis and keeps it cool. The clematis' large leaves are equipped with twining stalks by means of which the plant climbs.

The flowers of this particular specimen of Clematis 'H. F. Young' are slightly paler than normal, due to a prolonged and unusually early spell of hot, sunny weather.

15.14 Clematis & Teucrium

Clematis × durandii

sun/shade ○
type of plant hardy perennial
zonal range 6-9 (C-WT)
flowering time early summer to early autumn
flower colour deep violet-tinged blue
height 1.8m (6ft)

Teucrium fruticans

(shrubby germander)
sun/shade ○
type of plant slightly tender shrub
zonal range 7-10 (CT-WT)
flowering time early summer to early autumn
flower colour pale blue
height 90-150cm (3-5ft)
special characteristics evergreen, aromatic, grey-green foliage

Clematis × durandii might best be described as a 'nearly-climber'. It has a woody base but its non-clinging, herbaceous stems, unless supported in some way, simply scramble about at ground level. It looks especially attractive when grown over and through other plants – medium-sized shrubs with fairly open habits of growth being perhaps the ideal hosts. The rather angular stems of Teucrium fruticans provide just this kind of sparsely branched support.

However, it is not just the shape of this shrub that makes it such a good partner for C. × durandii. The success of the combination is due mainly to the germander's gentle colouring. With its white stems and grey-green leaves (all pungently aromatic), it manages to intensify the already strikingly deep blue of the clematis flowers. These lovely, thick-textured blooms are produced freely over a period of at least two months. The germander's contrastingly pale, small flowers appear in a series of flushes from early summer onwards.

If this combination is to grow well it must be given a warm site and good drainage. In addition, the clematis needs a soil that is at least reasonably fertile. The roots of this plant need to remain as cool and moist as possible and they should therefore be positioned on the shadiest side of the germander.

15.15 Chamaecyparis & Euonymus

Chamaecyparis lawsoniana 'Columnaris'

(Lawson cypress)
sun/shade ○ ◐
type of plant hardy conifer
zonal range 6-7 (C-WT)
height 6-9m (20-30ft)
special characteristics evergreen, blue-grey foliage

Euonymus fortunei 'Emerald 'n' Gold'

sun/shade ○ ◐
type of plant hardy shrub/climber
zonal range 5-9 (C-WT)
height 60cm (2ft), 1.8-2.4m (6-8ft) as a climber
special characteristics evergreen, variegated foliage

Many *Euonymus fortunei* varieties will eventually produce long, self-clinging, climbing stems as well as shrubby growths. Here a variety with yellow edges to its leaves is clambering among the dark, blue-tipped greenery of a large conifer, the lively foliage billowing out from the conifer's more restrained and much finer-textured growth. The foliage colour of *Chamaecyparis lawsoniana* 'Columnaris' varies a good deal and some specimens (which may be sold under the name 'Columnaris Glauca') are greyer and bluer than the form shown here.

Since both plants are evergreen, this partnership looks good throughout the year. In cold weather the leaf edges of the euonymus may supply some additional colour by becoming tinged with purplish-pink. Leaves exposed to full sun are most likely to assume these winter tints.

Both the plants illustrated here are slow-growing. This slim, upright Lawson cypress will reach about 2.4m (8ft) tall in ten years, increasing in size most quickly when planted in well-drained but moisture-retentive soils. The euonymus is a very tolerant plant that is happy in most soils.

For another cypress and euonymus combination, see 2.27.

15.16 Tropaeolum & Prunus

Tropaeolum speciosum

(flame flower)
sun/shade ○ ◐
type of plant hardy perennial climber
zonal range 7-9 (CT)
flowering time early to late summer
flower colour bright red
height 3-4.5m (10-15ft)
special characteristics decorative green foliage, fruit

Prunus laurocerasus

(cherry laurel, common laurel)
sun/shade ○ ◐
type of plant hardy shrub
zonal range 7-8 (C-WT)
flowering time mid- to late spring
flower colour creamy white
height 4.5-6m (15-20ft)
special characteristics evergreen, decorative green foliage, fruit

Older gardens often contain at least one or two specimens of common laurel. Nowadays the varieties of *Prunus laurocerasus* are much more popular than the species, yet this photograph demonstrates how the species can be transformed by the addition of a climbing plant. The twining stems of this climber are in fact very slender and if necessary can easily be removed. However, the laurel is a dense, vigorous plant, usually even wider than it is tall, and it is well able to withstand some competition.

The eye-catching blooms of the flame flower are, of course, the most conspicuous feature of this combination, but the laurel's leaves are large and handsome and they provide an excellent background of rich, glossy green. The flowers of the laurel consist of pale 'candles', each up to 12cm (5in) high. They are followed, from late summer onwards, by spherical fruits which are at first red and then black. At about the same time, the flame flower begins to produce its bright blue berries, too. The leaves of the flame flower are pretty and lobed.

The flame flower grows vigorously in areas with cool summers and high rainfall. Its roots should be moist and in shade. The laurel will grow almost anywhere except in wet or very chalky soils.

15.17 Clematis & Tropaeolum

Clematis 'Perle d'Azur'

sun/shade ○ ◑
type of plant hardy climber
zonal range 4-9 (C-CT)
flowering time midsummer to early autumn
flower colour light blue
height 3-3.6m (10-12ft)

Tropaeolum speciosum

(flame flower)
sun/shade ○ ◑
type of plant hardy perennial climber
zonal range 7-9 (CT)
flowering time early to late summer
flower colour bright red
height 3-4.5m (10-15ft)
special characteristics decorative green foliage, fruit

*C*lematis 'Perle d'Azur' produces masses of its 12cm (5in) flowers over a very long period – indeed, there are often respectable numbers of flowers in mid-autumn. In this combination, the scrambling, slender-stemmed flame flower – with its smaller, much hotter flowers and more airily shaped, lobed foliage – is a striking counterpoint to these relatively large, cool, tranquil flowers.

The flame flower is the ideal sort of climber to use in association with other plants. Although when well-suited it can grow very vigorously, its twining, herbaceous stems are so lightly constructed that they rarely hinder the growth of host plants. They are, in any case, easily removed. The plant is often seen glowing against yew. It also looks well on larger-leaved evergreens (see 15.16) and is a useful summer enlivener of winter jasmine. In late summer its flowers begin to ripen into bright, turquoise-tinted, blue berries.

Both of these climbers like their roots to be cool and moist and their upper growths to receive a reasonable amount of sun. The flame flower thrives in cool districts with high rainfall, and though it can be grown on shady walls, the clematis is really best planted on a sunny wall. In order to climb, the clematis must be given support for its twining leaf stalks to clasp.

15.18 Cotoneaster & Hedera

Cotoneaster horizontalis

(fishbone cotoneaster)
sun/shade ○ ◑
type of plant hardy shrub
zonal range 5-8 (C-WT)
flowering time early summer
flower colour pinkish white
height 60cm (2ft), up to 2.4m (8ft) against a wall
special characteristics decorative green foliage, autumn foliage, fruit, ornamental twigs

Hedera helix 'Glacier'

(ivy)
sun/shade ○ ◑
type of plant hardy climber
zonal range 6-9 (C-WT)
height 2.1-3m (7-10ft)
special characteristics evergreen, variegated foliage

*H*edera helix 'Glacier' is a moderately vigorous ivy with frosty-coloured little leaves that flatter many plants of warmer colouring. Here this white-edged, grey-green foliage is making shiny red cotoneaster berries seem particularly cheerful. It also looks well with the cotoneaster's neat, glossy leaves, both when these leaves are green, as here in early autumn, and later when they turn shades of rust and crimson (see 10.19). Even when the cotoneaster's dark twigs are leafless, their stiff fishbone arrangement is shown off to advantage by the pale leaves and relatively lax stems of the ivy, and in early summer the white edges to the ivy leaves enhance the white petals of the cotoneaster's tiny flowers.

As well as looking good all the year round, this combination of plants is very to grow. Almost any soil will be suitable as long as it is not waterlogged. Both plants can be used to cover shaded walls. The ivy climbs by means of aerial roots; the cotoneaster will fan its 'fishbones' upwards with support.

For other combinations featuring climbing plants, see:
GREY FOLIAGE 2.27*, 2.29 HOT-COLOURED FLOWERS 3.22 YELLOW FLOWERS 5.1 YELLOW FOLIAGE 6.10 GREEN FOLIAGE SECTION 8.1, 8.11 VARIEGATED FOLIAGE 9.16 AUTUMN FOLIAGE 10.11, 10.12 FRUIT 12.1, 12.8, 12.9, 12.10, 12.11, 12.18 FRAGRANT FLOWERS 13.1, 13.6 WINTER FLOWERS 14.4 GRASSES AND FERNS 17.19

* this combination features a mature specimen of *Euonymus fortunei* 'Emerald Gaiety' with climbing shoots. Most varieties of this euonymus will climb in maturity – see the index for additional combinations featuring these plants. See the index, too, for combinations that include *Cotoneaster horizontalis* and *C. atropurpureus* 'Variegatus', both of which will grow upright against walls.

15.19 Clematis & × Fatshedera

Clematis alpina

sun/shade ○ ◐
type of plant hardy climber
zonal range 5-8 (C-CT)
flowering time mid- to late spring
flower colour violet-blue
height 1.5-2.4m (5-8ft)
special characteristics fruit

× *Fatshedera lizei* 'Annemieke'

(syn × *F. l.* 'Lemon and Lime')
sun/shade ○ ◐
type of plant slightly tender shrub
zonal range 9-10 (C-ST)
flowering time mid-autumn
flower colour pale cream
height 1.8-2.4m (6-8ft) with support, 60-90cm
(2-3ft) unsupported
special characteristics evergreen, variegated
foliage

Shady walls are suitable for this most attractive blue and yellow combination of pretty flowers and handsome foliage. However, it is important for the sake of the fatshedera that if the position is shaded it is also sheltered.

Small-flowered clematis, such as *Clematis alpina*, often mix more happily with other plants than the large-flowered hybrids do, partly because their flowers are unlikely to overwhelm a combination, but also because the leaves of most small-flowered clematis are unobtrusive. In this combination, the almost ferny foliage of *C. alpina* does not draw attention away from the fatshedera's large, gleaming, strongly shaped and generously marked leaves, each of which is about 15-20cm (6-8in) long.

Clematis alpina has attractive, long-lasting seedheads (see 12.18) as well as pretty flowers. The knobbly flowerheads of the fatshedera usually coincide with the last of these seedheads.

Clematis alpina climbs by means of twining leafstalks. The fatshedera is basically a sprawling shrub, and its growths need to be tied to some support. The fatshedera will grow in any soil with reasonable drainage; the clematis requires a cool, moist rootrun and fairly fertile conditions.

Hedera colchica 'Sulphur Heart' (see 14.4) would be a hardier substitute for the fatshedera.

15.20 Hydrangea & Polygonatum

Hydrangea anomala ssp. *petiolaris*

(syn *H. petiolaris*)
(climbing hydrangea)
sun/shade ○ ◐
type of plant hardy climber
zonal range 5-8 (C-WT)
flowering time early summer
flower colour white
height 15-18m (50-60ft)
special characteristics autumn foliage

Polygonatum × *hybridum*

(Solomon's seal, David's harp)
sun/shade ◐
type of plant hardy perennial
zonal range 4-9 (C-CT)
flowering time late spring to early summer
flower colour white + green
height 75-90cm (2½-3ft)
special characteristics decorative green foliage

Some gardeners would feel that a climber as boldly proportioned as this hydrangea should be treated as a splendid solitary specimen and not combined with other plants. However, a strongly shaped but quietly coloured plant, such as Solomon's seal, placed at its base, adds variety without being distracting.

The distinctive arrangement of arching stems and horizontally held leaves makes Solomon's seal an exceptionally elegant plant. Its rows of small, pendent, green-tipped flowers echo subtly but most attractively the large, lacy, white flowers of the hydrangea. If sawfly have not decimated the leaves of Solomon's seal by late summer, the plant's foliage and thickets of stems turn butter-yellow in mid-autumn. This colour change also takes place in the leaves of the hydrangea (see 17.19).

To begin with the hydrangea grows slowly. Once established, its aerial roots will attach themselves to flat surfaces and the plant will be self-supporting. The ideal position for this climber is perhaps in some sun, but a shady wall is also suitable.

Both plants in this combination appreciate a fertile, moisture-retentive soil. Solomon's seal is particularly at home in cool, spongy soils, but it is a very accommodating plant. It will tolerate dry shade and can be grown in densely shaded places.

233

16 Plants for Water Gardens & Damp & Wet Soils

Constant moisture produces a special kind of jungly lushness that allows the creation of bold and exuberant plant combinations. Some of the largest-leaved and most handsome foliage plants grow in damp and watery places, the huge surface area of their leaves kept turgid by really moist growing conditions.

Many gardeners will be familiar with the vast, veined leaves of *Gunnera manicata* and the large-scale, shiny foliage of the lysichitons, or bog arums. Among the other large-leaved plants featured in this section are majestic moisture-loving ferns and several bold-leaved hostas. Even where plants have smaller leaves, plenty of moisture tends to produce strikingly generous quantities of growth.

However, not all water- and bog-garden plants are large and vigorous. Smaller-scale plants for damp soils include the popular, yellow-leaved form of creeping Jenny (see 13.20), *Caltha palustris* and its forms (see 16.13) and *Carex elata* 'Aurea' and *Ranunculus constantinopolitanus* 'Plenus' (see 16.2).

DECORATIVE FLOWERS FOR DAMP SOILS

There are also plenty of moisture-loving plants with very decorative flowers, including astilbes, daylilies and primulas, as well as some irises, globe flowers and bistorts. Many of these plants have pink, pale yellow or white flowers, but some of the primulas and astilbes in particular produce strongly coloured flowers (see 3.25 and 16.15, respectively). The range of flower shapes among these moisture-loving plants is good. There are, for example, the great, dark-stemmed spires of *Ligularia przewalskii*, the softer, fuller, plume-like flowers of astilbes, the elegant trumpets of some daylilies and the neat, spherical shapes of many globe flowers (see 1.31).

With a constant supply of moisture, plants like astilbes and primulas can be grown in full sun, where their flowering will be especially prolific. So often, in the absence of really moist growing conditions, these plants have to be given a shaded site in order to conserve what moisture is available. This necessary shading inhibits the production of flowers, at least to some extent.

FOLIAGE INTEREST

More colour, and some lively patterns, too, can be introduced into planting schemes for damp and wet places in the form of variegated or unusually coloured foliage. A number of moisture-loving plants have interesting leaves. There are, for instance, several varieties of cornus or red-barked dogwood with variegated leaves (see 1.22, 9.4, 13.4 and 16.3), and yellow-leaved and variegated elders (see 6.12 and 9.3, respectively). Smaller, non-shrubby plants with decorative foliage include some irises (see 3.15 and 16.12), several grasses (see 16.1 and 17.7) and many hostas. All these plants appreciate moisture and have attractively shaped, variegated foliage. By far the most striking glaucous- or grey-leaved plant for growing in damp places is *Hosta sieboldiana elegans* (see 16.19). Some willows, such as *Salix lanata* and *S. repens argentea*, have attractive, grey foliage. They, too, appreciate a position in moist or damp soils.

There are also numerous green-leaved plants with very handsome foliage that thrive in moist or damp conditions. These plants range in size all the way from *Gunnera manicata*, with its giant leaves, to small astilbes such as *Astilbe* 'Sprite' (see 16.3), which produce close-textured masses of glossy little leaves.

Unfortunately, few moisture-loving plants are evergreen (though see the variegated comfrey in 16.1 and the bamboo in 17.11). However, many plants suitable for the waterside and for the bog garden do produce foliage which grows densely and luxuriantly. They are therefore very efficient suppressors of weeds.

Some plants that thrive in damp and wet places have good autumn foliage colour. The various forms of *Cornus alba* are particularly useful since many of them have interesting foliage and brightly or richly coloured winter twigs as well as colourful autumn leaves. Other medium-sized plants which colour well in autumn include the royal fern (*Osmunda regalis*, see 16.8), the guelder rose (*Viburnum opulus*) and its forms, and some species of rodgersia (see 8.16).

PLANTS FOR WATER

There are plants in this chapter, such as the dogwoods, that are suitable for really wet soils, and others, including *Caltha palustris* and *Iris pseudacorus*, that will thrive in shallow water. However, many of these plants are quite adaptable. In ordinary, moisture-retentive conditions they may not grow with the same exuberance, but as long as they are given a reasonably deep and fertile soil that will not dry out in summer, they will grow quite satisfactorily.

What will not be available in ordinary beds and borders, however, is the reflective surface of water. The many handsome combinations in this section will look especially lovely when mirrored in glassy expanses of water and illuminated by soft, reflected sunlight.

16.1 Symphytum & Carex

Symphytum × uplandicum 'Variegatum'

(syn *S.peregrinum* 'Variegatum')
(comfrey)
sun/shade ○ ◑
type of plant hardy perennial
zonal range 5-9 (C-WT)
flowering time late spring to early summer
flower colour lilac-pink changing to blue
height 90cm (3ft)
special characteristics evergreen/semi-evergreen, variegated foliage, suitable for damp soils

Carex elata 'Aurea'

(syn *C. stricta* 'Bowles' Golden')
(Bowles' golden sedge)
sun/shade ○
type of plant hardy perennial (grass)
zonal range 5-9 (C-WT)
flowering time early to mid-summer
flower colour brown
height 60-75cm (2-2½ft)
special characteristics variegated foliage, suitable for damp and wet soils

Two sets of variegated leaves might seem to add up to a rather overelaborate combination. However, the very slender leaves of Bowles' golden sedge are so narrowly margined in green that the overall effect is of an arching spray of plain, strong yellow. The variegation fades substantially by late summer, but whether they are brightly or softly variegated, these grassy leaves always contrast interestingly with the much broader, more boldly variegated foliage of the comfrey.

Compared with its leaves the sedge's little rat-tail flowers are not particularly decorative, but the comfrey's simple, pink-budded flowers are charming. After these blooms have faded, the comfrey should be cut right back in order to encourage the production of a second crop of basal leaves. These leaves are large, hairy and of a soft grey-green, with pale cream edges. They form a dense clump about 30cm (12in) high and look fresh well into autumn, especially when the plant is grown in damp soil.

The sedge enjoys damp conditions, too. In addition, it may be grown in wet ground near water. It may be invasive in warm climates. Both plants will also do well in the slightly drier setting of a moisture-retentive, border soil, though here the comfrey's leaves will usually benefit from some shade.

16.2 Carex & Ranunculus

Carex elata 'Aurea'

(syn *C. stricta* 'Bowles' Golden')
(Bowles' golden sedge)
sun/shade ○
type of plant hardy perennial (grass)
zonal range 5-9 (C-WT)
flowering time early to mid-summer
flower colour brown
height 60-75cm (2-2½ft)
special characteristics variegated foliage, suitable for damp and wet soils

Ranunculus constantinopolitanus 'Plenus'

(syn *R. bulbosus* 'Speciosus Plenus', *R. speciosus* 'Flore Pleno')
(buttercup)
sun/shade ○
type of plant hardy perennial
zonal range 4-8 (C-CT)
flowering time late spring to early summer
flower colour rich yellow + green
height 30-45cm (12-18in)
special characteristics suitable for damp soils

Many of the plants that do well in damp or wet soils are large and have big, bold leaves, but those shown here are medium-sized, with comparatively fine-textured foliage. In late spring and early summer, each slender, green-margined leaf produced by *Carex elata* 'Aurea' is a good, strong yellow. This colouring is echoed here in the shiny, closely packed petals and green centres of the flowers of a non-invasive form of buttercup. These flowers are large – about 3cm (1½in) wide – and long-lasting. By the end of summer the sedge's variegation will have faded, but the dense mass of arching leaves will still look well with the buttercup's clump of rich green, deeply cut foliage. The flowers of the sedge are less decorative than those of the buttercup, consisting as they do of little rat-tail spikes.

Both these plants enjoy damp conditions, but they will thrive in fertile, moisture-retentive soils, too. The sedge may be grown in wet ground beside water. In warm climates it may be invasive.

The previous combination also features *Carex elata* 'Aurea', this time with a foliage plant.

16.3 Cornus & Astilbe

Cornus alba 'Elegantissima'
(red-barked dogwood)
sun/shade ○ ◐
type of plant hardy shrub
zonal range 3-8 (C-WT)
height 1.8-2.7m (6-9ft)
special characteristics variegated foliage, autumn foliage, ornamental twigs, suitable for damp and wet soils

Astilbe 'Sprite'
(false goat's beard)
sun/shade ◐
type of plant hardy perennial
zonal range 4-8 (C-CT)
flowering time midsummer to early autumn
flower colour pale pink
height 25-30cm (10-12in)
special characteristics decorative green foliage, suitable for damp soils

Tough and vigorous though this cornus is, its tapered foliage is an exceptionally graceful combination of cool grey-green and creamy white. The colouring is shown off to perfection here by some tightly packed, dark green astilbe leaves. These glossy little leaves are slightly bronze when young. The astilbe's flowers are also very attractive (see 1.37) and are followed by bright tan seedheads that last well into winter.

In winter, too, there are the bare, strikingly upright, maroon stems of the cornus. Young stems have the best colour, and the most satisfactory way of achieving plenty of colourful stems and a good quantity of foliage is to remove about half – rather than all – of the older stems each spring. Whatever the pruning method, the cornus is a fast-growing shrub which, once it is well-established, can put on several feet of growth in a season. Before the leaves of this shrub fall, they turn a mixture of soft oranges and pinks.

Damp and moisture-retentive soils suit both these plants. The cornus can also be grown in wet, waterside places, but the astilbe is not at its best in these conditions. The combination can be grown in either sun or partial shade, as long as the astilbe is positioned so that it can be shaded by the cornus.

16.4 Gunnera & Iris

Gunnera manicata
sun/shade ○ ◐
type of plant slightly tender perennial
zonal range 7-10 (CT-WT)
flowering time late spring to early summer
flower colour khaki-green
height 1.8-2.4m (6-8ft)
special characteristics decorative green foliage, suitable for damp and wet soils

Iris pseudacorus
(yellow flag)
sun/shade ○ ◐
type of plant hardy perennial
zonal range 5-9 (C-WT)
flowering time early summer
flower colour yellow
height 90-120cm (3-4ft)
special characteristics decorative green foliage, suitable for damp and wet soils, suitable for water gardens

In rich soils that are always wet or damp the exceptionally imposing leaves of *Gunnera manicata* may well be over 1.8m (6ft) in diameter. This massive plant can look magnificent all by itself, particularly if the planting site allows the veined and jagged foliage to be reflected in water. If it is to be successfully combined with other plants, it is important to remember just how big and bold it is. Single specimens of smaller plants can simply look like incongruous midgets beside these enormous leaves.

Here the sheer quantity of iris foliage ensures a proper balance in the planting. Each iris leaf is small and very slender, but the common yellow flag is a vigorous plant in the sort of damp and wet places that the gunnera likes best, and it will soon produce large swathes of growth. Its flowers have faded here, at the end of the first month of summer, but they are most attractively simple (see 16.10). The gunnera's flowers are extraordinary, almost primeval-looking, cone-shaped structures some 60-90cm (2-3ft) high, but when the foliage expands they are hidden from view.

The iris grows well in conditions ranging from shallow water to moisture-retentive borders. If a really moist position is not available for the gunnera, it must be given a soil that is at least deep and fertile. It usually needs a fairly sheltered site.

237

16.5 Sambucus & Ligularia

Sambucus racemosa 'Plumosa Aurea'

(elder)

sun/shade ○ ◑
type of plant hardy shrub
zonal range 4-7 (C-CT)
flowering time mid-spring
flower colour yellowish white
height 1.5-2.1m (5-7ft)
special characteristics yellow foliage, bronze when young, fruit, suitable for damp soils

Ligularia przewalskii

(syn *Senecio przewalskii*)

sun/shade ○ ◑
type of plant hardy perennial
zonal range 4-8 (C-CT)
flowering time mid- to late summer
flower colour yellow
height 1.2-1.8m (4-6ft)
special characteristics decorative green foliage, suitable for damp soils

Black stems seem an unlikely ingredient of a successful combination, but it is the tall, very dark and upright flower stalks of this ligularia against the elder's rounded outline and layers of pretty foliage that make this partnership so stylish. Of course, the ligularia's yellow flowers, which are just beginning to open here, and its rich green, jagged leaves are also important features; the flowers will reiterate the elder's colouring, while the foliage provides a plain green base to the composition.

The elder's finely cut leaves are pretty all spring – when the new growth is bronze – and throughout summer. If the plant is left unpruned, its flowers are followed by red berries (pruning encourages the production of plenty of foliage, but at the expense of flowers and therefore fruit).

In permanently damp soils both these plants do well. The elder is tolerant of a wide range of soil types and light conditions, but it is a slow-growing shrub that is most luxuriant with some moisture. The ligularia's substantial clumps of leaves soon droop sadly in hot, dry sites. A little shade makes conservation of moisture easier. It will also prevent the elder's foliage from becoming scorched.

For a photograph of this combination with the addition of a yellow-variegated hosta, see 6.12; 16.6 shows the elder with a particularly popular hosta.

16.6 Sambucus & Hosta

Sambucus racemosa 'Plumosa Aurea'

(elder)

sun/shade ○ ◑
type of plant hardy shrub
zonal range 4-7 (C-CT)
flowering time mid-spring
flower colour yellowish white
height 1.5-2.1m (5-7ft)
special characteristics yellow foliage, bronze when young, fruit, suitable for damp soils

Hosta fortunei var. *albopicta*

(plantain lily)

sun/shade ○ ◑
type of plant hardy perennial
zonal range 3-9 (C-WT)
flowering time midsummer
flower colour pale lilac
height 45-60cm (1½-2ft)
special characteristics variegated young foliage, suitable for damp soils

Although this combination of plants is at its most striking in spring, it still looks good even when the hosta's variegation softens to two tones of green after the plant has flowered. This photograph shows the hosta not long before flowering; for a photograph of it earlier in summer, see 8.16.

Throughout the growing season there are the pleasures of the elder's elegantly fringed foliage, with its bronze new growths, and the contrasting smoothness of the hosta's leaf outline. In midsummer the pretty, pale flowers of the hosta appear. If the elder is allowed to flower, it produces red berries from late summer onwards. Some gardeners feel, however, that it is worth sacrificing these berries by pruning established specimens of the elder right back in order to get plenty of well-coloured foliage.

As long as there is plenty of moisture both these beautiful plants can be grown in a sunny position, where their foliage colour will be particularly bright. In drier situations, general growth will be less luxuriant and, unless a partially shaded site is chosen, there will almost certainly be some disfiguring leaf scorch. In moist or damp soils, the hosta will form a substantial, ground-covering clump of leaves. The elder has an irregularly rounded shape. It increases in size fairly slowly, especially if it is pruned every year.

16.7 Aruncus & Alchemilla

Aruncus dioicus

(syn *A. sylvestris*)
(goat's beard)
sun/shade ○◐
type of plant hardy perennial
zonal range 3-8 (C-CT)
flowering time early to mid-summer
flower colour male flowers creamy white,
female flowers greenish white
height 1.2-1.8m (4-6ft)
special characteristics decorative green foliage,
suitable for damp and wet soils

Alchemilla mollis

(lady's mantle)
sun/shade ○◐
type of plant hardy perennial
zonal range 4-8 (C-CT/WT)
flowering time early to mid-summer
flower colour yellow-green
height 45cm (18in)
special characteristics decorative green foliage,
suitable for damp soils

With its long stems of almost tree-like foliage and its tall flowerheads, *Aruncus dioicus* makes an imposing plant for damp and waterside places. It is sufficiently vigorous to do well in drier conditions, too, provided the soil is fertile. Here it has been paired with the remarkably versatile and accommodating lady's mantle, which will grow almost anywhere apart from in waterlogged soils.

The resultant combination of fairly quiet colours is, nevertheless, strong and handsome because of the shapely foliage and the good, dense growth of both plants. There is a pleasing contrast between the foamy flowers of the alchemilla and the spikier outline created by the aruncus plumes. Unfortunately the aruncus is in flower for only a short period, but female forms, like the one shown here, do produce attractive seedheads. They also generate quantities of self-sown seedlings. Male plants bear flowers that are particularly erect and feathery.

The alchemilla produces a small second crop of flowers and plenty of new foliage in late summer if it is cut right back as soon as it begins to look slightly untidy. It is a prolific self-seeder. Its softly hairy, scalloped leaves look especially pretty after rain (see 1.32).

Alchemilla mollis features in various combinations (in this section, see 16.10 and 16.14).

16.8 Osmunda & Lysichiton

Osmunda regalis

(royal fern)
sun/shade ○◐
type of plant hardy fern
zonal range 3-9 (C-CT)
height 1.2-1.8m (4-6ft)
special characteristics decorative green foliage,
autumn foliage, suitable for damp and wet
soils, needs acid soil

Lysichiton americanus

(bog arum)
sun/shade ○◐
type of plant hardy perennial
zonal range 7-9 (CT-WT)
flowering time early to mid-spring
flower colour yellow
height 30-45cm (12-18in); leaves 60-120cm
(2-4ft) high after flowering
special characteristics decorative green foliage,
suitable for damp and wet soils, suitable for
water gardens

Set beside the relative insubstantiality of a fern, the very large leaves of bog arum seem even broader and bolder than usual. At this stage in their development, at the beginning of summer, the fern's fronds are still very upright and they retain tinges of their early orange-bronze colouring. Throughout the summer and into autumn, the bright green of their mature growth looks well with the richer colouring of the bog arum's veined leaves. As winter approaches, the fern's dense clump of foliage turns yellow and tan before dying.

Although it does not flower, the royal fern has plume-like fertile parts to some of its fronds. When ripe these are rust-coloured and decorative. The flowers of bog arum are very striking and shapely, resembling yellow, pointed hoods. They emit a musky smell when disturbed or at very close range and the plant is sometimes known as yellow skunk cabbage. The flowers are at their very best in mid-spring, when they coincide with the unfurling, crozier-shaped fronds of the fern.

Both plants in this combination need a constant supply of moisture and enjoy boggy conditions near ponds and streams. Bog arum can also be grown in shallow water. This plant is particularly large and lush in fertile soils. Once established, it will self-seed. The fern needs an acid soil.

239

16.9 Chaerophyllum & Cirsium

Chaerophyllum hirsutum

sun/shade ○ ◐
type of plant hardy perennial
zonal range 5-8 (C-CT)
flowering time late spring to early summer
flower colour pale cream
height 60-75cm (2-2½ft)
special characteristics decorative green foliage, suitable for damp soils

Cirsium rivulare 'Atropurpureum'

sun/shade ○ ◐
type of plant hardy perennial
zonal range 4-8 (C-CT)
flowering time early summer to early autumn
flower colour crimson
height 1.2m (4ft)
special characteristics suitable for damp soils

Both of these plants have erect stems, but the flower shape of each is quite distinct: whereas the cirsium has neat, dense little thistles, the chaerophyllum's flowerheads branch into wide, flat-topped masses of tiny blooms. These differences in flower form are emphasized by the contrasting flower colours, the one rich and deep, the other pale. The cirsium's spreading clump of pointed, dark foliage is not remarkable, but the chaerophyllum has toothed leaves that are ferny and an attractive, light green.

Either good, moisture-retentive border soil or a damp place – on the banks of a stream, for instance – will suit these easily grown plants. *Chaerophyllum hirsutum* is not very readily available, and though its pale flowers look well in this combination and would be especially appropriate in informal plantings, some gardeners will in any case find the pink-flowered form 'Roseum' (see 1.27) more decorative. In drier situations, one of the paler varieties of *Achillea* such as *A.* 'Hoffnung' or *A.* 'Moonshine', which have creamy buff and light yellow flowers respectively, would look well with the cirsium. The flowerheads of these plants are roughly similar in shape to those of the chaerophyllum.

16.10 Iris & Alchemilla

Iris pseudacorus

(yellow flag)
sun/shade ○ ◐
type of plant hardy perennial
zonal range 5-9 (C-WT)
flowering time early summer
flower colour yellow
height 90-120cm (3-4ft)
special characteristics decorative green foliage, suitable for damp and wet soils, suitable for water gardens

Alchemilla mollis

(lady's mantle)
sun/shade ○ ◐
type of plant hardy perennial
zonal range 4-8 (C-CT/WT)
flowering time early to mid-summer
flower colour yellow-green
height 45cm (18in)
special characteristics decorative green foliage, suitable for damp soils

The common yellow flag is a splendidly vigorous plant for informal areas of gardens where the soil is always wet or damp. Here it has been teamed with another vigorous and tolerant plant – the familiar and much-loved *Alchemilla mollis*. In this combination, the alchemilla's velvety, scalloped leaves and foamy heads of tiny flowers contrast very pleasingly with the iris's smoother shapes and simpler patterns. Mature specimens of the alchemilla produce large, dense mounds of leaves and numerous flowerheads which have plenty of visual impact beside the iris's generous sheaves of sword-shaped, ribbed foliage.

While there are striking contrasts between these two plants, the distinct yellowness in the foliage and flowers of the alchemilla provides an important link with the yellow blooms of the iris. These blooms mature into large, fat seedpods.

Here both plants are growing in a damp area near water. The iris will also grow in shallow water and in moisture-retentive borders. The alchemilla will thrive and produce large numbers of seedlings almost anywhere, though it will not grow in water or in permanently waterlogged soils.

16.11 Scrophularia & Persicaria

Scrophularia auriculata 'Variegata'

(syn *S. aquatica* 'Variegata')
(figwort, water betony)
sun/shade ○ ◖
type of plant hardy perennial
zonal range 5-9 (C-WT)
height 60-90cm (2-3ft)
special characteristics evergreen basal foliage, variegated foliage, suitable for damp and wet soils

Persicaria amplexicaulis 'Atrosanguinea'

(syn *Polygonum amplexicaule* 'Atrosanguineum')
(bistort)
sun/shade ○ ◖
type of plant hardy perennial
zonal range 5-9 (C-WT)
flowering time early summer to early autumn
flower colour deep red
height 90-120cm (3-4ft)
special characteristics suitable for damp soils

The bistort shown here has an exceptionally long flowering season. When its richly coloured flower spikes are combined with some paler, boldly variegated foliage, the result is a striking partnership that looks attractive for at least three months of the year. To keep the scrophularia tidy and its cream-variegated leaves in good condition, the plant's tiny brown flowers need to be pinched out. They are borne at the top of conspicuously dark, upright stems.

Both these plants thrive in rich soil that is moist or damp. The scrophularia may also be grown in wet, boggy ground near water. It produces particularly good quality foliage in a little shade. When well-suited, the bistort will quite rapidly form a large clump of big, weed-smothering leaves.

A similar combination of strong flower colour and decorative foliage can be produced earlier in the year by planting the crimson candelabra primula *P. pulverulenta* with variegated hostas. Damp soils are suitable for these plants, too.

For illustrations of the bistort's slim flower spikes with asters and with hydrangeas, see 1.5 and 3.24, respectively.

16.12 Iris & Lysichiton

Iris pseudacorus 'Variegata'

(yellow flag)
sun/shade ○ ◖
type of plant hardy perennial
zonal range 5-9 (C-WT)
flowering time early summer
flower colour yellow + brown
height 90cm (3ft)
special characteristics variegated foliage, suitable for damp and wet soils, suitable for water gardens

Lysichiton americanus

(bog arum)
sun/shade ○ ◖
type of plant hardy perennial
zonal range 7-9 (CT-WT)
flowering time early to mid-spring
flower colour yellow
height 30-45cm (12-18in); leaves 60-120cm (2-4ft) high after flowering
special characteristics decorative green foliage, suitable for damp and wet soils, suitable for water gardens

The bog arum's massive, veined foliage is regarded as a drawback by some gardeners, but it does lend big, bold shapes to bog or waterside plantings. It also provides an excellent background to the slender leaves of moisture-loving irises – as here – and the fronds of some ferns (see 16.8).

The spathes which precede these great, weed-suppressing leaves are pointed cowls of yellow. At very close range or if disturbed they have an unpleasant, musky smell and for this reason the plant is sometimes called yellow skunk cabbage. In this photograph the flowers of the iris are still in bud, in very early summer. After the flowers have faded, the leaf variegation of the plant gradually becomes less distinct. However, even when they are a uniform green, these narrow, very upright leaves look well beside the much broader foliage of the bog arum. Indeed, in informal settings, the plain foliage of *I. pseudacorus* itself (see 16.10) would look more appropriate with bog arums than the yellow-striped leaves of the form shown here.

Both the plants in this combination will grow in shallow water, as well as in wet or damp soil. Bog arum thrives in fertile soils. Established plants self-seed. The iris has generous seedpods and it too will self-seed, but the seedlings will usually be plain-leaved.

241

16.13 Iris & Caltha

Iris pseudacorus 'Variegata'
(yellow flag)
sun/shade ○ ◐
type of plant hardy perennial
zonal range 5-9 (C-WT)
flowering time early summer
flower colour yellow + brown
height 90cm (3ft)
special characteristics variegated foliage, suitable for damp and wet soils, suitable for water gardens

Caltha palustris
(marsh marigold, kingcup)
sun/shade ○ ◐
type of plant hardy perennial
zonal range 4-9 (C-WT)
flowering time mid- to late spring
flower colour rich yellow
height 23cm (9in)
special characteristics suitable for damp and wet soils, suitable for water gardens

As summer progresses, the yellow-striped leaves of this iris gradually lose their variegation (see 9.20 for the foliage in midsummer). Even when the leaves are completely green, however, this is an appealing conjunction of shapes. At all stages, the caltha's rounded foliage forms a pool of dark glossiness, like dimpled water, beneath the firm swordlike leaves of the iris. In spring and early summer, particularly when the caltha's bright, shiny flowers appear, this is a striking combination of yellows and greens. The iris's flowers are later replaced by large, fat seedpods, but any seedlings tend to have plain, green leaves.

Both these plants will grow in shallow water as well as boggy ground and damp borders. In rich mud the iris will be well over 90cm (3ft), but in a damp or ordinarily moisture-retentive soil it may only be 60cm (2ft) high.

Caltha palustris is a variable plant. Two of the more popular varieties are *C. p. alba*, which has yellow-centred white flowers, and *C. p.* 'Flore Pleno', which has tightly ruched, double, yellow flowers. The latter variety in particular would look attractive in this combination.

16.14 Persicaria & Alchemilla

Persicaria bistorta 'Superba'
(syn *Polygonum bistorta* 'Superbum')
(bistort)
sun/shade ○ ◐
type of plant hardy perennial
zonal range 4-8 (C-CT)
flowering time late spring to early summer and often late summer to early autumn
flower colour pink
height 75-90cm (2½-3ft)
special characteristics suitable for damp soils

Alchemilla mollis
(lady's mantle)
sun/shade ○ ◐
type of plant hardy perennial
zonal range 4-8 (C-CT/WT)
flowering time early to mid-summer
flower colour yellow-green
height 45cm (18in)
special characteristics decorative green foliage, suitable for damp soils

Although the combination of pink and yellow makes some gardeners wince, pink and yellowish green is nearly always an appealing association of colours. In this particular pairing, the shapes as well as the colours of the flowers look good together. *Alchemilla mollis* produces a pretty froth of flowers which becomes wider and looser as the summer progresses (the plant is shown here in early summer). In contrast, the bistort's pink pokers are dense and conspicuously upright.

Both these plants are vigorous and adaptable. The alchemilla will grow well – and produce numerous seedlings – in almost any soil that is not waterlogged. The bistort prospers in all moisture-retentive soils, including heavy clay. It will create an especially large clump of weed-suppressing foliage and be most floriferous in damp places. The alchemilla's velvety, scalloped leaves also make dense and efficient ground cover. Compared with the bistort's somewhat coarse greenery, however, these leaves are dainty and poised.

If the alchemilla starts to look shabby and untidy after its main flowering period, the whole plant may be rejuvenated by being cut right back. This treatment usually results in a small second crop of flowers as well as plenty of fresh foliage.

16.15 Astilbe & Hosta

Astilbe × arendsii 'Federsee'
(false goat's beard)
sun/shade ○ ◐
type of plant hardy perennial
zonal range 4-8 (C-CT)
flowering time mid- to late summer
flower colour deep pink-crimson
height 60cm (2ft)
special characteristics bronze young foliage, decorative green foliage, suitable for damp soils

Hosta plantaginea
(plantain lily)
sun/shade ○ ◐
type of plant hardy perennial
zonal range 3-9 (C-WT)
flowering time late summer to early autumn
flower colour white
height 60cm (2ft)
special characteristics decorative green foliage, fragrant flowers, suitable for damp soils

The numerous astilbe hybrids are popular plants for moisture-retentive and damp ground. The bright, glowing crimson of the variety shown here has been sharpened still further by being placed next to leaves of a tangy, light yellow-green.

As well as a piquant partnership of colours, this combination features some interesting contrasts in texture and form. The photograph shows the plants in midsummer, when the dense fluffiness of the astilbe's very upright flowerheads contrasts strongly with the relatively open, smooth shapes of the hosta's almost horizontally held leaves. Even the two sets of foliage look interesting together, the little leaflets of the astilbe creating a darker and much closer-textured mass of greenery than the hosta's big, bold, light green leaves. As an added attraction, the young leaves of this vigorous astilbe are attractively bronze-tinged. There are also long-lasting, russet seedheads.

In the rich, really moist soils that suit these two plants best, both the astilbe and the hosta will form dense and very substantial clumps of growth. In drier conditions both plants perform best if given a cool, shaded position.

The hosta's display of lovely, sweetly scented trumpets is rather undependable. A warm, sheltered site makes flowering much more likely.

16.16 Euphorbia & Hosta

Euphorbia sikkimensis
(spurge)
sun/shade ○ ◐
type of plant hardy perennial
zonal range 6-9 (C-WT)
flowering time mid- to late summer
flower colour yellow-green
height 1.2-1.5m (4-5ft)
special characteristics red young foliage, suitable for damp soils

Hosta fortunei
(plantain lily)
sun/shade ◐
type of plant hardy perennial
zonal range 3-9 (C-WT)
flowering time midsummer
flower colour pale lilac
height 60-75cm (2-2½ft)
special characteristics decorative green foliage, suitable for damp soils

Many spurges are plants for dry, sunny places, but some of the larger species and varieties revel in rich, damp soil and may spread widely in such conditions. Where its vigour and height can be accommodated, *Euphorbia sikkimensis* forms an impressive series of upright stems with slender leaves and open flowerheads. It is at its most striking, however, in early spring, when its new shoots emerge a bright pink-crimson. The photograph shows the plant in late spring when it is still a remarkable colour, although its shoots are lengthening and becoming much greener.

The slenderness and rich green of the leaves are enhanced here by the broad, veined foliage of a hosta which, at this stage, is still fairly upright and a lovely, fresh green. (The name *Hosta fortunei* covers a number of different forms, the leaf colour of which varies from soft, glaucous green to rich green.) As the summer progresses, the hosta forms a dense clump of almost horizontally held growth. This contrasts conspicuously with the slim, upright stems of the euphorbia. The hosta's flowers are held well above its foliage and consist of spires of small, pale trumpets.

Like the euphorbia, the hosta enjoys damp, fertile soils. In ordinary, moisture-retentive soils the two plants' general growth will be less luxuriant.

243

16.17 Matteuccia & Darmera

Matteuccia struthiopteris

(ostrich feather fern, shuttlecock fern)

sun/shade ◖
type of plant hardy fern
zonal range 2-8 (C-CT)
height 90-120cm (3-4ft)
special characteristics decorative green foliage, suitable for damp and wet soils

Darmera peltata

(syn *Peltiphyllum peltatum*)
(umbrella plant)

sun/shade ○ ◖
type of plant hardy perennial
zonal range 5-9 (C-WT/CT)
flowering time mid-spring
flower colour pink
height 60-90cm (2-3ft)
special characteristics decorative green foliage, suitable for damp and wet soils

The lush leafiness of water- and bog-garden plants is one of their great attractions, and many of these plants lend themselves to the sort of striking combination shown here. Both this fern, with its upright, spraying fronds, and the umbrella plant with its great, crinkled, scalloped discs of rich green are large-scale, dramatic plants. They combine to produce interesting contrasts in texture, shape and overall habit of growth.

The darmera's rounded flowerheads appear before its foliage and are a curious, bare-stemmed sight. Individual leaves of the plant can be over 30cm (12in) wide. In moist soils and full sun the foliage sometimes turns a brilliant red in autumn. The leaves make a good background not only for feathery ferns but also for the flowers of many moisture-loving primulas. In winter the fern's own 'flowers' or inner, fertile fronds are visible and though they are dark and withered they are decorative.

Both plants must have moisture and, although the darmera can tolerate some sun, a partially shaded site is best for this combination since the fern needs shelter and some shade. Where space is fairly limited, the darmera is a useful substitute for the huge-leaved *Gunnera manicata* (see 16.4). However, both plants are vigorous and can become invasive.

16.18 Hosta & Ranunculus

Hosta crispula

(plantain lily)

sun/shade ◖
type of plant hardy perennial
zonal range 3-9 (C-WT)
flowering time early to mid-summer
flower colour pale lavender
height 75-90cm (2½-3ft)
special characteristics variegated foliage, suitable for damp soils

Ranunculus aconitifolius

(bachelor's buttons)

sun/shade ○ ◖
type of plant hardy perennial
zonal range 5-8 (C-CT)
flowering time late spring to early summer
flower colour white
height 60-75cm (2-2½ft)
special characteristics suitable for damp soils

All hostas appreciate moist growing conditions, and the variegated forms in particular make very decorative, bold-leaved additions to plantings in damp areas. Here the white margins on the broad, elegantly pointed, wavy-edged leaves of *Hosta crispula* are most attractively echoed in the pretty sprinkling of neat white flowers produced by *Ranunculus aconitifolius*. The ranunculus also likes moisture-retentive and damp soils. Even after its branching flowerheads have faded, its clump of dark green, lobed leaves continues to look well with the larger-scale foliage and the white markings of the hosta.

If the hosta is not to end up looking rather battered after its tall stems of trumpet-shaped flowers have faded, it must have a position that is both shaded and sheltered. In ideal conditions, it slowly makes a dense mass of gracefully poised leaves about 60cm (2ft) high.

Gardeners who like double-flowered plants might like to substitute the more formal *Ranunculus aconitifolius* 'Flore Pleno' for the species in this combination. The double-flowered form has flowers that are especially long-lasting and make good cut material.

For other combinations suitable for damp soils, see:
HOT-COLOURED FLOWERS 3.26 PURPLE FOLIAGE 4.24 YELLOW FOLIAGE 6.12, 6.19 DECORATIVE GREEN FOLIAGE 8.16 VARIEGATED FOLIAGE 9.23 GRASSES AND FERNS 17.11

16.19 Athyrium & Hosta

Athyrium filix-femina
(lady fern)
sun/shade ◖
type of plant hardy fern
zonal range 4-9 (C-WT)
height 75cm (2½ft)
special characteristics decorative green foliage, suitable for damp soils

Hosta sieboldiana var. *elegans*
(plantain lily)
sun/shade ◖
type of plant hardy perennial
zonal range 3-9 (C-WT)
flowering time early to mid-summer
flower colour palest lilac
height 75-90cm (2½-3ft)
special characteristics blue-grey foliage, suitable for damp soils

Hostas and ferns nearly always look good together, principally because of the strong contrast between large, broad leaves and much-divided fronds. In the planting shown here there is also a mutually enhancing colour combination of a very fresh, rather yellowish green and a beautiful blue-grey. This combination has the effect of making the great ribbed and puckered leaves of *H. sieboldiana elegans* seem especially blue and the lacy fronds of the lady fern look almost lime-green.

The photograph shows the plants at the beginning of summer, a couple of weeks before the hosta's dense flowerheads open out. These are carried just above the solid clump of leaves. Later the flowers form attractive seedheads and the foliage briefly turns a buttery yellow before it dies.

Both of these plants thrive in damp places and look handsome beside water. In really moist soils that never dry out in summer they can be grown in sun as well as in light shade. However, the attractive bloom on the hosta's leaves will be less long-lasting in sun and the foliage will be less blue. Similarly, the erect and then arching fronds of this particularly pretty fern will not be quite as fresh and green for as long when the plant is grown in a sunny place. In rich, moist soils, this hosta often produces individual leaves as much as 30cm (12in) wide.

16.20 Geranium & Hosta

Geranium phaeum
(mourning widow, cranesbill)
sun/shade ◖
type of plant hardy perennial
zonal range 4-8 (C-WT)
flowering time late spring to early summer
flower colour dark purple
height 60-75cm (2-2½ft)
special characteristics semi-evergreen, decorative green foliage, suitable for damp soils

Hosta undulata var. *albomarginata*
(syn *H.* 'Thomas Hogg')
(plantain lily)
sun/shade ◖
type of plant hardy perennial
zonal range 3-9 (C-WT)
flowering time early to mid-summer
flower colour pale lilac
height 60-90cm (2-3ft)
special characteristics variegated foliage, suitable for damp soils

Hosta undulata albomarginata is one of the most popular and readily available of all hostas, and its versatility at combining flatteringly with many other plants is demonstrated by the number of times it appears in this book. Here the clean white edges of its foliage are enlivening the charming, very dark flowers of *Geranium phaeum*.

Apart from its distinguishing variegation, the hosta's bold leaves are also fairly slender, with smooth edges and pointed tips. The geranium's mass of lobed and veined greenery has much rounder outlines and the overall effect is light and airy. The photograph shows the plants in very early summer, shortly before the hosta's pale trumpet flowers appear on tall stalks above the plant's clump of foliage.

The hosta is a plant that grows especially well in damp soils, conditions that also suit the geranium. With moisture and a cool site both plants here will produce generous quantities of foliage.

The geranium self-seeds. The seedlings often vary in colour. There is, for example, a white-flowered variety, *Geranium phaeum* 'Album', which would look attractive combined with this or some other white-variegated hosta.

245

Grasses and ferns are two distinct, easily recognizable groups of plants. Grasses we associate with wide, open spaces, with airy freedom and sunshine; ferns seem plants of cool, shaded seclusion. The difference in planting requirements is not in reality so marked, as there are grasses for shady places and ferns that will readily adapt themselves to dry conditions and some sunshine.

Though the smooth curves of grass leaves and the filigree patterns of fern fronds seem so different, the repetition of restrained and elegant shapes is a striking characteristic that both grasses and ferns have in common. In both cases, these repeated lines ensure that the plants always contrast well with other genera. The repetition also gives a very natural look to grasses and ferns and this allows them to harmonize beautifully with a wide range of plants of all types.

The natural, flowing forms of most grasses seem particularly appropriate in the ecologically based plantings of matrix or prairie gardening. Grasses, along with large perennials, strike just the right note of graceful informality in these naturalistic plantings. However, such is the range of size, colour and texture among ornamental grasses, and the diversity in their habits of growth, that these plants have all sorts of different uses. There are, for instance, tall, plain green grasses, such as the various forms of *Miscanthus sinensis* and many bamboos (see, for example, 17.11). These imposing, often quite broad-leaved and lush-looking plants can act as calm counterpoints to strident colours.

COLOURED-LEAF GRASSES

Stiffly shaped or very brightly coloured grasses look more formal and more self-consciously decorative. Cultivars of *Festuca glauca*, for example, usually have narrow leaves of an intense blue-grey (see 2.1), often arranged in stiff, spiky clumps. *Deschampsia flexuosa* 'Tatra Gold', a very bright, yellow-green grass, is paired in 17.9 with *Ophiopogon planiscapus* 'Nigrescens', a grass-like plant with leaves that are almost black. There are also grasses with red- or purple-tinged leaves, and the ginger and russet tones of many species and forms of *Carex* (see 17.5) are particularly attractive. (Plants in the genus *Carex* are, strictly speaking, sedges and not grasses, but they are very similar to grasses in general appearance.) The range of variegated grasses is considerable. As with other variegated plants, the extra colour in variegated grasses can be used to echo similar colours in nearby leaves and flowers.

Whatever their colour, most grasses produce leaves of a predominantly fluid shape. This fluidity of form is combined with a highly attractive, mobile quality. Grasses shift and whisper, flutter and rustle in the breeze, making sounds as soothing as flowing water. Because they move so readily, grasses contrast very satisfactorily with less pliant, more static plants such as sedums (see 17.3), bergenias (see 8.2) and many conifers, and they also look well beside the hard surfaces of walls and paths. They also associate beautifully with expanses of water. Sedges – plants in the genera *Carex* and *Cyperus* – are particularly useful for planting in damp or wet ground or in shallow water.

FLOWERING GRASSES

Many grasses are very striking, flowering plants. Among the taller flowering grasses are the various forms of pampas grass (*Cortaderia*),

with their huge, silvery plumes, varieties of feathery-flowered *Miscanthus sinensis* and *Stipa gigantea* (see 17.2) with its glorious, glistening haze of oat-like seeds. Smaller flowering grasses include *Pennisetum orientale* (see 17.3) and *Milium effusum* 'Aureum' (see 17.12).

The flowers and subsequent seedheads of many grasses are at their very best at the end of summer and during autumn. Even when their flowers have faded and their seedheads have disintegrated, many grasses have considerable winter presence. Those that do not retain their leaf colour in the coldest months often turn beautiful shades of parchment, ivory and almond at this time (see 17.1). In addition, there are some grasses that turn warm shades of yellow, orange and red in autumn.

As well as being beautiful, grasses require very little maintenance; they are more or less completely pest- and disease-free and they often make good ground cover. However, it should be noted that running grasses can be invasive; clump-forming types may be considered less risky for the border.

FERNS

Ferns share grasses' ease of cultivation, but their colour range is more restricted and restrained. Although the primeval-looking fronds of some ferns can be tinged with pink or purple as they unfurl, and some ferns – notably *Osmunda regalis* (see 16.8) – are attractively coloured in autumn, almost all ferns are green. However, the particular shade of green varies considerably: there are bright greens, rich, dark greens and greens of muted, olive tones. All of these can be combined interestingly with the colours of other plants. One beautiful fern, *Athyrium niponicum pictum*, has maroon-tinged grey leaves (see 2.29).

Many ferns have the very finely divided, lacy foliage that contrasts wonderfully with the big, broad leaves of plants such as hostas (see 16.19) and bog arums (see 16.8). However, the regular, almost symmetrical habit of growth of many ferns makes them very striking plants, and this boldness in overall shape means they also look good with plants with quite finely textured foliage (see 17.15).

Some species of fern have varieties with fronds that are crested, closely curled or particularly finely divided. These extra intricacies introduce a striking density to the foliage (see 17.17 and 17.19). In contrast, the distinctive, undivided fronds of the hart's tongue fern are like rippled ribbons (see 5.18).

Despite their being associated mainly with cool, shaded places, there are ferns which are suitable for planting in sunshine. Some of these plants, such as those in the genera *Matteuccia* and *Osmunda*, will thrive in sun only if they are grown in really moist soils. A few ferns can adapt themselves to sunny conditions by becoming smaller and growing less lushly, and some will prosper in dry, shaded places. *Dryopteris filix-mas* (see 3.30 and 17.15) is outstanding in this respect, but *Polypodium vulgare* and *Polystichum setiferum* are almost as useful.

Ferns are plants of intriguing character: they appear simultaneously to be primitive and sophisticated, dainty and sumptuous. Because they have these seemingly contradictory qualities, ferns make good partners for a wide range of other plants but, at the same time, their understated beauty is rarely eclipsed.

17.1 Prunus & Helictotrichon

Prunus serrula
(ornamental cherry)
sun/shade ○
type of plant hardy tree
zonal range 5-8 (C-CT)
flowering time mid- to late spring
flower colour white
height 6-7.5m (20-25ft)
special characteristics fruit, ornamental bark
and twigs

Helictotrichon sempervirens
(syn *Avena candida*)
(blue oat grass)
sun/shade ○
type of plant hardy perennial (grass)
zonal range 4-9 (C-WT)
flowering time early to mid-summer
flower colour pale, blue-tinged yellow
height 90-120cm (3-4ft)
special characteristics evergreen, blue-grey
foliage

The gleaming, polished bark and peeling twigs of *Prunus serrula* can be spectacular features of winter gardens. However, the plant needs careful positioning to be seen at its best; it looks most conspicuous if it is placed where it will be lit by winter sunshine and where it has a contrasting background.

Here, in a Scottish garden in midwinter, the foliage of the blue oat grass has faded to a gentle flaxen colour. This creates an appropriately low-key, finely textured winter back-drop for the rich colouring and sleek appearance of the prunus. In spring and summer the leaves of the grass are an intense, chalky blue-grey of similar colouring to *Festuca glauca* and its forms (see 2.1). The combination then consists of an altogether more vibrant contrast of blue and almost-red.

The slender-stemmed flower panicles of the grass are carried well above the plant's tussocks of foliage. These tussocks are approximately 30-45cm (12-18in) high. The clustered, open-faced flowers of this wide-spreading, slim-leaved prunus are regularly followed, in late summer, by shiny, bright red fruits.

Both these plants will be happy on most well-drained soils. They both do well in alkaline conditions.

17.2 Stipa & Anemone

Stipa gigantea
(giant feather grass, golden oats)
sun/shade ○
type of plant hardy perennial (grass)
zonal range 5-10 (C-WT)
flowering time early to late summer
flower colour purplish turning to golden yellow
height 1.8-2.4m (6-8ft)
special characteristics evergreen/semi-evergreen

Anemone × hybrida 'Königin Charlotte'
(syn *A.* × *h.* 'Queen Charlotte', *A. japonica* 'Königin Charlotte', *A. j.* 'Queen Charlotte')
(Japanese anemone)
sun/shade ○ ◑
type of plant hardy perennial
zonal range 5-8 (C-WT)
flowering time late summer to mid-autumn
flower colour pink
height 75-90cm (2½-3ft)

Such is the stature of this impressively tall, erect-stemmed grass that it is often planted as a solitary specimen. However, the addition of another, carefully chosen, late-season plant can emphasize many of its good points. Here, in early autumn, the more or less circular flowers of a Japanese anemone highlight the grass's haze of oat-like seedheads, and at the same time the soft pink colouring of these flowers increases the general air of mellow ripeness exuded by the grass. Even the lobed leaves of the anemone make an important contribution to the success of this partnership, providing the grass's airy flower sprays – which tremble in the slightest breeze – with a thick, dark, anchoring clump of foliage. The grass's own slender, rather lax foliage forms a not particularly decorative but weed-proof mass about 60cm (2ft) high.

Medium or fairly light, well-drained soils suit *Stipa gigantea* best. The anemone is an adaptable plant which is particularly vigorous in heavy soils; it will, however, do well in most soils, as long as they are moisture-retentive. Some forms of this particular variety of Japanese anemone have more sepals than the specimen illustrated here and are semi-double in appearance. The seedheads of the grass remain attractive in the garden well into winter. They also make good dried material for use indoors.

17.3 **Sedum & Pennisetum**

Sedum 'Ruby Glow'

(stonecrop)
sun/shade ○
type of plant hardy perennial
zonal range 4-8 (C-WT)
flowering time late summer to early autumn
flower colour crimson
height 20-25cm (8-10in)
special characteristics blue-grey foliage

Pennisetum orientale

sun/shade ○
type of plant hardy perennial (grass)
zonal range 6-9 (C-WT)
flowering time midsummer to early autumn
flower colour purplish changing to mauve-grey
height 45cm (18in)

Here, in the middle of summer, the slender, subtly coloured flower spikes of *Pennisetum orientale* arch elegantly over the much more thickset growths of *Sedum* 'Ruby Glow'. The partnership is, perhaps, particularly appealing at this stage, since the as yet unopened flowerheads of the sedum are beautifully soft in colour. This colouring marries very successfully with the elusive greys and mauves of the grass. However, when the sedum flowers do open out into 10cm (4in) clusters of wine-red, their density and rich colour contrast strikingly with the paleness and slimness of the grass flowers. These soft, hairy bottle-brushes make good material for flower arrangements. They can be used both fresh and also dried, when they are a greyish buff colour.

As well as a very attractive association of colours, there are several differences in foliage texture and in habit of growth which make this combination so successful. The sedum's lax red stems are covered with succulent leaves of a dusky, purple-tinged blue-grey, while the long, thin foliage of the grass forms a thick tussock of much lighter green.

Well-drained, rather light soils suit both these plants. The grass lives longest and flowers most profusely in warm, sheltered places. However, in warm climates, its numerous seedlings can be a nuisance.

17.4 **Carex & Mentha**

Carex hachijoensis 'Evergold'

(syn *C. oshimensis* 'Evergold')
(sedge)
sun/shade ○ ◑
type of plant hardy perennial (grass)
zonal range 7-9 (CT-WT)
height 30cm (12in)
special characteristics evergreen, variegated foliage

Mentha × gracilis 'Variegata'

(syn *M. × g.* 'Aurea', *M. × gentilis* 'Variegata', *M. × g.* 'Aurea')
(ginger mint)
sun/shade ○
type of plant hardy perennial (herb)
zonal range 4-9 (C-WT)
flowering time midsummer to early autumn
flower colour lilac
height 30-45cm (12-18in)
special characteristics aromatic, variegated foliage

This intriguing piece of co-ordination involves two variegated plants which match in colour but differ in all other respects. Both plants have yellow and green foliage, but the mint's little pointed ovals are a breezy, cheerful mixture of acid yellow stripes and splashes on a bright green base, whereas the long, slender leaves of the sedge have a more elegant and orderly pattern of yellow central stripes and green margins.

These differences in leaf shape and variegation are given further emphasis by the contrasting habits of growth of the two plants. The jaunty variegation and bright colours of the mint leaves appear jauntier still when punctuated by conspicuous, dark red, upright stems, and the sedge's neat, symmetrical clump of arching growth adds extra, airy elegance to an already graceful plant.

The mint's modest little flowers, visible here in early autumn, do not make much impact, and the same is true of the sedge's brown spikes, which appear in spring. The mint, however, does have foliage which is freshly aromatic with distinct, gingery undertones.

Both these plants like a fertile, well-drained soil that remains moist throughout the growing season. In these conditions the mint is likely to spread vigorously.

17.5 Carex & Stachys

Carex comans Bronze Form

(sedge)
sun/shade ○ ◑
type of plant hardy perennial (grass)
zonal range 6-9 (C-WT)
height 30cm (12in)
special characteristics evergreen, bronze foliage

Stachys byzantina 'Primrose Heron'

(syn *S. lanata* 'Primrose Heron', *S. olympica* 'Primrose Heron')
(lamb's tongue, lamb's ear, lamb's lug)
sun/shade ○
type of plant hardy perennial
zonal range 4-9 (C-WT)
flowering time mid- to late summer
flower colour mauve-pink
height 23-30cm (9-12in)
special characteristics evergreen, yellow-grey foliage

The cinnamon tones and very fine, almost hair-like leaves of some of the sedges bring distinctive colour and texture to plantings. The unusual colouring associates particularly well with orange flowers. It also looks good with blue-leaved plants, and the combination illustrated here shows how grey leaves too can look striking with this pale, red-brown foliage. The greyness of *Stachys byzantina* 'Primrose Heron' is suffused with a light greenish-yellow which is particularly marked in spring (see 5.12). This yellowness blends most attractively with the sedge's warm brown.

Much of the success of this combination is due to marked contrasts in leaf shape and texture as well as a pleasing association of colour. The broad, simple ovals of these lamb's tongue leaves have a beautifully soft, dense covering of hairs. This covering extends over the erect flowering stems, too, so that the overall impression is one of pale woolliness coupled with bold foliage and fairly upright shapes. The sedge's thick, symmetrical tussock of fine, arching foliage looks and feels completely different.

As long as they are not too dry, most soils with reasonable drainage will suit the sedge. The lamb's tongue is particularly at home in light, well-drained soils, where its mats of foliage will be especially dense.

17.6 Acanthus & Carex

Acanthus mollis

(bear's breeches)
sun/shade ○ ◑
type of plant hardy perennial
zonal range 7-10 (C-WT)
flowering time mid- to late summer
flower colour mauve-purple + white
height 1.2-1.35m (4-4½ft)
special characteristics semi-evergreen, decorative green foliage

Carex hachijoensis 'Evergold'

(syn *C. oshimensis* 'Evergold')
(sedge)
sun/shade ○ ◑
type of plant hardy perennial (grass)
zonal range 7-9 (CT-WT)
height 30cm (12in)
special characteristics evergreen, variegated foliage

Slim-leaved grasses and sedges look beautifully fine-textured beside big, bold leaves. In the combination illustrated here, a neat fountain of light, creamy yellow-and-green foliage sprays out beneath thrusting shapes of deep, glossy olive. These two striking plants continue to show each other to mutual advantage almost all year long. In mild areas the acanthus's great clump of long, lobed leaves is virtually evergreen, and although the sedge can look weary at the end of winter it is very colourful at other times.

Leaves rather than flowers are the principal and most reliable attraction here. The sedge's little springtime spikes of brown are not very decorative, and the acanthus is rather shy-flowering in the northern hemisphere, except in warm, sheltered places or at the end of hot summers. However, when the tall spires of hooded, prickly flowers do appear, they make an impressive sight.

These two plants thrive in moist, fertile soils with good drainage. The sedge is not suitable for dry places. The acanthus is a vigorous plant which, once established, will spread and self-seed in a wide range of soils. Young plants benefit from some winter protection in cold districts.

This variegated sedge mixes well with other plants of yellow colouring (see 17.4).

17.7 Phalaris & Geranium

Phalaris arundinacea var. *picta* 'Picta'

(syn *P. a.* 'Elegantissima')
(gardener's garters, ribbon grass)
sun/shade ○ ◑
type of plant hardy perennial (grass)
zonal range 4-9 (C-WT)
flowering time early to mid-summer
flower colour cream
height 90cm (3ft)
special characteristics variegated foliage, suitable for damp soils

Geranium 'Johnson's Blue'

(cranesbill)
sun/shade ○ ◑
type of plant hardy perennial
zonal range 4-8 (C-WT)
flowering time early to mid-summer
flower colour clear blue
height 45cm (18in)
special characteristics decorative green foliage

In spring and early summer the white-striped leaves of this grass are irresistibly crisp and smart, and at this point in the year it is easy to forgive the plant its invasive ways. As the slim flower-heads mature the foliage becomes duller in colouring, but cutting back the older leaves will encourage freshly striped new growth to appear. Combined with geranium flowers of an exceptionally clear blue, it creates an early summer picture of beguiling, pristine coolness.

The simply shaped flowers of *Geranium* 'Johnson's Blue' open in succession over a period of several weeks. The leaves of the plant are pretty and deeply divided, and the slightly lax-stemmed clump of plain, green foliage contrasts attractively with the grass's dense mass of arching stripes. Like the grass, the geranium responds well to having its older growths cut back after flowering.

In rich, damp soils the running roots of gardener's garters will spread rapidly and widely. Even in the well-drained, moisture-retentive conditions suitable for this geranium, it will be very vigorous.

A good, less energetic substitute for gardener's garters in this combination would be *Miscanthus sinensis* 'Variegatus' (zones 5-10/C-WT/ST). Its foliage is about 1.2m (4ft) high, whereas the leaves of gardener's garters are about 60cm (2ft).

17.8 Tellima & Molinia

Tellima grandiflora Rubra Group

(syn *T. g.* 'Purpurea')
sun/shade ○ ◑
type of plant hardy perennial
zonal range 4-9 (C-WT)
flowering time late spring to early summer
flower colour green + purple-pink
height 45-60cm (1½-2ft)
special characteristics evergreen, decorative green foliage, autumn/winter foliage

Molinia caerulea ssp. *caerulea* 'Variegata'

(purple moor grass)
sun/shade ○ ◑
type of plant hardy perennial (grass)
zonal range 5-9 (C-WT)
flowering time late summer to early autumn
flower colour purplish
height 60cm (2ft)
special characteristics variegated foliage

One way of highlighting the slender leaves and the graceful, arching habit of many grasses is to plant them beside thick clumps or carpets of rounder leaves. In this combination, the steady, almost circular shapes of plain green which accompany this variegated grass make it seem especially slim-leaved, elegant and airy.

Edged very precisely in cream, these leaves are at first held erect but subsequently arch outwards from the dense centre of the plant. The veined and scalloped foliage of the tellima also grows thickly but the overall effect is much less finely textured.

In the last weeks of summer the tellima's leaves become tinged with pinkish-bronze (see 8.12). The winter foliage is a conspicuous purple-maroon. In autumn and winter the grass also changes colour, its leaves drying to a beautiful mixture of yellows and warm beiges. During autumn the seedheads of the grass, which are carried well above the 30cm (12in) clump of striped foliage, are a lovely straw colour. The tellima's dark-stemmed wands of flowers (see 7.14) appear much earlier in the year.

Moist, preferably acid soils suit the molinia best. The tellima is an adaptable, self-seeding, spreading plant that is happy in a wide range of soils and sites, including dry shade.

17.9 Ophiopogon & Deschampsia

Ophiopogon planiscapus 'Nigrescens'

sun/shade ○ ◐
type of plant hardy perennial
zonal range 6-10 (C-ST)
flowering time mid- to late summer
flower colour pale pink-mauve
height 15cm (6in)
special characteristics evergreen, purple foliage, fruit

Deschampsia flexuosa 'Tatra Gold'

(wavy hair grass)
sun/shade ○ ◐
type of plant hardy perennial (grass)
zonal range 4-9 (C-WT)
flowering time early to mid-summer
flower colour purplish-bronze
height 45cm (18in)
special characteristics evergreen, yellow-green foliage

For really startling contrasts in colour and texture this combination takes some beating. Setting brilliant, yellow-green bristles in front of heaps of almost sinister-looking, dark purple leaves shows both sets of foliage to advantage. With a strongly contrasting partner, the deschampsia looks dazzlingly exuberant and both its acidic colouring and the thinness of its leaves are emphasized fully. At the same time, the ophiopogon is made to seem especially dark and strange.

The sleek, arching foliage of the ophiopogon changes little during the year. The grass is yellowest in spring. As the leaves lengthen, the grass's habit of growth becomes more arching.

This photograph shows the grass in late spring, when its developing flower spikes are just visible. In summer these spikes open wide into glinting, bronzed panicles carried well above the 15cm (6in) tufts of foliage. This haze of gentle colour brings a quite different texture and colour to the combination. The ophiopogon's little clusters of bell-shaped blooms nestle among the dark leaves and are followed by long-lasting, black berries.

Deschampsia flexuosa and its forms like moisture-retentive, preferably acid soils. A good supply of moisture will also ensure that the ophiopogon forms a thick, ground-covering carpet.

17.10 Holcus & Ajuga

Holcus mollis 'Albovariegatus'

sun/shade ○ ◐
type of plant hardy perennial (grass)
zonal range 5-9 (C-WT)
height 15-23cm (6-9in)
special characteristics evergreen, variegated foliage

Ajuga reptans 'Atropurpurea'

(bugle)
sun/shade ○ ◐
type of plant hardy perennial
zonal range 3-9 (C-WT)
flowering time late spring to early summer
flower colour deep blue
height 15-20cm (6-8in)
special characteristics evergreen/semi-evergreen, purple foliage

Like gardener's garters (see 17.7), the grass shown here has running roots that can spread very widely, but it too is so freshly and cleanly variegated that its charms are difficult to resist. Each of the erect, velvety leaves has a thin, central stripe of green and broader margins of palest cream. From a distance, a patch of this creeping, mat-forming grass looks like a small white lawn.

Such close-textured paleness is especially striking when combined with dark foliage, and here it is accompanied by contrastingly broad, blunt-nosed leaves of a splendidly deep, rich purple. *Ajuga reptans* 'Atropurpurea' is another vigorous plant, especially in moist, fertile soils, and it is therefore unlikely to be overwhelmed by the grass.

In addition to its glossy carpet of foliage, the bugle produces erect spikes of bright blue flowers (see 5.8). These look clear and fresh with the crisply striped grass. The greenish summer flowers of the grass are best removed by light clipping.

For good, dense, ground-covering growth, this combination of plants needs a moisture-retentive but well-drained soil.

For a photograph of a grass similar in size and colouring to *Holcus mollis*, but without its invasive roots, see 17.14.

17.11 Fargesia & Hosta

Fargesia murieliae
(syn *Arundinaria murieliae, Sinarundinaria murieliae*)
(umbrella bamboo)
sun/shade ○ ◐
type of plant hardy perennial (bamboo)
zonal range 6-11 (C-ST)
height 2.4-3.6m (8-12ft)
special characteristics evergreen, decorative green foliage, ornamental canes, suitable for damp soils

Hosta 'Halcyon'
(Tardiana Group)
(syn *H.* 'Holstein')
(plantain lily)
sun/shade ◐
type of plant hardy perennial
zonal range 3-9 (C-WT)
flowering time mid- to late summer
flower colour greyish lilac-mauve
height 45cm (18in)
special characteristics blue-grey foliage, suitable for damp soils

Many grasses, and especially the bamboos, bring the alluring qualities of movement and sound to gardens. The umbrella bamboo's masses of elegantly slim and pointed leaves shift gently and rustle soothingly in the slightest breeze. Here the arching stems and the graceful, airy greenery of this bamboo have been contrasted with a much lower, steadier clump of broad, almost horizontally held foliage. This sturdy clump is not stolidly coloured, however, and the combination of striking blue-grey foliage and bright, light green bamboo leaves makes this pair of plants look remarkably cool and fresh.

The hosta's flowers are pale and carried not far above the foliage, but they are dense and therefore conspicuous. This non-invasive bamboo rarely flowers, but its canes are very decorative. At first they are bright yellow-green, in maturity becoming yellow or yellow-banded.

Ideally, this combination should be planted in a sheltered, lightly shaded place. However, *Fargesia murieliae* is more tolerant of sun and wind than many bamboos, and particularly so if it is given a damp soil. The hosta's leaf colour is bluest in shade; in a sunny site it should be planted on the shaded side of the bamboo. The hosta too appreciates a reliable supply of moisture.

17.12 Milium & Buxus

Milium effusum 'Aureum'
(Bowles' golden grass)
sun/shade ◐
type of plant hardy perennial (grass)
zonal range 5-8 (C-CT)
flowering time late spring to midsummer
flower colour yellow
height 60-75cm (2-2½ft)
special characteristics semi-evergreen, yellow-green foliage

Buxus sempervirens
'Aureovariegata'
(syn *B. s.* 'Aurea Maculata')
(box)
sun/shade ○ ◐
type of plant hardy shrub
zonal range 7-8 (CT-WT)
height 2.4-3m (8-10ft)
special characteristics evergreen, variegated foliage, fragrant flowers

The bright, tangy yellow of Bowles' golden grass is exhilarating with other intense colours (see the following combination), but it also combines very successfully with darker, more sombre foliage and flowers. In this instance, the broad, arching blades of this self-seeding grass have been positioned beside dense, bushy masses of glossy, leathery foliage. Each of these little rounded leaves – so different in shape and texture from the blades of the grass – is basically a rich, dark green. Overlaying this green are soft, irregular streakings of creamy yellow. This variegation is fairly low-key, but it is given much greater emphasis here by the yellow foliage of the grass. This is true even in summer, when the grass is lime-green. For its part, the weightier foliage of this slow-growing, variegated box creates an excellent background for the grass's floaty foliage and its airy, yellow-stemmed sprays of tiny flowers. The spring flowers of the box are very small, but they are sweetly scented.

Buxus sempervirens and its forms are easily grown in any well-drained soil. They thrive in alkaline conditions. Bowles' golden grass requires good drainage too but, in its case, the soil must be moisture-retentive as well. Both these plants can be grown in sunny sites, but the grass will only prosper in sun if the soil is permanently moist.

253

17.13 Milium & Pulmonaria

Milium effusum 'Aureum'
(Bowles' golden grass)
sun/shade ◖
type of plant hardy perennial (grass)
zonal range 5-8 (C-CT)
flowering time late spring to midsummer
flower colour yellow
height 60-75cm (2-2½ft)
special characteristics semi-evergreen, yellow-green foliage

Pulmonaria angustifolia 'Munstead Blue'
(blue cowslip or lungwort)
sun/shade ◖
type of plant hardy perennial
zonal range 3-8 (C-CT)
flowering time early to mid-spring
flower colour bright blue
height 15-23cm (6-9in)

The clear blue of these lungwort flowers sings out in early spring. Coupled with the brilliant yellow leaves of Bowles' golden grass, it seems particularly bright and pure. When the little flower sprays have faded, the lungwort's clumps of rich green foliage provide just the right sort of plain, smooth, rather restrained shapes that show the grass to advantage. Though Bowles' golden grass is yellowest in spring, the tufts of broad, arching blades are a striking, pale lime-green from midsummer onwards. When the plant has fully expanded, the foliage is usually about 30cm (12in) high. The wispy flowerheads are carried well above the leaves (see 17.12).

In the cool, moisture-retentive, humus-rich soils they are happiest in, both these plants will grow densely and provide good ground cover. Both will also self-seed. For another springtime combination using *Milium effusum* 'Aureum', see 5.9.

17.14 Arrhenatherum & Saxifraga

Arrhenatherum elatius ssp. bulbosum 'Variegatum'
(bulbous oat grass)
sun/shade ○ ◖
type of plant hardy perennial (grass)
zonal range 6-9 (C-WT)
flowering time mid- to late summer
flower colour greenish white
height 23-30cm (9-12in)
special characteristics variegated foliage

Saxifraga umbrosa var. primuloides
(syn *S. primuloides*)
sun/shade ◖
type of plant hardy perennial
zonal range 5-8 (C-CT)
flowering time late spring to early summer
flower colour pink
height 23-30cm (9-12in)
special characteristics evergreen, decorative green foliage

The rather upright stance and smart green-and-white stripes of this little grass are set off beautifully here by a dense mat of gleaming, rich green foliage and a multiplicity of tiny, crimson-eyed flowers. Even when the saxifrage has finished flowering, there is a very pleasing contrast between the two sets of foliage. Not only is there a striking difference in colouring, but there are also interesting dissimilarities in shape and texture between the grass's relatively simple and soft blades and the complex crinkles of the saxifrage's fleshy foliage.

Though the fresh colouring of this grass is reminiscent of *Holcus mollis* 'Albovariegatus' (see 17.10) the plant is much better behaved, its loose clusters of narrow leaves spreading only slowly (though in hot climates it may be invasive). It is most attractive in spring and early summer. After it has produced its slender panicles of oat-like flowers it tends to die back, but on any reasonably fertile soil it can be rejuvenated by cutting it back immediately after flowering. The resulting new growth will usually remain smartly variegated for the rest of the growing season.

Fertile soils with good drainage suit this grass best. If the saxifrage is to produce a dense carpet of growth, conditions must be both moisture-retentive and well-drained.

17.15 Acer, Dryopteris & Acaena

Acer palmatum f. atropurpureum

(Japanese maple)
sun/shade ○
type of plant hardy shrub/tree
zonal range 6-8 (C-WT)
height 3.6-4.5m (12-15ft)
special characteristics purple foliage, autumn foliage

Dryopteris filix-mas

(male fern)
sun/shade ○ ◑
type of plant hardy fern
zonal range 4-8 (C-CT)
height 60-120cm (2-4ft)
special characteristics decorative green foliage

Acaena saccaticupula 'Blue Haze'

(syn *A.* 'Pewter')
sun/shade ○
type of plant hardy perennial
zonal range 6-8 (C-WT)
height 10-15cm (4-6in)
special characteristics semi-evergreen, blue-grey foliage, fruit

Tough and very adaptable though it is, the male fern has considerable poise, too, and it is well able to hold its own among stylish plants such as the Japanese maple shown here. In this combination the lovely green laciness and bold, rather upright arrangement of the fern's fronds add panache to what would otherwise be a very pleasing but not particularly striking composition.

Apart from the good, strong shape and the excellent colour of the fern, the elegance and rich colouring of the maple and the smoky blue foliage of the acaena are important features here. *Acer palmatum* is a very graceful plant with a slightly layered canopy of spreading branches and shapely, lobed leaves. Its purple-leaved form is variable, but in the best specimens the foliage is a rich red-purple in summer and scarlet in autumn. The plant shown here is of fairly subdued but still attractive colouring. The purplish tan of its early autumn foliage is echoed softly in the red-brown seedheads of the acaena (which follow dull summer flowers).

The acaena's spreading, cool blue carpet of tiny leaves is in marked contrast not only to the rich colour of the maple's much larger-scale foliage but also to the warm, yellowish tones present in the fern's greenery. The low, horizontal line of this carpet introduces a contrast in shape, too. The fern's foliage stays green well into winter and the acaena can look fairly respectable even in midwinter (see 10.9). The male fern will grow almost anywhere. The acaena is a vigorous plant that is particularly dense and blue in sunshine and in well-drained soils, but it will tolerate less favourable conditions. The maple needs shelter from cold, drying winds and a well-drained but moisture-retentive and preferably acid soil. It is a very slow-growing plant.

17.16 Asplenium & Sedum

Asplenium trichomanes

(maidenhair spleenwort)
sun/shade ○ ◑
type of plant hardy fern
zonal range 3-8 (C-CT)
height 8-15cm (3-6in)
special characteristics evergreen/semi-evergreen, decorative green foliage

Sedum spathulifolium 'Purpureum'

(stonecrop)
sun/shade ○
type of plant hardy perennial
zonal range 4-8 (C-WT)
flowering time early to mid-summer
flower colour golden yellow
height 8-10cm (3-4in)
special characteristics evergreen, purple foliage

Though it is more usually seen growing in crevices in shady places (see 17.20), the maidenhair spleenwort is a very adaptable plant that will do well in sunnier sites. It is likely to prosper in sun if, as here, among the stones of a south-facing rockery, its roots can remain cool and moist. This fern tends to be quite small if it is grown in full sun, but the rather bright green of its foliage and the darkness of its stems ensure that it is always a striking plant. Its little springy tuft of more or less upright fronds contrasts well in this particular combination with a dense mat of fleshy foliage.

The basic leaf colour of the sedum illustrated here is a rich red-purple, but as the summer progresses this colour is overlaid with a lovely, gentle, white bloom. This pale wash is concentrated mainly in the centre of each neat rosette of foliage. (The photograph shows the sedum in early autumn. In spring the contrast between richly coloured outer leaves and pale inner leaves is more marked – see 13.13.) The olive-tinged green of the fern looks attractive with the sedum's foliage both when this foliage is distinctly purple and when it is greyer.

The sedum is easily grown in any soil with good drainage. Its rich yellow, short-stalked flower clusters add a burst of bright colour to this combination in summer.

255

17.17 **Viburnum & Dryopteris**

Viburnum plicatum 'Sterile'
(Japanese snowball)
sun/shade ○ ●
type of plant hardy shrub
zonal range 6-9 (C-WT)
flowering time late spring to early summer
flower colour pale green, changing to cream then white, finally pink-tinged
height 2.4-3m (8-10ft)
special characteristics autumn foliage

Dryopteris affinis Crispa Group
(syn *D. pseudomas* Crispa Group)
(golden scaled male fern)
sun/shade ○ ●
type of plant hardy fern
zonal range 4-8 (C-CT)
height 75-90cm (2½-3ft)
special characteristics decorative green foliage

This combination has a very limited palette of colours, but it certainly has plenty of impact. The slim, upright fronds of this crinkly-edged fern create an exciting burst of dense, dark colour beside a mass of pale, globular flowers. The overall outline of *Viburnum plicatum* 'Sterile', with its fans of splaying branches, is rounded, so there is a striking contrast in general habit of growth here, too.

When they first unfurl, the fronds of this fern are pale green. They retain the darker, rich green colour of their maturity until severe frosts set in. In autumn, the fern makes an interesting green accompaniment to the dying foliage of the viburnum, which turns shades of maroon, bronze and wine-purple. Even in summer, when both sets of leaves are green, the smooth outlines of the viburnum's veined foliage are quite distinct from the crisp, closely textured fronds of the fern.

Reasonably fertile soils that are moist and well-drained suit both these plants. In catalogues this viburnum tends to appear under a variety of names, including *V. plicatum tomentosum*, *V. tomentosum* and simply *V. plicatum*. It is not the same plant as *V. opulus* 'Sterile' (now known correctly as *V. o.* 'Roseum'), which is a form of guelder rose with ball-shaped flowers. However, this last plant would look well with the fern shown here.

17.18 **Asplenium & Lysimachia**

Asplenium trichomanes
(maidenhair spleenwort)
sun/shade ○ ●
type of plant hardy fern
zonal range 3-8 (C-CT)
height 8-15cm (3-6in)
special characteristics evergreen/semi-evergreen, decorative green foliage

Lysimachia nummularia 'Aurea'
(creeping Jenny)
sun/shade ○ ●
type of plant hardy perennial
zonal range 3-8 (C-WT)
flowering time early to mid-summer
flower colour bright yellow
height 2.5-5cm (1-2in)
special characteristics evergreen, yellow foliage, suitable for damp soils

This surprisingly bright and cheerful combination has been devised to light up the base of a shady, north-facing wall. The neat little fronds of the maidenhair spleenwort are a lively, slightly olive-tinged green and the whole plant, with its tight tufts of dark-stemmed growth, has a very sprightly air about it. This is particularly marked when the fern is grown in a moist, shaded place. In drier, sunnier conditions the plant is smaller and sparser but still very attractive (see 17.16). Teaming these bright bunches of slim fronds with a carpet of yellow rounded leaves introduces interesting contrasts in foliage colour and arrangement as well as brightening up what could be a dull corner.

Both these plants are especially at home in cool, shaded places. The combination could be grown in sun but, for the sake of the creeping Jenny in particular, the soil would have to be moisture-retentive. The sunnier the site, the more densely this vigorous plant grows. Where there is relatively little light, it has a loose, trailing habit of growth. Compared with the typical species, this yellow-leaved variety of *Lysimachia nummularia* does not flower very freely.

17.19 Hydrangea & Dryopteris

Hydrangea anomala ssp. petiolaris

(syn *H. petiolaris*)
(climbing hydrangea)
sun/shade ○ ◑
type of plant hardy climber
zonal range 5-8 (C-WT)
flowering time early summer
flower colour white
height 15-18m (50-60ft)
special characteristics autumn foliage

Dryopteris filix-mas Cristata Group

(male fern)
sun/shade ◑
type of plant hardy fern
zonal range 4-8 (C-CT)
height 60-90cm (2-3ft)
special characteristics decorative green foliage

Given time, this climbing hydrangea creates a magnificent covering for shady walls (though it is happy in sunnier sites, too). In these cool positions, ferns make flattering companions for this climber, their feathery fronds contrasting very pleasingly with the simple, rounded shape and smooth texture of the hydrangea leaves. This contrast in foliage texture is even more marked if the ferns' fronds have extra intricacies in the form of frills or crests on their leaflets.

The crested fern used in this combination is a long-lasting, rich, dark green and its fronds create a thick clump of rather upright shapes. It makes a striking 'full stop' at the base of the hydrangea – particularly so in mid-autumn, as here, when the hydrangea's leaves turn a beautiful, buttery yellow. Even in summer, when the hydrangea's foliage is mid-green and the large, lace-cap flowers appear (see 15.20), it looks good.

Dryopteris filix-mas itself (see 3.30) is a handsome plant that is very tough and adaptable. Its crested and frilled forms merit a partially shaded site and a well-drained but moisture-retentive soil. Once established, the hydrangea climbs by means of aerial roots to considerable heights. It grows especially well in moist, fertile soils.

17.20 Asplenium & Lamium

Asplenium trichomanes

(maidenhair spleenwort)
sun/shade ○ ◑
type of plant hardy fern
zonal range 3-8 (C-CT)
height 8-15cm (3-6in)
special characteristics evergreen/semi-evergreen, decorative green foliage

Lamium galeobdolon 'Florentinum'

(syn *L. g.* 'Variegatum', *Galeobdolon luteum* 'Florentinum', *G. l.* 'Variegatum')
(yellow archangel)
sun/shade ○ ◑
type of plant hardy perennial
zonal range 4-8 (C-WT)
flowering time early summer
flower colour yellow
height 30cm (12in)
special characteristics evergreen/semi-evergreen, variegated foliage

The maidenhair spleenwort's preference for alkaline conditions is evident in the way it colonizes old mortar in walls, its little clusters of wiry, dark-stemmed greenery making very fetching embellishments to masonry and brickwork. Here the adventitious, vertical wanderings of a lamium enliven this fern-covered wall by adding contrastingly large, silver-variegated leaves. In early summer hooded flowers appear among this silvery foliage, but they tend to be produced rather patchily.

The vigour of *Lamium galeobdolon* 'Florentinum' is notorious. Its trailing, rooting stems, once established in a garden, are often more or less impossible to eradicate. Where it already exists near a wall it might be encouraged to climb, as it has done here of its own accord. A safer alternative, however, might be to introduce some less energetic, self-seeding plants. On shady walls, the foliage rosettes and airy flower sprays of *Saxifraga × urbium* (see 8.22) would be very decorative. In sunnier sites, *Erigeron karvinskianus* would look attractive (see 1.16 where this little daisy is shown growing in a wall with various other plants) and other possibilities include some sedums and many sempervivums (houseleeks). In sun the fern will be quite small, but in cool, shady crevices it is considerably larger and lusher.

257

17.21 Athyrium & Epimedium

Athyrium filix-femina
(lady fern)
sun/shade ◖
type of plant hardy fern
zonal range 4-9 (C-WT)
height 75cm (2½ft)
special characteristics decorative green foliage, suitable for damp soils

Epimedium × versicolor 'Sulphureum'
(barrenwort, bishop's hat)
sun/shade ◖
type of plant hardy perennial
zonal range 5-8 (C-CT)
flowering time mid- to late spring
flower colour pale yellow
height 30-40cm (12-15in)
special characteristics evergreen, bronze young foliage, decorative green foliage, autumn/winter foliage

The exquisite laciness of the lady fern contrasts beautifully with large, simply shaped leaves (see 8.11 and 16.19). It also looks well with quite small leaves as long as they have smooth, simple outlines. Here a clump of downward-pointing, heart-shaped epimedium leaves steadies the flighty fronds of the fern. These leaves also provide an interesting contrast in texture, since they are smooth (and 'polished' here by a recent shower), whereas the fern's greenery is exceptionally intricate. Lastly, the epimedium's spreading habit of growth emphasizes the erect and then arching arrangement of the fern's foliage.

In the cool, damp places that the lady fern likes best, its foliage keeps its yellowish, fresh green colour for many months (it is shown here in mid-autumn). The epimedium's leaves emerge a wonderful, coppery chocolate in spring; in summer they turn a lively green; finally, in autumn, they become marbled and suffused with russety bronze. This marbling persists through winter, but the old leaves should be removed in spring to allow the little wiry-stemmed sprays of flowers to be seen properly.

Like the lady fern, this epimedium appreciates coolness and moisture, although it can be grown in a wide range of soils and it can tolerate some dryness.

17.22 Asplenium & Geranium

Asplenium scolopendrium Undulatum Group
(syn *Phyllitis scolopendrium* Undulatum Group)
(hart's tongue fern)
sun/shade ◖
type of plant hardy fern
zonal range 4-8 (C-CT)
height 30-45cm (12-18in)
special characteristics evergreen, decorative green foliage

Geranium macrorrhizum
(cranesbill)
sun/shade ○ ◖
type of plant hardy perennial
zonal range 4-8 (C-WT)
flowering time late spring to midsummer
flower colour magenta-pink
height 30-40cm (12-15in)
special characteristics semi-evergreen, aromatic, decorative green foliage, autumn foliage

For other combinations featuring ornamental grasses, see:
GREY FOLIAGE 2.1, YELLOW FLOWERS 5.9, DECORATIVE GREEN FOLIAGE 8.2 DAMP AND WET SOILS 16.1, 16.2

For other combinations featuring ferns, see:
GREY FOLIAGE 2.29 HOT-COLOURED FLOWERS 3.30 YELLOW FLOWERS 5.18 DECORATIVE GREEN FOLIAGE 8.11 FRAGRANT FLOWERS 13.7 WINTER FLOWERS 14.8 DAMP AND WET SOILS 16.8, 16.17, 16.19

While almost all ferns have finely divided, feathery foliage, the fronds of the hart's tongue fern are, in contrast, simple and strap-shaped, even in wavy-edged forms like those in the Undulatum Group. The slender, glossy fronds are held rather erectly in dense clusters. Here, both the striking leaf shape and the bold habit of growth of this fern are set off by a carpet of almost circular but distinctly lobed leaves.

The combination was photographed in mid-autumn, when the pale apricots, oranges and reds of the geranium's autumn foliage give a most attractive air of gentle mellowness to the whole scene. Even the fern's rows of red-brown spore cases add to this appealing impression of ripeness. Once the deciduous leaves of the geranium have died back, a lower mat of smaller, evergreen leaves is revealed. Both the deciduous and evergreen foliage create highly efficient – and powerfully aromatic – ground cover. The light green, summer leaves make a lively background for the branched heads of pretty, brightly coloured flowers (see 8.9).

These are two very accommodating plants. They are happiest in some shade and in well-drained but moisture-retentive soils. They will grow, rather less luxuriously, in quite dry, infertile conditions. The fern has a preference for alkaline and neutral soils.

PLANT HARDINESS ZONES

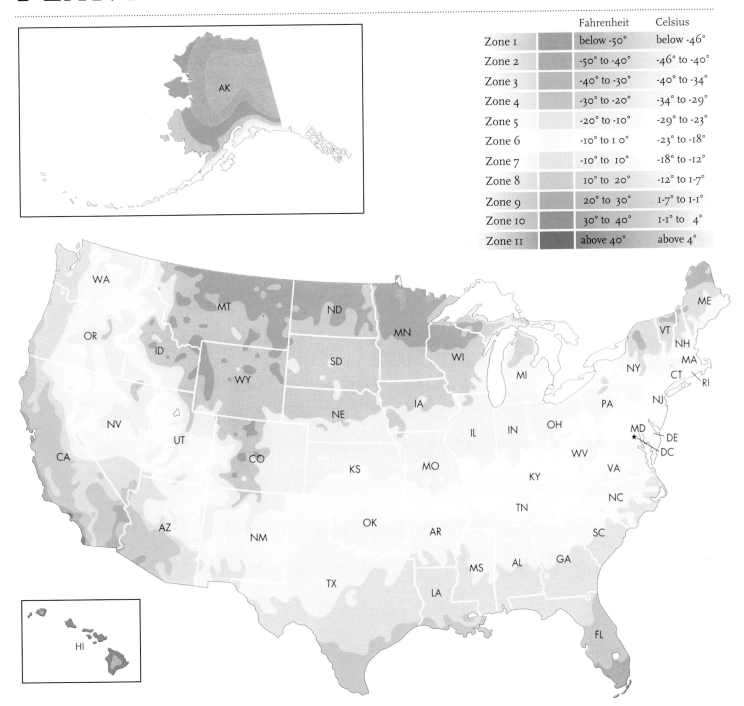

		Fahrenheit	Celsius
Zone 1		below -50°	below -46°
Zone 2		-50° to -40°	-46° to -40°
Zone 3		-40° to -30°	-40° to -34°
Zone 4		-30° to -20°	-34° to -29°
Zone 5		-20° to -10°	-29° to -23°
Zone 6		-10° to 1 0°	-23° to -18°
Zone 7		-10° to 10°	-18° to -12°
Zone 8		10° to 20°	-12° to 1-7°
Zone 9		20° to 30°	1-7° to 1-1°
Zone 10		30° to 40°	1-1° to 4°
Zone 11		above 40°	above 4°

The hardiness zone system developed by the USDA is based on the average annual minimum temperatures for each zone. All plants in the combinations are given a zone rating or are rated with a zonal range. In a range the lower zone indicates the coldest temperatures they will reliably survive and the higher one the hottest climate in which they will perform consistently. All the areas have their own microclimates which create variations by as much as two zones. Gardeners in the northern hemisphere living outside the USA can deduce the zone in which they live based on their own average minimum winter temperature. Gardeners in the southern hemisphere should consult the climate abbreviations given for each plant, and their explanation on page 17.

Nurseries & Plant Suppliers

The *RHS Plant Finder* has made tracking down particular plants very much easier than it used to be. This book, published annually by Dorling Kindersley, lists thousands of plants and hundreds of nurseries. *PPP Index* – the European equivalent to the *RHS Plant Finder* (compiled by Ann and Walter Erhardt and published by Verlag Eugen Ulmer) – provides information for finding plants in Europe, while North American gardeners can consult *The Andersen's Horticultural Library's Source List of Plants and Seeds* (compiled by Richard Isaacson and published by the Andersen Horticultural Library).

It can be very useful to have to hand at least a few catalogues of plant suppliers and nurseries that carry a wide range of stock and provide a mail order service, especially if you live in an area with relatively few garden centres or nurseries. For a comprehensive list of nurseries and plant suppliers see the annually updated *RHS Gardener's Yearbook* (edited by Charles Quest-Ritson and Christopher Blair, published by Macmillan).

British and Irish nurseries with a wide general stock and a mail order service include:

Burncoose & South Down Nurseries, Gwennap, Redruth, Cornwall TR16 6BJ. Tel: 01209 861112

Christie Elite Nurseries, The Nurseries, Forres, Moray, Grampian IV36 0TW. Tel: 01309 672633

Holden Clough Nursery, Holden, Bolton-by-Bowland, Clitheroe, Lancashire BB7 4PF. Tel: 01200 447615

Orchardstown Nurseries, 4 Miles Out, Cork Road, Waterford, Republic of Ireland. Tel: 00 353 51384273

Plaxtol Nurseries, The Spoute, Plaxtol, Sevenoaks, Kent TN15 0QR. Tel: 01732 810550

Scotts Nurseries (Merriott) Ltd, Merriott, Somerset TA16 5PL. Tel: 01460 72306

Seaforde Gardens, Seaforde, Co Down, Northern Ireland BT30 8PG. Tel: 01396 811225

Waterwheel Nursery, Bully Hole Bottom, Usk Road, Shirenewton, Chepstow, Gwent NP6 6SA. Tel: 01291 641577

Many gardeners who enjoy creating plant associations find that hardy perennials and bulbs are two particularly versatile groups of plants. Nurseries with a wide and interesting selection of bulbous plants include Avon Bulbs (Burnt House Farm, Mid-Lambrook, South Petherton, Somerset TA13 5HE. Tel: 01460 242177) and de Jager & Sons (The Nurseries, Marden, Kent TN12 9BP. Tel: 01622 831235). Nurseries with an especially good range of perennial plants include The Beth Chatto Gardens Ltd (Elmstead Market, Colchester, Essex CO7 7DB. Tel: 01206 822007), Four Seasons (Forncett St Mary, Norwich, Norfolk NR16 1JT. Tel: 01508 488344) and Stillingfleet Lodge Nurseries (Stillingfleet, Yorkshire YO4 6HW. Tel: 01904 728506). All these nurseries provide a mail order service.

Acknowledgements

A book of this sort would not be possible without the generosity of many garden owners, garden administrators and head gardeners. I have been treated with great kindness on my photographic travels. Garden owners have opened their gardens at special times for me, and they have taken much time and trouble over the identification of certain plants and they have unfailingly shown enthusiasm for this project. Many people have been very kind to me, and I thank them all. I would especially like to thank Lady Fraser, who very generously allowed me to visit her outstandingly attractive garden at Shepherd House near Edinburgh whenever I wished.

My occasional travelling companions Laura Osborne and Alison Wright made certain garden visits particularly happy and rewarding. My husband was a wonderfully efficient and encouraging chauffeur-cum-administrator on my more extended garden tours. From time to time each of my three children acted as photographic assistants. My editor at David & Charles, Anna Mumford, made some perspicacious comments at critical moments in the book's development. She and Alison Myer and Jane Trollope, also at David & Charles, were always kind and helpful. I am very grateful to all of them.

I would also like to thank Bill Tait (until recently supervisor of the Herbaceous and Alpine Department at the Royal Botanic Garden, Edinburgh) and Geoffrey Brookes (retired Landscape Officer of the University of Edinburgh), both of whom patiently disentangled some problems of plant identification. The identification of a few plants was also assisted by the holders of some National Plant Collections, and by Elizabeth Macgregor, Mrs Peter Cox and Mr Paul Whittaker. I am indebted to all these people.

The plant combinations were photographed in the gardens listed below. Not all of these gardens are open to the public, and some are open only occasionally. The owners of a few gardens that I visited asked that the names of their gardens should not be mentioned, usually because the gardens were about to change ownership and there was uncertainty about whether they would continue to be open to the public. Books such as *The Good Gardens Guide* (edited by Peter King and published by Ebury Press), Patrick Taylor's *The Gardener's Guide to Britain* (published by Pavilion Books) and *The RHS Gardener's Yearbook* (edited by Charles Quest-Ritson and Christopher Blair, published by Macmillan) give practical details about gardens open to the public. Details include opening times, admission charges and exact location. All three of these publications are regularly updated.

The so-called 'Yellow Books' for England and Wales and for Scotland are a further source of information, particularly about private gardens, many of which may be open only once a year. These handbooks, which are published annually, give details of gardens open for charities supported by the National Gardens Scheme and Scotland's Garden Scheme.

As an indication of approximate location, the names of English, Irish and Welsh gardens are followed by county names. In the case of Scottish gardens, the new local authority areas have been used.

† = garden administered by the National Trust

‡ = garden administered by the National Trust for Scotland

6 Hailes Street, City of Edinburgh (Mrs Molly Bullick)
23 Murrayfield Road, City of Edinburgh (Mr and Mrs James Buxton)
Aghaderg Glebe, Co. Down (the late Mrs J. D. Ferguson)
Allangrange, Highland (Major and Mrs Allan Cameron)
Alton Towers, Staffordshire (Alton Towers)
Arbigland, Dumfries and Galloway (Captain and Mrs J.B. Blackett)
Armagh Observatory, Co. Armagh (Trustees of Armagh Observatory)
Ballylough House, Co. Antrim (R.J. Traill)
The Bank House, Perth and Kinross (Mr and Mrs C. B. Lascelles)
Bank of Scotland, Comely Bank Branch, City of Edinburgh (Bank of Scotland)
Belsay Hall, Northumberland (English Heritage)
Benington Lordship, Hertfordshire (Mr and Mrs C. H. A. Bott)
Benvarden, Co. Antrim (Mr and Mrs Hugh Montgomery)
The Beth Chatto Gardens, Essex (Mrs Beth Chatto)
Bosvigo House, Cornwall (Mr Michael and Mrs Wendy Perry)
Branklyn Garden, Perth and Kinross ‡
Cally Gardens Nursery, Dumfries and Galloway (Mr Michael Wickenden)
Carolside, Scottish Borders (Mr and Mrs Anthony Foyle)
Castlewellan National Arboretum, Co Down (Department of Agriculture for Northern Ireland, Forest Service)
Cawdor Castle, Highland (The Countess Cawdor)
Chapel-on-Leader, Scottish Borders (Mr and Mrs Gavin Younger)
Colzium Estate, North Lanarkshire (North Lanarkshire Council)
Corbet Tower, Scottish Borders (Mr and Mrs G.H. Waddell)
Coulmony, Highland (The Hon Anthony and Mrs Laing)
Crathes Castle Garden, Aberdeenshire ‡
The Dillon Garden, Dublin (Helen Dillon)
The Dingle, Powys (Mr and Mrs Roy Joseph)
Edenkerry No 2, Midlothian (Mr and Mrs Colin Thompson)
Eggleston Hall Gardens, Co. Durham (Mrs W.T. Gray)
Etal Manor, Northumberland (Elizabeth, Lady Joicey)
Falkland Palace Garden, Fife ‡
Ford Hill, Northumberland (Mr and Mrs J. D. N. Stobart)
Glenwhan Garden, Dumfries and Galloway (Mr and Mrs William Knott)
Gordonstoun School, Moray (Gordonstoun School)
Greenfort, Co. Donegal (Mrs J. Braddell)
Harlow Carr Botanical Gardens, North Yorkshire (Northern Horticultural Society)
Hidcote Manor Gardens, Gloucestershire †
Hill of Tarvit, Fife ‡
Hodnet Hall, Shropshire (Mr A.E.H. and The Hon Mrs Heber-Percy)
Holehird, Cumbria (Lakeland Horticultural Society)
Hopleys, Hertfordshire (Mr Aubrey Barker)
House of Pitmuies, Angus (Mrs Farquhar Ogilvie)
Inveresk Lodge Garden, East Lothian ‡
Kaduna, Co Cork (Mrs Elizabeth Kavanagh)
Kailzie Gardens, Scottish Borders (Lady Buchan-Hepburn)
Kiftsgate Court, Gloucestershire (Mr and Mrs J.G. Chambers)
Lathrisk House, Fife (Mr and Mrs David Skinner)
Leeds Castle and Culpeper Gardens, Kent (Leeds Castle Foundation)
Levens Hall, Cumbria (Mr C. H. Bagot)
Malleny Garden, City of Edinburgh ‡
Micklefolly, Fife (Professor and Mrs L. J. Woodward)
Mindrum, Northumberland (The Hon. Peregrine and Mrs Fairfax)
Mount Stewart, Co Down †
Newby Hall Gardens, North Yorkshire (R. E. J. Compton)
Oak Lodge, East Lothian (Mr and Mrs Michael Kennedy)
Polesden Lacey, Surrey †
Portmore, Scottish Borders (Mr and Mrs D. H. L. Reid)
Powis Castle, Powys †
RHS Garden Wisley, Surrey (The Royal Horticultural Society)
Rowallane Garden, Co. Down †
Royal Botanic Garden, Edinburgh, City of Edinburgh (Trustees of the Royal Botanic Garden, Edinburgh)
Royal Botanic Gardens, Kew, Surrey (Trustees of the Royal Botanic Gardens)
Scottish National Gallery of Modern Art, City of Edinburgh (Trustees of the National Galleries of Scotland)
The Shackleton Garden/Beech Park, Co. Dublin (no longer open to the public; previously owned by Mr and Mrs Jonathan Shackleton)
Shepherd House, East Lothian (Sir Charles and Lady Fraser)
Sizergh Castle, Cumbria †
Stable House, Scottish Borders (Lt Col. and Mrs M. D. Blacklock)
Stevenson House, East Lothian (Mrs J. C. H. Dunlop/Brown Dunlop Country Houses Trust)
Suntrap Horticultural and Gardening Centre, City of Edinburgh (Oatridge Agricultural College; previously ‡)
Sutton Park, North Yorkshire (Sir Reginald and Lady Sheffield)
Traigh House, Highland (Mr and Mrs J. W. A. Shaw-Stewart)
Trelissick, Cornwall †
University of Edinburgh, Milne's Court and King's Buildings, City of Edinburgh (University of Edinburgh)
Wallington, Northumberland †
Wollerton Old Hall, Shropshire (Mr and Mrs John Jenkins)
York Gate, West Yorkshire (Gardeners' Royal Benevolent Society)
also the author's own garden in Edinburgh

Every garden I visited I found interesting. There were, however, a few gardens where the plant associations seemed outstanding. I found the following gardens especially interesting and inspiring: The Beth Chatto Gardens, Bosvigo House, Crathes Castle, The Dillon Garden, The Dingle, Hidcote Manor, Kiftsgate Court, Levens Hall, Mount Stewart, Powis Castle, Shepherd House, Stable House, University of Edinburgh (plantings at Milne's Court and King's Buildings especially), Wollerton Old Hall.

INDEX OF COMMON NAMES

INDEX OF BOTANICAL NAMES